Praise for
Steinbrenner: The Last Lion of Baseball

"Spectacular."
—*Boston Globe*

"Absorbing."
—*Forbes*

"For longtime baseball fans, this biography of the mercurial owner of the New York Yankees is as painful to read as it is informative. . . . [Madden] offers an insider's look at how Steinbrenner has run his team, even finding unexpected—certainly underpublicized—humanity in his subject."
—*Publishers Weekly*

"Riveting. . . . What we see, almost from the beginning of Steinbrenner's tenure, is a man of overweening self-importance and callousness with a breathtaking absence of empathy. Reading the book feels like the literary equivalent of passing a traffic accident; it is all but impossible to turn away."
—*New York Times Book Review*

"Definitive, indispensable. . . . Bill Madden brings the George we knew fully back to life, in all his sociopathic (and even felonious) glory."
—*Sports Illustrated*

"In *Steinbrenner: The Last Lion of Baseball* . . . Madden gives readers a definitive look into Steinbrenner's tumultuous reign over the most famous and successful sports franchise in America."
—*Daily News* (New York)

"Madden delivers the goods in this biography, a book comprehensive enough, detailed enough, big enough for its subject." —MLB.com

"Madden provides a definitive and captivating biography of 'the Boss.'" —*Kirkus Reviews*

"With the perseverance and patience of someone who has covered the Yankees for more than thirty years, Bill Madden takes the reader into the secret clubhouse of George Steinbrenner and intimately chronicles all the hubris and chutzpah that have marked the Boss's reign over the greatest sports franchise in the world."
—Gay Talese, bestselling author of *Honor Thy Father*

"In this authoritative biography, the Boss is revealed as great and small, shrewd and childlike, impossibly demanding and endearingly softhearted. Save for Steinbrenner himself (and he ain't talking), no one knows more about the Yanks than Bill Madden."
—Richard Ben Cramer, Pulitzer Prize–winning author of *Joe DiMaggio: The Hero's Life*

"With impressive reporting and an impeccable eye for detail, Madden has written the definitive biography of one of the most fascinating figures in baseball history. Buy it, read it, pass it on to your kids. They won't believe this stuff really happened."
—Jonathan Eig, author of *Luckiest Man: The Life and Death of Lou Gehrig*

LILLIAN MADDEN

About the Author

For more than thirty years **Bill Madden** has covered the New York Yankees and Major League Baseball for the *Daily News*. The author of several books on the Yankees, Madden is also the 2010 recipient of the Baseball Hall of Fame's J. G. Taylor Spink Award. He lives in New Jersey.

STEINBRENNER

The Last Lion of Baseball

. . .

Bill Madden

itbooks

AN IMPRINT OF HARPERCOLLINS PUBLISHERS

*it***books**

A hardcover edition of this book was published in 2010 by Harper, an imprint of HarperCollins Publishers.

HarperCollins books may be purchased for educational, business, or sales promotional use. For information, please write: Special Markets Department, HarperCollins Publishers, 10 East 53rd Street, New York, NY 10022.

FIRST IT BOOKS PAPERBACK EDITION PUBLISHED 2011.

The Library of Congress has catalogued the hardcover edition as follows:

Madden, Bill.
Steinbrenner : the last lion of baseball / by Bill Madden.
    p.   cm.
ISBN 978-0-06-169031-0
1. Steinbrenner, George M. (George Michael), 1930– . 2. Baseball team owners—United States—Biography. 3. New York Yankees (Baseball team)—History. I. Title.
GV865.S79M33   2010
796.357092—dc22
[B]   2010007871

ISBN 978-0-06-169032-7 (pbk.)

11   12   13   14   15   ID/RRD   10 9 8 7 6 5 4 3 2

For Lil, my "first read," who provided insight, inspiration, total support and unconditional love

For Steven and Thomas, a father's pride

And for all the New York Yankees newspaper reporters from the '70s through the '90s, who can feel entirely justified in multiplying their years on the beat by seven to take into account the "Steinbrenner factor"

Contents

Introduction

ON A COOL, OVERCAST afternoon in early March 1992, I had just finished having lunch in the dining room of George Steinbrenner's Bay Harbor Hotel, in Tampa, where I was staying for a few days while touring the spring training camps of those major league baseball teams based on Florida's Gulf Coast. I had not seen Steinbrenner since he'd been banished from baseball by Commissioner Fay Vincent in 1990, and had not spoken to him since he'd fired Lou Piniella as Yankees manager for the second time, after the 1988 season.

Throughout the '70s and '80s, I'd enjoyed a mostly pleasant working relationship with Steinbrenner in my capacity as a baseball writer for United Press International and then the New York *Daily News*, perhaps in no small part because my bosses and mentors at both places, Milton Richman at UPI and Dick Young at the *News*, were both legendary baseball writers and particular favorites of the forceful New York Yankees owner. During that time he had often solicited my opinion on player deals or manager firings he was pondering (which put me in good company with a lot of the bartenders and cabdrivers in Manhattan), and while his bullying of players, other baseball execs and writers usually left me no choice but to spank him in print, we'd managed to remain friends.

That ended when he fired Piniella after the 1988 season and, in an attempt to justify this, fed me a cockamamie story about how Lou had stolen furniture from the Yankees. That he would use me to discredit Piniella was, in my opinion, a new low, and I determined from that point on to have nothing more to do with him on a personal level other than report and comment in the *Daily News* on his activities as Yankees owner.

Two years later, I had little sympathy for Steinbrenner when he was tossed out of the game by Vincent for having paid a two-bit gambler for dirt on the Dave Winfield Foundation. It wasn't until months afterward that I learned from other baseball owners and attorneys who had worked on the case that Vincent's methods of getting rid of Steinbrenner had been just as underhanded as any of the shenanigans the Yankees owner had been guilty of over the years. I subsequently wrote a series of columns critical of the commissioner and the imperial manner with which he was governing the game.

By the spring of '92, it was starting to seem likely that Vincent was going to lift Steinbrenner's ban, and I remember feeling ambivalent about that. Left to his own means, general manager Gene Michael had been doing a commendable job of rebuilding the Yankees in Steinbrenner's absence, and everyone, fans and media alike, could remember what an absolute menace Steinbrenner had been in the '80s.

After lunch, I was walking up the long corridor that connects the Bay Harbor dining room to the main lobby when I suddenly saw him approaching from the other end. All I could think of was the opening scene in *Gunsmoke*, in which Matt Dillon stares down an outlaw off in the distance, getting ready to draw.

"Is that *you*, Madden?" he hollered.

"I plead guilty," I shouted back.

"What are you doing here, Madden?" he said as he kept walking toward me.

"I don't know, George," I said. "Other than I happen to like your hotel. Why? Am I on the banned list here?"

Then we were standing face-to-face. He smiled, extending his hand, and said, "Whatever happened to us, Billy?"

The way he said this momentarily caught me by surprise.

"What happened, George, was I never could understand why you fired Lou the way you did," I finally said, "and then, on top of that, you tried to tell me he was stealing from you."

"Oh, that was all a big mistake," he said. "I know I was wrong. The biggest mistake I ever made was letting Lou go. He knows how much I think of him."

After that chance meeting at his hotel, we gradually began to repair our relationship. On March 1, 1993, he was reinstated to baseball. I would like to say that his 29 months of exile had made him a more humble, softer person, but that wasn't exactly the case. Even as the Yankees, with the additions of Paul O'Neill, Tino Martinez, Jimmy Key, David Cone, and Wade Boggs and the development of players such as Derek Jeter, Bernie Williams and Mariano Rivera, evolved into another championship team for him, he continued to butt heads with his underlings and fellow owners, and I was most often right in the middle of it.

It was not until July 2005, when I wrote a story titled "Life with George" for a special section in the *Daily News* commemorating Steinbrenner's 75th birthday, that I first began thinking about doing a book on him. For years there had been periodic reports in the New York gossip columns that Steinbrenner was preparing to write his autobiography. But it never came to pass, and now, midway through his eighth decade, his health had begun to fail and it had become apparent that he was no longer capable of writing his own life story.

Over the years, Steinbrenner had successfully thwarted the attempts of freelance writers to write his biography simply by telling friends, associates and Yankee employees, past and present, that to cooperate would be at their own peril. But one night in 2005, over dinner at Elaine's, Steinbrenner's daughter Jennifer and her then-husband, Steve Swindal, broached the idea of doing her father's book.

"My father's getting up there now," Jennifer said, "and his book has never been written. Somebody needs to tell his story, and you're the person who should do it. No reporter has known him better than you."

At the time, she was talking about a collaboration—which I knew would be impossible. Nevertheless, I took her encouragement as tacit approval from the family to go ahead and pursue the project on my own. In late 2006, I began seeking out former Yankee employees and other close associates of Steinbrenner's, many of whom I hadn't seen or talked to in 20 years. On a few occasions, I was asked if Steinbrenner was cooperating with me on the book, to which I would invariably reply: "It's not really necessary. I was there."

Unfortunately, I'd joined the *Daily News* in 1978 and had not been around the Yankees on an everyday basis during the period when Gabe Paul was running the team for Steinbrenner. This posed a problem for me. As the baseball man who helped broker the sale of the Yankees from CBS to Steinbrenner in 1973 and became the architect of the 1976–78 championship teams with his trades for Chris Chambliss, Mickey Rivers, Ed Figueroa and Willie Randolph, along with his historic signing of Catfish Hunter, Paul was an integral character in the book. But engaging as I'd found him to be in the years after he left the Yankees to go back to Cleveland as general manager of the Indians, Paul was never very forthcoming about his relationship with Steinbrenner and his trials as president of the "Bronx Zoo" Yankees from 1973 to '77. He died in 1998 without ever having written his memoirs, and that was a great loss, because he was an important figure in baseball for over half a century and knew Steinbrenner better than anyone.

In an attempt to learn more about Paul's relationship with Steinbrenner, I contacted his son, Gabe Paul Jr., who, by 2006, had himself just ended a long executive career in baseball, as the point man for the northern Virginia group vying to relocate the Montreal Expos to Washington, D.C. Over lunch in Manhattan, Gabe Jr. confessed to having had little contact with his dad during Gabe Sr.'s Yankee years. However, he had kept many of his father's files, including Gabe Sr.'s handwritten diary of the entire proceedings—meetings, phone conversations, negotiations—of the CBS sale of the Yankees to Steinbrenner. "I'll be happy to provide you copies," he said.

It wasn't until a year later that I learned Paul had done much more than just keep a diary to preserve his place in baseball history. Gabe Jr. told me that, while cleaning out the garage of the family house in Tampa, he and his brother Henry had come across a large box full of reels of audiotapes. God bless him, ole Gabe made tapes, too—nearly a hundred hours of them—but only about his Yankee years with Steinbrenner.

After painstakingly transferring them onto CDs, Gabe Jr. invited me to listen to selected portions of them for use in the book. The tapes in their entirety are a whole separate book in themselves, detailing the love-hate dynamic between two iconic baseball figures, Steinbrenner and Paul, who, together, restored the Yankee dynasty. But for my purposes, the passages I was allowed to transcribe provided never-before-told detail of Steinbrenner's continued active involvement in the Yankees during his first suspension, the behind-the-scenes pursuit of Catfish Hunter, and the hiring of Billy Martin for the first time—all of which would be crucial to the book.

From there, it was a sentimental journey for me, revisiting the triumphs and trials of the most controversial owner in baseball history through more than 150 interviews of his friends, associates, employees and enemies. Throughout the process, I was frequently asked if I thought Steinbrenner should be in the Baseball Hall of Fame. I guess it depends on your perspective: his peers on the Hall of Fame Board of Directors saw to it that he wasn't even included on the executives ballot voted on by the Veterans Committee in 2007 and 2009. It is not my intention here to make the case for him one way or the other, but rather to faithfully tell his story with the cooperation and insight of all those who were there.

1

. . .

The Coming Storm

. . .

GEORGE STEINBRENNER'S KNEES WERE trembling. He had never felt so anxious, not even before all those obligatory phone calls to his father after the track meets, calls that often ended in rebuke and humiliation.

It was shortly before 3 P.M. on December 19, 1972, and he was waiting in the foyer on the 35th floor of the Columbia Broadcasting System building in Midtown Manhattan. He looked at the door leading to the office of CBS chairman William S. Paley, anticipating what he hoped would be the seminal meeting of his life. Steinbrenner was accompanied by Mike Burke, president of the CBS-owned New York Yankees, who had just briefed him over lunch on how to deal with Paley. The 72-year-old CBS chairman was a broadcasting and business icon, having assumed leadership of the company from his father in 1928, when it was a struggling Philadelphia-based radio network, and transformed it into the preeminent news-gathering and entertainment corporation in the postwar world.

Under Paley, CBS had launched the careers of Edward R. Murrow,

Walter Cronkite, Charles Collingwood and Eric Sevareid in the news division and George Burns and Gracie Allen, Jack Benny, Bing Crosby, Lucille Ball, Red Skelton and Jackie Gleason in the entertainment division. At the same time, Columbia Records, a division of CBS, had introduced the 33⅓ RPM long-playing vinyl disc and signed artists like Johnny Cash, Doris Day, Johnny Mathis, Tony Bennett, and Barbra Streisand. Indeed, almost every decision Paley made at CBS was inspired—with one notable exception: the deal he made in 1964 to purchase the Yankees from sportsman Dan Topping and real estate/hotel magnate Del Webb for $13.2 million.

When CBS purchased the team on November 2, 1964, the Yankees had won their fifth-straight American League pennant, and taken the St. Louis Cardinals to seven games in the World Series. But the team's stars were past their prime, and the once-fertile farm system was critically exhausted of talent. The team's legendary scouts, who for half a century had discovered and signed the Lou Gehrigs, Joe DiMaggios, Yogi Berras, Mickey Mantles and Whitey Fords, had all retired or died, and the amateur draft had evened the playing field for less affluent teams. Two years after CBS bought the team, the Yankees finished dead last in the 10-team American League, and by 1972 attendance at the Stadium had fallen to under one million for the first time since World War II.

By 1972, Paley concluded that CBS had failed in the baseball business—more embarrassingly, it had failed in New York—and in July he had discreetly put out the word that the Yankees were for sale.

The 42-year-old Steinbrenner, waiting outside Paley's office, had a résumé of business accomplishments in his own right. In 1963 he had bought control of his father's Great Lakes shipping company, Kinsman Marine Transit, and expanded its fleet. In 1967 he purchased a controlling interest in the larger American Shipbuilding Co., then based in Lorain, Ohio, and merged it with Kinsman. The company became the dominant grain carrier in the Great Lakes and, with the acquisition of the Great Lakes Towing tugboat company, quickly expanded into shipyards in Chicago and Toledo. In just five years, Steinbrenner had increased American Shipbuilding's revenues from $46.9 million, in 1967, to $73.7 million.

Through his shipbuilding enterprise, Steinbrenner had become a big player in Washington, beginning in 1968, when he lobbied Congress to amend the Maritime Act in order to get the Great Lakes more favorable tax benefits for its shipping industry. The Steinbrenners traditionally voted Republican, but the Democrats controlled both houses of Congress, so he happily accepted the job of chairman of the 1969 Democratic Congressional Dinner, one of the principal fundraising events in Washington, where he raised a record sum of $803,000 and developed close relationships with powerful Democrats, most notably Senator Edward Kennedy and House Speaker Tip O'Neill. The next year, Kennedy nominated Steinbrenner for chairman of the Democratic National Committee, but he declined, citing "personal and business obligations," and the post eventually went to former U.S. Postmaster General Larry O'Brien, who later became commissioner of the National Basketball Association.

Steinbrenner had decided he just couldn't divert the amount of time and energy away from his shipping business that the Democratic national chairmanship would have required. In addition, Steinbrenner, who was always careful to say that he was not registered with any political party, didn't want to limit his influence-seeking to the Democrats—not with a Republican, Richard Nixon, in the White House.

So Steinbrenner was no Cleveland bumpkin come to New York for an audience with one of the world's most powerful titans of business. It had been four years since *Fortune* had named him one of the country's 12 young "Movers and Shakers." As such, he had no reason to feel intimidated in Paley's presence. Or so he kept telling himself as he waited nervously to be summoned into the great man's office.

THEY CALLED THEMSELVES "Group 66," a name bestowed on them by their leader, George M. Steinbrenner, for no other reason than that was the year they first began gathering for lunch every Tuesday around table 14 at Al Bernstein's Pewter Mug, on 207 Frankfort Street. They were the young business dynamos and bright legal minds of Cleveland who, collectively, injected an energy and vibrant civic spirit into a city that had become economically, aesthetically and philanthropically stagnant.

Other members included: Thomas H. Roulston, president of Roulston & Co. brokerage firm, who'd assembled the group of investors that enabled Steinbrenner to purchase 470,000 of the outstanding 1,197,250 shares in

AmShip in 1967 and take control of the company; Robert D. Storey, a prominent black attorney who was director of the Cleveland Aid Society; Ted Bonda, one of the founders of APCOA parking; Sheldon Guren and Ed Ginsberg, partners in a Cleveland law firm; and Al Rosen, the former Cleveland Indians third baseman and American League Most Valuable Player in 1953 who was now an executive with the Bache & Co. brokerage firm.

Together, during the late '60s and early '70s, the group sponsored a number of charities and civic projects in Cleveland. Steinbrenner was the driving force behind a program for impoverished high school students that provided them with guidance counseling and scholarships and introduced them to the city's business leaders.

"Basically, we were just trying to get Cleveland out of the doldrums," said Rosen.

Symbolic of those doldrums was the mammoth and deteriorating 78,382-seat double-tiered, bowl-shaped Cleveland Municipal Stadium, on the shoreline of Lake Erie, along Cleveland's northern boundary. Originally constructed in 1928 in an attempt to lure the 1932 Olympics (which ultimately went to Los Angeles), the stadium became home to the Indians in 1932. In 1948, the year they won the world championship, the Indians set a major league attendance record of 2,620,027 at Municipal Stadium and continued to draw over a million fans every year through 1955.

But with the 1960s came a dramatic turn in the Indians' fortunes, both on the field and at the gate, and the team was bought and sold by a series of owners, none of whom could stem the team's financial difficulties. Throughout all the fiscally compromised Indians ownerships, one man, Gabe Paul, remained in charge of the baseball operations. Paul had been hired as Indians general manager in 1961 after spending 23 years in the Cincinnati Reds organization as traveling secretary and, later, general manager. A respected baseball executive, Paul was used to operating in a small market, but he longed to work for an owner whose resources would put the team on equal footing with his more privileged peers.

He got his wish in 1964, when, immediately after the Indians signed a favorable 10-year lease to remain in Cleveland Municipal Stadium, frozen-foods magnate Vernon Stouffer bought 80 percent of the club for $8 million. He gave Paul a 10-year contract along with a free hand to spend whatever it took to remake the team. Unfortunately for Paul, he never got to go on a spending spree for the marquee acquisitions he envisioned. Not long after the 65-year-old Stouffer bought the team, Litton Industries, a microwave oven company in which he purchased $21.5 million in stock in order to merge it with Stouffer Foods, began hemorrhaging money. Litton's stock, which had peaked at $120 per share at the end of 1967, had fallen as low as $18.50 by 1971, severely deflating Stouffer's personal fortune and his grand vision of restoring the Indians to the heights of a decade before.

The Indians' problems were a frequent topic of conversation at table 14 in the Pewter Mug every Tuesday. "How could you ignore it?" said Robert Storey. "We were all sports guys who cared a lot about our local teams. Plus, George was always talking about someday hoping to buy the Indians."

Rosen, a member of the Indians' board of directors, was particularly disgusted with the way Stouffer was running the team. Stouffer was one of Cleveland's most prominent and wealthiest citizens, but Rosen viewed him as a cantankerous old man who drank too much and whose personal business failings and lack of baseball knowledge had rendered him another in a long line of bad owners for the Indians and his friend Gabe Paul.

It was during the summer of 1971—when the Indians were on their way to the second-worst season (60-102) in their history and Stouffer was entertaining overtures from a New Orleans group to transfer 27 to 30 games there—that Sheldon Guren invited Rosen to a meeting at Cleveland Stadium with Art Modell, owner of the National Football League's Cleveland Browns. It seemed Edward DeBartolo, the prominent shopping-mall developer from Youngstown, Ohio, had purchased a large tract of land south of Cleveland on Route 8 and was interested in building a pair of racetracks, as well as two stadiums—one for baseball and one for football. Although the Browns were regularly filling Cleveland's Municipal Stadium with 80,000 fans every Sunday, Modell was an unhappy tenant in the decaying and outmoded edifice.

"The thought here," Guren told Rosen, "is that Art could fulfill one half of DeBartolo's plan by moving the Browns there, but we would need to fulfill the other part by purchasing the Indians from Stouffer. Do you think you could put together a group of investors?"

Rosen thought about it for less than a minute.

"I'm on it," he said. "Just give me a few days."

Excited over the prospect of wresting his distressed team from Stouffer, Rosen's first call was to Steinbrenner. Would George be interested in purchasing his hometown baseball team? "You bet I am," Steinbrenner said. "This has been my dream. I can do this. I have the people with the money."

Steinbrenner quickly enlisted Group 66's Ed Jeffrey (who was also on the Indians' board of directors) and Ted Bonda, who brought in his parking-lot partner, Howard Metzenbaum. Rosen was also good friends with Paul, who was anxious to keep his stock in the team and become part of a new ownership. "Count me in," said Paul, who brought to the group his close friend Steve O'Neill, the trucking magnate and Indians trustee who had more money than anyone else in the potential ownership group—a group that, according to Rosen, "had more money and more smarts than all the previous Indians owners combined. We had the ability and were prepared to restore the Indians to greatness."

Because Steinbrenner had a long-standing relationship with the Stouffer family—he'd attended Culver Military Academy, in northern Indiana, with Stouffer's son, Jimmy—Rosen and Guren felt he should be the group's point man in the negotiations. By this time, the elder Stouffer was feeling overwhelmed by the Indians' financial losses, his deteriorating image in Cleveland and the lack of support for his plight from his fellow American League owners. He was ready to sell. The negotiations between Steinbrenner and Jimmy Stouffer moved swiftly, culminating on December 6, 1971, with the group's offer of $8.6 million, by which the new owners would absorb the $300,000 debt that resulted from Stouffer borrowing against the team's 1972 television contract.

"The deal was struck, a handshake was given between George and Jimmy and now all that was left was for Vernon to give his final approval," Rosen said.

Later that day, Steinbrenner and Rosen waited at Steinbrenner's Am-Ship corporate office, on the 14th floor of the East Ohio Building, for a 5 o'clock phone call from Vernon Stouffer, who was in Scottsdale, Arizona. With them on that dark and frigid December afternoon was Marsh Samuel, who had done some public relations work for Steinbrenner and, more than 20 years before, for the Indians when they were owned by the flamboyant baseball promoter Bill Veeck. After alerting the media to come to the AmShip offices for an announcement, Samuel left Steinbrenner and Rosen alone and went to another office to prepare the press release.

The call from Vernon Stouffer came shortly after 5 P.M., and it was immediately evident to Steinbrenner that the old man had had more than two martinis over lunch in Arizona.

"I'm not doing this deal," Stouffer slurred to Steinbrenner, as Rosen listened in on another phone across the room. "You and your friends are trying to steal my team. You've already leaked the sale price to the press. I know I can get at least $10 million for it. So forget about it. I won't be pressured. I'm not selling to you."

Steinbrenner, his face white, hung up the phone and turned to Rosen. Remarkably composed considering what he'd just been told, he said glumly:

"You heard him, Al. He's not selling. I guess there's nothing left but to call Marsh and have him tell the media downstairs there's no deal."

But Steinbrenner was devastated.

"He couldn't believe what had happened," Rosen said. "He was really pissed, but there was nothing we could do and he realized it. You couldn't go public with the fact that you thought the old man was three sheets to the wind. That would only have shown us to be disrespectful to the Stouffer name or his son, Jim, who was only following his father's orders. It was just a terribly disappointing time for us."

If there had been one positive element of Steinbrenner's disappointing experience with Stouffer, it was the relationship he'd formed with Paul. A few days after his rejection by Stouffer, Steinbrenner called Paul, who he now knew had close ties to almost all the owners and top officials in baseball, and said: "Let me know if you ever hear of another franchise to come on the market. I'd still love to have you with me."

In the late summer of 1972, Paul and Rosen happened to sit next to each other on a flight from New York to Cleveland.

"I remember that conversation we had like it was yesterday," Rosen said. "Gabe looked at me and asked: 'Is your friend Steinbrenner real?' I said: 'What are you talking about?'"

"He asked me if I ever heard of a club for sale to let him know," Paul said, "and I know of a club for sale."

"What club is that?"

"The Yankees," said Paul.

GEORGE STEINBRENNER COULD not believe what he was hearing.

"You've gotta be kidding, Al," he said. "Are you sure?"

"I'm sure," said Rosen. "Gabe says CBS wants to get out of the baseball business. The team's not doing well, on or off the field, and they're tired of the losing."

"Did he say how much they want for them?"

"I think about $10 million," said Rosen.

The conversation with Rosen energized Steinbrenner, who immediately placed calls to some of the other well-heeled members of his Group 66, including Jess Bell, the CEO of Bonne Bell cosmetics, and Sheldon Guren and Ed Ginsberg. (Rosen had told him he was too busy handling his brokerage business in Cleveland to participate.) In addition to Paul and his wealthy friend Steve O'Neill (who told him they were prepared to sell their shares in the Indians), Steinbrenner was able to summon two other prominent Cleveland lawyers, Daniel McCarthy and Ed Greenwald, into the group.

As Guren said, "Ten million dollars was a lot of money to raise back then," so Steinbrenner had to reach beyond Cleveland to recruit additional investors, eventually wrangling oil-and-silver magnate Nelson Bunker Hunt, of Dallas; Leslie Combs III, a Thoroughbred breeder from Lexington, Kentucky; Chicago financier Lester Crown, whose family holdings included banking, real estate and hotels; John DeLorean, then vice president of General Motors in Detroit; Cincinnati banker and real estate developer Marvin L. Warner; and, from New York, theater entrepreneur James Nederlander, whose play *Seesaw*, which was about to open on Broadway, Steinbrenner had helped back. The last two limited investors were Thomas W. Evans, Steinbrenner's AmShip legal counsel, and, from Columbus, Ohio, Charlotte Witkind, heir to the Lazarus department store chain, which later became Macy's.

The original investors' breakdown gave Steinbrenner 11 percent ownership, the largest individual interest, with Hunt, Crown, Warner and O'Neill at 10 percent each and Ginsberg and Guren sharing 11 percent.

The rest had 6 percent or less. Steinbrenner's personal outlay was said to be $168,000.

By late summer 1972, Steinbrenner had assembled his group, and he instructed Paul to begin the dialogue with the CBS and Yankees officials. On September 17, 1972, Paul met with Yankees president Mike Burke over a late breakfast at the Plaza Hotel in New York. At the meeting, Burke informed Paul that CBS chairman Paley had given him the okay to assemble his own group of investors to buy the team, but that he'd been unsuccessful in coming up with a group sufficiently financed to meet Paley's expected asking price.

Paul assured Burke that his own investor group was "very substantial" and that they were prepared to do a cash deal, "no green stamps or delayed payments."

The next day, Burke sent Paul an internal memo with sales figures for the team. Paul forwarded them to Steinbrenner, who asked him to set up a meeting with him and Burke at the Carlyle Hotel in New York for Friday, September 29, at 8:30 A.M. Three days prior to the meeting, Steinbrenner had lunch with Paul at the Plaza, where he reiterated his intention to bring Paul in as team president.

But in a meeting with Burke over coffee and ice cream at the Plaza on September 17, the Yankees president was a bit discomfited by the news that, over the past few weeks, Paley had been wavering over whether to sell the team, concerned that it would reflect badly on CBS to sell while it was down. However, after returning from a vacation in Europe in late August, Paley was delighted to find the Yankees in the thick of the 1972 pennant race. His right-hand man, CBS president Frank Stanton, felt that it would now be the perfect time to sell with honor. As the meeting concluded, Paul was heartened when Burke told him that CBS was indeed looking to sell the team for a fair price.

"I'll be glad to meet with Steinbrenner," Burke said. "I'm sure we can work something out."

"What about your interest in the team?" Paul asked.

"I'll be in the picture at the start, but I don't think my participation is a must," Burke said. "I'll gladly bow out once the sale is completed."

"What do you think the price will be?" Paul asked.

"Oh, about $11 million," Burke replied, "but it could probably be knocked down."

"If Burke's right," Paul thought as he waited to hail a cab on Central Park West, "this is a helluva buy!"

Steinbrenner, Paul and Burke met at the Carlyle on September 29, at which time Steinbrenner said he would like his accountants to go over the Yankees' books. Burke agreed and said he would arrange to make the team's comptroller, Jack Collins, available to Steinbrenner's men.

Over the next few days, Burke began to ponder what his own role—if any—might be with the new Yankee ownership. On October 5, he telephoned Steinbrenner and said he would like to stay with the organization and leave CBS, but added that it wouldn't be a deal breaker if Steinbrenner didn't want him. "However," he said, "I do think you could make a more advantageous deal if the dealings were direct." In their previous conversations, Burke had insisted on a 5 percent stock share of the team as a fee for his role in brokering the deal with CBS, which Steinbrenner had flatly rejected, saying: "My investors will never go for that."

But now that he could see everything coming together, with Burke convincing Paley it was a good deal for CBS, Steinbrenner relented and began to formulate a plan in which he would offer Burke a stock option of 5 percent and install him as chief operating officer, with Paul as team president. He told Burke on October 4 that the stock option of 5 percent was okay, as long as the purchase price was $10 million and that he would be the COO. However, he neglected to add the part about Paul coming aboard as president and head of baseball operations.

Burke and Steinbrenner spoke by phone periodically over the next few weeks as the accountants and attorneys continued to pore over the books, which revealed a cash loss for the Yankees in six of the previous seven years. Finally, on December 18, the meeting was set with Steinbrenner and Paley.

In a phone call to Steinbrenner in Cleveland, Burke said: "He'll meet you in his office tomorrow afternoon at 3 o'clock. He wants to sell if the money is right."

NOW, STANDING WITH Burke outside Paley's office, Steinbrenner gazed admiringly at the original art hanging in the foyer. Over lunch at the Brussels, they had shaken hands on their own arrangement (Steinbrenner still hadn't mentioned that Paul would become team president) and agreed that the offer for the club would be $10 million in cash. Burke had dined on calf's liver; Steinbrenner had been too nervous to eat. He couldn't help but remember that awful day in Cleveland, a year and a half earlier, when Vernon Stouffer told him to take his offer for the Indians and stuff it. "What if this is all just another jerk-off?" he asked himself. "How do I know Paley isn't using this as a way of determining what the team is worth? What if he's decided CBS can't sell the team at a loss?" Suddenly Steinbrenner felt his knees tremble again as Paley's secretary interrupted his thoughts.

"Mr. Paley will see you now, gentlemen."

Years later, Steinbrenner would remember how eerie the whole scene was as they walked into Paley's office: Paley standing in front of the window, his back to them. Then, without turning around, he said: "So I understand you want to buy my baseball team?"

"I do," said Steinbrenner, trying to remain cool and calm.

"Well, I hope you didn't come here with Chinese money."

"I didn't," he said, more firmly. "I came here with cold, hard, genuine American cash. It's all the money I could raise."

"I assume you and Mike have worked out an arrangement that is satisfactory to him?" Paley asked.

"Absolutely," said Steinbrenner. "We wouldn't have gone into this deal without Mike as a partner."

When Burke, who'd been president of the Yankees since 1966 and had spearheaded the city's $100 million renovation of Yankee Stadium, slated to begin in 1974, informed Paley of being given a 5 percent interest and the title of chief operating officer, the old man smiled approvingly. "That's important to us," he said, looking directly at Steinbrenner. "Mike's identified with the Yankees more than CBS is, and we think continuity is important."

"Mr. Paley," Steinbrenner said, "I can assure you we wouldn't want it any other way. I've got a ship company to run. I won't have much time for baseball, so Mike'll have to carry the load. We're especially going to need him to follow up with the city on the stadium renovation project. All anyone has to do is walk around the city with him. He's 'Mr. Yankee,' and that's a helluva asset for us."

Paley ended the meeting by telling Steinbrenner he would be convening the CBS finance team in the next two or three days and that he'd get back to him. In a private conversation with Burke after the meeting, Paley said he was impressed with Steinbrenner and personally satisfied that the Yankees were being placed in good hands. There was, however, one caveat in his approval of the sale, as he told Burke: Paley said he wanted the point to be made clear at the press conference that CBS hadn't sold the team at a loss; that tax write-offs of player contracts plus the cash sale effectively made it a wash on CBS's original $13.2 million investment.

Steinbrenner, too, was impressed with Paley and how the meeting had gone, and flew home to Cleveland confident that, this time, there would be no last-minute double cross on the sale by CBS. Three days later, Burke called Steinbrenner in Cleveland to tell him that Paley had accepted their offer of $10 million and that they would meet again in New York on December 28 to finalize all the details, specifically the financial breakdown from all of Steinbrenner's partners and the execution of Paul's and O'Neill's sale of their stock in the Indians. For years, the final price was reported to be $10 million, but as Steinbrenner later revealed, the deal included a couple of parking garages that CBS had bought from the city. Soon after the deal was completed, the city bought the garages back from Steinbrenner for $1.2 million, making the net cost to his group $8.8 million. The negotiations were concluded on December 29, but the parties agreed to delay announcement of the deal until after the new year. Marty Appel, the Yankees' assistant director of public relations at the time of the sale, remembers sitting in the office he shared with Jackie Farrell, the director of the Yankees' speakers bureau, in the basement of Yankee Stadium on the afternoon of January 2 when his boss, Bob Fishel, walked in and began pacing nervously around his desk while fidgeting with some papers. Something was up, but what was it?

"We've got a major announcement to make tomorrow," Fishel said. "The team is being sold. Let's just hope we can get to tomorrow without it leaking out."

"It had to be the best-kept secret in history," recalled Appel. "Imagine something this big—CBS selling the Yankees—and nobody had even an inkling of it until the day of the announcement!"

When asked to prepare the press announcement, Fishel was told only that the buyer was a syndicate headed by Burke and a shipbuilding executive from Cleveland named George Steinbrenner. There were other investors, Fishel was told, but their identities weren't necessary for the initial announcement. Fishel, who had served as the Yankees' public relations director since 1954, was relieved that Burke was going to remain as part of the new ownership group.

"There's always a lot of uncertainty when a team changes ownership," he said, "and we don't know anything about these people Mike has aligned with."

OTHER THAN THEIR mutual interest in running the Yankees, Mike Burke and George Steinbrenner had almost nothing in common. Steinbrenner, the buttoned-up businessman and proud patriot whose close-cropped, perfectly coiffed hair was the product of almost daily trips to the barber, showed up at the office every day in a navy blue suit or sports coat, American designer dress shirt and striped tie—the same attire his father, Henry, had insisted he wear to grade school. Back then, as the only kid in the class wearing a jacket and tie, it had been cause for embarrassment and ridicule, but in the 1970s, *Penthouse* magazine called him the "best-dressed businessman in America."

By contrast, Mike Burke, with his flowing, shoulder-length white hair, fancied himself a '70s renaissance man in that he embraced the hippie movement of the day and had initiated a series of promotions at Yankee Stadium—Bat Day, Ball Day, etc.—directed toward the young fans, which the previous Yankee ownership would have never considered. (Indeed, Steinbrenner must have been shocked to learn that Burke was actually a war hero, serving with the United States Office of Strategic Services, where his activities took him behind enemy lines in Italy and France in World War II. In France he joined the Resistance in preparation for the D-Day invasion and was later awarded the Navy Cross, the Silver Cross and the French Médaille de la Résistance.) There is a picture in the 1973 Yankee yearbook that defines the contrasting styles and demeanors of Burke and Steinbrenner. Side by side at spring training, Burke looks relaxed in a pair of slightly yellowed white flannel jeans and a faded blue denim shirt, unbuttoned almost to his navel, a warm smile on his face, while Steinbrenner, appearing stiff in a blue blazer with a golf shirt buttoned to the top, scowls at something in the distance.

Prior to joining CBS in 1956, Burke had managed the Ringling Brothers Circus and was responsible for taking the circus out of the tents and into large indoor arenas. In 1968, a few of the American League owners, citing this flair for promotion, had nominated him to replace the fired William D. Eckert as baseball's commissioner. After none of the proposed candidates, including Burke, National League president Chub Feeney, Yankees general manager Lee MacPhail and Montreal Expos president John McHale, was able to garner the necessary three-fourths votes from each league, the owners settled on National League attorney Bowie Kuhn as a compromise candidate. Though the Yankees had sunk to their lowest depths under CBS, most baseball officials felt that it was due more to the neglect by the previous owners, Topping and Webb. Burke was regarded as an able leader of the major leagues' signature franchise with a style and personality perfectly suited for New York. Paley's esteem for him was evident. But would Steinbrenner be able to see past their outwardly differing styles?

ON THE MORNING of January 3, 1973, Bob Fishel and Marty Appel were frantically working their rotary phones, dialing the Associated Press and United Press International, all the New York and suburban newspapers and the radio and TV stations, alerting them to a "major" press conference that would be taking place at noon in the Yankee Stadium club. The night before, while sitting at his desk writing the release, Fishel had turned to Appel and repeated his sentiments of the day before: "I'm really glad Mike is still going to be part of this so it won't be such a dramatic transition."

Shortly before noon, they met Steinbrenner for the first time when he strolled into their office and asked to look at the press release. Upon giving it a cursory reading, he turned to Fishel and said, "Nice job," before heading upstairs to the stadium club.

In his opening statements to the reporters assembled in the stadium club, Fishel read the release and then turned the proceedings over to Burke, who, in keeping with his pledge to Paley, made a point of saying, "CBS substantially broke even on the deal, taking into account player-contracts depreciation and things like that. Some years were profitable, some were not. The first half of last season was disastrous, but in the second half our attendance doubled."

Unfortunately, Burke's effort to portray the sale as a good deal for both sides was immediately undermined by the enthusiasm of the new owner.

"It's the best buy in sports today," Steinbrenner crowed. "I think it's a bargain! But they feel the chemistry is right—they feel they haven't taken a loss on the team."

Burke was stunned and enraged at Steinbrenner's remarks.

"How *could* he?" he fumed to himself. "He was *told* of Mr. Paley's desires."

Years later, Burke said that Steinbrenner's "bargain" statement "in a stroke destroyed my relationship with Mr. Paley. The damage was irreparable. Explanation was pointless. Everyone knows you never erase from the mind the first impression of a newspaper story, and subsequently I learned that Paley held me responsible for Steinbrenner's boast and felt I had not been faithful to his request."

When asked later in the press conference about his future involvement with the team, Steinbrenner reiterated what he had said to Paley: "We plan absentee ownership as far as running the Yankees. We're not going to pretend we're something we aren't. I'll stick to building ships."

In the days following the January 3 press conference, arrangements were made for a second press conference to introduce the rest of Steinbrenner's investment group to the New York media. Paul had the trickiest job: divesting himself of his interest in the Indians before he could officially announce his involvement with Steinbrenner. In that respect, Paul's trade of Indians star third baseman Graig Nettles to the Yankees on November 17, 1972—at a time when he was working behind the scenes to help Steinbrenner with the CBS sale—later raised questions from the media and other baseball officials about a conflict of interest on his part. Whenever he was asked, Paul defended the trade by pointing out that, in outfielder Charlie Spikes, the Indians had received the Yankees' top prospect. In addition, he noted that in Buddy Bell, then a top minor league prospect who would go on to play in five All-Star Games, the Indians had a third baseman they considered to be potentially as good as or better than Nettles. In retrospect, the deal did make sense at the time for the Indians, who used an increasingly expensive but expendable commodity in Nettles to secure a highly regarded outfield prospect—and only began to call into question Paul's integrity when Nettles emerged as a third base force for the Yankees and Spikes failed to pan out for the Indians.

On January 9, Paul met in Cleveland with the new Indians owner, Nick Mileti, who had bought the team from Stouffer for $10 million, $1.4 million more than Steinbrenner's bid. They agreed to an amicable parting, with Paul, as his final act, signing a proxy authorizing the vote of his Indians stock for the ownership's latest reorganization. Later that afternoon, Paul flew to New York and met with Steinbrenner's freelance public relations man, Marsh Samuel, and Bob Fishel in the dining room of the Carlyle Hotel to go over the press release for the investors' press conference, which had been scheduled for the next day in a private room upstairs at the "21" Club.

Paul was dismayed to see that the press release Fishel presented him at the Carlyle listed him as one of the investors and made no mention of his being named team president. Steinbrenner had obviously still not clarified his front office alignment plans to Burke.

"What's this?" Paul asked Fishel.

"Well, we have to do it this way for internal reasons," Fishel replied. "Mike doesn't want to announce that just yet."

The next morning Steinbrenner called Paul in his hotel room and attempted to placate him over the confusion as to his role.

"Don't worry," he said. "Everything's the way we said it was. You're the president. Mike's the chief operating officer. He'll deal with the business stuff and the stadium renovation. I want you running the baseball operation."

"Will you tell that to Mike in front of me?" Paul asked.

"Absolutely," said Steinbrenner. "We'll talk it all over on the car ride over to '21'."

After the three of them climbed into the limo, Steinbrenner in the front seat, Paul and Burke went at it in the backseat.

According to Paul in his recorded notes, Burke complained that, in their December 29 meeting in which Steinbrenner had laid out his planned front office structure, "it didn't seem all that definitive."

Steinbrenner said nothing, allowing Paul to make his case in this clash of egos.

Pointing his finger at Burke in the backseat of the car, Paul said angrily: "Do you understand it now?"

"Yes," said Burke. "I'll simply say you're coming on in a very selective position."

"Fine," said Paul, "as long as you make it understood I'm coming aboard in a major executive capacity."

But at the press conference, Burke was seemingly deliberately nebulous in his reference to Paul's role in the organization. "Gabe is 63 and has a nice home in Florida where he and his wife, Mary, will retire in a few years," he said. "This is a nice swan song for him to end his baseball career." But as he later admitted in his 1984 memoir: "The New York sportswriters smelled a rat and duplicity added itself to my perception of Steinbrenner's emerging character. It was apparent that he and Gabe had reached an understanding about Gabe's role different from that described to me. It was a clear warning."

Paul's role, once it finally became known, didn't sit well with Burke's right-hand men in the front office, general manager Lee MacPhail and vice president of administration Howard Berk (who'd come over with Burke from CBS in 1964). MacPhail was driving Berk from the "21" press conference back to Yankee Stadium when he stopped at a red light and turned to Berk, his face flushed with uncharacteristic anger.

"Why did Mike play things so close to the vest?" MacPhail said. "Why didn't he let me in on this? If only I'd known, we could have put a group together and made this thing work!"

"I was as much in the dark as you were, Lee," said Berk. "I didn't know anything about it until the day after New Year's. He called me at home and said CBS had just sold the club to a fellow from Cleveland. I asked him who the guy was and he replied, 'His name doesn't matter. He's a terrific fellow, but he's going to be totally absentee.'"

For the next two months, Burke struggled in vain to get Steinbrenner to define his own role with the team in regard to just which areas he was in charge of—to no avail. His only recourse now was to get his lawyers involved, and discussions between them and Steinbrenner's attorneys dragged on into 1973 spring training. In the meantime, Steinbrenner was careful not to show any overt signs of exercising his authority, as the sale of the team had still not been formally approved by the American League owners. However, on one occasion Steinbrenner happened to be walking through the offices at Yankee Stadium when he spotted a vase of fresh yellow chrysanthemums on the coffee table outside Burke's office.

"What's this?" he snapped at one of the secretaries.

"Oh, sir, those are fresh flowers Mr. Burke always has in the office."

"Fresh flowers?" Steinbrenner thought. "That's the way this guy spends money? There's no way I'm letting him run my ball club."

One Saturday morning in early March, Berk's wife, Phyllis, was having breakfast by the pool at Fort Lauderdale's Schrafft's Hotel, where the Yankees were staying for spring training, when she overheard Steinbrenner, dining with two male friends, launch into a diatribe about Burke.

"He thinks he's gonna run this team?" Steinbrenner howled. "Him and his fucking fresh flowers and long hair? Wait till we take over this club! Then you'll see some discipline and some fiscal responsibility around here! I'll make that long-haired Irish sonofabitch dance to my tune."

Phyllis Berk was aghast at Steinbrenner's rant and immediately found her husband in the hotel lobby. After having the conversation relayed to him, Berk dialed Burke on the house phone and said it was urgent that he meet him in the lobby. A few minutes later, Burke got off the elevator and Howard and Phyllis Berk intercepted him as he was coming down the corridor.

"Looking around for a place for us to huddle, Mike opened a door to a broom closet, which we all crammed into," Berk recalled. "It was like a scene out of a bad spy movie."

Phyllis repeated what Steinbrenner had said. Burke looked at her husband and said firmly, "Don't worry, Howard. I'll take care of this."

By Monday Berk had returned to New York, where he got a call from his boss. Mike Burke told him that he'd spoken with Steinbrenner and that he was satisfied Steinbrenner wasn't looking to push him out. Again, he assured Berk that everything was okay.

"I couldn't believe Mike still didn't get it," Berk said. "He was a very bright and incisive guy, but in many ways he was also very naïve."

Burke used that meeting with Steinbrenner to work out the details of a formal agreement on his position with the team, with lawyers from both sides present. At the end of the session, Burke shook hands with Steinbrenner, satisfied that they had a firm agreement, and the lawyers—Bruce Haims for Burke and George Martin for Steinbrenner—drew up the long-negotiated contract on the flight back to New York. A couple of days later, however, Burke got a call from Haims with disconcerting news.

"Steinbrenner has repudiated the deal," Haims said. "All of it!"

"He what?" Burke exclaimed. "We shook hands on it!"

"He says the paper we drafted on the plane back from Fort Lauderdale is not what we agreed to at the meeting."

"Well, doesn't it?"

"Of course it does. As long as I've been practicing law, I've never experienced anything quite like this."

Burke was crushed.

"Okay," he said. "That wraps it for me. The man's word is worthless."

Years later, Haims ran into George Martin at a cocktail party in New York where the two men discussed the broken agreement and his long-ago adversary revealed the story behind the story.

"He told me that plane ride back to New York had been one of the most miserable experiences of his life," Haims said. "It seemed that after we'd concluded our meeting in Fort Lauderdale, Steinbrenner called Martin back into the room and told him: 'Everything we talked about here, forget it. We're not doing any of that. Just don't say anything to them.' That whole process of putting the contract together on the plane was a sham."

Burke would endure Steinbrenner's plotting and carping for another month, including a particularly rancorous exchange over the $100,000 contract he'd given the Yankees' star player, Bobby Murcer. A few days after that yearbook picture of Burke and Steinbrenner was taken, the owner telephoned Burke from Cleveland with another of his attorneys, Thomas Evans, patched in from New York.

Steinbrenner was furious about the Murcer contract.

"What did he make last year?" he demanded.

"Eighty-five thousand," Burke replied.

"So why would you give him a hundred?" Steinbrenner ranted. "What do you think this is, a money tree?"

Burke went on to explain that Murcer had led the Yankees in batting in 1972, that he had hit a career-high 33 home runs and was a fan favorite, one of the few the Yankees had. He went on to explain that Murcer was viewed as the second coming of Yankee legend and fellow Oklahoman Mickey Mantle, and that the six-figure contract would serve as a terrific psychological boost for him.

Steinbrenner was only mildly mollified by the explanation and ended the conversation by saying that Murcer had better live up to it. When, on Opening Day, Murcer struck out in the ninth inning with the tying and winning runs on base, Steinbrenner stormed into Burke's office immediately after the game and bellowed: "There's your goddamned $100,000 ballplayer!"

By now, though, Burke was immune to Steinbrenner's rages. This had been the case ever since that phone call from Haims, informing him that Steinbrenner had reneged on everything the two of them had agreed upon at their summit meeting in Fort Lauderdale only days before. So on April 25, barely more than four months after Steinbrenner had pledged his allegiance to him in William Paley's office, Mike Burke sat down at his desk in Yankee Stadium and put pen to paper on a letter of resignation as general partner of the Yankees.

2

. . .

Cleveland

. . .

H E WAS BORN ON the Fourth of July, 1930, in Rocky River,
Ohio, a red-white-and-blue circumstance of fate he trumpeted
so often and so proudly, it prompted skeptics to suggest that
perhaps George Steinbrenner made up his Independence Day birth in order to further enhance his credentials as a genuine American patriot. Could
it be a fiction, like the article published in the *Columbus Citizen* in 1954,
headlined THE AMAZING MISTER STEINBRENNER? According to the *Citizen,* a
panel of New York sportswriters had named Steinbrenner one of the 25
most outstanding athletes in the country in 1952, and he had played defensive halfback for the New York Giants, signing as a free agent upon
graduating from Williams. It's likely Steinbrenner was not the source of
that completely fictionalized article—in interviews through the years he
talked about only his hurdling successes, hardly ever mentioning his brief
flirtation with football during his senior year at Williams—and his birth
certificate bears out July 4, 1930, as the official date of his entry into the
world.

Steinbrenner grew up in Bay Village, Ohio, a suburb west of Cleveland along Lake Erie. His father, Henry, was by George's own account
"one tough German"—a strict disciplinarian and unyielding perfectionist. Henry Steinbrenner's great-grandfather Philip J. Minch was a German
immigrant who in the mid-1800s had settled in Lorain, Ohio, some 30 miles

west of Cleveland along the shores of the lake, and founded Minch Transit, a shipping company. Minch's daughter, Sophia, was college-educated at Oberlin. She became president of the company, expanding it and renaming it Kinsman Marine Transit, and relocated it as the first tenant in the John D. Rockefeller Building in downtown Cleveland. When Sophia died, the presidency of the company passed to her son George Steinbrenner II and then to his son, Henry.

Henry Steinbrenner had been a marine engineering honors scholar, a naval architect, and a world-class intercollegiate low hurdles champion at MIT who introduced his son to the hurdles at age 12. (Thomas Evans, George's Williams College classmate and early general counsel with the Yankees, recalled a visit to the Steinbrenner horse farm in Ocala, Florida, in the early '70s, where he saw the lonely figure of Steinbrenner's oldest son, Hank, who was not yet a teenager, practicing hurdles on a track off in the distance.)

George Steinbrenner was intimidated by his father, a fact he never denied, but he credited the old man with instilling in him the perfectionist, will-to-win competitiveness that would come to define his management style as president of American Shipbuilding Co. and, later, as owner of the Yankees. "Always work as hard, or harder, than anyone who works for you," Henry counseled him. Another lesson George took to heart: "It is always better to be the hammer than the nail." The fact that George was so dismissive of and often even abusive toward his employees can probably be directly attributed to his failure ever to win his father's approval. He once said: "I never really appreciated my dad or liked him growing up, but I appreciated him more as every day of my life went on, and now I can't give enough credit to my dad. Anything I ever accomplished I owe to him. Whatever's good in me is through him. Whatever's bad is me."

A close friend of Steinbrenner's said, "George was permanently scarred by his father's rigidity and lack of affection, and I have no doubt he'd have given up all his championship rings just to have gotten a hug and an 'I love you, son' from the old man. The sad part is he treated his own kids the same way."

In his mother, Rita, Steinbrenner could at least find sympathy and understanding, if not outward displays of affection. "It was my mom," he said, "who gave me compassion for the underdog and for people in need."

As a successful businessman and sports entrepreneur, Steinbrenner's acts of charity and philanthropy—the antithesis of the bully and tyrant that so characterized his public side—were far less publicized, most notably the hundreds of anonymous kids he put through college and the tens of millions of dollars he raised through his Silver Shield Foundation for the widows and families of New York City police officers and firefighters killed in the line of duty. In Cleveland, he ran the March of Dimes program and was director of Cleveland Now and chairman of the Junior Olympic Games, taking it upon himself to fund the trip to California for Ohio's participants in the Special Olympics. When the *Call & Post*, a newspaper that served the black community in Cleveland, sought sponsorship for its dinner honoring young black athletes in the city, George picked up the tab. Another time, he footed the bill to send a group of kids from Bay Village High to New York, putting them up at the Carlyle Hotel and arranging for tickets for them to a Broadway musical and the NIT basketball tournament.

The Steinbrenners were Christian Scientists, which meant they didn't believe in medical science or, for the most part, doctors. (It was because of this, friends surmised, that Steinbrenner refused to get an operation on his knee in his later years when his doctors warned him that the torn cartilage causing him so much pain would eventually lead to arthritis. Others said, however, that he was merely fearful of anesthesia. In any case, the arthritic knee finally rendered him wheelchair-bound in 2008.) Steinbrenner's childhood was one of grim regimentation—school, work, hurdles practice, piano lessons and precious little time left over for just plain recreation or social life. He often said the greatest pleasure of his youth was reading James Fenimore Cooper novels.

And, in fact, his work took up almost as much time as his schooling. Instead of an allowance, his father gave him chickens and told him to start his own business. "Earn your money through them," Henry instructed. George established a thriving little neighborhood poultry business, in which he would rise early, clean the coops, feed the chickens, and then go about selling the eggs door-to-door. He called it the George Company, and when he went away to school, he sold it for $50 to his two sisters, Susan and Judy, who renamed it the S&J Company. The two girls had an equally suppressed childhood under the strict rule of their father. Only in their adult years could they look back on it with a sense of humor, recalling how Henry would stiffly greet their gentlemen callers in a suit and tie at the front door before retiring to his reading room, only to make himself pointedly heard 15 minutes later, calling out, "Rita, is that goddamned kid still here?"

When George was 14, he was sent to Culver Military Academy, in Culver, Indiana, which had been established in 1894 "for the purpose of preparing young men for the best colleges, scientific schools and businesses of America." Culver's alumni include Jack Eckerd, founder of the pharmaceutical firm; actors Hal Holbrook and Adolphe Menjou; film director Joshua Logan; U.S. senator Lowell Weicker; comedian Jonathan Winters; yachtsman and businessman Bill Koch; Los Angeles Dodgers owner Walter O'Malley; playwright Luther Davis; and Alexander, the Crown Prince of Yugoslavia. Through the years, Culver became the Steinbrenner family school as all of George's four children—Hank, Hal, Jessica and Jennifer (a separate women's academy was established in 1971)—attended, as have their children. Because of George's donations, two buildings—the Steinbrenner Recreation Center and the Steinbrenner Center for Performing Arts—now bear the family name.

At Culver, Steinbrenner wasn't the honor student his father had been at MIT, although he was always proud to point out the A+ he earned in military science. Considering his passion for the military—he often extolled General George Patton as the one person he admired most in life, and also professed to be a student of Attila the Hun—it is clear that Culver had a profound impact on him.

Steinbrenner ran hurdles for the Culver track team and played football and basketball, but not baseball. When asked about that after he bought the Yankees, Steinbrenner replied: "Baseball was always my favorite sport as a kid, growing up as I did with the Cleveland Indians and all those great teams they had with Bob Feller, Early Wynn, Larry Doby and Bob Lemon in the '40s and '50s. I only wish I was better at playing it, but I wasn't. So I stuck to track, something I was good at, and football."

Upon graduation from Culver in 1948, Steinbrenner matriculated to Williams College in Massachusetts. It wasn't MIT—as Henry never failed to remind him—but in terms of educational prestige, it was regarded to be just a notch below the Ivy League schools.

At Williams, Steinbrenner majored in English, continued to run the hurdles and became fully engaged in the arts. In addition to playing in the college band for one year, he spent four years in the glee club and, with a classmate named George Kellogg, collaborated on a "dual pianos" act that they would perform before concerts and glee club recitals. Classmate Tom Evans recalls that "they were really quite good and were well received by the audiences."

Jack Horner, who sang in the glee club with Steinbrenner, said of him: "He was a tenor and he was distinguished. The one remarkable thing I remember was when he was able to obtain for Williams the original Brahms *Requiem* for the four-hands piano from Baldwin-Wallace College. Something like that was priceless, and I don't know how he was able to get it."

What Horner, who was close enough with Steinbrenner to have double-dated with him a few times, remembered most about him was the fear George had for his father.

"He had to call his father after every track meet," Horner recalled, "and inevitably every time his father would be ticked off because he didn't do better. I thought his father was a nasty guy."

In 1978, MIT built the $300,000 Henry G. Steinbrenner Stadium, a varsity game oval that serves as the venue for football, men's lacrosse, soccer and track and field. It was a gift to the school from George in honor of his father.

Suzyn Waldman, the Yankees' radio announcer, who grew up in Boston, recalled a Yankee road trip to the city in the early '90s. She and Steinbrenner were walking around the MIT campus, taking in the sights. Waldman had wanted to show Steinbrenner the Kresge Auditorium, where she had performed in shows as a youngster, and the Yankees owner asked her if she had ever seen the athletic facility. As the two of them approached the stadium, Steinbrenner told Waldman how he had brought his father to the dedication, which he'd planned as a surprise for the old man.

"How thrilled and proud he must have been," Waldman said.

"Actually," said Steinbrenner, "all he said was, 'That's the only way you'd ever get in this school.'"

After college, Horner settled in Bay Village, where he couldn't help but notice that the Steinbrenner family influence in the arts was everywhere—

most notably the Huntington Playhouse. which George helped rebuild in 1970 after a fire with a $10,000 gift and a community fund-raiser in which the 240 seats were sold for $100 apiece. George bought the whole first row of 16. "My son played in the high school band," Horner said, "in which all the tubas had been purchased by George."

George Steinbrenner a real-life Professor Harold Hill! Who knew?

For whatever reason, Steinbrenner never made much of his musical prowess, even though his friends and family said playing the organ at home was one of his favorite forms of leisure. For the most part, his Yankees employees were unaware of this side of him. Eddie Layton, the longtime Yankee Stadium organist, was practicing in the solitude of an empty stadium on the day before the Yankees were to open a season when suddenly he felt a shove.

"Move over!" Steinbrenner ordered.

The startled Layton got up and made way for Steinbrenner to slip behind the organ.

"What's this, George?" Layton said.

"This," said Steinbrenner, "is how you play the organ! You go walk around the stadium and see how the sound is and then come back here."

Layton began to walk around the stadium, first along the loge level and then to the upper deck, all the while listening in amazement to the Yankees owner's riffs. Layton remembered being particularly taken aback when Steinbrenner launched into one of his own signature Yankee "rally" songs, Chopin's "Tarentelle." It was as if Steinbrenner was letting him know that, even at the organ, he was the Boss.

When Layton returned to the organ booth, Steinbrenner was grinning.

"Well, Eddie, what did you think?"

"You're fired, George," Layton shot back, and they both burst into laughter.

In addition to his studies, the glee club, the dual piano act with Kellogg and running the hurdles in both the indoor and outdoor track programs, Steinbrenner's real passion, as he would later take pleasure in telling the media covering the Yankees, was sportswriting. He joined the *Williams Record* during his freshman year, and by the time he was a junior, he was co–sports editor, with his own column, Right from the Record.

Like Steinbrenner the bloviating baseball owner, Steinbrenner the neophyte sports columnist was not afraid to express his opinions or take swipes at his perceived enemies. He sprinkled his columns with phrases like "a strictly untitanic Colby team"; writing about rival Amherst's top-30 football ranking in the Associated Press, he said it was "as much out of place as Dolly Madison at a Sunday milk punch party."

Steinbrenner aimed the most brutal of his journalistic barbs at Amherst. In November 1951, he chided Amherst football coach John McLaughry for not allowing the varsity soccer team to participate in the Amherst football pep rallies. "I must admit, I find your arguments highly amusing, almost as I found your rating within the 'Top 30' teams in the Nation way back in early October," Steinbrenner wrote under the headline AN OPEN LETTER TO COACH MCLAUGHRY AT AMHERST. He continued, "I must admit that I do not believe that any coach should ever speak out openly against the supporting at rallies of any other team but his own. . . . And as for your assertion that, 'if we were over in England we would have to take a backseat to soccer' I have only this to say: You might have found the going a little better in England than you did 'here' this season."

But in what most surely was a precedent never repeated by Steinbrenner, three weeks later he penned an apology to McLaughry.

"Several matters on the agenda today," Steinbrenner began his December 8 Right from the Record column, "but first an apology that is long overdue on my part. Several weeks ago, I published a letter to Coach John McLaughry of Amherst. Since that time, there have been many compliments and many criticisms on that particular piece of journalism. Though it violates the gospel of a newspaper writer to abandon his convictions after they are in 'black and white' I am afraid I must cast my lot with those who have criticized my letter as 'cheesy' and 'totally unwarranted' journalism."

In his January 12, 1952, column, Steinbrenner criticized the selection of Princeton running back Dick Kazmaier as Male Athlete of the Year by the Associated Press. Though Kazmaier had won the Heisman Trophy in 1951 as the college football player of the year, Steinbrenner disparaged the AP sportswriters for overlooking pole vaulter Bob Richards, who'd become the second man in history to vault over 15 feet four times; Ben Hogan, who won his third Masters golf tournament that year; and Bob Feller, who won 21 games and pitched his third no-hitter for the Cleveland Indians. "I accuse the writers of the Associated Press of letting heavy publicizing and a degree of absurdity in building up of athletes to sweep them along to a decision of mediocrity," he wrote. Then, once again invoking his pet metaphor, he concluded: "These gentlemen are way wrong—their choice as much out of place as Dolly Madison at a Sunday milk punch party."

It's just as well that Steinbrenner's readership didn't extend much beyond the Williams campus. As a principal booster with the National Football Foundation, Steinbrenner would see Kazmaier at the College Football Hall of Fame induction dinner at the Waldorf-Astoria in New York every December. In a 2007 interview, Kazmaier told me he couldn't remember ever talking to Steinbrenner at the dinner. Nor was he aware that the Yankees owner had dissed him many years ago in the pages of the Williams paper.

"I'm frankly a little surprised he would have written that," Kazmaier said. "He hardly ever saw me play. I played against Williams only once, in 1950, and then I was only in about half the game, so George wouldn't have had a whole lot to judge me on."

I asked why he hadn't played much in the game, and Kazmaier replied: "Well, we beat them 66–0, and I only played in the first half. I believe it was the worst beating ever given a Williams football team, which, come to think of it, might have been George's motivation for writing what he did."

In January 1952, Steinbrenner's sportswriting career came to an end. In his final column he bade a fond adieu to his readers:

Now that it's all about to come to an end, I'm finding it hard to decide just what to say to you readers—be you many or few. I know there are some among you who would just as soon I said nothing. To this group I can only say that even though you have criticized my writing, I still consider you among my more rabid readers. To those of you who have found my columns of any interest at all, I extend my sincere gratitude for your support—to both of you!

"That's it," he concluded, "and now with due respect to my most faithful critic Philsy Gregware—good luck to all good sports and 'orchids to y'all.'"

No doubt Steinbrenner would have loved to defy ole Philsy and the rest of his critics, but he knew his father had not sent him off to Culver and then to Williams to be a sportswriter. The deal was to get a thorough, top-notch education and then come home to Cleveland and help Henry run Kinsman Marine. Henry had been preparing him for that during the summer months. In a 1981 interview with Marie Brenner of *New York* magazine, Steinbrenner recounted how he'd spent hours of his summer vacations crawling through the underdecks of ships, counting rivets and checking out what needed replacing in the filthy, close-quartered, stifling crannies.

Still, working full-time for the old man would wait a few more years. He graduated from Williams in June 1952—in the college yearbook he placed fifth in the voting for "Done Most for Williams" and second in "Shovels It Fastest"—and then, as the Korean conflict was coming to an end, he joined the Air Force and was assigned to Lockbourne Air Force Base in Columbus, Ohio, a two-hour drive from Cleveland. At Lockbourne, Steinbrenner was appointed aide to the commanding general and was assigned to oversee the base's struggling athletic program. According to articles in the *Columbus Citizen*, Steinbrenner succeeded in revitalizing all the athletic teams at Lockbourne, in the process reducing what had been a growing number of AWOLs due to low morale. Even though he admittedly knew nothing about baseball—years later he would tell Harry Reasoner on *60 Minutes*, "I just bought a good book and stayed one page ahead of the team"—Steinbrenner decided to coach the Lockbourne team, which played a pretty formidable schedule.

Bob Sudyk, who would go on to have a long, checkered relationship with Steinbrenner as a sports reporter for the *Cleveland Press*, remembers vividly one of the first Lockbourne baseball games under Coach Steinbrenner that spring.

"I was a freshman on the jayvee Ohio State baseball team," Sudyk said, "and we had driven over to Lockbourne for the game when our bus pulled up in the parking lot and we were confronted by this guy standing there waving his arms wildly and screaming at us. It was Steinbrenner. It seemed he thought he was playing the varsity and he was yelling at our coach for us to stay on the bus. He wasn't going to play us! Finally, our coach prevailed and we wound up playing them—and winning—which got George even more upset. He was yelling at the umpires the whole game, storming up and down, waving a rule book."

When he wasn't coaching baseball and overseeing the basketball and football teams at Lockbourne, Steinbrenner ran hurdles for the track team and even set an Air Force record for the 440-yard low hurdles. In a reincarnation of his boyhood poultry venture, he also demonstrated his budding business acumen by establishing his own coffee cart franchise, in which he used a half dozen Air Force pickup trucks to peddle coffee and doughnuts around the base.

UPON BEING DISCHARGED from the Air Force in 1954, Steinbrenner decided to stay in Columbus and enroll at Ohio State, where he studied for a master's degree in physical education. Ohio State, under the legendary coach Woody Hayes, was a football powerhouse, its 10-0 '54 team ranked first in the nation after beating Southern Cal, 20-7, in the Rose Bowl. The star of that team was Howard "Hopalong" Cassady, a speedy, 5-10, 177-pound junior running back. The following year, Ohio State dropped to number six in the country at 7-2, but Cassady was awarded the Heisman Trophy as the outstanding football player in the nation.

It was only natural that Steinbrenner would get caught up in the aura of big-time college football, and, in addition to attending every OSU home game, he would frequently be seen hanging around the practice sessions during the week, looking to pick up plays and strategies he could bring back with him to St. Thomas Aquinas High School, in Columbus, where he had become an assistant football and basketball coach. He got to know Cassady, with whom he also shared a couple of phys-ed classes. One day, Cassady remembered, Steinbrenner approached him after a class to inquire about a certain tall, slender, blond co-ed five years his junior named Elizabeth Joan Zieg, whose father, Harold, a prominent real estate developer in Columbus, was a wealthy Ohio State football booster.

"I was friends with the Zieg family and knew her dad especially," said Cassady. "At the time, she had been dating another player on the football named Doug Goodsell. George asked me if I would introduce him to her, and they started dating right away."

Steinbrenner courted Joan for over a year, frequently double-dating with Cassady, who later was asked to be part of their wedding party.

Steinbrenner and Joan (pronounced Jo-Ann) Zieg were married on May 12, 1956. The union, according to friends, was a stormy one almost from the beginning, with Steinbrenner's controlling and demanding persona quickly wearing thin with Joan, as well as his absences from the home because of all his other activities. Besides the Kinsman business and all his civic work with Group 66, his side venture into pro basketball further strained the marriage. On July 7, 1962, Joan filed for divorce in Cuyahoga County Domestic Relations Court. Two months later, however, she dropped the suit and it was reported by her attorney that the two had reconciled. If anything, they remained "reconciled" to each other as Joan, according to friends, developed just as much of a public temper as George and learned to give it as much as she had to take it. That's why, after Cassady had worked for the Yankees for nearly 40 years in various capacities, first as the team's first strength-and-conditioning coordinator and a scout and then a coach with the team's Triple-A farm team in Columbus, the joke among the front office underlings was that "George gave Hoppy a lifetime job so he could torture him for having introduced him to Joan."

Although they would go on to have four children, Hank, Hal, Jessica and Jennifer, and celebrated their golden wedding anniversary at a gala event at the Tampa Yacht Club in June 2006, Steinbrenner's closest friends attest it was anything but 50 years of marital bliss. More like a 50-year *War of the Roses* as George and Joan's public fights at parties and in restaurants were the talk of the Cleveland and Tampa social circuits. It was not uncommon for Joan to make an idle comment about something at dinner with friends, only to have George cut her short with a terse "Shut the fuck up, Joan" as everyone around them squirmed silently and uneasily in their chairs.

Steinbrenner's old friend Tom Evans remembered one such dinner confrontation vividly.

"My wife, Lois, and I were visiting George and Joan at the farm in Ocala," Evans related. "This was right after George and our group had bought the Yankees and the deal was just being announced. The year before, there had been rumors going around that, in order to raise money to buy a piece of the Chicago Bulls, George had sold Joan's stamp collection, which I guess must have been pretty valuable."

(Apparently, after Steinbrenner's losing venture as owner of the Cleveland Pipers of the American Basketball League, which had contributed to the strain on their marriage, he'd promised Joan he would never get involved in basketball again. However, when offered a share of ownership of the NBA Bulls in 1972, he couldn't resist, but may have figured that if he'd become a minority owner, Joan would never know.)

"Anyway, Lois and Joan were watching TV when suddenly the news report came on that the Yankees had been sold to guys who had interests in the Chicago Bulls. This came as a great surprise to Joan, and when George and I walked into the room, she lit into him with both barrels with some of the saltiest and most colorful language I've ever heard from a woman."

Steinbrenner steadfastly avoided appearing in public as a couple with Joan, especially in New York. Gabe Paul found himself in the middle of the Steinbrenners' ongoing domestic hostilities when Joan called him to complain about being banned from the private Yankee Club dining room upstairs at Yankee Stadium.

"I can't for the life of me understand why he won't let Joan eat in the dining room," Paul said at the time, in one of the first entries into the tape-recorded diary he kept during his years with the Yankees and Steinbrenner. "He's showing off with all his friends and cronies up there, but he won't let her up there and I've got to try to explain to her why. For all I know, he's got a broad up there."

As a matter of fact, on numerous occasions, that *was* the case—the "broad" in question being Barbara Walters, the celebrated TV journalist who was one of the few females in the Boss's inner circle of friends who attended big occasions at Yankee Stadium. Steinbrenner first met Walters in Cuba in 1977. She was there to interview Cuban premier Fidel Castro, and he was there with Yankee pitching great Whitey Ford on a top-secret mission to scout Cuban baseball players. As Walters related numerous times, Steinbrenner was furious when he spotted her and her camera crew in the hotel where they were staying, mistakenly thinking she was there to report on him. Over cocktails later that day, she explained that she was actually in Cuba to interview Castro, and that Steinbrenner's secret was safe with her.

Steinbrenner and Walters were often seen together around and about in New York, and Steinbrenner was fond of telling intimates how he and Walters would be walking down Fifth Avenue together and would make bets as to which one of them would be recognized first. And throughout the '80s and '90s, Walters was a frequent guest in Steinbrenner's private box at Yankee Stadium and in the Yankee Club.

Steinbrenner and Walters always insisted they were nothing more than good friends. But some members of Steinbrenner's inner circle of confidants back in the '80s suspected they might be something more. Joan Steinbrenner may have had her suspicions, too.

"They used to refer to each other as Spencer Tracy and Katharine Hepburn," said a Steinbrenner pal. It was common knowledge that the screen legends carried on an affair that endured until Tracy's death, in spite of the fact that he was married.

But Walters was always quick to dismiss suggestions that her relationship with Steinbrenner was romantic, and years later, in her 2009 memoir, she barely mentioned him.

As for Steinbrenner's secret mission in Cuba, he wasn't able to get himself any of Castro's players. Ford recalled how the two of them were sitting together at a game in Havana's stadium when one of Castro's uniformed emissaries approached them. Pointing to the premier sitting in his private box a few rows behind them, the emissary announced: "Premier Castro requests the pleasure of your company in his box."

But as Steinbrenner stood up, the guard put his hand on his chest.

"Not you," he said to Steinbrenner. "This man here," and he nodded at Ford.

"I felt bad for George," Ford said. "I sat up there for three or four innings talking baseball with Castro and I could see George was really pissed."

STEINBRENNER SPENT ONE year studying at Ohio State, where his involvement with OSU football and his coaching gigs at St. Thomas Aquinas had inspired him to continue working in sports. Instead of going home to Cleveland, he took a job as an assistant coach under Lou Saban at Northwestern University.

The 1955 Northwestern football team went 0-9, resulting in the dismissal of Saban and his entire coaching staff. Steinbrenner would remain friends with Saban, at one point hiring him as president of the Yankees, a position he held for barely a year before returning to football. The following year, now married to Joan, Steinbrenner moved on to Purdue University as the backfield coach under Jack Mollenkopf. The 1956 Purdue team fared better than Steinbrenner's first venture into Big Ten football, going 3-4-2. The Boilermakers' star quarterback, Len Dawson, would go on to become a member of the National Football League Hall of Fame.

"George wasn't nearly the vocal, animated guy he became later," Dawson told me in a 2008 interview, "but that may have been because Mollenkopf was about as vocal a coach as there was, and we didn't need two of them."

Although his time with Steinbrenner was limited to that 1955 season, Dawson recalled a conversation he had with his backfield coach midway through the year that had a profound impact on him. With the season fast becoming a lost cause, Dawson, who was a senior with an eye on the upcoming NFL draft, was dragging out a shoulder injury, sitting out practices.

One day, over lunch, Steinbrenner said not so subtly: "You know, Len, there are a lot of guys hurting on this team. How do you think the offensive linemen, who protect you, feel?"

"He made his point with me," Dawson said, "and it was a lesson I never forgot."

Much as Steinbrenner may have wanted to continue in his football-coaching career, by 1957 Henry Steinbrenner felt it was time his son began sowing the seeds of his expensive Culver and Williams education. The family shipping concern beckoned, and the old man regarded George's football coaching as folly. He would feel the same way about George's venture into pro basketball a few years later. "I raised you to be able to take over the family business," Henry told him, "not to be coaching football." Steinbrenner didn't fight him because he knew he was never going to get rich coaching football and he dreamed of being a big man in Cleveland—which could come about only if he was running the family business. When he returned home, Henry made him treasurer of Kinsman Marine, and told him to go out and find business for the company's five boats that serviced the Great Lakes with coal, iron and ore.

In his travels around the region, Steinbrenner made stops every other Tuesday in Buffalo. One day in 1957, after a luncheon at a private club down the block, Steinbrenner walked into a jazz club called the Royal Arms. After ordering an old-fashioned with extra sugar, Steinbrenner asked the bartender who owned the place. The bartender nodded at a man sorting checks at the end of the bar.

"After sending over a drink to me, we got to talking and George started going on about how he owned all these freighters out in the harbor," Max Margulis recalled. "I didn't believe him. I figured he was just a traveling salesman."

Steinbrenner stayed at the Royal Arms for the rest of the day, and that night Margulis took him downtown to dinner at the Normandy Steakhouse.

"I picked up the check, and that was the last one I ever picked up for him," Margulis said. "He said: 'I'll be back in two weeks to take you out. Bring your friends!'"

Two weeks later, Margulis was at the Royal Arms when Steinbrenner phoned and asked him to meet at the Normandy again for dinner.

"Bring your friends," Steinbrenner said. "We'll have some fun!"

It turned out Steinbrenner wanted to talk about getting into the restaurant business. Margulis warned him that it was "an awful business that you wind up being a slave to," but Steinbrenner wasn't deterred. Every time he'd come to Buffalo over the next few years, he'd pester Margulis about looking for a place they could buy. Margulis kept putting him off until finally, in 1964, the two of them, along with Max's friend Jim Naples, went in with Steinbrenner (who secured the loan) on a place called the Chateau.

"Before we opened, we discussed policy and we decided to serve only sandwiches at the bar and hot dinners in the dining room," Margulis said. "That was because the bar was four-deep from 4:30 to 8 o'clock. So who's the first guy to try and order dinner in the bar? George and two friends! The waitress comes over to me and tells me this, and I go to George and say: 'You know we can't serve dinner in the lounge!'"

"It wasn't long before George backed away from the restaurant," said Naples's son, Jim Jr., who, years later, went to work for Steinbrenner as the food-and-beverage manager at Yankee Stadium. "If he hadn't, Max would have killed him."

"George was George," sighed Margulis. "He made it very difficult to operate, constantly calling with changes he wanted to make in the menu, the prices, the decor. The problem was, he didn't have any understanding of the business."

But even after selling out his share of the restaurant when he moved to Tampa in 1973, Steinbrenner remained a loyal friend and benefactor to Margulis.

In 1977, Buffalo suffered one of the worst blizzards in its history, forcing Margulis to close the Chateau for 11 days. For the first two days of the storm, some 30 to 40 people were stranded in the restaurant.

"George called every day to check in on us," Margulis said. "I told him: 'We're okay. I just gotta get people back in the place.' Most of our customers were suburbanites who had found places closer to home during the storm."

"Don't worry, Max," said George. "I'll bring 'em back!"

During the last week of January 1978, just before the opening of spring training, two chartered jets filled with Yankees legends landed in Buffalo.

"Billy Martin, Phil Rizzuto, Mickey Mantle, Gene Michael, Lou Piniella, Mel Allen, Willie Randolph—all of 'em—came over to the restaurant, where we sold tickets at $100 apiece for a three-to-four-hour open bar and buffet," Margulis said. "Unfortunately, I made more enemies than friends, because we could only let 250 people in the place."

IN THE LATE '50s, Kinsman Marine Transit began to face formidable competition from the large steel companies' own fleets, and found itself in severe financial difficulties. By 1963, Henry Steinbrenner, then 59, was ready to retire. George realized that in order to succeed his father as company president, he was going to have to buy up all his relatives' shares. When Steinbrenner, with no capital of his own, was unable to obtain a loan for a down payment from any of the Cleveland banks, he went to New York, where he found a small bank that bought his argument about shipping on the Great Lakes still having a future and loaned him $25,000. After securing that sum, he was able to convince Union Commerce Bank in Cleveland to give him a more substantial loan in order to buy up the fleets of the other independent Great Lakes companies that were going out of business. He also bought four larger vessels from U.S. Steel. With the expanded and upgraded fleet, Steinbrenner managed to restore Kinsman to strong financial health by 1964 by shifting its fleet's shipping workload from the shrinking ore business to grain.

But consumed as Steinbrenner was with his work as Kinsman treasurer, he was never able to get past his yen for sports—a vocation effectively squashed by Henry's insistence that he abandon football coaching and focus on the family business. In the spring of 1960, Steinbrenner and his pals had been sitting around table 14 at the Pewter Mug discussing the plight of the Cleveland Pipers, a semi-pro team in the National Industrial Basketball League. Ed Sweeny, a plumbing-company executive who owned the Pipers, was beset with financial troubles and had put the team up for sale. Seeing an opportunity to get involved again in sports, Steinbrenner assembled a group of 16 of his business and civic associates, including Pewter Mug owner Al Bernstein, and together they offered Sweeny $125,000 for the Pipers. Steinbrenner, the principal investor, reportedly raised $250,000 for his share, plus operating expenses, by selling his Kinsman Marine Transit stock.

The Pipers were one of nine company-sponsored teams in the NIBL, which was considered to be a high-level "minor" league to the established National Basketball Association. Their coach, John McLendon, was one of the first African-American coaches in pro basketball and had quite a record of achievement, having won three consecutive small-college national championships at Tennessee A&I, as well as both the AAU and NIBL titles in 1961. Despite that success, in his 2007 biography of McLendon, *Breaking Through*, author Milton S. Katz reported that Steinbrenner had wanted a bigger-name coach, but the Pipers partners, citing the 45-year-old McLendon's popularity with the Cleveland fans, voted to keep him on. Several board members told Katz the vote was 15–1—with Steinbrenner the lone dissenting vote.

Although the NIBL was comprised of teams sponsored by some of the biggest and most respected companies in America—the Phillips 66 Oilers and the Akron Goodyears, to name two—Henry Steinbrenner was not impressed. He ordered his son to keep his new "hobby" separate from the Kinsman shipping business after Henry caught him talking Pipers business on the company phone and promptly cut the connection with a jab of his finger. George's response to that was to have a separate phone installed, with a red light on it that blinked for incoming calls, which he hid in his desk drawer when he wasn't in the office.

Bob Sudyk, who had taken a job as a sports reporter for the *Cleveland Press* after graduating from Ohio State, recalled a visit he made to the Kinsman office in an attempt to interview Steinbrenner shortly after his purchase of the Pipers.

"As I walked into the offices, Henry Steinbrenner immediately confronted me and demanded to know who I was and what I wanted," Sudyk said. "When I told him I was there to interview his son about the Pipers, he screamed, 'Get the hell out of here! This is a business!' He really intimidated me. I can only imagine what he did to George."

By 1961, however, the NIBL, unable to lure the top college players, was losing attendance to the NBA, which had gradually become integrated through the '50s and was now becoming dominated by prominent black players such as Wilt Chamberlain, Elgin Baylor and Bill Russell, who had emerged as exciting gate attractions. Steinbrenner, above all, recognized the shortcomings of the NIBL and, in 1961, he jumped at the offer from Harlem Globetrotters founder Abe Saperstein to have the Pipers join his fledgling American Basketball League, which he'd launched to challenge the NBA.

There were eight original franchises in the ABL, with Saperstein establishing himself as the owner of the Chicago team. A renowned promoter, Saperstein arranged for his Globetrotters to play exhibitions prior to the ABL games, and also invented the three-point field goal, which later became a staple of both the college and pro games.

By all accounts, Steinbrenner, in his first venture as owner of a sports team, was exactly what New York Yankee fans would experience 20 years later—manic, fiercely competitive, and frequently guilty of outrageous behavior, charging down to courtside from the stands to vent at opposing players and officials. The *Cleveland Press*, citing his referee-baiting antics in the stands, called him "congenitally unsuited" to own a sports franchise. Sudyk, who became the *Press*'s beat man with the Pipers, recognized Steinbrenner as the same wild man he'd first encountered at Lockbourne Air Force base 10 years earlier. "He would sit in the stands right behind the Pipers bench and scream at the officials throughout the game," said Sudyk, "and there were a couple of occasions when he'd charge right down onto the court and get in their faces."

More than anyone, it was the quiet, reserved McLendon who bore the brunt of Steinbrenner's rants. When Steinbrenner wasn't railing at the officials, he was openly criticizing McLendon's coaching and creating morale problems on the team with frantic personnel changes. In an effort to boost low attendance at Pipers games, Steinbrenner signed "name" players such as former Kentucky seven-foot All-American Bill Spivey, a central figure in the 1950s college point-shaving scandal who had been banned from the NBA, and 6-8 center Bevo Francis, who'd achieved fame at tiny Rio Grande State, in Ohio, for having scored 113 points in one game. Neither Francis, Spivey nor Larry Siegfried, the former Ohio State All-American guard who was the most acclaimed college player to sign with the ABL, fit into McLendon's fast-break system, and Steinbrenner bristled when the coach kept them on the bench.

Steinbrenner's most outrageous stunt occurred in the Pipers' first game of the 1961–62 season, when he sold forward Grady McCollum at halftime to the opposing team, the Hawaii Chiefs. Before the game, Chiefs coach Red Rocha had asked Steinbrenner if he would be interested in selling McCollum to him. Seizing an opportunity to pick up some quick operating cash, Steinbrenner told Rocha as the teams were walking off the court at halftime that he had a deal, and then went into the Pipers' dressing room and ordered McCollum to report immediately to the visitors' locker room to suit up for them for the second half. Shocked at such callous treatment of one of his players, McLendon told McCollum he didn't have to play against his teammates and to go sit up in the stands.

The tension between Steinbrenner and McLendon reached a breaking point on Sunday, January 14, 1962, when the Pipers lost the first-half ABL championship, 120–104, to the Kansas City Steers before a sparse crowd of just 2,313 at Cleveland's Public Hall. After the game, Steinbrenner stormed into the locker room, yelling that "heads will roll," and then had their pay-checks withheld the next day.

Sudyk found out from two of the Piper players that no paychecks had been delivered to the team offices and, as a result, the team had voted not to go to Pittsburgh for that night's game. When Sudyk's story of the Pipers players' boycott hit the streets at 10 o'clock the next morning, Steinbrenner flew into a fury and called McLendon to tell him the players would not be paid until they signed a letter denying Sudyk's story. Then he called Sudyk.

"This story is a pack of lies! I'll see to it that you never work at a paper again!" Steinbrenner screamed.

"After he got done yelling at me, he called my editor, Lou Seltzer, and tried to get me fired," Sudyk said.

The same morning, McLendon, disgusted over all that had just trans-pired, went to the *Cleveland Press* building and told Sudyk he was resigning.

Steinbrenner's fury shook Sudyk, but his phone call to Seltzer had the opposite effect: Sudyk actually received a raise.

A month later he was walking down Euclid Avenue in downtown Cleveland when he heard someone behind him shouting, "Sudyk! Sudyk!" Turning around, he was stunned to see Steinbrenner and thought, "Oh, God, what do I do now?" But when he caught up with him, Steinbrenner put his arm around Sudyk and said, "I've been trying to get a hold of you. Let's go get some drinks."

"We went into this little place and he apologized for everything he'd said to me," Sudyk said. "We talked all afternoon and then he took me to dinner with all his cronies. I have to say, he became a friend from that day on."

McLendon was similarly forgiving. In an October 2008 interview, his widow, Joanna, told me that McLendon never thought Steinbrenner was anti-black, just perhaps "anti-people," she said with a chuckle. "John just wasn't one to hold grudges or anything," she said. "He didn't like the way Steinbrenner treated him and the players, and that's why he did what he did. But I never heard him say anything harsh about Steinbrenner other than the fact that he treated everyone the same—like dogs."

McLendon wasn't the first Pipers employee that Steinbrenner drove from the job. Mike Cleary had been the Pipers' general manager since 1958.

At the beginning of the 1961 season, he was able to lure Dick Barnett, a star shooting guard, from the NBA's Syracuse Nationals—a wonderful coup for the less established league that was made possible, in part, by Barnett's having played for McLendon at Tennessee A&I. Steinbrenner had promised to give the *Cleveland Press*, which was the afternoon paper, the exclusive on Barnett's signing if it would agree to run the story on page one, and Cleary sent out the press announcement with an embargo for 6 A.M. But that night, the local TV station broke the embargo on its 11 o'clock sports report, which, in turn, compelled the morning paper, the Cleveland *Plain Dealer*, to run the story as well—but in the back pages of its sports section. The next day, when Steinbrenner picked up the *Press* (which had lost its exclusive), he was enraged to find just a tiny two-inch story on the Barnett signing.

"George called me and was berserk," said Cleary, "and that was the day I became the first general manager to be fired by George Steinbrenner."

Cleary wasn't out of work for long. A month after his firing, he was hired to be the general manager of the Kansas City Steers. Apparently, Steinbrenner felt that he didn't need to pay Cleary for his final two weeks as Pipers GM. After calling Steinbrenner on numerous occasions about the outstanding pay and never getting a response, Cleary decided to take matters into his own hands.

"When the Pipers came to Kansas City," he said, "I took four weeks' worth of pay out of the visiting team's gate receipts and wrote George a letter in which I said: 'You inadvertently forgot to give me my last two weeks' pay, and knowing how magnanimous you are, I'm sure you'd want to give me that plus two weeks' severance.' He called me back and said: 'Okay. You got me!'"

Cleary, who remained friends with Steinbrenner, said he was actually more fearful of the Pipers owner's father than he was of George.

"Every so often Henry would call me up and ask about our payroll checks," Cleary said. "He'd say: 'What's going on here? Why are you paying these salaries to these bums?' I'd try to be respectful to him and he'd scream: 'Don't give me that Mr. Steinbrenner shit! You think he's paying you that salary? That's *my* money!'"

With McLendon's resignation, Steinbrenner was able to bring in the big-name coach he'd wanted all along, in the person of Bill Sharman, the Hall of Fame Boston Celtics forward who had been coaching the ABL's Los Angeles Jets franchise until it folded at midseason.

"The day after the team folded, I got a call from George offering me the Pipers job," Sharman told me in 2007. "He said he'd promoted John [McLendon] to the front office, without giving a reason."

Under Sharman, the Pipers went on to win the overall 1961–62 ABL championship over the Kansas City Steers. Still, troubled by drooping attendance figures, Steinbrenner was becoming increasingly concerned about the league's viability. In order to attract more fans—and with an eye to gaining admittance to the NBA—in the spring of 1962 Steinbrenner pulled off a stunning coup when he signed Ohio State's 6-8 forward Jerry Lucas, the college basketball player of the year, to a unique player-management contract. By virtue of the NBA's territorial draft rule, Lucas was already technically on the reserve list of the Cincinnati Royals, who had selected him out of high school in 1962 and were just waiting for him to finish his college career to give him a contract.

After signing Lucas, Steinbrenner took the Pipers out of the ABL and entered into a secret deal with NBA commissioner Maurice Podoloff in which the NBA would take in Lucas and the Pipers and merge them with the Kansas City Steers, which would effectively kill the ABL. George McKean, the owner of the San Francisco Saints during the first year of the ABL, was supposed to go partners with Steinbrenner on the merged Pipers-Steers team. A meeting in which the parties worked out the details of the Pipers-Steers admission to the NBA took place on Podoloff's yacht on Long Island, and there was even a schedule printed for the 1963–64 season in which the Pipers were to open up against the New York Knicks.

"It would have been a pretty darn good team, too, with our five best players, the Pipers' best five players, plus Lucas!" said Cleary.

But McKean turned out to be underfinanced, having expended much of his resources to keep the Saints afloat, and when he and Steinbrenner fell behind in their payment schedule with the NBA, Podoloff killed the deal. The ABL ended up folding halfway through the 1962–63 season, leaving Steinbrenner with Lucas on the payroll and nowhere for the team to play.

"The NBA only wanted Cleveland because I was signed to a personal services contract with them," Lucas told me. "I signed with George because he offered me $40,000, which was $10,000 more than the Royals had offered me. But in the end, I never got a nickel of the $40,000 because the league folded."

Lucas sat out the 1962–63 season, then joined the Cincinnati Royals in the NBA the following year—for $30,000.

With the demise of the ABL, Steinbrenner faced over $125,000 in debts as well as personal losses of nearly $2 million.

"When the league folded, I was devastated," Steinbrenner told me in an interview I had with him on the occasion of his 25th anniversary as owner of the Yankees. "I didn't want to walk around the streets of Cleveland. It was embarrassing. But I was determined not to leave anyone holding the bag. It was my team, my debts, my problem. The easy thing would have been to just declare bankruptcy and walk away from it all, but as a businessman with a reputation to uphold, I just couldn't do that."

Over the next three years, Steinbrenner, using his Kinsman salary and the money derived from a separate company he formed to ship ore, paid off all of his partners and settled all of his debts. In 1984 he would counsel Ron Guidry to do the same when the star Yankee pitcher discovered that a series of bad investments by his agent had put him $400,000 in debt. "Essentially what George told me was, 'If you can remedy it, remedy it. But don't run away from it,'" Guidry told me.

WITH STEINBRENNER'S FIRST venture into professional sports a crushing failure, he poured his energy into the shipping business. After having completed his majority-interest purchase of Kinsman from his father and the other stockholders, George implemented new measures—expanding fleets, shifting the emphasis from ore to grain—to return the company to profitability. Next, he turned to his Group 66 pal Thomas Roulston, who headed a prominent Cleveland brokerage firm, and put together a deal to purchase 470,000 out of an outstanding 1,197,250 shares of stock in the American Shipbuilding Company for the purpose of merging Kinsman into it. On October 11, 1967, in the face of a threatened proxy fight, the board of directors named Steinbrenner to succeed William H. Jory as president and chief executive officer of the company.

It was in his new role as president of the largest shipping company on the Great Lakes that Steinbrenner began making frequent trips to Washington to lobby politicians to change the Merchant Marine Act, which had been in existence since 1936. "From the start, I knew the secret of American Ship was to get the Great Lakes included in the maritime act so they could get their share of assistance," Steinbrenner once told me. "I saw the whole Great Lakes fleet had to be rebuilt and the only way this could be done was with help from the government."

It took three years of schmoozing, cajoling and arm-twisting with the Democratic-controlled Congress, but Steinbrenner's lobbying effort to get the maritime act changed to include the Great Lakes finally proved successful. In the process, he developed close friendships with many of the leading Democrats, including Senators Ted Kennedy, Daniel Inouye and Vance Hartke and House Speaker Tip O'Neill. As chair of the annual Congressional Dinner in 1969 and 1970, Steinbrenner raised $803,000 the first year and over $1 million the second, setting new records for most money raised.

Suddenly, Steinbrenner, who was also contributing thousands of dollars to the 1970 Senate Campaign Committee of new Democratic pals through donations from AmShip, was a very high-profile Democratic activist in Washington—a fact his friends warned him could lead to repercussions for AmShip with a Republican, Richard Nixon, in the White House. Those fears proved to be well founded. On February 11, 1972, Secretary of Commerce Maurice Stans rejected AmShip's bid to be compensated for its $5.4 million cost overrun on the construction of an oceanographic survey ship, *Researcher*. Stans left the Commerce post a couple of days later to head up Nixon's campaign finance committee, but on May 2, 1972, his successor, Peter G. Peterson, determined that AmShip had to pay an additional $208,000 for late delivery of the vessel and another $22,000 in various construction penalties.

It was largely because of his concerns about the Nixon administration that Steinbrenner sought out and hired as AmShip general counsel his old Williams College classmate Thomas W. Evans, who had been Nixon's chief counsel in 1968 and was then deputy finance chairman of Nixon's 1972 reelection campaign.

After the Stans and Peterson rulings, a distressed Steinbrenner went to Evans and asked for his advice as to what do about his Republican problem.

"My impression was, he just wanted to be closely associated to presidential power," Evans said. "He told me he wanted to donate to Nixon's campaign and, in that regard, I introduced him to Herbert Kalmbach."

Kalmbach had replaced Evans as deputy finance chairman of Nixon's reelection campaign. His boss, Maurice Stans, had left the Commerce Department to become campaign finance chairman two days after rendering the decision against AmShip. Unbeknownst to Evans, Kalmbach was already engaged in a series of illegal schemes to raise money for Nixon—the heart of the Watergate scandal that, in 1974, would bring down the Nixon presidency and result in dozens of felony convictions, among them that of George M. Steinbrenner III, Chairman and Chief Executive Officer, American Shipbuilding Co.

3

. . .

"Lead, Follow, or Get the Hell
Out of the Way"

. . .

THOUGH HE HAD PROMISED to "stick to my shipbuilding business," George Steinbrenner did not wait for the American League
owners' formal approval of his purchase of the Yankees to begin
scrutinizing firsthand his new team and its on-field and off-field personnel.

In later years, Steinbrenner had a motto, engraved on a wooden nameplate atop his desk at Yankee Stadium—LEAD, FOLLOW, OR GET THE HELL
OUT OF THE WAY—which was in keeping with his "General George Patton" management style. And in the months leading up to his final approval by the AL
owners at their June meeting, Steinbrenner had made it quite apparent he
was going to be anything but the absentee owner he professed to be at the
January 3 press conference. The Yankees front office staff could sense that
their new boss was creating an environment far different from the benign
ownership of CBS, with many of them quickly concluding it was probably
best to just exercise the third option and stay out of his way.

At the same time Mike Burke began plotting his exit, Howard Berk,
the VP of administration, was deciding whether he'd be able to follow
the new owner or if he should exercise the clause in his contract allowing
him to return to CBS in the event the Yankees were sold. Steinbrenner's
stinging condemnation of Burke overheard by Berk's wife by the pool at
Schrafft's had certainly been dire enough warning of what was to come,
but, on Opening Day at the Stadium, Berk got his own initial firsthand

indoctrination of this when Steinbrenner ordered him to move a VIP lunch of over 200 people from the stadium club upstairs to another dining room on the main level.

What ultimately convinced Berk that he couldn't work for Steinbrenner was the rainout of the Yankees' April 27 game with the Minnesota Twins.

All afternoon, as the rain came down in torrents, Berk was on the phone, getting the latest updates from the weather service at Newark Airport. After consulting with the umpires, Berk announced that the game was going to have to be postponed. As soon as Berk made the announcement, Steinbrenner, who was in Cleveland, had him on the line, screaming: "How the hell can you call that game? It's not raining there!"

"I'd been hollered at before by a lot better people," said Berk, "but this was so illogical! Finally, I just shouted back at him: 'How in the hell can you tell me it's not raining here when you're not even in the city?'"

Berk gave his notice the next day, earning him the distinction of the first Yankee official to leave the employ of George Steinbrenner. Two days later, it was announced that Mike Burke had decided to step down as Yankees chief operating officer and would become a consultant while remaining a limited partner. In the various news reports and even in the *Official Baseball Guide* the following year, Burke's departure was reported as a firing.

In his letter of resignation to Steinbrenner, Burke wrote:

"The scope of responsibilities and authority proposed to be assigned to me are so limited as to be incompatible with even the narrowest definition of 'chief operating officer' and I must conclude that you do not want me to operate the Yankees. Slowly and sadly, I have come to this conclusion. It represents a stunning, personal setback."

Burke concluded by saying that he would not serve as general partner, would not be directly involved in the day-to-day operations of the club and would continue on the Yankee payroll for a maximum period of four months, during which time he would actively seek other employment.

Upon learning of Burke's departure while listening to a Yankee broadcast on the radio, a startled Howard Berk immediately called his old boss.

"I'll never forget his words to me," Berk recalled. "He said: 'I was tired of going to the mat every day. Life's too short. It's just not worth it.'"

Three months later, on July 27, Mike Burke was named president and chief operating officer of Madison Square Garden, with an annual salary of $100,000. In 1981, he sold his 5 percent share of the partnership for $500,000. The listed buyer on the sale agreement was Leonard Kleinman of Shaker Heights, Ohio—Steinbrenner's tax attorney, who was merely serving as an agent for the principal owner.

STEINBRENNER WAS STILL waiting to be approved by the American League owners when that spring's juiciest story broke: the stunning announcement by Yankee pitchers Fritz Peterson and Mike Kekich that they had decided to trade wives and, by extension, their families. The ever-cynical Dick Young wrote in the New York *Daily News*, "At least they did it before the inter-family trading deadline."

While it was left to general manager Lee MacPhail and manager Ralph Houk to provide the Yankees' public posture on the embarrassing wife-swap story, on most other issues Steinbrenner was fully engaged behind the scenes. Houk, who had enjoyed a unique autonomy as Yankee manager during the lean years of CBS's stewardship, found out quickly he was now working for a very different kind of owner.

On Opening Day against the Cleveland Indians, Steinbrenner was sitting in the club box behind the Yankees dugout, frowning as the Yankees stood at attention, caps off, for the national anthem. "The hair," he grumbled: "unacceptable." He began jotting down uniform numbers of the players he deemed in need of a haircut. After the game, he presented Houk with the list, which had a half-dozen numbers scrawled on it, including "1" for Bobby Murcer, "15" for Thurman Munson, "17" for Gene Michael and "28" for Sparky Lyle. "Tell these players they have to get their hair cut," he told Houk.

The next day, in a clubhouse meeting before the game, Houk carried out the new owner's edict, to the number.

"It was really kind of funny," recalled third baseman Graig Nettles, who had just come over to the Yankees from the Cleveland Indians the previous November and had taken an instant liking to Houk, reputed to be the ultimate "players' manager." "There's Ralph, standing there in front of us and announcing: 'I've been instructed to inform the following players to get their hair cut,' and then he reads off just the numbers. We thought it was funny that George didn't even know us by our names—only by our numbers and our hair."

A few months into the season, Steinbrenner was sitting in a box next to the visitors' dugout watching the Yankees take pregame infield practice at Arlington Stadium, in Texas, when Gene Michael, running out onto the field, suddenly tossed his glove up in the air and let out a shriek as a hot dog flew out of it, landing right in front of Steinbrenner. It turned out Michael was terrified of bugs and snakes and was often the butt of his teammates' practical jokes. In this case, infielder Hal Lanier had slipped the hot dog into one of the fingers of Michael's glove. From Steinbrenner's standpoint, though, pregame hijinks were an indication that Houk's players weren't taking the game seriously. In a fit of agitation, he wrote down Michael's uniform number and demanded that Houk discipline the tall, lanky shortstop.

"We knew George meant business when he came into the clubhouse afterward, accompanied by a Texas state trooper, demanding to know who was responsible for the prank," laughed Sparky Lyle, the free-spirit Yankee closer.

Michael remembered the incident as the first time Steinbrenner really took notice of him personally. After his playing days were over, he would serve two terms each as Steinbrenner's manager and general manager and went on to become the owner's most respected talent evaluator in the Yankee organization. "Even Ralph could hardly keep a straight face when he called me over and told me how pissed George was," said Michael.

Houk wasn't laughing as Steinbrenner continued to meddle for the rest of the '73 season, however, especially after the Yankees went into a second-half funk, going 20–34 in August and September. On August 17, the Yankees took an 8–1 drubbing from the Rangers in the first of a three-game series in Texas and right fielder Johnny Callison dropped a fly ball for a critical error. Steinbrenner, who was again in the stands, called general manager Lee MacPhail and bellowed: "Get that sonofabitch Callison out of here. He can't play. I want him gone, do you hear me?"

MacPhail protested but was forced to release Callison. It was the same with Bernie Allen, a utility infielder abruptly sold to the Montreal Expos after Steinbrenner deemed him unsuitable for his team. In the book *Dog Days*, by Philip Bashe, Allen recalled his exile to the Montreal Expos. "I went into the clubhouse to pick up my stuff and Ralph called me into his office and said: 'Bernie, I just wanted you to know that Lee and I had nothing to do with this.'"

(In retrospect, though he may have been impulsive and heavy-handed, Steinbrenner was right about both Callison and Allen, neither of whom played again beyond the '73 season.)

MacPhail and Houk were also privately revolted by Steinbrenner's hiring of Max Patkin, the so-called Clown Prince of Baseball, to perform his goofy gyrations and mimic routine from the first base coaching box during a few games that first season. Patkin had earned a living taking his routine through the minor leagues, and MacPhail and Houk, both of whom were steeped in Yankee tradition, regarded his presence as a bush league carnival act, certainly not befitting baseball's most revered franchise.

By now MacPhail had realized that his position as Yankee general manager under an impetuous, meddling owner and an established baseball executive, Gabe Paul, was not tenable. He had been desperately disappointed that Mike Burke had not solicited his interest in putting together an ownership group when CBS decided to put the Yankees up for sale, and now Burke was gone altogether, leaving MacPhail with no buffer between him and the aggressive new owner. He was therefore very interested to hear that 67-year-old Joe Cronin, who had served as American League president since 1959, planned to retire at the end of the 1973 season. For the American League owners, the search for a successor to Cronin was brief and uncomplicated, beginning and ending with MacPhail, whose nearly 25 years of baseball experience as Yankee farm director and general manager of both the Baltimore Orioles and the Yankees had earned him universal respect within the baseball establishment. Plus, as everyone well knew, he was eminently available.

MacPhail would remain on the job as Yankee GM until the end of the year. One of his final acts was to trade a fading, 36-year-old relief pitcher named Lindy McDaniel to the Kansas City Royals for outfielder Lou Piniella. It was a trade that would have lasting consequences, most of them positive, for both the Yankees as a team and Steinbrenner personally.

"For the last deal of my career, it wasn't too bad," said MacPhail.

Shortly after the '73 season, Bob Fishel, the vice president of public relations who was himself a Yankee institution, having presided over countless historic press conferences, including the 1960 Casey Stengel firing, Roger Maris's 1961 home run record chase, the return of Houk to the field in 1966 and the selling of the team by Dan Topping and Del Webb to CBS and then by CBS to Steinbrenner, announced that he, too, was leaving to join MacPhail in the same media relations capacity at the American League. Fishel's then-25-year-old assistant, Marty Appel, remembers feeling both shock and trepidation at his boss's departure.

"He told me he was leaving out of loyalty to Lee," said Appel, "but instead of feeling excited about being promoted, I felt a little scared. There had never been anyone as young as I was heading up public relations for a major league team, and now, instead of reporting to Bob, I was reporting directly to Steinbrenner."

As time passed, Fishel told friends that the real reason he left was Paul's presence as front office chief. "He just didn't trust Gabe and considered him an outsider, and he hated being around him. That became even more unbearable when Gabe took him off the road in '73," Appel recalled.

Ralph Houk also resigned after 1973, severing his 35-year relationship with the Yankees, where he had gone from backup catcher to coach, manager, general manager and manager again. But it was not quite as seamless as the resignations of his close colleagues, MacPhail and Fishel. In fact, there was very likely some behind-the-scenes skullduggery about it, although no one would ever fess up to it and nothing was ever proved, even in the aftermath of a league inquiry.

Nicknamed "The Major" (in reference to his Army rank in World War II, when he earned a Silver Star for bravery in leading his battalion's resistance to German panzer divisions in the town of Waldbillig during the Battle of the Bulge), Houk had replaced the popular Casey Stengel as Yankee manager in 1960 and become the first manager in baseball history to win world championships in his first two seasons. But in Houk's second term as Yankee manager—he'd gone upstairs as general manager in 1964, only to return to the field in April 1966, after the team started the season 4-16 under his handpicked successor, Johnny Keane—his standing with the fans deteriorated in conjunction with the quality of his teams. When the

Yankees went into their late-season collapse in '73, Houk was booed lustily by the home fans almost every time he came out of the dugout to make a pitching change.

Between the booing from the fans and Steinbrenner's meddling, Houk was ready and actively looking for a change of venue. Sometime in early September, after firing his manager, Billy Martin, Detroit Tigers general manager Jim Campbell contacted Houk to solicit his interest in coming over to Detroit. Houk never admitted to what would have been a case of tampering, even though it was an open secret he was planning to resign as Yankee manager at the end of the season and that the Tigers were his likely new employer. Houk always insisted it was more the continual booing he took from the fans that last season than Steinbrenner's interference that prompted him to leave. What was somewhat surprising—especially given his future lack of regard for managers—was Steinbrenner's overture to Houk to stay, in a meeting they had in the manager's office after the last game of the season.

"I've decided to resign, George," Houk said. "This losing and the booing has really been hard on me. It's time I moved on."

"You're making a mistake, Ralph," Steinbrenner said, "because I'm gonna go out and get ballplayers that'll make this team great again."

"Looking back, that's exactly what he did, and maybe I have a little regret about that," Houk told me in a 2002 interview. "But if I'd stayed, I'm sure he'd have gotten me too, just like all the rest of 'em."

The Yankees never made an issue of Campbell's likely tampering with Houk, probably because Steinbrenner had been guilty of the same thing that season with Oakland A's manager Dick Williams, who'd managed the A's to consecutive world championships in 1972 and '73. Like Houk, Williams worked for a meddlesome, irascible owner, Charles O. Finley, who quarreled publicly with the Oakland players and regularly called Williams in the middle of the night.

The final straw for Williams was Finley's infamous "firing" of second baseman Mike Andrews in the middle of the 1973 World Series, against the New York Mets. Andrews, a late-season acquisition, committed two errors in the 12th inning of Oakland's 10–7 loss in game two. Because Andrews had been nursing a sore shoulder, Finley seized the opportunity to try to replace him on the roster with another second baseman, Manny Trillo, by coercing him into signing a statement that he was too injured to play.

Finley's ploy was swiftly rejected by Commissioner Bowie Kuhn, who fined him $5,000 and ordered Andrews restored to the A's roster. For the disgusted Williams, the Andrews incident became his justification for re-signing as A's manager immediately after the last game of the Series.

As they stood side by side at the World Series trophy presentation ceremony, Finley said, "Even though you're not going to be with us next year, I want to thank you for the great job you've done for the three years you've been with me," to which Williams replied, "Thank you, Charlie, very much, and I'm going to miss being with you, but I've made a decision and I'm going to stick with it."

It appeared to be an amicable parting of ways, except that Williams had been secretly negotiating with the Yankees months before the World Series, and Finley quickly came to surmise as much. For, sometime in early August, as the Yankees began slumping badly, Steinbrenner decided to make a manager change at the end of the season. Hearing of Williams's dissatisfaction with Finley, he asked Gabe Paul to look into it. Wily to all the inner doings in baseball, Paul instinctively knew the man to talk to: Nat Tarnopol.

Growing up in Detroit, Tarnopol had been a star shortstop in high school and was offered contracts by both the Chicago White Sox and the Detroit Tigers in the late '40s. The low wages earned by baseball players at that time and the anti-Semitism directed at Jewish athletes, especially his boyhood hero, Hank Greenberg, prompted Tarnopol to pass on the offers, and instead he embarked on a career in the music industry, becoming, at age 25, manager of the legendary rhythm-and-blues singer Jackie Wilson and later taking control of the record label that produced Wilson's albums.

Once an established music mogul, Tarnopol used his wealth and influence to ingratiate himself with baseball players, especially the Jewish big-leaguers like the Yankees' Ron Blomberg. In the '70s he was a regular at Yankee Stadium and in Gabe Paul's office, suggesting trades and lobbying the Yankee president to have an "appreciation day" for Blomberg. Though he considered himself a Yankee insider, Tarnopol wasn't friendly with just the home team. He would often entertain friends on visiting teams at his mansion in upstate Purchase, New York. Among them was Irv Noren, a former Yankee outfielder in the '50s and now one of the A's coaches. When the A's came to New York on August 23 for a three-game series, Tarnopol called Noren at his hotel room to inform him of the Yankees' interest in his boss, Dick Williams.

At Noren's urging, Williams immediately called Tarnopol, who bragged to him that he'd talked to Paul and could get him the Yankee manager's job if he was interested. Williams definitely was.

"I'm no idiot," Williams told me in 2007. "I didn't quit Finley in the middle of the World Series without knowing I had another team in my pocket!"

Once Williams made his resignation official at the World Series, Steinbrenner instructed Paul to proceed with negotiations to sign Williams. But then, on October 23, two days after the World Series, Finley confronted Steinbrenner at an owners meeting in Chicago.

"I know what you're up to," Finley said after calling Steinbrenner aside in one of the conference rooms, "and I'm letting you know right here and now, Williams can resign all he wants to, I'm not letting him out of his contract. If you go ahead and try to sign Williams, I'll charge you with tampering!"

In a series of interviews immediately after that meeting, Finley reiterated that he was not going to let Williams out of his contract without being properly compensated, citing a similar 1968 circumstance in which the Mets had given the Washington Senators pitcher Bill Denehy and $250,000 in exchange for their releasing Gil Hodges from his contract so he could return home to manage New York.

The stalemate continued into the December winter baseball meetings in Houston, where Paul, realizing that the precedent set by the Hodges deal favored the A's, offered Finley a package that included two minor league players and $150,000 in exchange compensation for Williams. Finley flatly rejected the offer, saying that neither of the minor leaguers was a major league prospect. A frustrated Steinbrenner instructed his in-house counsel, Tom Evans, to pore over Williams's contract for any loopholes. On December 17, Evans reported back to Steinbrenner.

"I've studied every aspect of this contract, George," Evans said. "I can't find where you have any legal standing for hiring Williams."

Steinbrenner thanked Evans and hung up the phone. The next day, the Yankees held a press conference at Feathers-in-the-Park restaurant, near their new, temporary Shea Stadium offices, introducing Dick Williams as their new manager. In the contract negotiated by Paul, Williams was to receive an annual salary of $90,000 for three years and, in a separate agreement made personally by Steinbrenner, the Yankees would indemnify him for any damages he might incur if Finley filed a lawsuit claiming he had breached his contract. Because of the legal complications, Steinbrenner decided not to attend the press conference, leaving Paul to handle the tough questions. At one point, Paul was asked if the Yankees believed they were on solid legal ground in hiring Williams.

"We absolutely believe that," Paul said. "Our lawyers right here have assured us of this."

He then pointed to two men sitting in the front row of the press conference, neither of whom Evans, watching on TV, recognized.

"Right there and then was how I found out our firm was no longer George's general counsel," Evans said.

The next day, Finley filed a federal lawsuit in San Francisco seeking to prevent Williams from managing any team other than the Oakland A's for 1974. Nevertheless, on Sunday, December 16, Paul got a call from Steinbrenner expressing confidence in the Yankees' position.

"I just talked to Bowie," Steinbrenner said, referring to the commissioner, "and he told me he's delighted we've signed Williams. He also encouraged us to compensate Williams for any indemnification with Finley."

Thus, the stage was set for the first of many occasions when George Steinbrenner would be called to defend himself and his actions before the higher authorities of baseball. In this case, it was American League president Joe Cronin, who summoned him to Boston for a hearing on December 18 to determine the legality of the Tigers' hiring of Ralph Houk as their manager and the Yankees' subsequent hiring of Williams. It had been the strategy of the Yankees' new attorney, Martin Saiman, that they not contest the possible tampering on the Tigers' part for Houk in order to strengthen their own case for signing Williams.

Until the hearing, Williams had never met Steinbrenner. His only contact with the Yankees had been with Gabe Paul, who instructed him not to say a word "to anyone—*anyone*," when he arrived in Boston. Keeping that in mind, Williams purposely kept his head down as he walked across the hotel lobby to the check-in desk. When he suddenly heard a voice from behind one of the columns in the lobby shouting, "Dick! Dick!" he pretended not to hear it. Finally, as he was checking in, he felt a tap on his shoulder.

"Dick," said the voice behind him, "I'm George Steinbrenner. Didn't you hear me?"

Turning around, Williams said: "Hell, yeah, I heard you. But you told Gabe to tell me that I was not to talk to anyone! How was I supposed to know you were *you*?"

After hearing testimony from Campbell and Houk on the first day, Cronin gathered all the Yankees and A's parties the following morning for what would be a much lengthier session on December 19. In presenting the Yankees' position, Paul said that "without prejudice, in exchange for hiring Dick Williams we're prepared to offer Oakland the contract of pitcher Larry Gowell and $150,000, payable over three years, or the contract of pitcher Tom Buskey and $150,000, or the contracts of Buskey, Gowell and outfielder Ron Swoboda and $125,000."

Finley, sitting across the table, shot back: "I have no interest in any of those players. The players I want are outfielder Otto Velez and pitcher Scott McGregor. If the Yankees don't want to give me both of them, I'll take Velez and $100,000, or I'll take Velez and another outfielder, Terry Whitfield, plus a pitcher, Doug Heinold." (Heinold was the Yankees' number-one draft pick in 1973.)

Paul, his face flushed with anger, was clearly taken aback. Velez and McGregor were the Yankees' two top prospects. In a press conference later that day, he referred to them as "our crown jewels" and expressed his outrage at Finley's overreaching. Cronin apparently was unmoved by the Yankees' complaints.

On December 20, the Yankees received a teletype from Kuhn informing them that, after consulting with Cronin, he had decided to grant Houk the right to sign with Detroit. A few minutes later, a second teletype came in informing them that Williams's contract with the Yankees had been disapproved. When Paul called Steinbrenner to tell him the double dose of bad news, the Yankees owner reacted with predictable indignation.

"This is outrageous!" Steinbrenner bellowed into the phone. "We need to get new lawyers! How could they blow this?"

Though publicly he vowed that "this is not a dead issue," Paul knew the game was over. After hanging up with Steinbrenner he decided immediately to begin pursuing their second choice, Bill Virdon, who had just been fired as Pittsburgh Pirates manager one year after guiding them to a 96-win first-place finish in the National League East. Paul had admired Virdon both as a player who'd been one of the best defensive center fielders ever and as a manager with a reputation for being a sound tactician and strict disciplinarian. Paul had even tried to convince Steinbrenner to sign Virdon weeks earlier, as soon as it became clear that Finley was going to contest them over Williams.

A week after the notification from Kuhn, Paul instructed Lee MacPhail, who was finishing out his term as Yankee GM, to call Virdon and ask if he'd be interested in managing the Yankees, with the agreement that he'd step down once Williams became available. Somewhat surprisingly, Virdon said he was amenable to taking the job under those circumstances, as long as there were certain monetary guarantees in his contract, which he would discuss with Paul shortly after the new year. Two days after he spoke with Virdon, MacPhail got a phone call from Kuhn in which the commissioner said he had never given Steinbrenner his blessings to sign Williams—as Steinbrenner had maintained in that phone call to Paul on December 16— and that it had been a mistake to give him any encouragement to have Williams institute a suit against Finley. When informed of the conversation by MacPhail, Paul was dumfounded.

"Why would [Steinbrenner] have told me all that?" Paul wondered on his tape-recorded diary entry that day.

Paul's meeting with Virdon was scheduled for January 3, but the day before, he got a phone call from Steinbrenner, who was again in a fury, this time over the fact that his scheme to have Williams sue Finley (with the Yankees paying his legal expenses) was all falling apart.

"You and MacPhail let me down!" Steinbrenner exploded into the phone. "We had an agreement with Williams that was something we all wanted and signed off on!"

Rather than arguing with Steinbrenner, or even mentioning that Kuhn had denied ever having okayed the Yankees' signing of Williams, Paul just listened. When Steinbrenner finally stopped speaking, Paul reminded him of the meeting with Virdon the next day.

"I will not go for Virdon!" Steinbrenner screamed. "*You* guys want him! I don't want him!"

Now Paul was furious. It was too late in their conversation with Virdon for Steinbrenner to back out like this. This was no time for Steinbrenner to be embarking on one of his petulant tirades. They had a manager to hire! After hanging up the phone in exasperation, he said to himself: "I should've told him to stick this job up his ass. Here he is acting like he had nothing to do with all this when he instigated all of it and made up conversations he had with Kuhn. This guy has to be crazy!"

Paul decided to keep the meeting the next day. Much to his surprise, Steinbrenner himself strode into the Yankee offices at 9 o'clock sharp that morning. "He was in good spirits, with no hint of the belligerency of the previous night, and he was immediately taken by Virdon," Paul said in his tape entry that day. "We covered all the bases—coaches, managing techniques, discipline. This was the same guy George had wanted no part of the night before!"

It was then left to Paul to complete the financial arrangements with Virdon.

"I have been authorized to offer a salary of $40,000 for you to manage the team and $25,000 if you have to be a coach," Paul said. Virdon insisted on the $50,000 he'd been making in Pittsburgh, while agreeing to have it reduced to $40,000 if the Yankees hired Williams and he had to become a coach. Upon having Virdon's request relayed to him, Steinbrenner told Paul to go ahead with those terms on a one-year contract.

As for Williams, he had resigned himself to sitting out the year and collecting Finley's money when, on June 27, 1974, the California Angels fired their manager, Bobby Winkles. The Angels' owner, Gene Autry, who had poured millions of dollars into the team but enjoyed little success since its inception in 1961, immediately contacted Finley about Williams. This time, Finley didn't ask for any compensation—at least not publicly. "I'm letting Dick go to the Angels not for his sake but because of my affection for Gene Autry," Finley said.

According to Williams, though, that was not entirely true.

"Years later, Finley bragged to me that he got $100,000 from Autry for me," he told me.

With Mike Burke, Howard Berk, Lee MacPhail, Bob Fishel and Ralph Houk all out the door and Dick Williams briefly in and then out as well, the first year of George Steinbrenner's Yankee stewardship had been one of uneasy transition.

Gabe Paul would tell friends that he'd never been around anyone quite so mercurial and ill-tempered in all his years in baseball. The initial wave of defections from the Yankees was not limited to just the front office and the dugout. Three of the original limited partners, Nelson Bunker Hunt, Sheldon Guren and Ed Ginsberg, divested themselves of their Yankee stock after that first year. For Guren and Ginsberg, Steinbrenner's attorney pals from Group 66 in Cleveland, a bad real estate venture in Texas forced them to sell their shares back to Steinbrenner. Hunt, on the other hand, was one of the wealthiest men in the country but had no interest in being involved in baseball. As he explained to me in a February 2008 telephone interview, "I only invested with George as a favor through a mutual friend of ours and always it was with the understanding that I could sell it back as soon as I wanted."

Those three original partners got out before they could discover what another limited Yankee partner, John McMullen, would learn later in the decade. When asked in 1979 why he was selling his Yankee stock, McMullen, who a few months later purchased the Houston Astros for $13 million, famously replied: "I came to realize there is nothing in life quite so limited as being a limited partner of George Steinbrenner."

4

. . .

Watergate and Catfish

. . .

B Y THE END OF his first season as Yankees president, Gabe Paul was beginning to wonder what he'd gotten himself into with "this Steinbrenner," as he frequently referred to him. In his years as general manager of the Cincinnati Reds and Cleveland Indians, Paul had run the day-to-day baseball operations largely without interference by the owners, who trusted Paul's judgment on players and salaries and generally left him alone while concentrating on their other businesses.

Paul had taken Steinbrenner at his word when the new Yankees owner had said he would be too busy with his shipbuilding business and would be leaving the running of the team "to the experts." "It didn't take long for him to become an expert," Paul bemoaned. As the 1973 season went on and Lee MacPhail began phasing himself out as Yankees GM, Paul found himself constantly putting out brush fires started by Steinbrenner, from the Dick Williams fiasco to the barring of Joan Steinbrenner from the Yankee Club.

"Thank God," Paul thought, "he's had this Watergate business to consume himself with."

What had at first appeared to be an isolated break-in at the Democratic campaign headquarters in the Watergate Hotel, in Washington, D.C., was by the summer of 1973 raging into a major scandal, with the Nixon administration accused of a litany of crimes ranging from conspiracy, burglary and wiretapping to obstruction of justice and illegal campaign fund-raising.

It was the latter criminal activity in which George Steinbrenner allowed himself to become ensnared, and as his first season as owner of the New York Yankees played out, he was beginning to feel the walls of justice closing in on him.

When Richard Nixon's former attorney, Thomas Evans, who was then general counsel at American Shipbuilding Co., introduced Steinbrenner to Herb Kalmbach, the deputy finance director for the Committee to Re-elect the President (CREEP), in March of 1972, he didn't know how much money Steinbrenner intended to donate. Nor did he have any idea that Kalmbach was already engaged in a patently illegal scheme to raise money for Nixon.

At Steinbrenner's first meeting with Kalmbach, the deputy finance chairman informed the Yankees owner that if he wanted to make a donation to the president, to get his attention, it would have to be a meaningful one—as in $100,000. When Steinbrenner didn't blanch at the figure, Kalmbach provided him a list of some 40 separate organizations that were branches of CREEP—groups with patriotic names such as Dedicated Americans for Effective Government and Loyal Americans for Government—that would funnel the money to Nixon's campaign. Kalmbach further instructed him to write 33 separate checks for $3,000 and one additional check for $1,000, since, according to federal law, gifts exceeding $3,000 required the disclosure of the donor's name.

The law was scheduled to be amended on April 7, 1972, after which the names of all political contributors would have to be disclosed. But under Kalmbach's direction, Steinbrenner was able to beat the deadline by one day. On April 6, he delivered checks from six of his American Shipbuilding Co. employees made out for $3,000 apiece and, in violation of Kalmbach's instructions, two more for $3,500 each. (It was those last two checks, in excess of Kalmbach's explicit instructions, that alerted the Watergate investigators and ultimately led to Steinbrenner's indictment.) The origin of this largesse from the AmShip employees turned out to be bonus checks totaling $42,325.17 from Steinbrenner, which, after taxes, wound up to be $25,000. For the remaining $75,000, Steinbrenner wrote out 25 personal checks for $3,000, each of them to a different committee on the list Kalmbach had provided him.

"The concept of getting money through corporate employees was

George Steinbrenner's idea and *not* my idea," Evans told me emphatically in a 2008 interview. "It was something George had developed when he was raising money for Democrats. I only learned that he had used this mechanism with Kalmbach months after he had done it."

Evans explained that, in 1968, he'd developed 33 or more committees for fund-raising purposes, each of which had separate charters and separate officers and could act in its own behalf. But sometime in the 1970s, someone developed a similar list that had the same officers for each committee.

"That meant that they were, in fact, all one committee—and that was a violation of the law," Evans said.

On November 13, 1973, two employees of the American Shipbuilding Co., Matthew E. Clark Jr., the director of purchasing, and Robert E. Bartlome, the company's secretary, testified before the Watergate Committee in Washington that a total of $25,000 in corporation funds was given to the Republicans through a sham bonus plan in 1972, and that other false bonuses had been given to "loyal" AmShip employees in 1970 and '71 and subsequently passed on as political contributions. Clark and Bartlome went on to testify that attempts had been made to cover up their illegal contributions through such devices as placing false backdated memorandums in the company's files and listing some of the expenditures on the company's books as "research."

Clark and Bartlome said that when they were subpoenaed to appear before the Watergate Committee in 1973, they, along with the other AmShip employees involved, agreed they would not perjure themselves. According to the two, when they informed Steinbrenner of their intentions at a meeting in the company offices, he put his head down on the desk and moaned: "I'm ruined! This company is ruined!" But then, Clark said, Steinbrenner handed him $200 in cash and said: "Have a nice weekend."

Steinbrenner had hired the high-powered Washington attorney Edward Bennett Williams, whose previous clients included Frank Sinatra, *Playboy* publisher Hugh Hefner, mob boss Frank Costello and Teamsters union chief Jimmy Hoffa. Through Williams, Steinbrenner exercised his constitutional right under the Fifth Amendment not to testify.

It would be another five months—on April 5, 1974—before Watergate Special Prosecutor Leon Jaworski handed down a 15-count indictment of Steinbrenner. The indictment charged the 43-year-old Steinbrenner with having set up a phony bonus system for trusted employees who then wrote out checks for campaign contributions. It also alleged that he'd authorized the employees to submit fictitious expense vouchers to receive reimbursement.

"I'm a fighter, not a quitter. I am totally innocent and we will prove it in court, where this case belongs," Steinbrenner said in response to the indictment, which stunned Yankees employees who had been unaware of how deeply involved the Yankees owner had actually been in the Watergate affair.

All through that summer of '74, Steinbrenner spent most of his time working with Williams on his defense. Finally, on August 23, in a U.S. district court in Cleveland, he entered a guilty plea of illegally authorizing $25,000 in campaign contributions to the Committee to Re-elect the President as well as illegally contributing $1,000 to the reelection campaign of Democratic senator Vance Hartke of Indiana and $500 to the campaign of Democratic senator Daniel Inouye in 1970. In addition, he pleaded guilty to a second count of being an accessory after the fact by attempting to cover up the contributions. The Associated Press reported that Steinbrenner was the 17th person and American Shipbuilding Co. the 14th corporation to be convicted or indicted for illegal federal campaign contributions in conjunction with the Watergate scandal.

Under the provisions of the original indictment, Steinbrenner could have received up to six years in prison and been fined as much as $15,000. But with the renowned Williams handling his defense, he was spared any jail time at his August 30 sentencing before Federal Judge Leroy J. Contie Jr. Rather, he was fined $10,000 on the felony illegal campaign charges and $5,000 on the misdemeanor "accessory after the fact" charge. In addition, AmShip was fined $10,000 on each of the two felony counts.

In what sounded much like the familiar refrain he would make after tough Yankee losses in years to come, Steinbrenner said of his sentencing: "All things considered, I can't be critical, because what happened, happened. [The prosecutors] were fair and tough. I'm not sure if I'll invite them to my next party, but thank God the country has guys like that."

(Steinbrenner remained a convicted felon, unable to vote, until

January 19, 1989, when President Ronald Reagan, in one of his final acts before leaving office, pardoned the Yankees owner for his 1972 illegal campaign contributions—along with industrialist Armand Hammer, who had also been found guilty of making illegal contributions to Nixon, worth $54,000.)

Clearly embarrassed by his now very public involvement in the Watergate scandal, Steinbrenner became an infrequent visitor to his favorite Cleveland haunts, the Pewter Mug and Mushy Wexler's Theatrical Grill, or the Cleveland social events where he'd always been a fixture. Then in late 1974, Steinbrenner revealed that he was moving AmShip's headquarters, as well as his family, to Tampa. He explained the move as being made primarily because his wife, Joan, wanted to live in a warmer climate. Privately, however, he told friends that he was sick and tired of being "abused" in the Cleveland newspapers and not appreciated for all the humanitarian work he'd done for the city.

What he never explained was why he broke the law for $25,000 when he could have contributed the entire $100,000 himself, without involving his AmShip employees in this elaborate fake bonus scheme. And what was his ultimate motivation? To win favor with the Nixon administration after he'd previously gotten considerable financial and tax relief for the Great Lakes shipping industry from the Democrats?

"I honestly don't think it was any of that," said Evans. "I honestly believe George just wanted to be closer to power. It was strictly an ego thing with him."

Steinbrenner got away with a slap on the wrist from the government, but his indictment and guilty plea created a much more serious problem for him with baseball. Commissioner Bowie Kuhn had been monitoring Steinbrenner's legal proceedings. In his 1987 memoir, *Hardball,* Kuhn wrote, "Illegal contributions may be one thing, but obstruction of justice is quite another."

As Kuhn noted, the latter was a serious charge for which people went to jail. The last baseball owner to go to jail, St. Louis Cardinals owner Fred Saigh (sentenced to 15 months in 1953 for tax evasion), was ordered by then-commissioner Ford Frick to sell the team. This was not a prospect Kuhn relished having to deal with, and when Steinbrenner hired Williams, the commissioner privately hoped the Yankees owner would be able to totally exonerate himself.

In a meeting with Kuhn shortly after revelations of his involvement first broke in the news, Steinbrenner maintained that the offenses he was alleged to have committed occurred in 1972, before he bought the Yankees, and that they therefore had nothing to do with baseball. Kuhn replied that those facts would not prevent him from taking serious disciplinary action if Steinbrenner were convicted. Though confounded by Kuhn's stance, Steinbrenner pledged to give the commissioner "every cooperation on this," while reassuring him that "there will be no reason for you to do anything."

Once the indictment came down, Steinbrenner decided to remove himself from the daily affairs of the Yankees, citing his need to concentrate all his time and energy on his defense. "Perhaps anticipating a suspension," Kuhn said, "George beat me to the punch and, in the process, earned some credit with me. Also to his credit, he never tried to hide from the seriousness of the matter."

Kuhn was admittedly surprised when Steinbrenner was able to plead guilty to a single felony count of the indictment, but he was still greatly troubled by the obstruction of justice to which the Yankees owner had also pleaded guilty. In a meeting in his office with Steinbrenner and Williams a few days after the sentencing, Kuhn said he was not persuaded by Williams's argument that, since Judge Contie had settled for a fine and no jail time, there should be no suspension.

Kuhn mulled his decision for a couple of weeks, all the while having trouble getting past the fact that Steinbrenner had pleaded guilty to a felony that could have included jail time. Finally, on November 27, in a 12-page ruling, Kuhn announced that he was suspending Steinbrenner for two years, declaring the Yankees owner "ineligible and incompetent" to "have any association whatsoever with any major league club or its personnel." Kuhn went on to say in the ruling that "an essential element of a professional team sport is the public's confidence in its integrity. Attempting to influence employees to behave dishonestly is the kind of misconduct which, if ignored by baseball, would undermine the public's confidence in our game."

Steinbrenner was in his office in Tampa when he was notified of Kuhn's decision. He immediately called Yankees P. R. man Marty Appel in a rage.

"How dare he call me incompetent!" Steinbrenner screamed at Appel. He then began dictating a statement of his own, as the 24-year-old neophyte PR director frantically scribbled down his words.

"Naturally, we are shocked beyond belief by Mr. Kuhn's decision. It is certainly a wonderful Thanksgiving Day present. I will be meeting with my attorney, Edward Bennett Williams, in the next few days. We haven't yet had time to carefully study the full decision. But we understand that Mr. Kuhn has found that I am 'ineligible and incompetent.' It is impossible to understand how the commissioner of baseball could call me incompetent."

"As much as George seemed hung up on that 'incompetent' word, I think he knew down deep it was a legal term, and he just used it as a PR opportunity to win some sympathy points," said Appel.

A few days later, Kuhn sent a letter to Steinbrenner clarifying the terms of his suspension, stating: *"For as long as [Steinbrenner] remains on the Ineligible List, he shall not exercise any of the delegated power, duties or authority of the General Partner; visit or be physically present in the Yankee offices or clubhouse; confer, consult, instruct, advise, or otherwise communicate, either directly or indirectly, with the person or persons to who such powers, duties and authority are delegated. These prohibitions shall not be interpreted as prohibiting Mr. Steinbrenner from associating with such persons on a purely social basis, during which there shall be no discussion of the affairs, financial or otherwise, of the New York Yankees."*

Those "persons" to whom Kuhn referred were Patrick J. Cunningham, the Bronx Democratic leader, whom Steinbrenner quickly named acting general partner and general counsel, and Gabe Paul, who, as team president, would continue to handle all the day-to-day baseball and business operations of the Yankees. At the time, Cunningham was a major political figure, and Kuhn was satisfied that, between him and Paul, the Yankees were in capable hands. He was also satisfied that the underlying terms of the suspension—preventing Steinbrenner from having any public communications regarding baseball as well as from attending baseball meetings—were a "significant deprivation for a man of George's ego."

For Gabe Paul, the one upside to the Watergate scandal was that Steinbrenner finally became the hands-off owner he had promised to be when he bought the team. On April 27, Paul executed a multiplayer trade with his old assistant general manager in Cleveland, Phil Seghi, in which the Yankees sent pitchers Fritz Peterson, Steve Kline, Fred Beene and Tom Buskey to the Indians in exchange for first baseman Chris Chambliss and pitchers Dick Tidrow and Cecil Upshaw. It proved to be a complete fleecing of his former team on Paul's part, as Chambliss and Tidrow became important cogs in the Yankees' 1976–77–78 championship teams while, of the four pitchers Cleveland obtained, only Peterson would have another good season (with a 14-8 record in 1975) and all but Buskey had retired by 1977.

Under Bill Virdon, the backup manager choice to Dick Williams, the 1974 Yankees, who were picked to finish somewhere near the bottom of the American League East, wound up in second place, 89-73, two games behind the Baltimore Orioles, thanks to a fierce late-season rally. In mid-August the Yankees had been in fourth place with a 60-61 record, but they won 29 of their next 41 games—including a sweep of the Indians, their second-to-last opponents of the regular season—and boarded an airplane to Milwaukee with a chance to win the division. That chance was gone by the end of the flight, where the Yankees partied a little too hard. Things got really rambunctious as they checked into the Pfister Hotel, where reserve catchers Rick Dempsey and Bill Sudakis got into a fistfight. All of a sudden, players were wrestling and rolling all over the floor. Bill "Killer" Kane, the Yankees' traveling secretary, said the scene was "like one of those old-fashioned furniture fights in the westerns with tables and lamps crashing to the floor and bodies flying over the couches." Bobby Murcer, the Yankees' best player, who led the team with 88 RBI, broke his finger attempting to separate the combatants.

The next day, the Yankees lost 3–2 to Milwaukee when Lou Piniella, Murcer's replacement in right field, dropped a fly ball that started a tying rally for the Brewers in the eighth inning, and the Orioles beat the Tigers in Detroit to win the division. Disappointing as the ending was, Steinbrenner, who was traveling with the team and had witnessed firsthand the Yankees' three-game sweep of the Indians in Cleveland (in which they scored 28 runs), was ebullient over the way his team had played. In Cleveland, adhering to the terms of Kuhn's suspension, he had waited outside the clubhouse to extend congratulations to his players, but in Milwaukee, with the season over, he was unable to restrain himself.

"I don't care what they do to me," he said to reporters as he strode into the visiting clubhouse after the final game. "I want to be with these guys. They played like champions."

"It was all very harmless," said Phil Pepe, the Yankees beat writer for the New York *Daily News*. "The season was over and George just wanted to celebrate with his players, and Bowie let it pass. Nothing was ever said, at least not publicly."

Nevertheless, Gabe Paul thought Steinbrenner's eagerness to socialize with his players was a detriment to the operation of the team. In terms of player-management relations, Paul was strictly old school. He believed the players were nothing more than chattels of the team; in order for the club to maximize profits, salaries had to be held in line. Above all, he would say, you can never fall in love with your players. It was therefore no surprise that, to a man, the Yankee players detested him—and no surprise that Paul resented the camaraderie Steinbrenner enjoyed with them.

In particular, Murcer, the team's star center fielder (whose $100,000 contract had been cause for one of Steinbrenner's celebrated flaps with Mike Burke), had a very chummy relationship with the owner. Murcer had introduced Steinbrenner to fellow Oklahoman Mickey Mantle and could occasionally be seen dining with the Yankees owner in Manhattan. According to Murcer, during that time, Steinbrenner assured him, "As long as I own this team, you'll be here."

But when the Yankees moved to Shea Stadium in 1974 because of the renovation of Yankee Stadium, Murcer's performance suffered dramatically. He had the perfect left-handed swing for Yankee Stadium's short (344 feet) right field porch, but at Shea, where the right field fence was some 30 feet farther away, his fly balls invariably turned into routine outs in front of the warning track. After averaging 25 home runs per season for his first seven years with the Yankees, he hit just 10 in 1974, only two of them at home. In addition, Virdon, noticing a deterioration in Murcer's defensive skills in center field, moved him to right (replacing him in center with Elliott Maddox, a singles hitter the Yankees had obtained that spring from the Texas Rangers). The move to Shea and the move to right had been a double-barreled blow to Murcer's ego, and it didn't help him either that Steinbrenner had become disconnected from much of the day-to-day baseball operations.

Between Murcer's slippage as an elite player and Steinbrenner's pre-occupation with his Watergate defense, Gabe Paul saw an opportunity to rid himself of a player he felt had way too much influence with the owner. At the 1974 World Series in Los Angeles, between the Dodgers and the Oakland A's, Paul's longtime friend Cappy Harada, a scout for the San Francisco Giants, told him that the Giants were shopping their two-time All-Star right fielder Bobby Bonds, the fourth player in baseball history to hit 30 homers and steal 30 bases in a single season.

Paul swiftly arranged a meeting with Giants owner Horace Stoneham at Candlestick Park in San Francisco on October 14, where he proposed a trade: Murcer for Bonds, straight up. Stoneham said he'd have to discuss it with his chief scout, Charlie Fox, and suggested they talk further at the World Series gala in Oakland the next day.

Stoneham had a reputation for being a heavy drinker, so Paul felt it would be the perfect venue in which to extract a favorable deal from the Giants owner. However, when they met at the cocktail party, Stoneham said he'd have to get Doc Medich, one of the Yankees' best pitchers, in the deal—which Paul flatly rejected. That night, he called Steinbrenner to inform him where things stood.

"Just take it easy, Gabe," Steinbrenner said. "We can't chase it."

Paul agreed. The next day, Stoneham called him back.

"Do you still want to make the Murcer-for-Bonds deal?"

"Absolutely," said Paul.

"Okay," said Stoneham. "We'll do it, one for one."

After agreeing to wait until after the World Series to announce the trade, Paul immediately called Steinbrenner, who was delighted: "This is one of the greatest deals we ever made!"

However, the next morning, Steinbrenner called Paul with a new idea. He'd had lunch in Cleveland the day before with Ken Aspromonte, the man-ager of the Indians, who had told him the Kansas City Royals were look-ing to move their first baseman, John Mayberry, and their center fielder, Amos Otis.

"Mayberry and Otis would be even better than Bonds for Murcer," Steinbrenner said. "Can't we do this?"

"No, George, we can't," said Paul. "We can't renege on our word with San Francisco."

"Well, Aspromonte tells me that Murcer is overrated."

"George," Paul screamed, "that's what we've been telling you for a long time!"

"Now all of a sudden he's got Aspromonte as one of his new advisers," Paul groused in private into his tape recorder. "Imagine Kenny coming in here and looking over my shoulder. That's all I need. I hired him in Cleveland, for God's sakes!"

At least he'd been able to convince Steinbrenner about the honor in keeping an agreement with another owner.

Four days after the 1974 World Series, on October 21, the Yankees called a press conference to announce the Murcer-for-Bonds deal. Marty Appel remembered the glow on Paul's face as he summoned him into his office at 9 o'clock that morning.

"I want you to hear this phone conversation," Paul said after instructing his secretary, Pearl Davis, to call Murcer at his home in Oklahoma City, where it was 8 o'clock.

"Bobby? Gabe Paul here. Did I wake you? Oh, I'm sorry. But you know that old saying: Only whores make a living in bed. Anyway, I've got some news for you, which you may not like at first but will be a terrific opportunity for you. We've decided to go in a different direction here. We've traded you to the San Francisco Giants."

On the other side of the line, the groggy Murcer was bewildered.

"Did I just hear that right?" he said.

The conversation continued uneasily for another couple of minutes before Paul told Murcer that if there was anything the Yankees could do for him to let him know, and ended the call. Upon hanging up, he looked at Appel and said, grinning, "Well, what did you think of *that*?"

But because of Paul's haste to call Murcer to inform him of the trade, news of the deal leaked out before the Giants were able to hold their press conference, which was scheduled for that morning in San Francisco. This prompted an angry, drunken phone call from Stoneham to Paul at about 4 o'clock in the afternoon New York time.

"You beat the announcement," Stoneham slurred. "How could you? I'm getting killed out here. They're saying I wanted Medich in the deal and when I couldn't get him, I went ahead and did it anyway. I never asked for Medich!"

Paul speculated that Murcer had probably called Players Association chief Marvin Miller to ask about his rights and that was how the story had leaked out.

"What are you telling me?" Stoneham said. "That he doesn't want to report?"

"No, no. Everything's okay. He's going to love San Francisco. I told him what a great opportunity it is for him."

Nevertheless, Paul decided to call United Press International columnist Milton Richman and ask him to write a nice column about Stoneham and how the Giants owner had only wanted Murcer in the deal. The following February, Murcer reluctantly reported to the Giants' spring training camp in Phoenix, where he would go on to have an All-Star season (hitting .298) but an otherwise miserable two-year existence in chilly San Francisco before being traded to the Chicago Cubs.

A month after unloading Murcer, Paul was able to rid himself of another of Steinbrenner's favorites: Gene Michael, the light-hitting backup shortstop, who had turned down the club's contract offer of $45,000 for 1975. Instead of negotiating any further, Paul called Michael and informed him he was being released.

"You gotta be kidding!" Michael said.

"No," Paul said, "this is what we've decided to do."

"Does Mr. Steinbrenner know about this?" Michael demanded.

Paul, clearly annoyed by Michael's assertion that Steinbrenner would have never approved of him being released, said: "There's no retreat on this. I don't care who you call."

After hanging up, Paul thought: "The guy was a damn fool to turn down $45,000. I just hope Steinbrenner doesn't do something equally foolish by bringing him back."

In spite of the embarrassment of Watergate and the subsequent restraints of his exile, Steinbrenner had a right to feel good about the direction the Yankees were heading in the first two years of his stewardship. The trades for Nettles, Chambliss, Tidrow, Bonds and Piniella, a .300 hitter and the 1969 Rookie of the Year, had laid the foundation for a championship-quality team. As big as the acquisitions of Bonds and Piniella were, Steinbrenner was hard at work after the 1974 season to secure a player whose very signing would have monumental consequences on baseball.

On the eve of the 1974 World Series, Jerome Holtzman of the *Chicago Sun-Times* reported that Oakland A's owner Charlie Finley—who had successfully blocked Steinbrenner from hiring his manager, Dick Williams, the previous year—had been charged with a breach of contract by his star pitcher, Catfish Hunter. On behalf of Hunter, the Major League Baseball Players Association had filed a grievance against Finley, citing the failure of the A's owner to make a $50,000 annuity payment that was part of the deferred salary in Hunter's contract. (In January 1974, following his third-straight 21-win season, Hunter had signed a two-year contract with the A's, at $100,000 per, with a unique arrangement in which $50,000 in salary each year would be deferred in annuity payments to the Jefferson Standard Life Insurance Co. of Greensboro, North Carolina.) With the union's backing, Hunter argued that Finley's failure to make the payment had rendered the contract void, which would thus make the pitcher a free agent.

Initially, the story was viewed as just another dispute between the cantankerous Finley and one of his players. Though Oakland, with its bumper crop of homegrown talent—including Hunter, slugger Reggie Jackson, third baseman Sal Bando, shortstop Campy Campaneris, outfielder Joe Rudi and reliever Rollie Fingers—was baseball's best team in the early '70s, winning back-to-back world championships in 1972–73, Finley was constantly feuding with his players.

Hunter had a strong ally in Players Association executive director Marvin Miller. Since assuming the leadership of the union in 1966, Miller had won a slew of new rights for the players that led to unprecedented improvements in salaries and benefits. Throughout his contentious labor negotiations with the owners, Miller's ultimate goal was the elimination of the reserve clause in the standard player's contract, which effectively bound players to their teams for life. The issue had gone all the way to the Supreme Court in 1970 when St. Louis Cardinals outfielder Curt Flood lost a suit in which he contended that the team had no right to trade him without his consent.

Finley, who'd made his fortune in the insurance business, should have known better than to make the initial deal with Hunter. The reason he'd refused to pay the $50,000 annuity was that he came to realize it was not tax-deductible, like a regular salary, and that he wouldn't be able to deduct the payments to the insurance company until years later, when Hunter began receiving *his* deferred payments. It was a blunder that finally gave Miller his opening in his effort to win the most precious right of all for the players—free agency.

At first Finley downplayed the story, saying, "It's not even worth commenting on, but you can be assured that we do not owe any player any money." A few days later, he appeared to backtrack somewhat, telling *The Sporting News* that the situation was "just a little misunderstanding."

Hunter said nothing. He was in the middle of the World Series against the Dodgers (earning a save in game one and winning game three with a 7⅓ inning, one-run effort), but his agent, Jerry Kapstein, confirmed to reporters that Finley had reneged on the contract.

Because there was no precedent for such a case, nobody could predict whether Hunter might actually be awarded free agency. (Kapstein, for one, didn't believe the case would lead to his client winning free agency, and when Hunter later learned that his agent had expressed this opinion to reporters, he fired him.)

American League president Lee MacPhail downplayed that possibility, revealing that Finley, in his presence, had attempted to make restitution with Hunter prior to the American League Championship Series. This was only partially true. At an October 4 meeting at Finley's office inside the Oakland Coliseum, the A's owner had offered Hunter a check for $50,000, to which Hunter replied, "I can't take it. I've been advised by my attorney that the check must be sent directly to the Jefferson Insurance Company."

MacPhail contended that the offer by Finley was sufficient grounds for Hunter not being awarded free agency, but baseball's arbitrator, Peter Seitz, disagreed. On December 13, Seitz ruled that not only would Finley have to pay the $50,000 in the annuity method specified in the contract, but that Hunter was now a free agent and could negotiate with any team in baseball.

The players were overjoyed. The owners were outraged, though that didn't stop them from trying to sign Hunter. All of a sudden, the best pitcher in baseball was available to the highest bidder. Kuhn set December 18 as the starting date for the historic auction.

All the negotiating took place at the Ahoskie, North Carolina, offices of Catfish Hunter's attorney, J. Carlton Cherry, about an hour's drive from Hunter's farm in Hertford, North Carolina. With the exception of one team, the San Francisco Giants, club officials began making the pilgrimage to this tiny rural hamlet to meet with Hunter and his new celebrity country lawyer. Even notoriously tightfisted Minnesota Twins owner Calvin Griffith wanted in. "I think this is one of those once-in-a-lifetime happenings," Griffith said. "I think most of our players would be glad to see us get Hunter, because it would add $25,000 to their contracts if he pitches us to the World Series."

On Friday, December 20, Gabe Paul flew from New York to Tampa to discuss the situation with Steinbrenner. As he would later tell Yankee confidants, Paul did not believe this was a violation of Steinbrenner's suspension agreement with Kuhn, since a Hunter signing would involve a sizable investment on the part of the team that could not be made without the knowledge and approval of the principal owner. By then, speculation in the papers and TV had put the top bid over $2 million for five years, and Paul told Steinbrenner that they needed to be prepared to go $3 million or more if they were going to lure the country boy to New York. The one advantage the Yankees might have, Paul said, was Clyde Kluttz, a former big league catcher and a onetime neighbor of Hunter's who was now a scout for the Yankees. It was Kluttz, as a scout for Finley, who had signed Hunter to his first professional contract with the A's in 1964, before they moved from Kansas City to Oakland.

"You do what you feel you have to do," Steinbrenner told Paul. "We have to get this guy."

On December 23, Paul caught a 7:25 A.M. flight out of Tampa, changed planes in Atlanta, took a charter flight to Raleigh and then drove to Ahoskie for a one o'clock meeting. As he began the discussion with Cherry, Paul remembered being "flabbergasted" to hear the lawyer say the bids were getting higher than he and Hunter ever expected; that teams had told them they were prepared to bid between $3 million and $5 million. And Kluttz had told him it would probably take $2 million to sign Hunter.

Paul's meeting with Cherry lasted almost two hours, while Montreal Expos executives John McHale and Jim Fanning were waiting anxiously in another room. At the conclusion of the meeting, Paul, as usual, made a relatively low offer of $1.5 million over five years that he quickly realized was not even close to the offers from other clubs. Cherry told him he'd get back to him, prompting Paul to say the Yankees were prepared to be competitive with whatever offers other clubs made for Hunter. In the meantime, Paul instructed Kluttz to hang out in Ahoskie to monitor the developments and continue to lobby Hunter and his friends and family.

For a week, Kluttz stayed in his hotel room in nearby Elizabeth City, reading the papers and watching TV all day before venturing out at night to visit Hunter's friends in Hertford, subtly selling the virtues of New York. Every other day, he would stop at Hunter's house and give his New York pitch firsthand. At one point, Hunter asked him about living in New York. Kluttz said, "I hated it too. But people's people. The city's fast, and you wouldn't want to live downtown. But just get a place in the country. There's plenty of country not far from the city."

Hunter then asked Kluttz about San Diego, where the Padres (whose manager, John McNamara, had managed the A's in 1969 and '70) had offered $3 million over five years.

"San Diego's nice," Kluttz said. "But how many players from San Diego have ever made it to the Hall of Fame?"

That prompted another question from Hunter that Kluttz had been prepared for.

"How about Steinbrenner?"

"Look," said Kluttz. "It can't be any worse than playing for Finley. You're going to get a lot more press in New York, and you can handle the media. And you're going to make a whole heckuva lot more money up there off the field. New York is where everything's happening."

After that conversation, Kluttz sensed that he was winning Hunter over to signing with the Yankees, but he worried that another team might make an outrageous offer at the last moment. He called Paul and told him he'd better get back to Ahoskie to nail the deal. At Steinbrenner's suggestion, Paul brought with him Ed Greenwald, a Cleveland attorney and one of Steinbrenner's limited Yankees partners, to handle the contract negotiations.

On Sunday, December 29, Paul, Kluttz and Greenwald checked in at the Temple Motor Inn, in Raleigh, and drove to Ahoskie the next morning. On the trip, Kluttz briefed Paul on what he knew about the offers Hunter was considering. Before leaving New York, Paul had called Cherry and upped the Yankees' offer to $2.6 million.

"It's obvious to me Hunter wants New York," Kluttz said, "but San Diego was so strong with him, he might accept."

To Paul, that sounded as if the Yankees might be out. They pulled the car over at a Gulf station where Greenwald rushed to a phone booth and called Steinbrenner.

"I think we're probably going to up our offer to $2.8 million," he said.

"It's Gabe's decision," Steinbrenner said. "But there'll be no problem with the bank."

As they arrived at Cherry's office, Cleveland Indians owner Ted Bonda and his general manager, Phil Seghi, were just walking out. From the tone of Cherry's voice, Paul sensed that the Padres had also upped their offer. Nevertheless, he informed Cherry of the Yankees' intention of going to $2.8 million. The lawyer smiled but didn't say anything.

"Well," Paul said after a few tense moments, "I guess we'll be on our way. We'll wait to hear from you."

"You will," said Cherry.

From Ahoskie, Paul, Greenwald and Kluttz drove to Suffolk, Virginia, where two charter planes were waiting, one to take Paul back to New York and one to ferry Greenwald to Cleveland. While they were waiting at the airport, Kluttz put in a phone call to Hunter. Upon hanging up, he turned to Paul and said: "He wants to come to New York to look around the area."

Paul shrugged. "There has to be a breaking point here," he thought to himself.

The next morning, Kluttz called Paul from the Tomahawk Motel, in Ahoskie, where he had met with Hunter.

"He wants a $50,000 insurance policy up front for his kids, and then

$100,000 for each of the next five seasons," Kluttz said. "If you're willing to do that, I'd say you've got him."

Paul was exasperated.

"This cat-and-mouse game has got to stop," he sighed. "We can't keep upping the ante like this!"

At that point, Kluttz put Hunter on the phone.

"Mr. Paul," Hunter drawled, "if you all are willing to take this offer, I promise I'll sign."

Paul told Hunter he'd have to get back to him after discussing the deal with other Yankees officials. He then called Greenwald, who discussed it with his Cleveland law partner and fellow Yankees limited partner, Daniel McCarthy.

"You're going to need to make a decision, Gabe," Greenwald said. "I just don't know."

"Well," said Paul, "the way I look at it, we'll all be dead in 20 years and this is a chance to change the course of baseball in New York from a secondary position to one of dominance. It's worth it. I say let's do it."

Greenwald called Steinbrenner. But instead of being elated over winning the Hunter sweepstakes, Steinbrenner erupted.

"How much?" he screamed at Greenwald. "I don't know if the banks are going to go for this! What's the matter with you? You've let them manipulate you into looking like fools."

"But, George—" Greenwald interrupted.

"Shut up," Steinbrenner yelled. "You're just a fucking errand boy!"

A shaken Greenwald called Paul back to report Steinbrenner's reaction.

"I'm quitting," Greenwald said. "I can't take being talked to like that. I'm going sell my shares. McCarthy too. I'll draw up the contract if you want and get the hell out of it and let Pat Cunningham do the rest."

"Just hang in there, Eddie," Paul said. "Cunningham's a political guy who's just serving as George's surrogate. We can't have boy scouts doing this job. It'll be all screwed up."

Paul then called Steinbrenner, who had calmed down and was now prepared to go through with the deal.

"Greenwald has to be in this, George," Paul said. "It's a very complicated deal."

"All right," said Steinbrenner, "but I don't want Greenwald speaking at the press conference."

"Don't worry about the press conference," Paul said. "We'll handle that."

The next day, December 31, Greenwald flew back to Ahoskie, where he met with Cherry, Hunter, Kluttz and Cherry's law partner, Joe Flythe. After going over the terms of the deal, all five flew to New York on Steinbrenner's private AmShip plane. During the flight, Greenwald drew up the contract in longhand. But when they got to New York, Paul reported that Steinbrenner had told him he still didn't have the bank clearance. It didn't arrive until 8:15 P.M., and it wasn't until 8:25 that Hunter finally signed the contract.

Meanwhile, Marty Appel was frantic. Earlier in the day, Paul had instructed the first-year Yankees PR director to round up the local media for a 6 P.M. press conference at the Yankees' office inside the Parks Administration building. By the time Hunter finally signed, several dozen newspaper, TV and radio reporters had been waiting in the group sales office for over two hours, angry that they had ditched their plans for New Year's Eve. Paul didn't tell Appel why the press conference was being delayed, and as the eight o'clock hour came and went, Appel began feeling a sense of dread.

As soon as Hunter signed his name on the contract, Appel hastily escorted him down the corridor with Paul, Cherry, Flythe and Kluttz to the group sales office for the press conference. Terms of the deal were never announced by the Yankees, and the next day reports varied from $3.2 million to $3.75. In fact, the contract was worth $3.35 million, broken down thus:

- $500,000 in salary for five years
- $250,000 deferred salary
- $100,000 signing bonus
- $1.5 million in deferred bonus
- $750,000 life insurance policy
- $50,000 for each of Hunter's two children
- $200,000 in attorneys' fees

Steinbrenner became the first owner to award a seven-figure contract—and only two years after chewing out Mike Burke for raising Bobby Murcer's salary to $100,000. In absentia, Steinbrenner had rocked the foundation of baseball. Hunter became the highest-salaried player in baseball history; more important, his example had demonstrated what free agency would mean for the players. "What we saw happen here," said San Diego Padres president Buzzie Bavasi after the Hunter deal was announced, "fully demonstrates the importance of the reserve clause. This manifests why we can't afford to change the reserve rule. The richest clubs would offer the top players the biggest salaries and the biggest bonuses."

Bavasi's fears for the owners' control over the players were well founded, as Marvin Miller had only just begun to fight. At Miller's prompting, over the next year, pitchers Dave McNally and Andy Messersmith would also challenge the reserve clause and become free agents, opening the floodgates of free agency and providing George Steinbrenner with the vehicle he needed to restore the Yankees to greatness.

Considering the magnitude of the Hunter deal, it was curious that only Paul and a couple of midlevel front office executives from the Yankees were present at the press conference. But this was the way Steinbrenner wanted it. And instead of Greenwald, who could have explained the contract for the media, Steinbrenner arranged for his friend Neil Walsh, a New York City commissioner, to present Hunter with a fishing rod as a welcoming gift from the city.

Paul was particularly irritated by Walsh's presence at the press conference—"just another of Steinbrenner's cronies who doesn't know anything about baseball but is allowed to get involved nevertheless."

A couple of weeks after the Hunter press conference, Paul was informed by Steinbrenner that Neil Walsh's insurance company would be drawing up a policy on Hunter. Paul showed the policy to Greenwald, who said, "I don't like this, Gabe. There are tremendous premiums in this. It's just not a good policy for us."

"I don't know what to tell you, Ed," said Paul. "It seems like everything that Neil Walsh recommends to Steinbrenner is the greatest thing since indoor plumbing."

Then, a couple of weeks before 1975 spring training, Walsh informed

Paul that, with Steinbrenner's approval, he was bringing in a disc jockey and friend of his from the West Coast, Johnny Magnus, "the host who loves you the most," to help out in the group sales and promotions departments. "This is what George wants," Walsh said. "I told George the Yankees need a promotions and PR guy—somebody who knows how to do this kind of work—and he agrees."

Paul couldn't believe what he was hearing.

"We have no plan of organization," Paul complained on his daily taped diary entry. "It all depends on what bar he goes to and who gets his ear last. This Steinbrenner is just not gonna stay out of it! All this stuff about us having no problem with the banks, and we didn't get the approval until 8:15 that night and then almost blew the Hunter deal! I love this guy, but he's not a guy to be working with or be in business with! Everything is falling apart internally. Especially all this stuff with Walsh—the insurance policy, Magnus—it's an unsound way of doing business."

A few days after his conversation with Walsh, Paul received a letter from Magnus expressing a desire to go into the broadcast booth.

"This is insane," Paul said. "Now this guy thinks he should be one of our broadcasters? He's telling me what a good idea it would be to introduce the players by their astrological signs. Enough!"

Nevertheless, in early February Magnus flew to New York to meet with Paul about the job. Paul, however, had arranged to be out of town and turned the meeting over to his assistant, Tal Smith, with instructions to tell him there were no vacancies in the broadcast booth at the present time. Thirty-four years later, Magnus was still smarting from his brief Yankees experience.

"I was crushed," he recalled. "Neil had called me in the middle of the night from Elaine's restaurant in New York to tell me I had the job, but when I got there Tal Smith said he didn't know anything about it. I never got to meet Steinbrenner. I felt like the victim of some caper."

But that was only one of the many tempests Paul continually had to snuff out.

On January 18, he'd been asked to lunch by Jimmy Nederlander, one of the limited Yankees partners. It seemed Nederlander and the other limiteds were becoming increasingly unhappy at Steinbrenner's obvious disregard for them. For years Nederlander had been one of Steinbrenner's closest friends. Together, along with Joseph Kipness (owner of Joe's Pier 52, the famous Manhattan restaurant frequented by New York's sports and theater celebrities), they had enjoyed a great relationship as producers for a number of Broadway shows, among them *Applause* and *Seesaw*. But being a partner of Steinbrenner's in the baseball business, Nederlander was discovering, was, by contrast, quite unrewarding.

"We never have meetings or get any information as to what's going on with the team," Nederlander complained to Paul. "It's the same thing I hear at AmShip, where George just bought a plane without consulting with anyone."

Paul didn't have the heart to tell Nederlander that Steinbrenner had instructed him not to invite any of the limited partners to the New York baseball writers' dinner that week.

"They'd be more upset if they knew what he uses that plane for," Paul replied, a note of disgust in his voice. "Junkets for Neil Walsh and all his other cronies."

Nederlander was especially disturbed by Steinbrenner's frequent cash calls to his partners. Despite the Yankees' improvement on the field, they were losing millions while playing at Shea during the renovation of Yankee Stadium, and the partners were concerned as to whether they could afford the Hunter contract.

"I understand your concern, Jim," Paul said. "I'm working for nothing here, and I have to put up too."

THREE DAYS AFTER his lunch with Nederlander, Paul and Steinbrenner were called to a meeting at Bowie Kuhn's office. It was Steinbrenner's hope that the commissioner was going to reduce his suspension. Instead, Kuhn wanted to know the depth of his involvement in the Hunter deal.

"I had nothing to do with it," Steinbrenner insisted. "That was all Gabe's deal."

Kuhn seemed to accept Steinbrenner's answer and noted that he was satisfied that Paul was conducting the Yankees' baseball business with a free hand. Paul, managing to keep a straight face, said nothing, but gave a silent thanks that the commissioner hadn't asked him how often he'd been talking to Steinbrenner or how little the content of the calls had been of a "social nature."

He wasn't particularly fond of Kuhn anyway, but in the weeks and months to come, Gabe Paul would begin to think more and more that "this Steinbrenner," whom he worked for and covered for during the owner's exile from baseball, was merely crazy.

5

. . .

Three for the Tabloids

. . .

I F NOTHING ELSE, YOU must never forget there are three things that sell this newspaper: cops, tits and the Yankees."

The man explaining this to me was Buddy Martin, the executive sports editor of the New York *Daily News*. It was a June afternoon in 1978, and we were in the Lantern Coffee Shop, on 42nd Street. Through the window I could see the *Daily News* building across the street. It was the city's largest-circulation daily newspaper, and I was interviewing to become its new baseball writer. "At this place," Martin continued, "the prototypical *Daily News* every day will have cops, crime and mayhem on page one, interspersed with stories about sex and hookers along with semi-naked photos of pop tarts on the inside gossip pages, and George and Billy going at it on the back page. *That's* the winning trifecta here!

"Oh, and one other thing. When you hear how Steinbrenner thinks he owns our back page? The fact is he probably does."

Martin was preparing me for life at a New York City tabloid, a place where, after five years of owning the Yankees, George Steinbrenner had created a permanent niche for himself. He had done this by systematically restoring the Yankees to a championship-quality team. There had been the trades for Lou Piniella, Graig Nettles and Chris Chambliss early on, followed by the momentous free agent signing of Catfish Hunter. All of a sudden, not only were the Yankees getting considerably better under the direction of Steinbrenner and Gabe Paul, but they were also developing a personality.

Of course, when it came to personality, Steinbrenner loomed over all. Winning breeds celebrity, and as the Yankees began to matter again in the mid-'70s, the man behind their renaissance became as much a presence on the New York social scene as he was on the sports pages.

When he wasn't sitting in his private box on the mezzanine level at Yankee Stadium, Steinbrenner was hobnobbing at Upper East Side spots like Elaine's, P. J. Clarke's, McMullen's and the private Le Club.

In the spring of 1975, Steinbrenner was indeed the most visible face of these reborn Yankees, thanks largely to the historic signing of Hunter while he was supposed to be serving a suspension.

WITH THE ADDITIONS of Catfish Hunter and Bobby Bonds—bona fide baseball superstars—to a Yankee ball club that had finished a surprising second in 1974, it appeared George Steinbrenner and Gabe Paul now had a team capable of returning to the franchise's old glory. But amid the lingering good feelings from the team's finish the year before and the optimism that Hunter's and Bonds's presence brought for 1975, a pall was cast on the final week of spring training in Fort Lauderdale, when one of the veteran team leaders, Mel Stottlemyre, the fifth-winningest pitcher in club history and ace of the pitching staff from 1964 to '73, was without warning handed his unconditional release.

Stottlemyre had sustained a torn rotator cuff in his shoulder on June 4, 1974, but hoped that a winter of complete rest would enable him to pitch again, and Paul had agreed to wait until May 1 to make that determination. During spring training, however, as Stottlemyre showed no improvement, Paul realized that if he released him prior to April 1, the Yankees would have to pay him for only 30 days of the season, or one sixth of his contract, in severance. Stottlemyre had continued on an exercise and soft-tossing program throughout the spring, unaware of the Yankees' intentions, and was thus blindsided when Paul called him into his trailer office on March 29 and informed him he was being let go.

"But you told me I had until May 1," Stottlemyre said.

"Well, that was merely an arbitrary target date," Paul said uneasily. "If you want, I'll call around and see if there's any interest from other clubs."

Stottlemyre couldn't believe what he was hearing; couldn't believe the Yankees were doing this to him after all he'd meant to them over the past decade. That night, his head was still spinning when the phone rang in his apartment. It was Steinbrenner, who had not been around the team all spring because of his suspension.

"I'm not happy about what happened today," Steinbrenner declared, "but I want you to know I had nothing to do with it. Gabe's running the team, and I'm not allowed to get involved."

Steinbrenner then recommended that Stottlemyre contact a friend of his, Charlie Beech, a professor of kinesiology at Michigan State, who could put him on an arm-strengthening program that might save his career.

"I'll pay you $40,000 to go work with him, even if you aren't able to pitch again," Steinbrenner said.

Stottlemyre thought this was a very magnanimous gesture on Steinbrenner's part and spent three days with Beech at Michigan State in late March. He then flew to Los Angeles to work out with Mike Marshall, the former Cy Young Award–winning relief pitcher, who had a doctorate in physiology from Michigan State.

Ultimately, none of the programs were able to strengthen Stottlemyre's shoulder to the point that he could pitch again, and he went home to Seattle concluding his career was over.

At least, he thought, there was still $40,000 coming from Steinbrenner. But as weeks and then months went by, there was no check. Nor did Stottlemyre hear anything more from the Yankees owner. As he said years later, he was too proud to call him. It wasn't until 21 years later, when Joe Torre hired him in 1996 as a pitching coach, that he finally got his money.

While negotiating the contract, Stottlemyre told Joe Molloy, who was then Steinbrenner's son-in-law and serving as the Yankees' acting general partner, that he would have to have an additional $40,000 "as a way of bringing closure to his bitterness toward Steinbrenner." Molloy, not wanting such an embarrassing story to become public, agreed to defer the $40,000 with interest. Stottlemyre wound up with nearly $80,000 in "deferred bonus" money for serving as the Yankees' pitching coach from 1996 to 2005.

Other than Stottlemyre, who could have used the Yankees owner's intervention, it was rather refreshing for everyone else around the team that Steinbrenner was still on suspension and not inflicting his wrath upon them. Still, the owner managed to assure his players that he was still very much around.

On Opening Day 1975, sitting in the box seats watching pregame batting practice, Steinbrenner summoned manager Bill Virdon and handed him a cassette tape.

"I want you to play this for the team," he said. "It'll get 'em going today."

Virdon looked at Steinbrenner quizzically but said nothing as he stuffed the tape into his pocket. When the Yankees finished batting and infield practice and returned to the clubhouse, Virdon was standing by a table in the middle of the room, where the traveling secretary ordinarily would be sitting with a stack of envelopes, filling all the players' ticket requests. This time the table was bare except for a tape recorder.

"I've been instructed to play this tape," Virdon announced before touching the play button.

"Basically, it was just George delivering one of his patented 'I sign your checks and I expect results' speeches," remembered Graig Nettles. "It was George doing his Knute Rockne thing without being there in person."

While the tape played for a full four minutes, Virdon just stood there, smiling, as his players tried to keep from laughing.

"The one thing I do remember about it," said Lou Piniella, "was that at the end, George made like he was on *Mission: Impossible* by saying, 'This tape will self-destruct in 30 seconds.' *That* was funny!"

Though *The Sporting News* named him manager of the year for guiding the Yankees to within one game of the American League East title in 1974, Virdon's strict, detached managing style had worn thin with most of the players, especially the veterans who were used to having their egos constantly massaged by Ralph Houk. Virdon's base-running drill at the conclusion of each spring training workout—in which the manager stood at home plate like a drill sergeant and gave a thumbs-up to go into the locker room or a thumbs-down to take another lap—was a particularly grueling ritual the players hated.

After another Virdon spring training boot camp, the Yankees began the 1975 season by losing their first three games, including the home opener, in which Hunter surrendered a three-run homer to Detroit's Nate Colbert in the fifth inning and lost to the Tigers, 5–3. In his second start, against the Red Sox four days later, Hunter was unable to hold a 3–0 lead and was beaten again, 5–3. By the end of April, the Yankees were 9-10 and Hunter was 0-3 in four starts with a 7.66 ERA.

It wasn't until June—when they went 20-9 and actually climbed into first place for a brief spell—that the '75 Yankees began to look like a team capable of contending with the Red Sox and the defending division champs, the Baltimore Orioles, for the AL East title. But then a series of injuries decimated their outfield and served to undercut career seasons by Nettles, Chambliss and catcher Thurman Munson, and even the return to form by Hunter, who wound up winning 23 and hurled more complete games (30) than any American League pitcher since 1946.

On June 7 in Chicago, Bobby Bonds, who was leading the AL with 15 home runs and 45 RBI, fell down in the outfield while making a game-saving catch against the White Sox and injured his right knee. X-rays later revealed torn cartilage, but Bonds played through the rest of the season, though at a clearly diminished capacity. Six days after Bonds hurt his knee, Elliott Maddox, who'd hit .303 as Bobby Murcer's center field replacement in 1974, slipped and fell on the wet sod of Shea Stadium and tore the ligaments in his right knee. Maddox, who was hitting .307 at the time, missed the rest of '75 and most of '76 and later filed a $1 million negligence suit against the city of New York, citing the field condition at Shea for having prematurely ended his career. (The suit was ultimately dismissed.) Also during June, Piniella suffered a mysterious inner ear infection and designated hitter Ron Blomberg tore the rotator cuff in his shoulder while taking an unusually hard swing of the bat. The two players, who in 1974 had both hit over .300 and, with Maddox, accounted for 185 runs and 163 RBI, were also lost for most of the season.

Under the terms of his suspension, Steinbrenner was prohibited from making any public comments about his team or baseball in general. But with the mounting injuries, coupled with the team's nine losses in 10 games from June 20 to July 5, his growing frustration was apparent in the way he scowled and waved his arms in disgust from the field box next to the Yankees' dugout. Behind the scenes, Steinbrenner vented furiously to Gabe

Paul, who came to expect nightly phone calls from the banished Yankees owner that were of anything but "a social nature."

Most of the time, Steinbrenner's wrath was directed at Virdon, whom he blamed for losing control of the team. Virdon's stoic demeanor especially irritated Steinbrenner, who complained to the *Daily News'* Yankees beat man, Phil Pepe, that he wanted to see a more animated manager. "I don't like a manager who walks out to the mound with his hands in his back pocket and his chin on his chest like he's carrying the weight of the world and doesn't know what to do," Pepe quoted him as saying. "I like a guy who charges out to the mound and waves decisively to the bullpen; a guy who knows exactly what the problem is and what to do about it! I want a guy who shows some *fire!*"

On July 21, 1975, precisely such a manager became available when the Texas Rangers fired Billy Martin. For Martin, the notorious "bad boy" who had played second base for the Yankees in the '50s, it was the third time he'd been fired as a manager, all for the same reason: a personality clash with ownership. (As a player with the Yankees, despite his reputation for being a clutch performer on the '52, '53, '55 and '56 World Series teams, the owners regarded Martin as a bad influence on the team's biggest stars, Mickey Mantle and Whitey Ford. It was after Mantle, Ford, Yogi Berra, Hank Bauer and pitcher Johnny Kucks had been involved in a fight at the Copacabana nightclub while celebrating Martin's birthday in May 1957 that "Billy the Kid" was traded to the last-place Kansas City Athletics.)

Martin brought the same flinty, uncompromising persona to managing. Just as he had immediately made winners of the Minnesota Twins in 1969 and the Detroit Tigers in 1971, in late 1973 Martin took over a Texas team that had lost 105 games that year and led them to an 84-win season the following year, only to find himself fired again because of his hard drinking and his combative personality.

Indeed, when Steinbrenner made those remarks to Pepe, he probably had Martin in mind. The suggestion that Martin manage the Yankees had actually been made two years earlier by Mike Burke. As the former Yankees general partner recounted to friends, he'd told Steinbrenner, in their final meeting at the Yankee Stadium offices in April 1973, that if George ever got the chance, he should hire Martin as his manager. When he was with the Yankees, Burke would have dinner with Martin when Billy was in New York, and he told Steinbrenner that in 1972 he had tried to hire Martin away from the Tigers at the risk of tampering charges.

"Billy's driving ambition is to manage the Yankees and become baseball's first $100,000 manager," Burke told Steinbrenner. "He never got over being traded by them when he was a player. The Yankees are in his blood."

With the Yankees staggering into the All-Star break at 45-41 after losing 12 of their previous 18 games, Steinbrenner might well have ordered Paul to fire Virdon then, had he not been preoccupied with league politics.

At the All-Star Game in Milwaukee, the owners scheduled a meeting to vote on Bowie Kuhn's reelection as commissioner of baseball. In the weeks leading up to it, there had been grumbling about Kuhn's job performance, particularly from the American League, where Charlie Finley was attempting to muster a coalition to oust the commissioner. The *Chicago Sun-Times* reported in June that a "Dump Bowie" club was being formed, with Finley, Steinbrenner and Baltimore Orioles owner Jerry Hoffberger as its charter members. Their dissatisfaction with Kuhn stemmed from a feeling that, as the former National League attorney, he had favored the rival league and was, in fact, controlled by Los Angeles Dodgers owner Walter O'Malley.

Under the terms of the major league rules of procedure, a commissioner needed the support of 75 percent (9 out of 12) of the clubs from each league to be elected. Since Kuhn had suspended him, Steinbrenner's vote against was seen as a given, and it was reported just prior to the meeting that Finley had also enlisted the support of the Texas Rangers' Brad Corbett, giving him the necessary four votes to fire the commissioner. Nevertheless, American League president Lee MacPhail told Kuhn before the meeting he was embarrassed by the Finley cabal and vowed to work behind the scenes on his behalf.

Though he was not permitted to take part in the meeting, Steinbrenner was granted permission by Kuhn to attend the All-Star Game and discuss the commissioner's reelection with Yankees officials—a development Gabe Paul viewed as suspicious. For his part, Steinbrenner told a group of reporters gathered at the Pfister Hotel in Milwaukee: "I would never vote against the commissioner because of anything he did within the perimeter of his authority. People seem to think the Yankees will vote against him because of my suspension, but that is not true. I will not enter into any retaliatory attempts of any sort."

Paul, of course, knew different. In their conversations that summer, Steinbrenner had frequently expressed his disdain for Kuhn, and Paul had agreed with him. "I don't think he's done a good job," Paul said. "He hasn't solved any of the problems baseball has, and he's too pompous." They agreed that Paul and acting Yankees general partner Pat Cunningham would cast a "no" vote against Kuhn on behalf of Steinbrenner.

But the night before the reelection vote was to take place, Walter O'Malley, the powerful and influential owner of the Los Angeles Dodgers, called Corbett and convinced him to change his vote to a "yes." This, in turn, prompted Pittsburgh Pirates owner Dan Galbreath, who shared horse-racing interests with Steinbrenner, to call the Yankees owner and inform him of the changed political landscape. Realizing immediately that, with Kuhn's reelection certain, it would now be in his best interest to vote for Kuhn, Steinbrenner asked Galbreath if he would lobby the commissioner to lift his suspension. Galbreath agreed to talk to Kuhn on his behalf—but only after the election.

During this last-minute maneuvering, Paul, who had again assured Hoffberger that the Yankees would be voting against Kuhn, became concerned when he saw MacPhail going into Cunningham's room at the Pfister in the morning before the vote was to take place. What had particularly disturbed him was a letter Kuhn had sent to Cunningham a few weeks earlier in which the commissioner said Steinbrenner had a "free pass" to talk to Cunningham about the reelection matter. "He's barred from everything else, but he can talk about the commissioner's reelection," Paul said in his tape entry that day. "What a fine kettle of fish."

As they sat down at the meeting in the Pfister ballroom, Cunningham turned to Paul and said that Steinbrenner's attorney, Edward Bennett Williams, had called to inform him the night before that if they didn't vote for Kuhn there was no way he'd ever get the suspension lifted.

Paul was furious.

"Clearly, Pat, there's been a deal made here and I've been double-crossed," Paul said. "What am I supposed to say to Hoffberger now?"

It turned out not to matter, because he never got the chance. No sooner was the vote announced as 22–2 in favor of Kuhn's reelection than Hoffberger got up and stormed out of the room, momentarily stopping in front of Paul and sputtering loud enough for everyone in the room to hear: "Tell your goddamned boss he doesn't have a gut in his body!"

If Steinbrenner thought his vote for Kuhn would hasten his own reinstatement, he was mistaken. It would be another eight months before the commissioner allowed him to resume control of the Yankees.

In the meantime, Steinbrenner returned to New York from Milwaukee, his "free pass" from Kuhn having expired with the commissioner's reelection, and continued to watch the Yankees lose. Coming off a 3-6 road trip after the All-Star break, they won the first of a four-game series at home against the Red Sox, only to lose the next three. The Sunday, July 27, doubleheader, in which they were shut out in both games before a crowd of 53,631, the largest at Shea all year, was the breaking point for Steinbrenner. In the fifth inning of the first game, Virdon allowed .220-hitting Yankees shortstop Fred Stanley to bat with the bases loaded and none out. When Stanley grounded into a force-out at the plate, Steinbrenner could be seen screaming into the dugout.

That night, Steinbrenner showed up unannounced at Gabe Paul's apartment in Manhattan with an edict. As Paul opened the door, Steinbrenner stormed in and began ranting.

"Get rid of Virdon!" he hollered. "Do you understand me? Get rid of him! You can't talk me out of this anymore!"

Until that point in the season, Paul had resisted Steinbrenner's impulses, but now even he privately conceded to himself that Virdon probably needed to go. At the same time, however, he was growing increasingly weary of Steinbrenner's tantrums and ill-conceived ideas. In one of their conversations the previous week, Steinbrenner had told Paul that he wanted to pay for baseball scholarships at the University of South Florida, "so they'll hold their players for us." Paul had to explain that there was no getting around the draft in baseball, in which amateur players were selected by teams in the reverse order of the previous year's standings.

As he listened to Steinbrenner's latest rant about Virdon, Paul thought to himself: "It's getting harder and harder to defend Virdon. But this guy is relentless about this. I really ought to recommend Martin to him and serve him right! At least Virdon can control himself."

On July 28, the Monday after the disastrous Red Sox series that left the Yankees 10 games out of first place, Steinbrenner called Paul from Tampa and said, "It's definite. We're getting rid of Virdon. I want you to announce it immediately."

"George," Paul said, "you can't make an announcement until you have your replacement."

A few days earlier, once it had become apparent to him that Virdon wasn't going to be able to survive Steinbrenner's resolve, Paul had taken it upon himself to dispatch his top scout, Birdie Tebbetts, to the Yankees' Triple-A farm in Syracuse for the purpose of evaluating the manager there, Bobby Cox. It was Tebbetts's opinion, Paul said, that Cox wasn't ready for the big league job.

"All right," Steinbrenner snapped, "then what do we have to do to get Martin?"

Paul again summoned Tebbetts and asked him to find out where Martin was. Tebbetts placed a call to Rangers general manager Dan O'Brien, who informed him that, as far as he knew, Martin was on a fishing trip somewhere in the wilds of Colorado and couldn't be reached.

"Okay," Paul said to Tebbetts, "then I want you to go out to Colorado, find him, and bring him back to New York right away. Nobody must hear about this. Fly him back to New York under an assumed name and bring him directly to Shea Stadium."

"But how am I supposed to find him?" Tebbetts said.

"I don't know, just find him, but you'll likely find him in some bar," said Paul before hanging up.

Tebbetts flew to Denver, where he rented a car and drove through the mountains to a small mining town called Grand Junction, where some of Martin's friends told him he was staying. Tebbetts parked his car and walked down Main Street, peering into every bar until he spotted Martin sitting with a friend in a smoky saloon at the end of the street. Though he was surprised to see Tebbetts, Martin had heard the rumors that the

Yankees were probably going to be making a manager change and he was immediately excited when Paul's man pulled out a $75,000 contract for him to look over.

"Billy was out of a job, his marriage was breaking up, and he badly wanted to come back to the Yankees," Tebbetts remembered. "I bought him a one-way ticket to fly back to New York with me. There were no complications."

But as the Yankees would soon come to realize, there was nothing about Billy Martin that was uncomplicated.

While Tebbetts was in Colorado corralling Martin, Paul got a call from Rangers owner Brad Corbett. Corbett had purchased the team in April 1974 from Bob Short, who had signed Martin to a contract with a "special services" codicil that guaranteed additional income above his base salary for things such as personal appearances. Martin wouldn't be able to perform special services for Short or the Rangers if he was working for another team, but either way, they were obligated to pay him the extra money.

"Can we work out something on this?" Corbett asked.

"We want a clean contract," Paul said. "Why don't you simply take over Virdon's contract and we'll take over Martin's?"

"No, that's not going to work," Corbett said. "We already have a manager in Frank Lucchesi."

For the next five days, Paul, Corbett, Short and Martin haggled over the contract.

Finally, Paul worked out new contract terms for Martin, in which, to make up for the lost "special services" money on his Rangers contract, Billy would get a percentage of the money the Yankees recovered on Virdon's contract once the former manager was hired by another club. Fittingly, the next day was Old-Timers' Day, the perfect venue for the Yankees to announce the return of their prodigal son, Billy Martin, as their new manager.

Knowing Steinbrenner's penchant for tipping off his favorite reporters, it was not surprising to Paul that, despite all his efforts to keep the Martin hiring under wraps, news of the manager change began leaking out that night. Around 7 P.M. he got a call from Milton Richman of United Press International.

"I understand the *Daily News* is reporting tomorrow that Virdon's out and Martin's in," said Richman. "You've got to play fair with me, Gabe. Steinbrenner gave me this four days ago and I agreed to sit on it."

"I'm not going to lie to you, Milton," Paul said. "Do what you feel you have to do."

It turned out Steinbrenner had been an equal-opportunity leaker. Apparently forgetting he'd promised Richman the scoop, he called Phil Pepe at the *Daily News* to tell him about the impending managing change. Pepe and *News* columnist Dick Young quickly composed their front-page story for Saturday's editions, MARTIN YANKS' PILOT—TAKES OVER FROM VIRDON. Richman only found out the deal was done because UPI's headquarters was in the *Daily News* building and a UPI staffer, having drinks in Louie's East, the bar next door, overheard one of the *Daily News* printers talking about the big story coming tomorrow.

"I have no illusions as to why George gave me the story," said Pepe. "He gave it to me because I was the guy from the *Daily News*, where he knew he'd get his biggest splash."

Pepe compared covering Steinbrenner to a bakery. "With George, you got your ticket and he'd leak you stories, but the first time you wrote a story he didn't like, you went to the back of the line for a new ticket to get a return call from him," Pepe said.

With the press conference set for 9:30 Saturday morning, Paul sent word over to Virdon's office at Shea Stadium after the Yankees' Friday-night 5–4 win over the Indians for the manager to come see him in the Parks Administration building across the street. A half hour later, Virdon came into his office, a look of resignation on his face.

"Bill, this doesn't look very good," Paul said, avoiding coming right out and telling him he was fired.

"I understand, Gabe," said Virdon. "You have to do what you think is necessary."

With that, Virdon departed without bothering to say goodbye to the players.

"I really wasn't aware it was in the process," Virdon told me in 2008. "You have to remember, because George was on suspension, I didn't have much dealing with him. In that respect, I was the lucky one of all his managers. Other than the tape incident, he didn't really bother me much."

The Old-Timers' Day celebration of Martin's return was an overwhelming success, culminating with a 5–3 Yankees win over the Cleveland Indians. The ovation for Martin was almost as loud as those for the Yankee icons, Joe DiMaggio and Mickey Mantle, and the newspapers all hailed the hiring of the popular, combative Martin as a master stroke. That night, when Gabe Paul got back to his apartment, he found a note under his door, written in longhand.

"If there was any doubt in your mind today, the excitement and the electricity we produced in the stadium I haven't seen in a long time. You deserve the credit for having the guts to do it. We're going to put a lot of fannies in the seats. This was a triumph for you and Birdie, but particularly you. You're the big winner. You deserve it and I wanted you to know that!" It was signed "George."

Paul was touched, and stunned. He couldn't ever remember such an expression of gratitude and praise, spoken or written, from Steinbrenner. As he read the note again, and thought back to the Kuhn vote two weeks earlier, Paul shook his head in amazement at how quickly things had changed with "this Steinbrenner."

The good feelings didn't last long. Paul awoke the very next morning to a call from Steinbrenner, who was now furious over a column by Dick Young in the *Daily News* critical of the Martin hiring. It seemed a few days before telling Richman about Martin's hiring, Steinbrenner had intimated to Young that Virdon's job was safe. Young was in the process of writing a column to that effect when Pepe told him of the "Martin in, Virdon out" scoop Steinbrenner had just given him. Feeling he'd been misled by the Yankees owner, Young wrote a Sunday "day after" column strongly suggesting the Martin hiring was a mistake and that the Yankee players were not reacting well to it. The column, which was headlined, YANKEE PLAYERS GRIM . . . GONNA BE PROBLEMS, was the only negative article about the manager change in any of the New York papers the next day.

"I don't want anyone here talking to Dick Young anymore," Steinbrenner told Paul. "He's got to learn to take the good with the bad."

But Young was on to something. Barely a week into his tenure as the new manager, Martin and the Yankees arrived in Oakland for a weekend series against the Athletics, with Steinbrenner along for the trip. Though most of the visiting American League teams stayed at the Hyatt, because of the price and its proximity to the Oakland Coliseum, where the A's played, the hotel's bar had a reputation back then for turning a blind eye to drugs, prostitution and other assorted vices. The Yankees had lost three straight to the Angels in Anaheim prior to arriving in Oakland, and the team closer, Sparky Lyle, had blown a couple of saves.

Calling Paul from his room phone, Steinbrenner ranted: "I told Billy I don't want Lyle pitching anymore. And this hotel! There's too many whores running around this place! The manager is supposed to control that, and I don't see Billy doing anything about it."

In fact, Martin was in the middle of it. Since he was a native of Berkeley, Oakland was as good as home to him, and the Hyatt bar was one of his favorite drinking spots. Whenever Martin visited with one of his teams, he seldom left the hotel except to go to the ballpark.

The Yankees finished September with a 16-10 record, and Steinbrenner and Martin were optimistic that, with a few additions to the roster, a championship could be in the offing for 1976. Right after the '75 World Series, Paul met with Pat Gillick, the Yankees' director of scouting and development. The 32-year-old Gillick had been given expanded duties that August when Paul's assistant, Tal Smith, resigned to become general manager of the Houston Astros. (The move met with considerable resistance from Steinbrenner, who initially wanted compensation for him.) Paul and Steinbrenner soon came to respect Gillick's player evaluation ability and had asked him to size up the Yankees' needs and offer whatever suggestions he might have to fill them.

With Steinbrenner listening on speakerphone in Paul's office, Gillick mentioned that the Yankees had finished next to last in runs in the American League in '75, and said the Yankees needed to add more speed to their lineup. Gillick was also concerned about the Yankees' "up-the-middle" position players, with the exception of Munson behind the plate. Their shortstop, Jim Mason, had hit an anemic .152 in '75; Sandy Alomar, the aging second baseman, hit only .239; and the knee injury to Maddox made center field a question mark.

"It's my recommendation," Gillick said, "that now would be the time to trade Bonds—while he still has good value. We have a lot of needs—pitching, infield, possibly center field—and he could help us fill a few of them."

"But isn't he our biggest asset?" Steinbrenner asked.

Paul pointed out that, despite Bonds's courageous play for the Yankees after sustaining the knee injury, he was a heavy drinker who didn't take care of himself. Gillick was interested in a young second baseman from Brooklyn, Willie Randolph, who played for the Pittsburgh Pirates' Triple-A team in Charleston, West Virginia. "I think we should try to get him if we can," Gillick said.

"Okay," said Steinbrenner, "see what you guys can do."

Pirates general manager Joe Brown had been calling Paul for weeks, hoping to trade for the Yankees' number-two pitcher, Doc Medich, who had 16 wins in '75. At the December winter meetings at the Diplomat Hotel in Hollywood, Florida, Paul ran into Brown and told him that he'd consider trading Medich, but he'd have to get a left-handed pitcher in return—perhaps Ken Brett, who'd been a fifth starter for the first-place Pirates. "I also need a second baseman," said Paul, "and you've got a kid, Randolph, at Triple-A, who we like a little."

"Let me think about it," said Brown. "I'll get back to you before the meetings are over."

By the last day of the meetings, Paul still hadn't heard from Brown, and was beginning to assume the deal was dead. Finally, as Paul was packing up his bags in his room that morning, the Pittsburgh GM called him.

"I think we can do the Medich deal," Brown said. "We'll give you Brett and Randolph, but you've got to take Dock Ellis too."

The right-handed Ellis had won more than ten games in six straight seasons for the Pirates, from 1969 to '74, including an impressive 19-9 record for their 1971 world championship team, but his frequent temper tantrums and erratic behavior had become a constant source of irritation to the team's management. (His latest clubhouse tantrum, in mid-August, had been directed at Pirates manager Danny Murtaugh, after which Ellis had been suspended for 30 days without pay.) Brown's sudden inclusion of Ellis in the discussions momentarily caught Paul by surprise.

"I don't know," he said. "What else do you want?"

"Nothing," said Brown. "Just take him. I've got to get him out of town."

So Paul was able to get two starting pitchers and a top prospect in Randolph for Medich. His next call was to the California Angels, who were anxious to acquire Bonds and offered in return their speedy center fielder Mickey Rivers, who had led the AL with 70 stolen bases and 13 triples, and Ed Figueroa, a 27-year-old right-handed pitcher from Puerto Rico, who had a 16-13 record in '75. In the cab ride from the Diplomat to the airport, Gillick looked at Paul with a smile of satisfaction.

"Well, boss," he said. "We pretty much filled just about all of our needs in two deals."

In retrospect, those two trades were among the best in Yankee history, as Rivers provided them a leadoff catalyst and was an All-Star center fielder the following year, Figueroa won 55 games over the next three years, Ellis was 17-8 in 1976 and Randolph was the Yankees' second baseman for the next 13 seasons, earning five All-Star nominations.

Gillick, however, did not stay around the Yankees to enjoy the fruits of his player evaluation acumen. In late July 1975, Peter Bavasi, president of the expansion Toronto Blue Jays, called Steinbrenner to ask permission to talk to Gillick about becoming the first general manager of the fledgling franchise. At first Steinbrenner refused, but when Gillick found out, he told him: "If you don't give me permission to talk to them, I'm leaving anyway at the end of the year when my contract is up." Steinbrenner eventually relented, albeit with the written promise from Gillick that he wouldn't take any of the Yankees scouts or uniformed personnel with him.

As MUCH AS those winter trades would help the Yankees, there were events unfolding in baseball that would have far greater impact on the team and on Steinbrenner. A year after Catfish Hunter's groundbreaking victory against the Oakland A's, players-union chief Marvin Miller was mounting yet another challenge to the reserve clause, this time targeting section 10A in the basic player's contract, which effectively bound players to their teams for life. Noting the wording of the clause—*"If prior to March 1, the Player and the Club have not agreed upon the terms of the contract then, on or before 10 days after, the Club shall have the right by written notice to renew this contract for the period of one year"*—Miller argued this should be interpreted as a one-year-only renewal and not, as the clubs had insisted for 75 years, an automatic annual "roll-over" renewal.

Miller had urged those players whose contracts had been renewed after the 1974 season not to sign new contracts. Two pitchers, Andy Messersmith of the Los Angeles Dodgers and Dave McNally of the Montreal Expos, agreed to take part in Miller's experiment, playing the entire 1975 season under renewed contracts and then rejecting multiyear offers from their clubs at season's end. It was the union's position the players "had completed their renewal years and now should become free to negotiate with any of the 24 clubs with respect to their services for 1976."

Despite fierce opposition from the owners, who maintained that matters regarding the reserve system were "expressly exempted" from the grievance procedure, the issue came before baseball arbitrator Peter Seitz, who had ruled in Hunter's favor a year before. On December 23, Seitz again found for the Players Association, maintaining that the owners had left him no choice after rebuffing his recommendation that they negotiate a settlement with the players. In response, the owners exercised their right under the Basic Agreement and fired him.

But they couldn't reverse his decision. By finishing off the reserve clause, Seitz had swung open the gates to free agency. In exile, George Steinbrenner had no involvement in the owners' desperate legal maneuverings to preserve the players' servitude, but now he stood prepared to take full advantage of their blundering.

It turned out that McNally, who'd been hurt for much of '75, elected to retire after the season, passing on his chance to test free agency. Messersmith, who had won 20 and 19 games respectively over the previous two seasons for the Dodgers, looked to cash in big time. Not surprisingly, when all the owners' legal efforts had been exhausted and Messersmith's free agency was upheld at the start of spring training in 1976, the Yankees were first in line at his doorstep.

This time, Steinbrenner, who knew that Kuhn was still mulling over whether to reinstate him early, allowed Paul to conduct all the negotiations with Messersmith's agent. On March 31, Messersmith and the Yankees agreed to a four-year, $1 million contract, but no sooner had the announcement been made than a dispute arose over the interest on the deferred money in the deal. It was left to Kuhn to resolve the issue, and the commissioner ruled that the contract was not binding. A week later, Messersmith instead signed with the Atlanta Braves. "It's all right," Paul told Steinbrenner after Kuhn ruled against the Yankees on the Messersmith contract. "It was going to be a lot of money and, after the deals we made with Pittsburgh and California, we're okay with our starting pitching."

In contrast to 1975, where injuries had contributed to unfulfilled expectations (and the ultimate undoing of Bill Virdon), Billy Martin's first full season as Yankees manager in 1976 was a success from the beginning, starting with a 10-3 April. As Paul had maintained, the Yankees had the best pitching staff in the American League (3.19 ERA)—further bolstered by a midseason trade with the Orioles for veterans Ken Holtzman and Doyle Alexander—and with the leadership of catcher Thurman Munson (who won MVP honors with a .302 average, 17 homers and 105 RBI), they stayed in first place most of the season and easily won the AL East by 10½ games. While Munson, Nettles (93 RBI), Chambliss (96 RBI), Oscar Gamble (17 homers) and Roy White (14 homers) provided firepower up and down the lineup, it was the speed of Rivers and Randolph (who combined for 80 stolen bases) that prompted the media to dub Martin's aggressive and opportunistic bunch "the Bronx Bandits."

From Steinbrenner's point of view, nothing was sweeter about the 1976 season, the first year of the renovated Yankee Stadium, than the "fannies in the seats"—2,012,434 of them all told, the first time since 1950 that Yankees attendance had surpassed the two-million mark. "Remember three years ago, when our group bought this club from CBS, I said it would take us three years to build this team back to where it once was?" Steinbrenner crowed. "Nobody believed it, but here we are. Do you know how hard it is to build a business in three years?"

Still, the season was not entirely without some contentious times. When the Yankee players reported to spring training in Fort Lauderdale, there was a notice on the bulletin board headlined "Neatness Counts," in which a new club grooming-and-appearance policy was outlined: "No beards. No beads. No mutton chops. No long hair. No long stirrups." It was signed "George Steinbrenner and Billy Martin." Some of the players were annoyed. Sparky Lyle complained that it had cost him $50 to have his hair curled, "and they said it was still too long." And it took an hour and $30 for Oscar Gamble to shear his trademark Afro into a shape that fit acceptably under his cap. But most of the players reacted with amusement over the new regulations, playfully shouting out "ten-*shun*" whenever Steinbrenner would walk into the clubhouse.

The players still didn't quite know what to make of Martin, especially after the cocky address he gave them on Opening Day in Milwaukee. "You just do what I tell you and we're gonna win," he said. "That's a promise, so don't worry about it. Just do what I say."

On the second day of the season, Martin showed them what he meant. The Yankees were leading 9–6 with one out in the ninth inning when the Brewers loaded the bases. Dave Pagan, the Yankees' rookie right-hander, gave up an apparent game-winning grand slam to Don Money. Elliot Wahle, Gillick's assistant in the Yankees farm department, remembered the reaction in the team front office back at Yankee Stadium.

"We had just moved back into the Stadium," Wahle said, "and a lot of boxes and things were piled up in the hallway outside our offices, including a TV from Gabe's old office in the Parks Administration Building at Shea. The TV was on and we were all listening to the game from our offices."

Steinbrenner, who'd had his suspension lifted a month earlier, was also back in his office, from which he would emerge periodically to check the score. Right after Money hit the home run, Wahle heard a tremendous crash in the hallway and scrambled to the doorway to see what had happened.

"There was the TV . . . in smithereens, glass all over the floor and smoke coming out of it," Wahle said. "George had kicked in the screen, leaving everyone dumbfounded."

It was unfortunate Steinbrenner had chosen to kill the messenger, in this case the TV, because he and everyone watching in the Yankees office missed what happened next: Martin charged out of the dugout and began screaming at the first-base umpire, then the home-plate umpire. He had noticed that, prior to Pagan's last pitch, the first-base umpire had called time-out, thus nullifying the home run, and the Yankees wound up winning the game, 9–7.

"If nothing else," Wahle said, "George let everyone know he was back with all his uncontrolled fury."

Three months later, Wahle would personally feel that fury when Gillick offered him a job as his assistant GM with the Blue Jays.

Since Wahle was the assistant farm director, he did not fall under the category of scout or uniformed employee, positions that Gillick was prohibited from hiring away from the Yankees. But when he informed Steinbrenner of his decision to follow Gillick to Toronto, he was not prepared for the Yankees owner's reaction.

"You ungrateful sonofabitch!" Steinbrenner screamed. "How can you do this? Oh, fuck it. It doesn't matter. I can get 2,000 people to do your job better than you—and for less money. So just get the fuck out of here. If you're not out of your office in one hour, I'll just call security and have the cops throw you out!"

Wahle was trembling as he went back to his office and began frantically emptying desk drawers into cartons. Sure enough, an hour later, two security guards appeared at his door to escort him out of the stadium. He figured he'd probably never talk to Steinbrenner again, but two months later, at an owners meeting at the O'Hare Hilton in Chicago, Wahle stepped into an elevator that had just one other occupant.

"How's everything going in Toronto, pal?" said Steinbrenner, smiling. "It's good to see you."

Steinbrenner's suspension had been lifted by Bowie Kuhn on March 1, 1976, with the commissioner noting, among other things, that the financial problems incurred by the Yankees having to play two years at Shea Stadium "would be significantly alleviated by his reinstatement and attendant benefits to the team and Yankee fans." In a letter to Steinbrenner, Kuhn welcomed him back and urged him to "get on with making the Yankees a competitive team."

Those last words would come back to haunt the commissioner. Steinbrenner, with his free spending on players and constant criticism of umpires and fellow owners, gradually replaced Finley as Kuhn's most difficult and exasperating owner. In his 1987 memoir, Kuhn cited the litany of Steinbrenner's offenses against baseball *after* he'd lifted the Yankees owner's suspension and concluded: "He was like the *Titanic* in search of an iceberg; only in George's case it was never wise to bet on the iceberg. . . . He behaved as if he were guided by a compass that pointed unerringly to trouble."

After experiencing a relatively injury- and trouble-free 1976 season under Billy Martin and coasting to the American League East title, the Yankees earned the right to represent the American League in the World Series by beating the Kansas City Royals in a stirring best-of-five AL Championship Series. The climax was Chambliss's ninth-inning walk-off home run, which touched off a near riot at Yankee Stadium as thousands of jubilant fans stormed onto the field, preventing the Yankee first baseman from even touching home plate. Arriving at Cincinnati's Riverfront Stadium for their workout the next afternoon, the Yankees showed the effects of having partied all night. As they staggered off the bus and walked across the Riverfront Stadium outfield, pitching coach Bob Lemon tripped over a duffel bag full of baseballs and sprawled onto the turf as everyone roared with laughter.

It was as if, by bringing Yankee fans their first pennant in 12 years, they had already won the World Series. They were outmatched against the Reds, losing in a four-game sweep. Behind the scenes, Steinbrenner ranted continually at Paul and anyone else who happened to be around him. Most of his ire was directed at Mickey Rivers, whose lackadaisical play over the last month of the season—which was directly related to his financial and marital woes—had worn thin on everyone around the team.

"Mick the Quick" had proven to be a valuable acquisition in '76, a top-of-the-order igniter the like of which the Yankees had never had. Off the field, however, his life was a mess—he would gamble away his paychecks on losing horses at Aqueduct Racetrack, which in turn created a hostile environment on the domestic front with his missus. As the season wore on, Paul would hear regularly from Rivers, asking for advances on his salary, and from the center fielder's wife, Mary, who would call to complain about her husband's missing paychecks. One time that season, Mary Rivers actually showed up unannounced at Steinbrenner's office, demanding that the owner have the checks sent directly to her.

Another time Mary Rivers took her wrath out on her husband's car—and, in the process, a few others belonging to his teammates. She had come to the Stadium on the day of a game hoping to retrieve Rivers's paycheck. John Addeo, the Yankees official in charge of the players' parking lot, remembered seeing Mary Rivers angrily getting into her husband's car but paying little heed to her until, a few moments later, he heard cars being smashed at the other end of the lot.

"It was unbelievable," Addeo said. "I run over there and she's smashing Mickey's car into the other cars in the lot. It was like bumper cars at the amusement park!"

Rivers was 0 for 9 in the first two Yankee losses to the Reds in Cincinnati. On the off-day at Yankee Stadium, Steinbrenner called Paul to his office and began railing about the team's missing-in-action leadoff man.

"Rivers is killing us!" Steinbrenner shouted. "You've got to get rid of him, Gabe! Trade him!"

Paul couldn't believe his ears.

"What are you talking about, George?" he said. "You can't trade players in the middle of the World Series! Besides, he's what *got* us here the first five months of the season."

"Well, then, we've got to get rid of the wife," Steinbrenner said. "She's the problem. She's the one causing all this trouble!"

"What do you suggest we do about her?" Paul asked.

"I know what to do," Steinbrenner snapped. "I'm going to get the Black Muslims on this." That would take care of it.

Paul had no idea what Steinbrenner was talking about. Only years later would it be learned that, shortly after purchasing the Yankees from CBS, Steinbrenner had been approached by the Black Muslims militant group, who made a secret deal with him to provide a little extra security around Yankee Stadium. For now, Paul merely thought Steinbrenner was talking crazy.

"*Black Muslims?*" he said to himself. "This man will stoop to anything!"

The Yankees went down easily, 6–2 and 7–2, in the two games at Yankee Stadium, bringing a quick end to the Series. Martin, who had lost nearly 20 pounds during the season, was not willing to let it go. He had been thrown out of the final game of the Series for tossing a baseball onto the field and verbally baiting home-plate umpire Bill Deegan. After the game, sitting red-eyed and crying in his office, he told reporters, "People say it was a great year, but how can it be a great year when we lost four straight?"

Sparky Lyle agreed. The stellar closer conceded that the Yankees hadn't been prepared for the Reds. "We were coming off the high of beating the Royals, and the World Series was over before it started," Lyle said.

Lyle and the rest of the Yankees were sitting in the somber, silent Yankee clubhouse when Steinbrenner strode in.

"All he said was: 'You oughta hang your heads!' and then he walked out."

At least Steinbrenner could now turn his attention to the new frontier of the off-season and the pursuit of free agents in the wake of the McNally-Messersmith decision. Beginning the morning after the last game of the World Series, Steinbrenner, Paul and occasionally Martin had a series of meetings to discuss the 22 players who had played out their contracts and been declared free agents. Among them were: Reds pitching ace Don Gullett, who had beaten the Yankees in the first game of the World Series; Baltimore Orioles All-Star second baseman Bobby Grich; and four stalwarts from Charlie Finley's three-time world champion Oakland A's: shortstop Bert Campaneris, third baseman Sal Bando, outfielder Joe Rudi and closer Rollie Fingers. Steinbrenner, Paul and Martin all agreed that Gullett should be their first objective. He would further solidify what was already one of the deepest starting rotations in the American League and also deal a blow to the team that had just vanquished them in the World Series.

As for the rest, Martin wanted to pursue Rudi to play right field and Grich to play shortstop. "Rudi's one of the best outfielders in the game," Martin contended, "and even though Grich is a second baseman, he has the range to play short, and we got no production out of shortstop this year."

Steinbrenner looked at Paul. "What do you think, Gabe?" he said.

"I like Grich," Paul said, "and Billy's right about Rudi. He's a good player."

"Maybe," said Steinbrenner, "but none of these guys you're talking about are stars. One guy we haven't talked about is Reggie Jackson."

Jackson, who had twice led the American League in homers for Finley's Oakland A's and was named Most Valuable Player in 1973, was the only marquee player on the free agent list. Once Finley realized he wasn't going to be able to sign him, he had traded Jackson to the Baltimore Orioles midway through the 1976 season. Shortly after the trade, the Orioles were in New York for a series against the Yankees, and Jackson, never one to miss an opportunity to regale the media masses, got to talking with a group of Yankees beat reporters from the tabloids about his impending free agency.

"All I know is," Jackson said very calculatingly, "if I ever played in New York, they'd name a candy bar after me."

At the World Series in New York a few months later, Jackson made his intentions even clearer. He had decided to attend game three at Yankee Stadium and was on his way to have dinner in the Yankee Club when the receptionist at the door stopped him from entering.

"I'm sorry, Mr. Jackson," she said. "Your name is not on the list here. I can't let you in."

Recognizing Jackson waiting at the door, Fred Matthews, the manager of Steinbrenner's Bay Harbor Hotel, in Tampa, who had been brought to New York by the owner to oversee the luxury boxes and the restaurants for the Series, rushed over to intervene. As the receptionist began explaining the situation, Matthews wrote Jackson's name on the back of the list and instructed her to let him in.

"Forget it," snapped Jackson. "Next year, I'll own this fuckin' place!"

Steinbrenner had most assuredly heard about the incident.

"The way I see it," he continued to Paul and Martin, "we need a cleanup hitter and we also need a star."

Martin blanched. "George," he said, "we've *got* a cleanup hitter in Chambliss, and we won this year without a star."

But Martin could see where this conversation was going, especially when Paul said nothing. Steinbrenner had made up his mind. The Yankees owner was going to take full advantage of free agency, just as he had with Catfish Hunter two years before. Steinbrenner would bring Reggie Jackson to New York, where they would name a candy bar after him.

And the New York tabloids were going to eat it up.

6

. . .

Turmoil and Triumph

. . .

I T TOOK GEORGE STEINBRENNER all of a week to get his man.

Reggie Jackson already had a pretty good idea about what life would be like in the "great metropolis," as his friend Howard Cosell was so fond of calling it. Jackson knew what sort of off-the-field marketing and promotional opportunities New York offered. Still, having played almost all his major league career in Oakland, Jackson had begun to think of himself as a West Coast guy, and Los Angeles and San Diego both appealed to him.

On November 4, 1976, Major League Baseball conducted its first "reentry draft" at the Plaza Hotel in New York. The 24 existing clubs (the expansion Toronto Blue Jays and Seattle Mariners were not allowed to participate) were selecting for the right to negotiate with the 22 players who had played out their "renewal" years, each of whom could be selected by up to 12 teams and become free agents in the aftermath of the McNally-Messersmith decision.

As soon as the draft was over, Steinbrenner instructed Gabe Paul to set up meetings with the agents for Cincinnati Reds ace left-hander Don Gullett and Jackson, both of whom had been selected by the maximum 12 clubs. Paul was to concentrate his efforts on Gullett, while Steinbrenner said he would personally handle the Jackson recruiting effort. Paul reported back to Steinbrenner that Jackson was planning to make some trips to the other clubs that had drafted him, but because his Arizona-based agent, Gary Walker, refused to travel by airplane, that would take some time.

"It's my understanding," Paul told Steinbrenner, "Jackson has told the agent he'd like to know by Thanksgiving where he's going to play next year."

"Okay," said Steinbrenner. "Tell them I'd like Reggie to come to New York at the beginning of that week. I'll take it from there."

On November 18, Steinbrenner and Paul completed the first part of their free agent quest by signing Gullett to a six-year, $2 million contract. That night, Steinbrenner took Thurman Munson to dinner at "21" for a dual purpose. He wanted to celebrate their acquisition of the preeminent pitcher on the free agent market and, more important, he wanted to sound out the Yankee captain as to whether the team would welcome Reggie Jackson.

Steinbrenner told Munson that he was inclined to sign Jackson despite his reputation for being a "hot dog" and a me-first player, but that Paul and Martin preferred to sign Grich to play shortstop.

"Go get the big guy," Munson said. "He's the only guy in baseball who can carry a team for a month, and don't believe all the other stuff you've heard about him. He plays hard all the time. We can always trade for a shortstop."

This was all Steinbrenner needed to hear, though Munson had an ulterior motive for encouraging him to sign Jackson. The previous spring in Fort Lauderdale, Munson had met with Steinbrenner at the owner's apartment in the Galt Ocean Manor hotel, where the two had discussed the coming era of free agency. As a catcher who hits .300 and drives in 100 runs, Munson noted, he figured to get top dollar on the open market.

"But my desire is to remain a Yankee," Munson had told Steinbrenner, calculatingly. "All I ask is that, other than Catfish, I will always be the highest-paid player on the team."

"That's sounds fine to me," Steinbrenner said.

For good measure, Munson had asked Bill "Killer" Kane, the team's traveling secretary, to accompany him to the meeting as a witness.

Now, buoyed by Munson's endorsement of a potential clubhouse rival, Steinbrenner arranged to spend a day in New York with Jackson, showing him the sights and the power spots while schmoozing with him about the advantages of playing for the Yankees in the country's biggest media market.

On the Monday before Thanksgiving, Jackson arrived in New York after having previously visited with Expos owner Charles Bronfman, the Seagrams whiskey heir, in Montreal, and in San Diego with Ray Kroc, the McDonald's hamburger magnate who owned the Padres. In his mind, Jackson had set a figure of $3 million for five years as the baseline for his first free-agency contract. But Bronfman knocked him and his agent off their feet by offering $5 million. Years later, Jackson would say that the reason he didn't sign with the Expos was that he just couldn't see himself living outside the U.S.

Steinbrenner had no idea how high Bronfman had already raised the Reggie stakes when he picked Jackson up in his limo to go to lunch at "21." Meeting them there were three of the most prominent real estate moguls in New York: the Fisher brothers, Zack and Larry, and Tony Rolfe. Steinbrenner had also invited his close pal Bill Fugazy, who had made his name as a power broker in New York with his high-profile travel and limousine business. Jackson had never been to "21" but was well aware of its reputation as a place where New York's most powerful businessmen met for lunch. Accordingly, he made sure to wear a tie (which was definitely not his custom, especially at lunch), though he later admitted to being taken aback at the saloon-like decor: checkered tablecloths and uncarpeted wooden floors.

During lunch, Steinbrenner told Jackson that his friends, the Fishers and Rolfe, would find him an apartment in Manhattan, and Fugazy assured him that he'd have a limo at his disposal anytime he needed a ride. Jackson, in his 1984 autobiography, wrote that he was awestruck by the whole scene: "These guys seemed to represent all the business and radiate all the action of the Big Apple." The final touch, Jackson wrote, was when, on the way out, he spotted a pipe in the smoking case by the front door that was priced at $60. When he casually commented that it seemed an exorbitant price for a pipe, Larry Fisher insisted on buying it for him.

Standing on the sidewalk in front of "21," Steinbrenner suggested to Jackson that the two of them take a little walk. As they headed east along 52nd Street, then turned left onto Second Avenue and headed uptown, passersby gradually began to recognize them: the owner of the Yankees and the most celebrated free agent in baseball strolling Manhattan together, smiling and waving as a cabbie hollered, "Sign him, George!" or a cop on the corner greeted them, "Welcome to New York, Reggie." All the while Jackson wondered to himself if Steinbrenner hadn't staged this whole thing for his benefit.

When they got to 71st Street, Steinbrenner said, "Here's the brownstone where I live. Let's go up and talk."

Once they were settled in the living room, Steinbrenner wasted no time cutting to the chase.

"So what exactly are you looking for, Reggie?" he asked.

"Gary and I want $3 million."

"Oh, I can't pay you that much!" Steinbrenner protested, laughing. "It'll screw up my whole salary structure!"

From there, they began to feel each other out, Steinbrenner reiterating the financial advantages of playing in New York and Reggie asking if the owner had talked to any of the Yankees players about signing him. Steinbrenner finally said he was prepared to offer Jackson $2 million for five years, to which Reggie, his meeting with Bronfman still fresh in his mind, laughed. "You're not even close, George—and that doesn't even include the Rolls-Royce I'd like to have as a sort of signing bonus."

They didn't agree to terms, but both knew what they wanted, and that was each other. They agreed to get together again in a few days, on the Wednesday before Thanksgiving, at the O'Hare Airport Hyatt, in Chicago. This was convenient for Steinbrenner, who afterward would continue on to Culver Military Academy in Indiana to spend Thanksgiving with his son Hank. What he didn't know was that Jackson and his agent had chosen this site because it was a convenient midway point for all of Jackson's suitors to fly in with their final bids. When Steinbrenner walked into the Hyatt and saw Baltimore Orioles general manager Hank Peters sitting in the lobby, he was stunned. He quickly realized what was happening and thought: "I don't know how many other people are here, but I'm going to be the last to leave."

When he sat down with Jackson and Walker in their room, Steinbrenner said he'd considered what Jackson had said to him two days earlier in New York and was increasing his offer to $2.9 million for five years. When Jackson reminded him that he wanted a Rolls-Royce as part of any deal he made, Steinbrenner shrugged. He wouldn't buy the car himself, he said, but he'd throw in an extra $60,000 to cover the expense of it, scribbling all the details down on a Hyatt cocktail napkin. Smiling, Jackson reached for the napkin and wrote on the back of it: "I will not let you down. Reginald M. Jackson." Thus, for $2.96 million Reggie Jackson became a New York Yankee.

Jackson would, within a year's time, live up to his pledge to Steinbrenner, but it would be a tumultuous relationship that barely lasted to the press conference in which the Yankees announced Jackson's signing. The Sunday after Thanksgiving, Steinbrenner phoned Yankees public relations director Marty Appel and instructed him to book a room for Jackson at the Americana Hotel, on 52nd Street, where visiting teams stayed when they played the Yankees and where the press conference would be held the next day.

But at 1:30 A.M. Appel was awakened by the ringing of his telephone. On the other end of the line was Steinbrenner, screaming at him to "get your ass into the city and straighten out this problem with Reggie or else it's gonna be *your* ass!" Appel learned that Jackson had brought along a female companion, but his room at the Americana had two twin beds in it. Frantically, Appel called the night manager of the hotel, who informed him that Jackson was threatening to leave town. Worse, the manager told Appel that all the rooms at the Americana came with twin beds.

At Appel's urging, the manager corralled Jackson as he was heading out the door and put him on the phone.

"Stay right there, Reggie," Appel pleaded. "I'll be back to you in five minutes with a new room."

Appel called the Plaza, where he was able to secure a suite for Jackson. But upon calling back to the Americana, the manager told him he'd found a foldout double bed for Jackson, who had retired for the night. Relieved he still had a job, Appel managed to get a few of hours of sleep before hustling to the Americana to prepare for the 11 A.M. press conference. But when he arrived, he discovered that Steinbrenner had instructed Yankees in-house counsel Joe Garagiola Jr. to change some of the language in the contract at the last minute. Naturally, Jackson's attorney, Steven Kay, balked at this, and by 10:15 the contract still wasn't signed. Finally, Steinbrenner came into Kay's room, where the negotiations were going on, and resolved the impasse by ordering Garagiola to remove the language from the contract. In front of Jackson and Kay, he blamed the whole misunderstanding on Garagiola. The embarrassed Garagiola said nothing, but at that moment privately concluded that if he was going to continue practicing law, it would be in a private practice or for somebody other than George Steinbrenner.

At the press conference, Jackson, wearing a pale gray suit with brass buttons, blue shirt, silk tie and alligator shoes, heaped praise upon Steinbrenner for winning him over to the Yankees. "He took it on his own to hunt me down. It was like trying to hustle a girl in a bar. I got the feeling I was his personal project to be with the Yankees." It was when Jackson later told the media, "Sometimes I just underestimate the magnitude of me" that the other Yankee players in the room looked at each other with raised eyebrows.

Steinbrenner had invited a carefully selected entourage of Yankees to show support for his newest star: iconic coaches Yogi Berra and Elston Howard (the first black Yankee), Roy White (the most prominent black player on the team) and Munson. Conspicuous by his absence was Billy Martin. Nobody knew why Martin wasn't there, but it later became very apparent that the manager resented the way Steinbrenner had been fawning over Jackson. After watching the press conference on TV, Martin complained to his friend Nick Nicolosi, manager of the Sheraton Hotel in Hasbrouck Heights, New Jersey, where he was staying, "George takes Reggie to all the best restaurants in New York and he never once even took me to lunch." When Jackson said, "It's going to be great with the Yankees because George and I are going to get along real good," Martin groused, "He's gonna find out real quick that George isn't the manager."

The following spring in Florida, Martin was admittedly bitter about the addition of his new $2.9 million right fielder, and his mood gradually worsened as Steinbrenner began nitpicking over his management style—things like not riding on the team bus to the Grapefruit League games (Martin drove his own car) and not playing his regulars enough. Things came to a head on March 26 in St. Petersburg, after the Yankees lost to the Mets in a game that was telecast back to New York. In the days leading up to it, Steinbrenner had continually harped about the importance of winning spring training games under the misguided belief that the team's Grapefruit League performance affected ticket sales back home for the regular season—making the Mets game, in his mind, doubly important. After the game, a seething Steinbrenner, with Gabe Paul in tow, stormed into the clubhouse and began venting about the loss to Martin, who was sitting in the corner of the room with his pal Mickey Mantle.

Enraged at being dressed down in front of his best friend and his players, Martin shouted back, "Get the fuck out of here, George! I won't have you yelling at me in front of my players!"

"I'll do whatever I want," Steinbrenner yelled.

"No, you won't, George," said Martin. "Not here. You can't come in here and yell at me and my players."

"Oh, no?" said Steinbrenner. "Do you want to be fired right here, right now?"

"If that's what you wanna do, George, then go ahead. Fire me!" Martin screamed, edging closer to Steinbrenner.

As Martin kept approaching, Steinbrenner walked backward until they were both almost up against the wall in the trainer's room, at which point Paul, worried that Martin might throw a punch, stepped between them alongside the trainer's table. Instead of hitting Steinbrenner, Martin slammed his fist into a tub of ice water, splattering ice all over the 67-year-old Paul. As the players listened to the fracas out in the clubhouse, Yankees trainer Gene Monahan scurried out of the trainer's room, "his face whiter than his trainer's garb," according to Sparky Lyle. The shouting died down and, a few minutes later, Martin walked out of the training room and left with Mantle. Steinbrenner came out next, turned to Yogi Berra in the coaches' room and told him he would be taking over as manager.

"Huh-uh," said Berra. "This is Billy's club, George."

"We'll see about that," Steinbrenner said. Then, pointing to "Killer" Kane, the traveling secretary, he said, "You get Billy to my apartment in Tampa at 9 o'clock tomorrow, and don't be late!"

When Kane returned from dinner to the Bay Harbor Hotel in Tampa (where the Yankees were staying for a series of Grapefruit League games on

Florida's west coast), he was distressed not to find Martin at his usual perch in the bar. He did find Berra, who suggested he get a key to Martin's room and wait for him there. Berra volunteered to wait with Kane, and they sat in Martin's room telling baseball stories until 5 A.M., when a bleary-eyed Billy finally walked through the door.

"What are you two guys doing here?" Martin said.

"George wants to see you at his apartment at 9 o'clock," Kane said, "and he asked me to take you there."

"Oh, shit," Martin grumbled. "Just what I need. More bullshit from this guy."

After a few hours of sleep, Kane picked up Martin and delivered him to Steinbrenner's Tampa apartment for what would prove to be the first of many meetings between the owner and the manager in which a temporary understanding would be reached—only to last until the next Yankees loss or conflict between Martin and Jackson. At this meeting, Billy was able to convince Steinbrenner that it made no difference if he traveled to the spring training games in his own car instead of the team bus.

"There was no need to yell at me in front of my players, George," he said.

"All right," said Steinbrenner, "but I want you to understand, Billy, there's a reason why I take these spring training games as seriously as I do. I have to be concerned with ticket sales up north."

"Fine, George," said Martin. "From here on out I'll be playing the regulars longer anyway."

Gabe Paul could see that Steinbrenner's meddling was already wearing on Martin, and the regular season hadn't even begun. Paul felt the same way—and had for the past two years. His latest headache derived from a phone call he had received from Steinbrenner in which the owner told him he was signing Hopalong Cassady, the Heisman Trophy winner he knew from his days at Ohio State (who was already on the payroll as a conditioning consultant), to a three-year contract as a scout.

"This is just another example of George paying off his obligations at the club's expense," Paul complained in his recorded diary. "This guy is supposed to be a *scout*? He asked Yogi Berra what the sign was for the sacrifice fly!"

Paul's exasperation with Steinbrenner nearly reached the breaking point at the end of spring training, when he was trying to complete an important trade with the Chicago White Sox for shortstop Bucky Dent. At the winter meetings the previous December, Steinbrenner had heard that White Sox owner Bill Veeck was looking to trade Dent, who was a year away from becoming a free agent.

"We need to get back on this, Gabe," he told Paul. "The shortstops we have here in camp aren't going to cut it. Find out what Veeck wants for Dent and make a deal."

Paul, however, found Veeck and his general manager, Roland Hemond, to be hard bargainers despite their eagerness to move a shortstop they were not going to be able to afford after the '77 season. In addition to Oscar Gamble, a left-handed hitter the Yankees deemed expendable, Hemond kept asking for a parcel of the Yankees' top pitching prospects for Dent, particularly Ron Guidry, the lithe, hard-throwing left-hander from the Cajun country of Louisiana. Though he had been slow to find a niche as either a starter or reliever in five years in the farm system, Guidry had nevertheless impressed Paul in two brief stints with the Yankees in '75 and '76, and the Yankees' scouts and minor league coaches agreed that it would be a grievous mistake to give up on him. Steinbrenner, however, wasn't hearing it.

The previous spring he had witnessed a rough outing by Guidry and, within earshot of the 25-year-old lefty, had grumbled, "He'll never be more than a Triple A pitcher!" Guidry was so upset that he packed his bags, got in his car, and began driving home to Lafayette, Louisiana. Only at the urging of his wife, Bonnie, did he change his mind about quitting and turn the car around to head back to Fort Lauderdale.

Now, however, Steinbrenner was even more adamant about Guidry's expendability.

"We've got to have the shortstop, Gabe," he said after Paul reported back to him about the White Sox' demands. "They want Guidry? Well, goddammit, then give him to 'em!"

"Over my dead body," Paul shot back. "I won't do it. If you want to do it, then you do it yourself."

"Oh, no, I'm not getting involved," Steinbrenner said. "You handle it. I want Dent. This deal is on you to get it done."

Despite his boss's impatience, Paul held out, and on the last day of spring training he was able to secure Dent from the White Sox for Gamble, two minor league pitchers and $250,000. One of the pitchers, LaMarr Hoyt, would go on to win a Cy Young Award for the White Sox in 1983. But by that point Guidry would win 122 games for the Yankees and his own Cy Young Award for going 25-3 in 1978, and compile a 3-1 record and 1.69 ERA in four World Series starts.

When the '77 season began, with Jackson in right field and Dent at shortstop, the growing friction between Martin and Steinbrenner was exacerbated by the Yankees' 2-7 record in their first nine games. They would win 14 of their next 16, but the atmosphere continued to be uneasy all around as tension remained, and not just between the manager and the owner.

From the first time he walked into the Yankee clubhouse in Fort Lauderdale, Jackson realized that his "magnitude of me" press conference back in November had not sat well with a lot of the Yankee players, who viewed Munson as their leader and felt the need to remind Jackson that they'd been American League champions the year before without him. When he arrived that first day, he sat at his locker for five tense minutes, unacknowledged, before Catfish Hunter, his old Oakland A's teammate, walked over to Jackson, put out his hand and said, "Welcome to camp, Buck."

Munson himself was no longer quite so enamored with the addition of Jackson either, once he learned the details of the right fielder's contract. Minus the $400,000 signing bonus, Jackson's annual salary was $332,000. Munson, under the terms of the four-year contract he'd signed in the spring of '76, was to earn $155,000 in 1977, $165,000 in '78 and $195,000 in '79, which meant he'd be making barely half as much as Jackson in any given year—and that didn't include the extra $60,000 for the Rolls-Royce. But when Munson went to Steinbrenner at the beginning of the '77 season to remind him of their verbal agreement, the Yankees owner put him off, arguing that $132,000 of Jackson's annual salary was deferred and that his actual take-home pay amounted to $200,000. As such, he said, there was no reason to make any adjustment in Munson's salary. Munson was outraged at his callous disregard for what they'd agreed to and stormed out of Steinbrenner's office.

"Killer" Kane was working on his travel budget in the solitude of his basement office, just down the corridor from the Yankee clubhouse, when Munson burst through the door, grabbed a chair and hurled it against the wall. "That lying, no good sonofabitch!" the burly catcher shrieked. "Fuck him! I'm not gonna forget this! I'm done here!"

"I never saw Thurman as mad as he was that day," Kane said in a 2009 interview. "He scared me, to be honest. There was nothing I could say to him. But it was right after he felt George betrayed him that he started making a real big deal about family and wanting to be closer to home. And then he bought that damn plane."

As for Reggie Jackson, the cold reception from his new teammates left him feeling like an outsider, and Martin's refusal to bat him in his accustomed cleanup spot—using him instead as the number-five hitter—was only making him more miserable. Then, on May 23, the new issue of *Sport* magazine hit the newsstands. In an article titled "Reggie Jackson in No-Man's Land," writer Robert Ward quoted Jackson saying, "'this team . . . it all flows from me . . . I'm the straw that stirs the drink. . . . Munson thinks he can be the straw that stirs the drink but he can only stir it bad.'" Copies of the magazine were all over the Yankees clubhouse, and the players reacted to the story with predictable disgust, their initial feelings about Jackson now confirmed.

It would take a whole season, and one glorious October night at Yankee Stadium, for Reggie to heal the rift and finally win their admiration. In the meantime, he could not seem to avoid controversy during that summer of '77, even though competing for column inches in the tabloids were the Son of Sam murders, a citywide blackout, the riots in Bushwick and a contentious four-way mayor's race.

On June 18 in Boston, the simmering hostility between Martin and Jackson broke out into a full-blown conflagration. In the sixth inning of the game between the Yankees and the Red Sox, which was being played before a national TV audience, Jackson was slow to retrieve a ball hit to right field by the Red Sox' Jim Rice. Rice made it to second for a double, and directly after the play, as he walked to the mound to make a pitching change, Martin could be heard shouting, "I've had enough of this shit!" He brought in Sparky Lyle to relieve Mike Torrez and sent reserve outfielder Paul Blair to replace Jackson in right field. As Blair trotted past the mound, Lyle asked him where he was going.

"The manager told me to go to right field," Blair said.

Lyle, who detested Jackson, couldn't contain his glee. "Hooo, boy!" he exclaimed. "I can't wait to see *this*!"

Stunned by Blair's arrival in right field, Jackson threw up his hands as if to say "Are you kidding?" and when he reached the Yankees dugout he immediately confronted Martin. The cameras showed them jawing at each other, nose to nose.

"You want to show me up by loafing on me?" Martin seethed. "Fine, then I'm gonna show your ass up. I ought to kick your fucking ass!"

"Who the fuck are you talking to, old man?" Jackson shot back.

That remark brought the veins popping out of Martin's neck, and he charged at Jackson as Yogi Berra and Elston Howard moved in quickly to restrain him. Jackson, who was being held back by outfielder Jimmy Wynn, had the last word as he was shuffled down the runway to the clubhouse:

"You never wanted me on this team," he shouted. "Why don't you just admit it?"

Realizing that the scuffle was being picked up on the NBC telecast, Martin ordered one of the batboys to throw a towel over the dugout camera. But at his farm in Ocala, Florida, Steinbrenner had watched the entire ugly scene, and now he was on the phone to Paul in just as much of a rage as Martin and Jackson.

"We've been embarrassed on national TV!" Steinbrenner railed. "Billy's out of control. I want you to set up a meeting with them tomorrow morning, straighten them both out and get this under control. I can't have this!"

He then told Paul to expect him in Detroit, where the team was going next, so he could speak to Martin in person.

Jackson and Martin, who was hungover, met at 9 o'clock the next morning for breakfast in Paul's suite at the Boston Sheraton, where each man gave his version of the events of the previous afternoon. Martin insisted that Jackson hadn't hustled on the ball, which is why he had pulled him from the game. Jackson adamantly maintained that he had not loafed on the ball, his agitation rising at having to defend himself again. Martin, on the other hand, was getting even angrier as he listened to Reggie giving his version of the events. Finally he stood up and yelled at the outfielder, "You're a fucking liar! Get up, boy. I'm gonna kick your ass right here!"

Paul sternly told Martin to sit down. Jackson turned to Paul and said, "You're a Jew, Gabe. How do you think I should feel after being called that name?"

" 'Boy' is just an expression," Martin said.

"Just everyone calm down here," Paul sighed before concluding the meeting by informing both of them that he'd be reporting everything they'd discussed to Steinbrenner, who would meet them in Detroit. After Martin and Jackson departed for Fenway Park (where Jackson would be back in the lineup and the Red Sox would complete a three-game sweep by thumping the Yankees, 11–1), Paul telephoned Steinbrenner. Steinbrenner was even angrier at Martin than he'd been the night before and told Paul that he wanted to fire the manager. What he didn't mention was that he had just talked to Milton Richman of UPI and informed him that this was precisely the reason for his trip to Detroit: to fire Billy Martin.

Richman's story was all over the airwaves and the newspapers Monday morning when Steinbrenner arrived at the Pontchartrain Hotel, in Detroit, and ran into Jackson in the lobby. While he didn't know what Steinbrenner's actual intentions were, Jackson realized that if the owner fired his popular manager, the fans would see him as the villain.

Steinbrenner listened as Jackson explained that the team was already split wide open and that if he fired Martin for what had happened in Boston, the season would likely be lost. It was enough to convince Steinbrenner that perhaps the timing and circumstances dictated against making a change. A few hours later, he met in his room with Jackson and Martin, demanding assurances from both that they could coexist on the Yankees. Before dismissing them, Steinbrenner warned Martin that he'd "better shape up" and get control of himself, and he told Jackson, who had complained to him about other players making remarks about blacks and Jews, that he had to "stop being consumed with racial prejudice."

After being swept in Boston, the Yankees' woes continued as they lost two out of three in Detroit. The first game in Detroit was televised nationally on ABC, and Paul was forced to hike up three levels of old Tiger Stadium to do an interview with Howard Cosell because the press elevator was broken. Paul's was face was flushed and sweat was pouring through his shirt as he explained to Cosell and the assembled reporters that he and

Steinbrenner had met with Jackson and Martin, and that Billy would remain as manager.

The team returned home to play the annual Mayor's Trophy Game for New York charities with the crosstown Mets on Thursday. With the Red Sox coming in for a big weekend series, Paul figured the exhibition game would be a welcome respite from a season that seemed to be getting crazier by the day. But reading the newspaper stories, he became further aggravated, especially by one in the *Daily News*, written by backup baseball writer Bill Verigan, that had obviously been a direct feed from Steinbrenner.

"George Steinbrenner has taken charge of the Yankees," Verigan wrote. "When he came riding into Detroit this week, he took a good look at his team, and what he saw appalled and saddened him. But he seemed saddened the most by what was happening to the team president, Gabe Paul, who is supposed to be Billy Martin's superior and the team's general manager."

The article went on to say Steinbrenner had made the decision to retain Martin and that Paul was "too indecisive and weak" to deal with Billy.

Paul was outraged by what he viewed as a blatant undermining of his credibility by Steinbrenner. And when Steinbrenner called him from Tampa later that morning, Paul was ready to unload.

"I'm a little worried about your health, Gabe, after all this," Steinbrenner said. "Are you okay?"

"My health," said Paul angrily, "is not bothered by Martin. It's bothered by the things *you* do! I'm sick and tired of you getting credit for saving Billy's job. That Verigan article today, which demeans me, is all bullshit and you know it! Why would you say something like that?"

"I don't know what you're talking about, Gabe," Steinbrenner snapped back. "I never said any of that. Do you *believe* me?"

"No."

"Okay," said Steinbrenner, "then I'll write a statement refuting everything in the story."

"Fine."

After hanging up, Paul was more disgusted than ever. "This guy takes full credit for all the trades, but never says he was under suspension when we got Randolph, Ellis and Brett," he muttered into his tape recorder, "or that he wanted Guidry out of there in Fort Lauderdale when he said Guidry didn't have any guts, and then wouldn't take the responsibility for trading him."

Further irritating to Paul was a $50,000 salary advance Steinbrenner had given to Mickey Rivers—after Paul had strongly advised him against it. "Rivers is now just going to keep going back to the Big Rock Candy Mountain Man for more money!"

Steinbrenner's sudden concern for Paul's health might have been piqued by an episode involving one of the Yankees execs, a few weeks earlier. The exec, who was a bit of a gadfly, was always coming up with bizarre promotion ideas, such as "Polaroid Camera Day." A guy named Bill Press had come to him with 40 Polaroid cameras and the idea of having ushers at locations all around the stadium take pictures of every fan in the ballpark alongside a Yankee player. Not surprisingly, the promotion ended up an exercise in chaos, as there was no way they could accommodate every single fan. But as the exec explained to Steinbrenner a few days later, at least the Yankees would not have to pay Press his fee—he'd just been found in the trunk of a car at Kennedy Airport, his severed testicles stuffed in his mouth. The day after being berated by Steinbrenner for another of his promotions gone wrong, the exec came to work and collapsed from a heart attack. Yankees officials frantically attended to him until the paramedics arrived and rushed him to the hospital.

When informed of the heart attack, a shaken Steinbrenner flew up from Tampa to make a personal hospital visit to his stricken exec, assuring him that all his needs would be taken care of. Later that day, Dave Weidler, the team comptroller, who was the exec's closest friend in the front office, also paid a visit to the hospital and smiled in amusement at the mountains of fruit baskets and floral arrangements with Yankees logos filling the room. Steinbrenner obviously felt guilty over his tirade, but as Weidler found out, the heart attack wasn't his fault. It seemed the exec had been living a double life, alternately cohabitating with a wife and kids in the suburbs and a mistress in Manhattan.

"As I sat there next to him in the hospital," Weidler said in a 2007 interview, "He leaned over and whispered to me with a sense of pride that, before he'd come to work that day, he'd had a ménage à trois downtown."

• • •

THE TRUCE BETWEEN Martin and Jackson remained an uneasy one as the Yankees stayed barely above .500 through June and into July while the manager continued to resist batting Jackson in the cleanup spot. After a 9–8 loss to the Brewers in Milwaukee on July 13, Munson and Lou Piniella decided to take matters into their own hands. Steinbrenner had accompanied the team on the road trip and, after the game that night, the two players went to his room at the Pfister Hotel to talk about the state of the ball club. In particular, they said, Billy had to be persuaded to restore Jackson to the cleanup spot. As the three were talking, Martin, who had been downstairs in the bar, passed in the hallway. Upon hearing the voices coming out of Steinbrenner's suite, he pounded on the door and demanded to be let in. According to Piniella, he and Munson had spontaneously asked Steinbrenner to meet with them; they hadn't planned it behind Martin's back. When Martin was let into the room by Steinbrenner, he was upset at the sight of the three of them together. After a tense couple of minutes, Steinbrenner was able to assure his manager that they were only talking about what needed to be done for the team's best interests. By the end of the meeting, Martin had agreed to restore Jackson to the cleanup spot and Steinbrenner had agreed to back off his public criticisms of him.

When Paul heard about the meeting, he was incredulous.

"George actually *invited* the players up there!" he said in his tape diary. "And then he lays the law down to Martin about the batting order. How can the manager be overruled by his players?"

But as the Yankees finished the first half of the season by losing all three games to the Royals in Kansas City, Steinbrenner decided it was time for one of his patented "Yankee pride" lectures. Addressing the team in the clubhouse before the final Sunday game, he warned: "Either you're going to make a comeback or forever be remembered as the team that choked." He then handed out checks for $300 to each of the players, telling them to "go out and have a good time over the All-Star break."

By this time, however, Paul had become convinced that Martin had to go; that he was too unstable to handle the situation with both the irrational owner and his insecure star player. And after a sloppy 5–4 loss to the Brewers in the second game of a doubleheader at Yankee Stadium on July 21, in which they blew a 4–0 lead in the ninth inning, Steinbrenner was inclined to agree. Meeting with Paul in his office after the game, Steinbrenner asked for his general manager's opinion.

"If you ask me, Billy is a mirage as a tactician," Paul said. "He's not resourceful or planned enough. We're the only club in the American League that doesn't have pitching charts."

"What about the players and how they feel about him?" Steinbrenner asked.

"I don't know or care what the players think of him," Paul said. "They're selfish and only out for themselves. I just think Billy is too emotionally unsound and I don't think we can win with him. If we had made the change in June, it would've looked like Reggie is calling the shots and he'd have never recovered from it, but now it's not so much about Billy and Reggie as it is about the team not performing to its capability."

"Who do you think we should get?" Steinbrenner asked.

"I think we should go with Dick Howser and let the chips fall where they may."

"It's your decision," said Steinbrenner.

"My only concern," said Paul, "is that Howser might not want the job on a one-year basis. He's gonna want a two-year contract beyond this, and I don't blame him."

The next morning, Saturday the 23rd, Paul met with Howser and offered him the manager's job, but was not surprised when the third-base coach turned him down. What *did* surprise Paul was a story by Dick Young in the *Daily News* the next day revealing that Howser had been offered Martin's job. When Paul couldn't reach Steinbrenner, who was conspicuously unavailable to anyone that day, he was sure the owner had again leaked the story to the *News*.

Finally, that Sunday night, Steinbrenner called, claiming he was in North Carolina on a business trip, though Paul later learned that the owner had been laying low at the home of his friend Mike Forrest, the furrier, in New Rochelle, a half hour from Yankee Stadium.

"I've thought about this, Gabe," Steinbrenner said, "and the way I see it, we have three options here: Say nothing and do nothing, keep looking, or make a move with either Yogi, Bobby Cox, Jack Butterfield or Gene Michael, who would be my choice."

Paul thought about this before responding. Steinbrenner had already offered Berra the job in the spring, and Yogi had turned it down out of his loyalty to Billy. Butterfield was the farm director and, while highly regarded as a player evaluator, he had no professional managing experience and was relatively unknown to Yankee fans. Paul also didn't think Cox was ready. And Michael, just two years removed from playing, was serving as an executive assistant to Steinbrenner in the front office and had never before managed a minor or major league team.

"*Jack Butterfield?*" Paul thought. "Is he kidding? I should let him do it. They'd blow up the ballpark!"

"What do you think, Gabe?" Steinbrenner asked.

"I think no way on Butterfield. Yogi probably won't take it either. And you can't do this to Gene Michael. He's just not ready."

"Well," said Steinbrenner, "I guess that brings us back to options one and two."

Without a viable replacement, they agreed that Martin would stay. Paul would call Howser and instruct him to deny everything in the Young story. Later that day, before the Yankees' game with the Royals, Paul went down to the clubhouse to give Martin the news of his latest reprieve.

"You're the manager," Paul said.

"For the rest of the season?" Martin asked.

"In baseball, things change from day to day, Billy. No promises. Just go out and manage your way."

The Yankees went on to finish July with seven wins in eight games. But when they lost two out of three to the California Angels in the first series of a West Coast road trip to open August, and then lost two more to the last-place expansion Mariners in Seattle, the team and the season were again in turmoil. As the Yankee players trudged into the visiting clubhouse at the Kingdome following a 9–2 trouncing, Piniella let loose on his teammates. Over the previous weeks, numerous players on the team had been complaining about a variety of issues personal to them—Munson about his salary, Rivers about his advances, Ed Figueroa about Martin periodically skipping him in the rotation, Jackson about life in general—and Piniella, renowned for his hot temper, had finally had enough.

"Okay, all you complainers," he shouted as he entered the clubhouse, "the writers are all here now, so tell 'em all how unhappy you are. Go on! Get it all out in the open! This is your opportunity. We just got beat nine-fucking-two by a horseshit, fucking expansion team and nobody seems to care about that!"

The room went quiet. Some of the players would later contend that it was a turning point in their season. The next day, they beat the Mariners handily, 7–1, salvaging the last game of the road trip and beginning a stretch of 27 wins in 30 games that moved them into first place to stay. Other players would maintain that August 10 was the day their season changed. That was when Martin finally inserted Jackson into the cleanup spot, for only the 11th time in 110 games. From then on the slugger would bat fourth for the rest of the season. Martin explained the change by citing the fact that Reggie had had 20 RBI in the past 23 games batting fifth, while Chambliss had had only nine RBI in 29 games in front of him. "I was just waiting for the right time," he said.

From that date, Jackson drove in 49 runs and hit 13 homers in the last 53 games, 41 of which the Yankees won. They finished the season 100-62, 2½ games ahead of the Red Sox and Baltimore Orioles. Once again, they beat the Kansas City Royals in five games in the American League Championship Series, earning a return trip to the World Series. The ALCS hero was Lyle, who pitched 5⅓ innings of shutout relief in game four in Kansas City and came back the next day to close out the clincher with another 1⅓ innings of scoreless ball, the Yankees scoring three runs in the ninth to win, 5–3. During the celebration in the clubhouse afterward, Martin sneaked up behind Steinbrenner and dumped the remaining contents of a champagne bottle over the owner's head.

"That's for trying to fire me." Martin grinned.

"What do you mean 'trying'?" Steinbrenner said.

As for Reggie Jackson, the ultimate triumph was yet to come.

The Yankees' ALCS victory over the Royals was tempered by the fact that Gullett, after compiling a 14-4 record during the regular season, had come up with a sore shoulder during the series. And, in the final game, there was more controversy between Martin and Jackson. In spite of his batting surge that had carried the Yankees to the AL East title, Jackson arrived at the ballpark to discover that not only was he out of the cleanup spot, he was out of the lineup altogether. Benched!

To that point, Jackson had been 1 for 14 in the ALCS, and the Royals' game five starter, Paul Splittorff, had been particularly successful against him over the years. Just the same, Martin had called Catfish Hunter into his office and asked him about Jackson versus Splittorff. "Reggie can't hit that guy with a paddle," Hunter said.

Initially stunned at seeing he was not in the lineup—especially since Martin hadn't bothered to tell him personally—Jackson turned surprisingly conciliatory when told by the writers that Hunter had told Martin he couldn't hit Splittorff. "The worst thing in the world would have been to leave me in the lineup and have me go 0 for 4," Jackson said. "At the very least, [Martin] showed some guts."

Nevertheless, Jackson contributed a key eighth-inning RBI pinch hit off Royals reliever Doug Bird to help the Yankees into the World Series against the Los Angeles Dodgers.

After forging a 3-1 lead in games in the World Series, Martin sought to close it out in L.A. with Gullett, who had pitched gamely in limiting L.A. to five hits in 8⅓ innings in game one. But the 26-year-old lefty was clearly hindered by his throbbing shoulder and left the game in the fifth inning, after the Dodgers had battered him for eight hits and seven runs en route to an easy 10–4 win, sending the Series back to Yankee Stadium for game six. Though at the time it was just another mark in the box score, the final Yankee run was a homer by Jackson in the eighth inning.

The scene for game six on that cool, clear night of October 18 was charged from the outset. As 56,407 fans began filing into Yankee Stadium, giddy with thoughts of hopefully witnessing the first Yankee world championship since 1962, Jackson put on an awesome pregame power show, knocking 35 to 40 balls into the right-field seats during batting practice. Even the crusty baseball scribe Dick Young marveled at the performance.

"You look pretty locked in," Young said to Jackson as he came out of the cage. "I've never seen anything like that. But don't you think you should save some for the game?"

It turned out Jackson had saved three swings, which was all he needed for three consecutive home runs off three different Dodger pitchers—Burt Hooton, Elias Sosa and knuckleballer Charlie Hough—to carry the Yankees to an 8–4 Series-clinching victory. Jackson's three home runs tied Babe Ruth's record for most homers in a World Series game. Coupled with the one he'd hit in the eighth inning of game five, Jackson had hit four home runs on four straight pitches, and his five total home runs for the Series was also a record, earning him the sobriquet "Mr. October."

Afterward, in the Yankee clubhouse, the unbridled affection displayed between Jackson and his teammates belied the acrimonious tenor of the regular season. Graig Nettles, who had made no secret of his dislike for Reggie during the year, said of his teammate: "He was awesome. A very impressive performance under pressure, as good as you can do. He even caught everything that came to him in the outfield!"

At one point during the revelry, Steinbrenner, Jackson and Martin, the unholy trinity, found themselves together in the manager's office, drenched in champagne, hugging and swearing eternal allegiance to one another.

"You can't do anything to me now—I've got a five-year contract," Jackson teased Steinbrenner.

"You're damn right," said Steinbrenner, "and you're not going anywhere else."

Later, Steinbrenner declared, "Next year we'll be even tougher to beat," before leaving Martin and Jackson to rhapsodize with each other over Reggie's magic night.

"Three home runs," Jackson said. "Do you realize I did that?"

"Yeah," said Martin, grinning, "and you broke my Series record for extra-base hits, and that pisses me off!"

As they laughed, Jackson addressed the remaining writers in the room. "I love Billy Martin," he said. "The man did a helluva job this year. There's nobody else I'd rather play for."

If Gabe Paul had been there, his eyes would have been rolling. Much as he had personally reveled in winning his first world championship after 58 years in the game, the season-long travails with Steinbrenner and

Martin had left the veteran executive feeling drained. At the beginning of the World Series, other Yankees employees witnessed Paul sitting in his office, crying, after Steinbrenner had withheld his tickets for his brother, Sol. Prior to that, he'd once again had to go to the mat to dissuade Steinbrenner from placing Gullett and Hunter on the disabled list before the Series.

Five years of trying to run the Yankees despite constant turmoil and stress, all created by the owner, had exacted a huge toll on Paul. He was sorry he'd ever gotten Steinbrenner into baseball, even though it had finally led to his own triumph as an executive. But now he'd had enough.

Back in Cleveland, the Indians were once again searching for a new guardian angel to rescue them from having to leave the city. The latest underfinanced Indians owner, parking-lot mogul Ted Bonda, reported a $1.1 million loss for 1977 and was desperate to sell. Art Modell, owner of the NFL Browns, who shared Municipal Stadium with the Indians, had suggested to Bonda that he call Steve O'Neill, the multimillionaire trucking magnate who'd sold his minority share in the Indians back in 1973 to join Paul as a limited partner of the Yankees.

The thought of coming back home to Cleveland and buying the Indians as an act of civic responsibility was appealing to O'Neill, who, like Paul, was fed up with being a limited partner of Steinbrenner's. He would buy the club, O'Neill told Bonda, with the idea of bringing Gabe Paul back to Cleveland to run the club.

The day after the winning of the World Series, Paul was back in his office at Yankee Stadium, pondering his future and reflecting on the season. The '77 Yankees, he concluded, had defied all the known laws of baseball. They had won in spite of clubhouse dissension, a crazy manager and an even crazier owner.

In one of his final entries in his recorded diary, a clearly dispirited Paul ruefully summed up his feelings about Steinbrenner: "The guy is a mental case, a liar, an egomaniac and a crook, and that's a pretty good parlay!"

Dreary Cleveland and more losing Indians teams never looked so good to him.

7

. . .

Days of Whine and Rosen

. . .

STEINBRENNER WAS STILL BASKING in the glow of his first world championship when he assembled his high command at Yankee Stadium during the first week of November to discuss the newest class of free agent players about to hit the market.

It had been two weeks since Gabe Paul had informed him of his intentions to join Steve O'Neill in Cleveland. Paul took pains to explain to the media that his decision was based solely on his allegiance to O'Neill, and Steinbrenner had publicly expressed disappointment at losing a person he said he considered a "mentor," but both men knew they could no longer coexist in New York. Too much friction and ill feeling had built up from all their arguments over the last five years. Still, Paul agreed to stay around through the reentry draft and winter meetings to help the transition of baseball operations. After that, Cedric Tallis, whom Paul had brought in from the Kansas City Royals to be his assistant in 1974, would take over as general manager.

Paul, Tallis, Gene Michael, Birdie Tebbetts, Jack Butterfield and Bill Bergesch, another assistant GM, were sitting with Steinbrenner at the big round table in his office, which was covered with a mound of scouting reports and statistics sheets.

"All right," Steinbrenner said, "I want to know who're the best players here."

Paul nodded to Tebbetts, his chief scout, whose primary assignment that season had been to follow the pending free agents around the league. Tebbetts noted that two Minnesota Twins outfielders, Lymon Bostock and American League RBI leader Larry Hisle, were clearly the class of the hitters, but he wondered whether the Yankees, with Jackson, Rivers, Piniella and White, really needed to spend a lot of money on another outfielder.

"What about the pitchers?" said Steinbrenner.

Everyone at the table agreed that Rich "Goose" Gossage, the 26-year-old Pittsburgh Pirates right-hander whose 100-mile-per-hour fastball was complemented by an equally devastating hard slider, was unquestionably the cream of the crop that included the Yankees' own Mike Torrez (who had won 14 games in 1977) and one of their exes, Doc Medich. There was, however, one problem. Gossage was a closer who'd saved 26 games and struck out 151 batters in 138 innings, and, in Sparky Lyle, the Yankees already had the premier closer in the American League, coming off a Cy Young Award–winning season.

"There was a lot of debate about how two closers could be a real problem," remembered Gene Michael. "Would we be able to give each of them enough work? How would Sparky deal with it? In the end, though, I guess George was the driving force."

The way Steinbrenner saw it, he'd built the Yankees into a championship team by taking advantage of the new era of free agency and signing the best of them: Catfish Hunter, Reggie Jackson and Don Gullett. Now Gossage was the best free agent of this year's class, and Steinbrenner saw no reason to abandon his philosophy. If two of everything was good for Noah, why not him?

"We're going after Gossage," he declared. "I'll handle this. Don't worry about Lyle. I've taken care of him."

Steinbrenner had met with Lyle at Yankee Stadium a few days after the World Series and rewarded the left-hander for his Cy Young season (in which he'd gone 13-5 with a 2.17 ERA, saved 26 games and led the American League in appearances) with an extra year on his contract and a bonus of $35,000. The 34-year-old Lyle was pleasantly surprised by the owner's magnanimity; he had never been one of the owner's favorites, given his penchant for practical jokes and the fact that he frequently showed up late for spring training. However, Lyle later began to understand that Steinbrenner's generosity had been designed not so much to reward him as to placate him for signing Gossage—at even more money—to share his job.

"George had clearly made up his mind to go after Goose, probably even before the season ended," Lyle said in a 2008 interview. "In retrospect, I can understand why he did it. I was getting older and didn't throw 97 miles per hour, and Goose was in his prime. But at the time, I was pretty upset."

A couple of days after the meeting about newly available free agents, Steinbrenner flew to Las Vegas with his pal Bill Fugazy for the Ken Norton–Jimmy Young heavyweight title fight at Caesars Palace, November 5. While there, he made a point of looking up his old friend Al Rosen, from Group 66 in Cleveland. Rosen had left Cleveland a couple of years earlier, in the wake of the same failed Texas real estate deal that had forced Sheldon Guren and Ed Ginsberg to sell their original 11 percent share of the Yankees back to Steinbrenner. Rosen's friend Billy Weinberger, the president of Caesars, had offered him a greeter's job at the casino. But Rosen was miserable in Las Vegas. He despised everything about the town and yearned to return to a job that actually mattered. Over dinner at Caesars Palace the night before the fight, Rosen said as much to Steinbrenner.

"Well, you know Gabe's leaving me," Steinbrenner said. "I'd love to have you come to New York and take over as president of the Yankees."

"That's something I'd really like," said Rosen. "I've been wanting to get back into baseball for a long time."

Though Tallis had been the architect of those Kansas City Royals teams that played the Yankees in the '76 and '77 American League Championship Series and had even been voted executive of the year by *The Sporting News* in 1971, Steinbrenner viewed him as more of an administrator than a baseball talent evaluator. Rosen, on the other hand, had played the game and played it exceedingly well, winning American League Most Valuable Player honors with the Indians in 1953. He'd been a hero in Cleveland, especially to Steinbrenner.

"I want you to run the operation, just like Gabe did," Steinbrenner told his friend. "Cedric will remain the general manager, but you'll be the one in charge of the baseball end of it."

"I'm ready to go," said Rosen.

Rosen had hated the Yankees his entire life—in the '50s the Indians had consistently battled them for the pennant—but he was ecstatic at the opportunity. Two weeks after his meeting with Steinbrenner in Las Vegas, he arrived in New York, where he worked by day with Paul, Tallis and Bill Bergesch at Yankee Stadium, going over scouting reports, waiver rules and contracts, and by night accompanying Steinbrenner on the Manhattan social scene with the owner's friends, Bill Fugazy, the Fisher brothers and Mike Forrest. They went to Regine's, or Elaine's or McMullen's. One night, at Le Club, an exclusive private establishment operated by another of the Yankees owner's cronies, Patrick Shields, Steinbrenner introduced Rosen to the actress Candice Bergen, who was drinking champagne at the next table.

"George was the king of New York," Rosen said in a 2008 interview, "and I felt like one of the free agents he was recruiting. And then, on my first official day as the team president, it all changed."

Rosen had been staying at a hotel in Hasbrouck Heights, New Jersey, while he prepared to move his family from Cleveland after the first of the year. With Major League Baseball closed down the week between Christmas and New Year's, he flew home to Cleveland to help his wife, Rita, pack their belongings. He was home one day when he got a phone call from Steinbrenner in Tampa.

"What are you doing?" Steinbrenner said.

"I'm home here for the holiday week, packing up all my things and getting ready for the move," Rosen said. "There's nothing going on in baseball. Everyone's closed."

"*We're* not closed," Steinbrenner said angrily. "Now get your ass back to New York and be in your office tomorrow!"

Tallis had also gone home to Kansas City for the holiday week and gotten the same phone call from Steinbrenner. "And for the next five days Cedric and I just sat in our office staring across the desk at each other at phones that never rang, and telling baseball stories," recalled Rosen. "I don't know where George was. We never heard from him the rest of the week."

Meanwhile, Steinbrenner's pursuit of Gossage was far less flashy than his courtship of Reggie Jackson the year before. Perhaps because he'd been told that Gossage was a country boy from Colorado Springs, Steinbrenner didn't see a need to bring him to New York and try to sell him on the charms of the big city.

"Basically, George just blew everyone else away with his money offer," Gossage told me. "I don't even remember much negotiating with any other teams."

On November 22, Gossage and his agent, Jerry Kapstein, met with Steinbrenner in Tampa and agreed to a six-year contract worth $2.748 million. Lyle's reaction to reporters' calls about the signing was predictable, even though Steinbrenner, in anticipation of this, had already sweetened his deal. "I want out," Lyle said. "It's nothing personal, but I'll be damned if I'm going to sit out there in the bullpen and go stale because I can't get enough work."

But instead of trading Lyle, Steinbrenner added yet a third closer at the winter meetings in Hawaii, signing 27-year-old right-hander Rawly Eastwick to a five-year, $1.1 million contract. While nobody could quarrel with Steinbrenner for paying what he did for a pitcher of Gossage's quality, the Eastwick signing shocked the rest of baseball. Eastwick had led the National League in saves in '75 and '76 with the Cincinnati Reds' world championship teams, but he'd been injured for much of '77 and had been traded to the St. Louis Cardinals. He was now viewed as damaged goods, hardly a million-dollar pitcher.

"I remember we discussed Eastwick at the winter meetings and we all pretty much agreed we shouldn't sign him," Rosen said. "But George wouldn't listen. I think he just signed him because of the name familiarity."

It was the same way with Andy Messersmith. Two years after his trailblazing free agency, in which he almost signed with the Yankees, Messersmith was out of favor with the Atlanta Braves and their wacky owner, Ted Turner, after suffering an elbow injury that required season-ending surgery in '77. When he had signed Messersmith in April 1976 to a three-year, $1 million contract, Turner proclaimed: "Andy will be a Brave as long as I am. His contract is forever, until death or old age do us part." But after getting only a 16-15 performance from the right-hander's first two seasons in Atlanta, Turner was now anxious to recoup the remaining $333,333 on his contract, and delivered Messersmith to Steinbrenner for a mere $100,000.

For Al Rosen, those winter meetings proved to be quite an introduction to life with Steinbrenner's Yankees. Steinbrenner seemed bent on putting his own imprint on the championship team his outgoing president had built. Paul left for Cleveland right after the new year. On the first day of spring training in Fort Lauderdale, Steinbrenner was talking to a couple of reporters and bristled as they began praising Paul for the job he'd done with the Yankees. "He was in baseball for 40 years, 25 of them as a general manager, and did he ever win a pennant before?" Steinbrenner said, his voice rising. "You think he made all those moves with this team himself? You think all of a sudden he got brilliant?"

Because he'd been out of the game so long, Rosen chose to stay in the background, mostly observing at the winter meetings in Hawaii and offering his opinions only when asked. He knew that once he was entrusted with running the baseball operations and had a better familiarity with all his scouts, he would be asserting himself (and inevitably butting heads with Steinbrenner). For now, he was more concerned about how he was going to deal with Billy Martin.

Perhaps because he had become immune to Steinbrenner not bothering to seek his opinions on players, Martin kept to himself in Hawaii, spending his nights in the hotel bar with baseball friends and the days sleeping off his hangovers on Waikiki Beach. He would later refer to Eastwick and Messersmith as "George's boys."

Martin's indifferent attitude at the meetings didn't faze Rosen. Going all the way back to their minor league playing days in 1949 in the Pacific Coast League, when, according to Rosen, Martin sucker-punched him in a fight, he viewed Billy as an incorrigible troublemaker. "I couldn't warm up to Billy Martin if I was embalmed with him," Rosen once said.

Martin felt the same way about Rosen, but managed to contain his animosity when the team assembled for spring training in February 1978. After all, unlike Rosen, Martin was a true Yankee, wasn't he? And he'd just managed the Yankees to the world championship. Rosen, on the other hand, hadn't been around the game in over 20 years. Nevertheless, Steinbrenner had made it clear how much he respected Rosen. "It's not so easy," he said, "for Billy to look at Al Rosen in the face and say, 'What do you know about baseball?' which he can do with me."

Martin was not surprised when Sparky Lyle failed to show up for the early spring training camp for pitchers and catchers that Steinbrenner had ordered. In truth, Martin felt empathy for his yeoman closer, who was about to be displaced by Steinbrenner's new marquee free agent, Gossage. Martin had not forgotten how Lyle had saved him, and the Yankees' season in '77, with his sterling relief work against the Royals in the ALCS the previous fall. Nor did he relish the task of trying to keep both closers sufficiently busy and happy. And also by now, Lyle had come to realize that, at $135,000, his salary ranked eighth on the Yankee pitching staff, what with the raises given Ron Guidry and Ed Figueroa and the additions of Messersmith at $333,333 and Eastwick at $220,000.

When Lyle finally arrived, a week after the early camp had begun, Steinbrenner arranged to have him greeted as he emerged from the jetway at the Fort Lauderdale airport by the Hollywood Hills High School marching band playing "Pomp and Circumstance," the closer's trademark entrance anthem at Yankee Stadium. For once, the practical joke was on Lyle, but it proved to be the only bit of levity in another otherwise uneasy spring.

For starters, it didn't take long for Gossage to incur the enmity of Billy Martin. The morning before one of his first spring outings, Gossage was shocked when Martin approached him and said he wanted him to deliberately throw at the head of Texas Rangers outfielder Billy Sample. Martin had managed Sample in Texas and, for reasons he didn't bother to tell Gossage, didn't like him. Gossage resisted, telling Martin, "I can't fight your battles for you."

"I tell you to drill a guy and you say you're not gonna do it?" Martin hissed. "You're a worthless piece of shit!"

"I guess he was trying to test my loyalty, but from that day on, I never had any use for Billy," Gossage told me. "He was a big reason for me leaving the Yankees like I did six years later."

Since early that spring, Gossage had been hobbled by a staph infection in his right foot, one of the pitching staff's many ailments that preseason. Gullett and Hunter were still experiencing severe pain in their shoulders. Then, on March 2, the *Daily News'* Phil Pepe broke the story that Catfish Hunter had diabetes.

"How could you do this to us?" Steinbrenner railed at Pepe. "You're helping the enemy by putting something like that in the paper!"

"I don't work for you, George," Pepe shot back. "I work for the *Daily News,* and this was news."

"Ah, well," Steinbrenner sighed. "At least we got the back page."

And when Messersmith, who was having an excellent spring, took a fall while covering first base and separated his pitching shoulder, Steinbrenner was apoplectic. Suddenly, the multimillion-dollar starting rotation he had assembled was decimated.

"You couldn't tell George that injuries were a part of the game," said Rosen. "He was mad at everyone. He blamed Pepe for the Catfish diabetes story, he blamed the team doctors and trainers for the Gullett and Hunter shoulder injuries and, for all I know, the groundskeepers in Sarasota for not having softer grass where Messersmith took his fall. It was a mess, and it didn't help that Billy hated Ken Holtzman, one of our few healthy starters, and wouldn't pitch him."

Finally, on March 25 in Fort Lauderdale, after the Yankees had played sloppily against the Mets in another game that was telecast back to New York, Steinbrenner blew a gasket, much as he had after the Mets game the previous spring in which he and Martin nearly came to blows. This time the Yankees had actually won, 9–6, but only after a six-run ninth inning against the Mets' secondary relievers. Earlier in the game, incensed over five Yankee errors, Steinbrenner had stormed from his private box on the rooftop of Fort Lauderdale Stadium, down through the stands and right into the Yankees dugout, where he began voicing his disgust with the team's sloppy play. Martin was outraged at Steinbrenner's intrusion into the dugout in the middle of a game.

"George, you've got to get out of here," he shouted, and was surprised when, this time, Steinbrenner didn't challenge him. Instead, he retreated down the runway into the clubhouse. After the game, however, the owner was not at all mollified by the ninth-inning rally.

"The manager had better start pulling this team together," he said pointedly to reporters. "I know the players say these spring training games don't mean anything, but they do to me. When I look out there and see all those errors on the scoreboard, I care. Billy Martin and Al Rosen tell me they're on schedule, but personally I don't think that they are."

Rosen and Martin, of course, had no control over the injuries. Gullett would make only eight starts in '78 before undergoing career-ending shoulder surgery in July; Messersmith came back in late May but made only six starts before reinjuring his shoulder. And while Hunter (who'd struggled to a 9-9 record in '77 when his shoulder soreness first cropped up) was able to start the season in the rotation, he spent two stints on the disabled list and was only 2-3 at the All-Star break.

As a result of all the injuries, Martin was forced to move Dick Tidrow into the starting rotation from the bullpen (where he'd served as an able setup man for Lyle in '77) and enlist two rookies, right-handers Jim Beattie and Ken Clay, into emergency starting duty. Holtzman was placed on the disabled list, then traded when he filed a grievance over it with the league and made disparaging remarks about Martin and Steinbrenner. Fortunately, Rosen was able to find a taker for the disagreeable left-hander's services in Bob Kennedy, his old '50s Cleveland Indians teammate who was now the general manager of the Chicago Cubs. In exchange for Holtzman, Rosen was able to extract from Kennedy a hard-throwing minor league right-hander named Ron Davis who, the following year, established himself as an equally intimidating setup reliever for Gossage.

Meanwhile, Rosen's relationship with Martin was deteriorating further. Ten days prior to the Holtzman deal, Thurman Munson's aching knees prompted the gritty captain to ask for a rare couple of days off. Uncertain whether he'd have to place Munson on the disabled list, Rosen called up catcher Mike Heath from Triple-A Tacoma—without informing Martin, who, when he found out, was furious at being undermined, as he saw it, by the new team president. In the pressroom after the game that night, Rosen was informed by pitching coach Art Fowler, who'd been drinking with Martin at a table across the room, that the manager was really upset. Moments later, Rosen confronted Martin at his table.

"I understand you're bad-mouthing me for the Heath situation, Billy," Rosen said. "Do you want to just settle this thing right here?"

Martin refused to respond to Rosen's challenge, but the two exchanged some heated words before eventually calming down when they realized that everyone in the room was listening to them. While explaining that he'd been unable to locate Martin and that the decision to recall Heath had to be made immediately, Rosen promised that in the future he would make every effort to inform him beforehand of any player moves.

In mid-June, the Yankees made their first trip to Fenway Park to face the first-place Red Sox. Steinbrenner accompanied the team on the trip and was incensed when they were clobbered, 10–4, in the opener. Two days later, rookie Jim Beattie, who hadn't pitched in nine days, lasted just two innings in another rout, 9–2, that dropped the Yankees into a third-place tie with Milwaukee, eight games behind the Red Sox. As Beattie exited the game, Steinbrenner erupted at Rosen and Tallis in the visiting-team box.

"Get Beattie out of here!" he screamed. "I want him on a plane to Tacoma now!"

Assuming he meant after the game, Rosen and Tallis said nothing. Steinbrenner couldn't believe it.

"Don't just sit there," Steinbrenner hollered at Tallis. "I told you what to do. Get your ass down to that clubhouse and get him out of here! Do you hear me?"

After the game, Steinbrenner lambasted Beattie to the reporters.

"Did you guys see the way Beattie pitched?" he said. "He looked like he was scared stiff!"

When asked about the overall state of the team and particularly Martin's handling of it, Steinbrenner snapped, "It's Al Rosen's decision. But I'll tell you one thing. I won't put up with this shit much longer."

Beattie was recalled in mid-July and given a regular spot in the rotation. After a month's exile in Tacoma, he was pitching much better, and would go on to win games in both the '78 American League Championship Series against Kansas City and the World Series against the Dodgers. Years later, the Dartmouth-educated Beattie served as general manager of the Montreal Expos and Baltimore Orioles, and the writers and other baseball execs always speculated that he never forgave Steinbrenner for that public slight. But in a 2009 interview, Beattie dispelled that notion.

"What nobody ever knew," he said, "was that in September of that year I got married, and when we came in off a road trip, there was an envelope waiting for me with $1,000 in it as a wedding gift from George. For a guy making $21,000, that was a pretty nice gift."

Between the patchwork starting rotation and the nagging injuries to many of the regulars—Munson played through his aching knees all season, while Bucky Dent and Mickey Rivers each missed a couple of weeks in the first half—Martin's Yankees continued to fall behind in the pennant race.

They were swept by the Brewers in a three-game series in Milwaukee to fall 11½ games behind the Red Sox at the midseason break. The sweep also enabled Milwaukee to jump ahead of the Yankees into second place in the American League East. All of this made for a very satisfying three days for Brewers owner Bud Selig, who sat side by side throughout with a fuming Steinbrenner in his private box in County Stadium.

During the final game on Sunday, Gullett was forced to leave after just two thirds of an inning, his shoulder throbbing, and the reporters, who could see Steinbrenner and Selig through the glass partition that separated the press box from Selig's, asked Mickey Morabito, the Yankees' public relations man, if they could talk to the Yankees owner. Morabito dutifully went into Selig's box and emerged a minute or so later.

"I've been told to tell you guys he isn't here," Morabito said, smiling.

"Doesn't he realize we're looking right at him?" one of the reporters asked.

"All I know is, he told me he's not here," Morabito said, now unable to contain his laughter.

Later, as the Yankees fell further behind in the game, the writers asked Morabito to make another attempt at getting Steinbrenner to talk to them. This time, Steinbrenner could be seen shouting and gesturing at the PR man, then suddenly rising from his chair. In his attempt to make a hasty retreat from Selig's box, Morabito forgot about the low overhang separating it from the press box and conked his head, toppling to the floor. As he lay there, dazed, Steinbrenner continued berating him.

"It was just an astounding scene," remembered Selig. "I thought Mickey might be dead. Here was the poor kid lying there on the floor and George, oblivious to the situation, standing over him and still screaming at him."

Over the All-Star break, Steinbrenner resolved to right the ship. In a meeting with Rosen, Tallis and Martin, he said that 34-year-old Roy White, the longest-tenured Yankee, and backup center fielder Paul Blair should both be released, and that Munson, because of his knees, should be taken out from behind the plate and moved to right field, with Reggie Jackson becoming the designated hitter. Mike Heath would take over as catcher. In addition, Lou Piniella would be benched, occasionally shar-ing the DH duties with Jackson, and Gary Thomasson, a reserve player obtained from the Oakland A's at the June 15 trading deadline, would take over in left field.

"We're playing horseshit and we're going to go with the younger players," Steinbrenner declared. Then, to the surprise of the men in the room, he added: "And from now on, Cedric will be more prominent in the baseball operations and Al Rosen will concentrate more on the business affairs."

This was just another example of Steinbrenner's mercurial behavior— that he would diminish a friend whose knowledge of baseball he had declared invaluable only a few months earlier.

Martin managed to talk Steinbrenner out of releasing White and Blair, but said that the other moves Steinbrenner wanted to make all seemed reasonable. Given Billy's penchant for rebelling at any interference with his managing, Steinbrenner was pleasantly surprised. Steinbrenner went down to the clubhouse for the first time that season, accompanied by Martin, in a seemingly united front as they addressed the players to announce all the changes.

With Martin standing behind him, Steinbrenner laid out his plan for turning the season around: "I'm not gonna lie down and die like a dog and neither are you guys," he said firmly. "I expect you to accept whatever role you're given without griping and do it as best you can. I'm paying you guys a lot of money and we're gonna do it the way I want to do it. And the way Billy has agreed is the proper way to do it. If you don't like it, I'll try to accommodate you elsewhere."

The next day, Steinbrenner and Martin taped a Miller Lite TV commercial that had been arranged by Martin's agent, Doug Newton. The ad, in which they argued about whether Miller Lite tasted good or was less filling, concluded with Steinbrenner saying: "Billy, you're fired!" to which Martin responded: "Oh, no, not again!"

Ironically, in another three weeks, they'd be doing it for real.

OF ALL THE changes Steinbrenner implemented, the one that would provoke the most protest was moving Reggie Jackson from right field to designated hitter and once again in and out of the cleanup spot. Jackson regarded this as a slight on his defensive skill, an insult compounded by the fact that now he wasn't even the everyday DH. Similarly upset was Lou

Piniella, the other half of the new DH platoon and the one Martin used only against left-handed pitchers. Piniella, too, still considered himself a regular. With each passing day, Jackson became more and more miserable.

Jackson had been trying to get a meeting with Steinbrenner for two weeks when, on July 17, the owner finally agreed to hear him out. Steinbrenner was sitting at the big round table in his office at the Stadium with Rosen and Tallis when Jackson and his business agent, Matt Merola, entered the room. When Reggie voiced his refrain about not being able to play for Martin, suggesting that it would probably be in everyone's best interest that he be traded, Steinbrenner abruptly cut him off.

"I agree with Billy about your outfield play," he said. "That's why you're the DH. But I do want you batting cleanup."

"But I'm not even doing that every day," Jackson countered.

Until then, Jackson had considered Steinbrenner his biggest ally, and maybe his only one. But when the owner told him that it had been his decision to make Jackson the DH, Jackson's insides began to boil. "How could this guy turn on me like this?" he thought. "How did I get to here from last October?"

From there, the discourse became more and more heated until, according to Jackson, Steinbrenner inadvertently uttered the "boy" term in the course of scolding his disgruntled slugger.

"Who the hell do you think you're talking to here?" Jackson screamed, leaping up.

As Merola and Rosen sought to calm Jackson, Steinbrenner said, "I think you should just leave, Reggie."

"I don't feel like leaving."

Steinbrenner stared hard at Jackson, then stood abruptly and walked out. A few minutes later, his head spinning at having accomplished nothing while instead making matters worse, Jackson left with Merola and took the elevator down to the clubhouse. Once he was gone, Steinbrenner returned to the office and said to Rosen: "I'm sick and tired of his whining. He needs to just shut up and start producing."

JULY 17 WOULD turn out to be the nadir of the 1978 Yankee season—and the beginning of the end for Billy Martin as Steinbrenner's manager.

The Yankees were playing the last night of a three-game series against the Kansas City Royals, having lost eight of the previous ten games. At Steinbrenner's request, Jackson was hitting cleanup. After going hitless his first four times up, Jackson came to the plate in the tenth inning with the score tied 5–5, with one out and Thurman Munson on first. When he looked over at third-base coach Dick Howser, Jackson was dumbfounded to see that he was being given the sacrifice sign. This was the first time all season he'd been asked to sacrifice, and when the first pitch from Royals reliever Al Hrabosky came in high and inside, he backed away.

Noticing that the Royals infielders had picked up the sacrifice sign and moved in, Martin called it off. Jackson, however, decided to bunt anyway. He didn't care that he was openly defying Martin's orders. It seemed that everyone was trying to humiliate him now, and in his personal frustration he bunted and missed the next pitch, then bunted the next two foul, striking out, much to the amazement of Royals catcher Darrell Porter, who said later to reporters that he couldn't understand what Reggie was trying to do. Martin was not amazed—he was livid. After the Yankees lost the game, 9–7, in the 11th inning, putting them 14 games behind the first-place Red Sox, the manager unleashed a torrent of fury in his office as Cedric Tallis sat there nodding in agreement.

"How dare he defy me?" Martin screamed. "Who the fuck does he think he is? I'm running this team. This time he's gone too far. I'm finished with him!"

Afterward, Martin fumed to the gaggle of reporters as they furiously scribbled down his words. "There's not gonna be anybody who's gonna defy the manager in any way. Nobody's bigger than this team!"

He then read a prepared statement that said Jackson was suspended without pay "for deliberately disregarding the manager's instructions during his at-bat in the 10th inning." Asked later if he planned to talk to Jackson about the incident, Martin said, "I don't talk about it. If he comes back, he does exactly what I say, period. I'm not getting paid $3 million. I don't disobey my boss's orders."

When the writers approached Jackson's locker for his reaction, he complained, "I was just trying to move the runner over and help the team. How can they say I'm a threat to swing the bat when I'm not even an everyday player? I can't win here. No matter what I do, I come off as a big greedy moneymaker against a poor little streetfighter."

The next day, an off-day before the Yankees embarked on a seven-game road trip to Minnesota, Chicago and Kansas City, Martin announced that Jackson's suspension would last five days, adding: "This is probably the best thing that's happened in a long time. It'll pull the team together."

At first, it looked like Martin was right. Ron Guidry and Ed Figueroa threw back-to-back shutouts against the Twins, then the Yankees won the first two games in a three-game series against the White Sox. But on the day of the final game in Chicago, Martin's ebullient mood turned sour with Jackson's return to the team. Seeing the mob of reporters around Jackson in the visiting clubhouse of Comiskey Park, Martin grew angrier and angrier. He began filling out the lineup card. In the cleanup spot, he penciled "Roy White, DH." That'll serve him, he said to himself. When Jackson looked at the lineup card and saw that he wasn't playing, he simply shook his head.

Even the 3–1 getaway victory (making it a perfect 5-0 road trip without any help from Jackson) failed to improve Martin's mood. The day before, Martin had been further aggravated after a conversation he had with White Sox owner Bill Veeck in Comiskey Park's Bards Room. Veeck was in a playful mood, drinking beers with some friends, when Martin came in after the 7–2 Yankee victory and joined him at his table.

"I suppose I have only myself to blame if we get swept by you, Billy," Veeck said, "considering you could have been managing for me this weekend."

"What do you mean?" Martin asked.

"Oh," said Veeck, "didn't you know? Last month George wanted to trade you to me. We were going to trade managers, you for Lemon, but I felt I needed to get a player in the deal as well."

"That sonofabitch," thought Martin. Steinbrenner had tried to get rid of him behind his back.

When the team bus arrived at O'Hare International Airport on Sunday, Martin called *New York Times* beat reporter Murray Chass aside. Earlier, Jack Lang of the *Daily News* had shown Martin a copy of his story in which

Jackson had refused to admit he was wrong in the bunting incident. Now Martin wanted Chass's opinion as to whether that constituted conduct detrimental to the Yankees.

"I'm saying, 'Shut up, Reggie Jackson, we're winning without you,'" Martin said. "If he doesn't shut his mouth, he won't play, and I don't care what George says." As Martin spoke, Chass was writing everything down in his notepad. And, lucky for the reporter, the Yankees' charter flight to Kansas City was delayed, giving him time to dictate his new story back to his office from a pay phone. It also gave Martin more time to further drown his anger in drink.

A half hour later, Chass was waiting at a newsstand with *New York Post* reporter Henry Hecht when Martin approached him.

"Did you get all that in the paper?" he said.

When Chass assured him he had, Martin smiled with satisfaction. But he was not through whining about Jackson. As the three of them walked to the gate where the Yankees' plane was boarding, Martin, his eyes reddening, continued his diatribe.

"You know he's a damn liar," he said of Jackson.

Then, just as they arrived at the gate, Martin said, "The two of them deserve each other. One's a born liar, the other's convicted."

Damning words that would live in Yankee infamy. Martin would later say he didn't know why he'd included Steinbrenner in his wrath; perhaps his conversation with Veeck the previous day was still fresh in his mind. But he did, invoking the aspect of Steinbrenner's life that the owner was most sensitive about: his Watergate felony conviction.

When the plane landed in Kansas City, Chass and Hecht rushed to the pay phones. The first call Chass made was to Steinbrenner, who was home in Tampa.

"He said *what?*" Steinbrenner shrieked. "Let me have that again?"

After Chass repeated Martin's quote, Steinbrenner hung up and immediately called Rosen, who had just retired to bed in his Manhattan apartment. Steinbrenner told him the story, then said, "Now I want you to get on a plane to Kansas City and fire Billy."

According to Rosen, Steinbrenner was so upset, he made no mention of who was supposed to replace Martin. But Rosen had just the man in mind:

Bob Lemon (whom Veeck had fired anyway after his manager trade discussion with Steinbrenner).

"Bob was just the calming influence I knew the team needed," Rosen said, "and I think George had enough confidence in me to make the decision."

First, however, Rosen had to make sure Steinbrenner wasn't going to change his mind. Armed with a statement dictated by Steinbrenner that Martin was being relieved of his duties out of consideration for his health, Rosen checked in at the Crown Center Hotel in Kansas City shortly before 3 P.M. Monday. He was preparing to go to Martin's room when Mickey Morabito intercepted him in the lobby.

"Billy's resigning," said Morabito. "He's written a statement that he's going to read to the press downstairs in the lobby."

After meeting with Martin in his room, along with Cedric Tallis (who had accompanied the team on the road trip), Rosen led the quartet downstairs, where Martin, his hands shaking and fighting back tears beneath his dark glasses, read his letter of resignation.

"I owe it to my health and my mental well-being to resign. At this time I'm also sorry for the things that were written about George Steinbrenner. He does not deserve them, nor did I say them. I've had my differences with George, but we've been able to resolve them. . . ."

Now who was lying?

Back in Tampa, Fred Matthews, the manager of Steinbrenner's Bay Harbor Hotel, was going over some bills in his office when the house phone rang. It was Steinbrenner calling from the bar.

"What are you doing?" he asked.

"Nothing much, I'm just winding up some stuff," Matthews said.

"I'm in the lounge. C'mon down."

As they sat at the bar listening to the soft jazz of the Bill Himes Trio, Matthews noticed that Steinbrenner seemed melancholy and, uncharacteristically, ordered a second drink.

"You got a problem, Boss?" he said.

"Yeah," said Steinbrenner, "I just fired Billy."

"He just sat there for about an hour, listening to the music," Matthews recalled. "He just wanted company."

Meanwhile, with Martin gone, Rosen announced that Dick Howser would manage the Yankees for the Monday-night game in Kansas City. He then called his old friend and Cleveland Indians teammate, Lemon, who was home in Long Beach, California, where he was working as a scout for the White Sox.

"The conversation took all of five minutes," Rosen remembered. "I told him I needed him and he said: 'Where do you want me to be, Meat [Lemon's term of affection for all his friends]?' He never asked why I needed him or how much he was going to be paid. He just said he'd be on the next plane to Kansas City."

Rosen was ecstatic over the turn of events. He had replaced Martin, whom he detested, with his best friend. But his satisfaction would prove to be short-lived, as he had no way of foreseeing or comprehending the perverse "love-hate" dynamic that was developing between Steinbrenner and Martin.

According to Martin's agent, Doug Newton, Billy made the decision to resign because he wasn't about to give Rosen the satisfaction of firing him. After listening to Martin's almost incoherent ramblings, the alarmed Newton called Steinbrenner.

"I'm very concerned about my client's mental state right now," Newton said. "He's resigning without any consideration for how it will affect him financially."

"We'll take care of him in that regard," Steinbrenner said. "But there must be conditions. Do you think Billy could say he resigned because he has a drinking problem?"

"No fucking way!"

"Well, we have to handle this in such a way that it can't be on my head and make me look bad," Steinbrenner said. "I'll take care of Billy and find something for him, but you've got to make sure Billy says this was in the best interest of the New York Yankees."

It was agreed then that Martin would cite health reasons for having resigned and that the Yankees would pay him for the remaining year and a half on his contract under the condition that he not have any derogatory things to say about anyone in the organization, particularly Steinbrenner. But then, the next morning, as Rosen was lining up Lemon, Steinbrenner phoned Newton back. The owner was having pangs of guilt—which would be a familiar pattern in all of his future manager firings.

"Doug," he said, "I don't feel good in my gut, I don't feel right that Billy's not the manager of the Yankees."

"Well, Billy doesn't feel good either," Newton replied. "His heart is broken."

"I want to keep him in the organization," said Steinbrenner. "Do you think he'd entertain being a scout or a front office assistant or something?"

"All he wants to be is manager."

"Well, I want him to be the manager again."

"If that's the case, George," said Newton, "if you want him to come back and be the manager, why don't you just announce that he's coming back as manager next year, and do it in front of 50,000 fans on Old-Timers' Day?"

"By God, that's a helluva idea."

On Thursday of that week, two days before Old-Timers' Day at Yankee Stadium, Newton, Martin and Steinbrenner held a secret meeting at the Carlyle Hotel to discuss a hitch in their plan. In his anxiousness to bring Martin back for the 1979 season, Steinbrenner had forgotten he'd promised Lemon a full year as manager. He couldn't go back on his word, he told Newton by phone before the meeting.

"Okay," Newton said, "so why don't we just say Billy will be coming back in 1980. We'll make it a three-year deal starting then. If nothing else, that'll give you guys some extra time to really get to know and understand each other better and it'll give Billy more time to get straightened out. As long as you pay him, it'll be great for everyone."

"Okay, that's how we'll do it," said Steinbrenner.

Newton remembered how, at the Carlyle, Steinbrenner and Martin had both been overcome with emotion as they talked about their reconciliation.

"They both cried," he said, "and then there was the feeling of excitement in the room about this wonderful, fantastic extravaganza of an announcement we were going to make."

They decided that Martin would hide out in an apartment in Hasbrouck Heights, New Jersey, owned by a friend of Billy's, until Saturday morning, when a limo would deliver him and Newton to Yankee Stadium. Just to be sure they wouldn't be recognized, Steinbrenner suggested they wear dark glasses and raincoats.

They followed through with the raincoats, even though it turned out to be a sunny, hot day. When they arrived at the Stadium, a couple of Yankee security guards spirited them through a side door and downstairs to a boiler room just down the corridor from the visitors' clubhouse, where they waited for the ceremonies to begin. As public-address announcer Bob Sheppard began introducing the old-timers, most of whom were assembled in the Yankees dugout, Martin and Newton made their way down the corridor toward the Yankees clubhouse. Suddenly, Newton froze as Rod Carew, of the visiting Minnesota Twins (whom Martin had managed a few years earlier), came out of the clubhouse and recognized them.

"What in the hell are you doing here?" Carew said.

"I'm gonna be the manager again in about two more minutes, pal," Martin said, grinning. "But don't let it out. I've been sworn to secrecy. I'm only telling you 'cause it's about to happen."

Carew smiled and hugged Martin. A couple of minutes later, Martin walked down the runway to the Yankees dugout and ducked into a bathroom to wait for his introduction. Other than Yankees security chief Pat Kelly, Mickey Morabito and his assistant Larry Wahl in the public relations department, Steinbrenner had told no one of the surprise announcement, not even Rosen, who admitted to being a little puzzled when the owner had asked him that morning if he would agree to suit up with the old-timers in the uniform of his old team, the Cleveland Indians.

"Why would you want me to do that?" Rosen had asked. "I mean, I'm the president of the Yankees. How's it going to look if I'm out there in an Indians uniform? I'll probably get booed."

"No, no," said Steinbrenner. "It'll be fine. I just want you to stand next to Lem. You were his teammate and it'll look good, the two of you standing there side by side."

As he stood there on the first-base line next to Lemon, listening to the gradually increasing ovations for his former rivals—Yankee deities like Phil Rizzuto, Roger Maris, Whitey Ford, Yogi Berra, Mickey Mantle and, finally, Joe DiMaggio—Rosen had to admit the Yankees had a tradition like no other team.

But as DiMaggio tipped his cap to the near-capacity crowd of 46,711, Sheppard wasn't finished. The "Yankee Clipper" was accustomed to being the last man introduced on Old-Timers' Day, and as such, he looked quizzically up at the press box as the venerable PA announcer intoned:

"And now, ladies and gentlemen, your attention please! The Yankees would like to announce today that Bob Lemon has agreed to a contract to continue as manager of the Yankees through the 1978 and 1979 seasons." This was greeted by a chorus of boos from the crowd, boos that grew even louder when Sheppard announced that Lemon would become general manager in 1980. Then, as signs of BILLY WILL ALWAYS BE NO. 1 and BRING BACK BILLY! were being hoisted throughout the ballpark, Sheppard implored, *"Your attention, please! Your attention, please! And the Yankees would like to introduce and announce at the same time that the manager for the 1980 season and hopefully for many seasons after that will be num-buh one, Billy Martin!"*

With that, Martin raced out of the Yankees dugout, tipping his cap to a thunderous ovation from the crowd. For seven minutes they stood and cheered deliriously. Watching this, *enduring* this, Rosen was at first stupefied and then, just as quickly, enraged. The moment the ceremony concluded, he raced off the field into the old-timers' dressing room and literally ripped the Indians uniform off his body, the shirt buttons popping onto the floor. After quickly changing his clothes, Rosen took the elevator upstairs and stormed past the reception desk into Steinbrenner's office, where the owner was sitting at his desk watching the Old-Timers' Game on TV.

"How could you do this kind of thing?" Rosen screamed. "You've embarrassed me in front of everybody! How do you expect me to run this ball club?"

"Oh, I'm sorry, Al," Steinbrenner said weakly. "I couldn't tell you because we had to keep this thing under wraps. It's just something I felt I had to do. I didn't feel right about the way everything had been done with Billy."

"George, what you've done to me, and, even more importantly, to Lem, is just unconscionable," Rosen shot back. "The poor man was booed out there! We've just got everything calmed down around here and you pull a stunt like this! I know why you didn't want to tell me: You knew how I'd react. Well, you're right, George. This is bullshit."

Rosen wasn't the only one who felt that way. DiMaggio was fuming at being upstaged by Martin, who Joe had always believed was ill suited to manage the Yankees because of his often undignified behavior. "Unbelievable," he said, shaking his head, when reporters asked for his reaction immediately after the ceremony. Instead of going upstairs to Steinbrenner's box (where he would customarily sit to watch the game), DiMaggio left the Stadium in a huff with his friend Barry Halper, one of the limited Yankees partners. And in the Yankee clubhouse, Reggie Jackson, having watched the ceremony on the TV in the players' lounge, was numb with shock. One week Martin calls him a felon, Jackson thought, and now he hires him back? It was at that moment, Jackson wrote in his memoir, that he understood for the very first time that "deep down Steinbrenner was a man with very few principles and a man to whom real loyalty could never be very meaningful."

"You'd need a psychiatrist to try and figure out George's relationship with Billy," Rosen told me in a 2007 interview. "George always felt Billy was like a wayward son."

For Rosen, Old-Timers' Day 1978 would go down as one of the worst days of his life. After the game, in which the Yankees beat the Twins, 7–3, he and Lemon went out to dinner and "then really tied one on." He had never felt so betrayed.

"That day," Rosen said, "was the first indication to me that this was not going to be a long-standing relationship."

8

. . .

From Here to Eternity

. . .

BILLY MARTIN MAY HAVE thought Steinbrenner had brought him back like Lazarus, but barely a week later, as events quickly unfolded, the former and supposedly future Yankees manager might as well have been dead again.

Whether he took seriously the outrage expressed by Al Rosen or merely lost patience with the details of something not scheduled to happen for nearly two years, Steinbrenner's focus returned to the pennant race from almost the moment Martin and his agent, Doug Newton, left Yankee Stadium that Saturday. In their haste to hash out an agreement on just how, when and for how much Billy would return as manager, the parties had neglected to write up a formal contract. For weeks afterward, Newton would call Steinbrenner to ask about the contract, only to be put off. As August passed and the Yankees, under Lemon's steady hand, continued to mount what would be a comeback for the ages, Newton couldn't even get Steinbrenner to return his calls.

Because the Old-Timers' Day bombshell had been so spontaneous, reporters hadn't had time to sort everything out that afternoon either, and in the days immediately following, Martin had gone into seclusion. After numerous requests for interviews with Martin, Mickey Morabito, the Yankees' public relations director, suggested to Al Rosen that they bring him in for a small press conference. "Just the beat writers," Morabito said. With Steinbrenner's blessing, Morabito arranged a lunch at Alex & Henry's restaurant, in the Bronx, for August 9. That morning, they brought Martin to Yankee Stadium and briefed him in Rosen's office as to what sort of questions he should expect to be asked and how to answer them. After all, they wouldn't want him to say anything that would create problems with the owner, who was in Tampa. Unfortunately, in spite of all of Morabito's good intentions, he overlooked one very critical element of any event involving Billy Martin—alcohol.

As he watched Martin down a couple of rounds of drinks before lunch and loosen up with the reporters, Morabito began to think he may have made a huge mistake. It didn't take long for one of the writers to ask Martin about the comment he had made about Jackson and Steinbrenner at O'Hare—"One's a born liar, the other's convicted." "I didn't mean what I said about George," Martin replied, "but I did mean it about the other guy. I never looked at Reggie Jackson as a superstar. I never put him over Chris Chambliss, or Thurman, or Willie Randolph, and there were times I even put Chicken Stanley over him."

As Martin spouted off, Morabito sank into his seat. He could just see the headlines in the New York tabloids the next day. BILLY: REGGIE'S NO SUPERSTAR . . . BILLY RIPS REGGIE, SAYS HE'S STILL A BORN LIAR. There was no point pleading with the writers to treat Martin's remarks as off the record. Morabito hadn't set any ground rules for the luncheon, and now he was going to have to live with the consequences. On the way back to his office, Morabito braced himself for the call from Steinbrenner, whom all the reporters had, of course, phoned for reaction to Martin's latest public blast of Jackson.

The call came just minutes after Morabito got back to his office.

"What the hell happened up there?" Steinbrenner demanded. "I told you this wasn't a good idea, that Billy's not stable enough to handle these kinds of situations. You and Rosen have really screwed up!"

Morabito attempted to explain. "I understand, sir, it's just . . . I thought . . . with all the media requests for Billy . . . we could—"

"You think you're so fucking smart," Steinbrenner shouted, cutting him off. "We'll see how this comes out in the papers! If it isn't too negative, fine. But if it's more of this Billy-Reggie shit, you're gone! I can't have this!"

Morabito didn't have to wonder how it would play out in the papers the next day. He knew he was gone. To fill time while he waited in his office that night for the early editions of the *Times, Daily News* and *Post* to hit the stands, he got some boxes from a utility room and began packing up his personal belongings. But then he received a phone call from a friend downtown informing him of a most unexpected development: There *were* no New York newspapers—they had all gone on strike! The Newark *Star-Ledger, Newsday* and the Westchester-Rockland papers would report Martin's assailing of Jackson, but Steinbrenner didn't pay attention to them.

The newspaper strike, which would continue for 88 days into November, had saved Morabito—and the Yankees, Bob Lemon would later say.

The easygoing Lemon had had a positive, calming effect on the Yankees, just as Rosen had predicted to Steinbrenner. After Martin's firing, the Yankees finished July 11-4, then went 19-8 in August. At the same time, the first-place Red Sox began to slip, losing nine of 10 from July 20 to 28, cutting their lead to only 4½ games over Milwaukee. The Yanks were coming, and it didn't take Paul Revere sounding it to every Middlesex village and farm for New England and Red Sox Nation to be alerted to the fact that the summer of '78 suddenly had a pennant race. Martin was gone, Jackson was content for the first time and the injured had healed, most notably Catfish Hunter, whose chronically sore shoulder was cured (miraculously, as it was reported) by an arm manipulation performed by Dr. Maurice Cowen, the Yankees' team physician.

Still, as of August 25 the Yankees were 7½ games behind the Red Sox. Lou Piniella told his teammates, after they lost three out of the last four games of a West Coast road trip in mid-August, that they had better close some ground before going to Boston for a showdown four-game series the first week of September. Lemon reiterated when they got home August 25 that it was important to keep the pressure on the Red Sox in the next two weeks, and his team responded. By winning 10 of their next 14, the Yankees were able to cut the deficit to four games by the time they arrived in Boston on September 7. Now it was the Red Sox who were beset with nagging injuries and feeling the toll of the long season. In what became known as "the Boston Massacre," Lemon's rejuvenated troops, unencumbered by the clubhouse hostilities to which they had become accustomed under Martin, swept the four-game series by a combined score of 42–9.

With the Yankees and Red Sox now tied for first and just three weeks remaining in the season, American League president Lee MacPhail began making provisions for a playoff. On September 15, he summoned Al Rosen to his office at 280 Park Avenue to conduct a coin flip by which the home field for a one-game playoff would be determined. When Rosen entered MacPhail's office, Red Sox general manager Haywood Sullivan was already on the speakerphone from Boston.

"You're right there, Al," said Sullivan, "so why don't you just go ahead and make the call."

With that, MacPhail flipped a 50-cent piece into the air and Rosen called out "Heads."

"Sorry, Al," MacPhail said. "It's tails. If we need to have the playoff, it'll be played at Fenway Park."

All the way back to his office, Rosen dreaded having to make the call to Steinbrenner about this unhappy turn of events. Though he fully anticipated a scathing rebuke, he was not prepared for the owner's incredulous reaction.

"I'm sorry to tell you, George, but we lost the coin flip," Rosen said.

"You *lost?*" Steinbrenner said. "How could you lose? What did you call?"

"I called heads. Why?"

"*Heads?*" Steinbrenner shrieked. "You fucking imbecile! How in the hell could you call *heads* when any dummy knows tails comes up 70 percent of the time? I can't believe it! I've got the dumbest fucking people in baseball working for me!"

Click.

Rosen, who by now was accustomed to having to hold the phone away from his ear as Steinbrenner ranted, placed it back in the cradle and shook his head in disbelief. "Is he crazy?" he thought. "Did he just say what I thought he said? Is there anyone so irrational?"

Perhaps there was: Mickey Rivers. On September 22, the Yankees were locked in a desperate head-to-head race with the Red Sox and were playing the Indians in Cleveland. Before the game, a Cuyahoga County deputy sheriff came into the visiting clubhouse at Municipal Stadium with a subpoena for Rivers. It seemed the outfielder was once again late with his alimony payments to his ex-wife, Mary (she of the bumper-cars infamy in the Yankee Stadium parking lot a couple of years earlier). After the sheriff departed, a few of the players sauntered over to Rivers's locker to ask what the problem was.

"No big deal," Rivers said. "Mary's just upset 'cause she don't like some of the 'vestments I've been making. She lives here. We had lunch today at the racetrack." In fact, Rivers wasn't staying at the team's hotel—he was staying with his ex-wife.

That night, however, Rivers made a call to his agent and attorney, Nick Buoniconti, to ask him for advice. When Rivers informed him he was staying with Mary in Cleveland, Buoniconti said, "Mickey, you don't need a lawyer. You need a psychiatrist!"

When Rosen reported the incident to Steinbrenner, the owner shrugged and told him that they needed Rivers to get through the season even if meant continuing to give him advances on his salary.

"What are we doing here?" Rosen asked. "We might as well just pay him by the game!"

After Steinbrenner's apoplexy over the coin flip, Rosen felt sure that the season was fated to come down to a playoff—and it did, when the Red Sox rallied to win their last eight games of the season and the Yankees and Catfish Hunter were beaten by the Cleveland Indians on the final day, leaving both teams with a 99-63 record. Though Hunter had won 12 of his previous 14 starts since the arm manipulation, he was driven from the game after just 1⅔ innings, having given up five runs and two homers. The Indians went on to a 9–2 win behind five-hit pitching by an undistinguished left-hander named Rick Waits. During the game, Bill "Killer" Kane, the team's traveling secretary, was in the press box checking all the hotel reservations for the trip to Boston when he was told Steinbrenner wanted to see him in his office.

Kane remembered the eerie scene as he walked into the big man's office. The shades had been drawn on the windows that looked out onto the field and Steinbrenner was sitting alone at his desk, in the dark.

"He couldn't bear watching what was going on down on the field," Kane said. "He was beside himself."

And in need of someone on whom to take out his anger and frustration.

"I just want to make sure you've got everything arranged for Boston," Steinbrenner said.

"Yeah, everything's set, boss," Kane said.

"Where's the plane?" Steinbrenner asked.

"Newark."

"*Newark*?" exclaimed Steinbrenner. "Oh no, no, no, we're not taking off from Newark. We've got to go out of LaGuardia! Newark's too far away."

"We've been flying out of Newark all season, George," Kane said.

"I don't care," said Steinbrenner. "I want the plane moved to La-Guardia."

"We can't move the plane!" Kane protested.

"I don't want to hear anything more. Get it moved. Do you hear me?"

"I hear you, George, but it can't be moved."

"Well, if you can't get it moved," said Steinbrenner, "I'll get someone else who can. Now just get out of here. You're finished."

"Fine," shot back Kane, "you do that. Go find somebody else. I don't need to take your shit anymore," and he stormed out of the office.

After Kane left, Steinbrenner phoned down to the ticket office for Jerry Murphy, who had helped out as traveling secretary for a couple of road trips the year before. The 25-year-old Murphy had originally been hired by the Yankees as a batboy in 1971 and worked off and on in various capacities in the front office while he was going to college at Fordham, in the Bronx. Steinbrenner took a liking to him and eventually made him his executive assistant. When Murphy reported to Steinbrenner's office on this occasion, he had no idea he was about to get a promotion.

"You're taking the team to Boston," Steinbrenner said.

"I'm what?" Murphy said. "I don't understand. Killer's the traveling secretary."

"Fuck Killer," Steinbrenner said.

"I don't want to fuck Killer!"

"Oh," said Steinbrenner, "so you want to fuck *me*?"

"I don't want to fuck *anybody*! I can't just take over this job on a moment's notice."

Exasperated, Steinbrenner told Murphy to go down to Kane's office to make sure all the arrangements for the trip to Boston were in order.

When news of the Yankees' loss reached Fenway Park, the scoreboard operator flashed a message: THANK YOU, RICK WAITS. A couple of hours later, the Yankees were boarding their charter flight—in Newark—for the short hop to Boston. Steinbrenner, now in an even fouler mood, was sitting by himself in the front of the plane when Piniella sidled up the aisle and stood over him.

"Oh, what's your problem, George?" he said. "Cheer up. We're going to go up there and kick their ass tomorrow, and you're gonna get another payday out of it!"

MONDAY, OCTOBER 2, dawned bright and seasonally cool in Boston, a crisp early-autumn day, perfect for a championship baseball game. For a baseball man like Al Rosen, it didn't get any better than this: Fenway Park, New York and Boston playing one game for the season, and his man, Bob Lemon, in charge of the Yankees. Thirty years earlier, as a 24-year-old rookie with the Indians, Rosen had been in Fenway under the very same circumstances as part of a Cleveland win over the Red Sox in a one-game playoff for the American League pennant. But today Rosen had a dilemma. It was Rosh Hashanah, and as a practicing Jew he was torn about attending the game instead of being at temple. "So much of my heart and soul had gone into that season, especially with everything I'd been through with George, I just decided I had to be there," Rosen told me in 2007. "I got only one letter from somebody who castigated me for sitting there in the Yankee box in front of all those people. I wrote him back and said: 'How did you know I was at the game? You should've been in temple!'"

The game turned out to be a classic. Ron Guidry, who had fashioned one of the single greatest pitching seasons of all time in 1978—his record was 24-3 at that point—started for the Yankees against former Yankee Mike Torrez. Steinbrenner had dismissed Guidry as "nothing more than a Triple-A pitcher" 18 months earlier, when Gabe Paul had refused to include him in the deal with the White Sox for shortstop Bucky Dent, so it was somewhat ironic that his new ace would hold the Red Sox to two runs over 6⅔ innings, while the slap-hitting Dent knocked a three-run homer over the Green Monster to give the Yankees a 3–2 lead, which they never relinquished, eventually winning the game 5–4. When the team got back to

New York shortly before 8 P.M., an ecstatic Steinbrenner took "Killer" Kane aside in the Yankee Stadium parking lot.

"C'mon, Killer," Steinbrenner said, putting his arm around the traveling secretary, "let me take you to dinner."

BECAUSE THEY HAD used Guidry in the playoff, the Yankees' pitching rotation was off-kilter as they went into the postseason. It didn't matter. Rookie Jim Beattie held the Kansas City Royals to one run over 5⅓ innings in the Yankees' 7–1 win in the opener of the American League Championship Series, and after losing game two when Ed Figueroa was pummeled for five runs in the first two innings, the Yankees overcame a three-homer onslaught by George Brett off Catfish Hunter to win game three, 6–5. In that game, Thurman Munson, who went 3 for 4, responded with a monstrous two-run homer in the eighth inning into the left center field bullpen to put the Yankees up for good. The home run, which proved to be the turning point of the series, was Munson's first in 54 games and only his third all season at Yankee Stadium. It traveled an estimated 475 feet and prompted Royals manager Whitey Herzog to exclaim: "That darn Thurman sure hit it, didn't he?"

For most of the 1978 season, Munson had been miserable. His knees ached, the pain in his shoulder hampered his throwing, and while Steinbrenner had redone his contract the previous year, making it a five-year deal worth $1.7 million through 1981, he was still annoyed at being put off so long by the owner and was talking more and more about wanting to play closer to his home in Canton, Ohio. But when the Yankees won game four, earning them a World Series rematch against the Dodgers, Munson seemed rejuvenated, hitting .320 with another seven RBI. The Dodgers were winning the series 2–1 when a controversial play in game four changed the series. With the Yankees trailing 3–1 in the sixth inning, Reggie Jackson, running from first to second, broke up a double play by swiveling his hip and blocking with his right leg L.A. shortstop Bill Russell's relay throw to first. Dodgers manager Tommy Lasorda argued in vain that Jackson had deliberately interfered with the ball and the Yankees went on to win the game, 4–3. They clobbered the Dodgers 12–2 the next night, then wrapped up their second-straight world championship with a 7–2 win in Los Angeles two nights later.

During the celebration in the visitors' clubhouse afterward, Steinbrenner sought out Munson, whom in 1976 he'd made the first Yankee captain since Lou Gehrig, and asked him to accept the World Series trophy from Commissioner Bowie Kuhn.

"I want a duplicate of this trophy for my den," Munson said. "I don't care what it costs, George, just tell the jeweler to make another one just like it, okay? Now, don't give me any shit about this or I'll demand to renegotiate!"

Here they were, two stubborn, hard-nosed adversaries, now standing side by side on the victory podium, laughing and hugging, Steinbrenner in a suit and Munson in his skivvies and dirty socks, as someone drenched them from behind with champagne. It was a moment, Steinbrenner said afterward to reporters, he would cherish forever. "He asked me if I'd inscribe CAPTAIN OF THE YANKEES on the trophy," Steinbrenner said. "Anything he wants. And I know he's talked about wanting to go home, but he isn't going anywhere. Even if he wanted to, I wouldn't let him."

IN THE WEEKS following the World Series, George Steinbrenner's first act of business was getting rid of the Yankees' disgruntled reliever, Sparky Lyle, who all season had made his feelings known about having to share the closer's role with Goose Gossage.

Trading Lyle, it turned out, was one of the rare issues upon which Rosen and Steinbrenner found themselves in agreement. "Sparky wanted out of there as badly as George wanted him out of there," Rosen said. "Even though the 'two closers' situation worked out okay, everyone pretty much agreed that Sparky and Goose couldn't continue to coexist." During the ALCS, Rosen's top scout, Jerry Walker, had raved to him about a young left-handed pitcher he'd seen with the Texas Rangers' Double-A farm team in Tulsa earlier that summer. "It must have been 110 degrees the day I saw him," Walker said, "and this kid was throwing harder in the ninth inning than he had in the first! It was unbelievable!"

His name was Dave Righetti. Rosen wrote it down, while making a mental note to tell Steinbrenner that when they began shopping Lyle their first call should be to his friend Brad Corbett, owner of the Rangers. "I guarantee you Corbett's probably never heard of this kid Righetti," Rosen told Steinbrenner, "and this will be an opportunity for us to get a real good pitching prospect."

When Steinbrenner, with Rosen sitting across from him in the Yankee Stadium office, called Corbett on November 10, he found the Texas owner only too eager to acquire the services of a former Cy Young Award–winning closer and Yankee icon. As they talked, the proposed trade got larger and larger, until nine players would be changing teams, the principals being Lyle and catcher Mike Heath going to the Rangers, and Gold Glove–winning center fielder Juan Beniquez coming to the Yankees. After an hour of talking, everything was just about agreed upon when Steinbrenner said, "We have to get one more player to make it an even five-for-five, Brad."

"That's fine," Corbett said. "Do you have any player in mind?"

"Uh, yeah," said Steinbrenner. "You've got a pitcher, a left-hander, I think, at Tulsa—what's that guy's name, Al? Spaghetti? Oh, right, Righetti. We'd like to have him, and we'll throw in some cash to help offset Lyle's salary."

"You got a deal, George," said Corbett.

When the trade was announced the next day, Graig Nettles famously said: "In one year, Sparky went from Cy Young to sayonara."

Righetti went on to have a distinguished career with the Yankees, first as a starting pitcher who hurled a no-hitter against the Red Sox on July 4, 1983, and then as a closer who led the American League with 46 saves in 1986 and was selected to two All-Star teams. Rosen would look back fondly on that day when he and Steinbrenner teamed up on one of the best trades in Yankees history.

"That day was like we were back in Cleveland together," Rosen said. "It was fun. Unfortunately, there was otherwise very little fun working for George. It [1978] had been a very trying season in which we prevailed against all the odds and adversity, but George never allowed himself the sheer enjoyment of it. Afterward, it was like he wasn't interested. George had his demons, which I can only assume came from his father, who was also never happy or satisfied."

Indeed, the good feelings were gone barely a month later, when Steinbrenner and Rosen tried to get Rod Carew, the seven-time batting champion the Minnesota Twins were eager to deal because he would become a free agent after the 1979 season.

For Steinbrenner, the sudden availability of the Panamanian-born Carew, who had grown up just across the Harlem River from Yankee Stadium in Washington Heights, was irresistible. He ordered Rosen to aggressively pursue a trade for the 33-year-old first baseman at the December winter meetings in Orlando, Florida. But on the third day of the meetings the San Francisco Giants announced that they had made a deal with the Twins for Carew, pending the superstar first baseman's approval. Rosen remembered the day—December 7, the 37th anniversary of the Japanese bombing of Pearl Harbor—as one of the worst in his time with the Yankees. Moss Klein, the Yankees beat reporter for the Newark *Star-Ledger,* was talking with Rosen in his suite about another matter when the telephone rang. Hearing the screaming voice on the other end of the phone and realizing it was Steinbrenner, Klein got up to leave, but Rosen motioned to him to stay. For a few minutes Klein stood uncomfortably as the red-faced Rosen, unable to get a word in, let Steinbrenner rage. Finally, Rosen said, "There's no point in talking until you've calmed down, George," and hung up the phone. Smiling at Klein, he said, "No big deal. This is my life now as president of the Yankees."

But then Carew rejected the trade to San Francisco, citing a desire to remain in the American League, and Twins owner Calvin Griffith, in turn, rejected an offer from the California Angels, giving Rosen a chance to make his move. He offered to give the Twins first baseman Chris Chambliss, Beniquez, the center fielder they had just acquired from the Rangers, plus two top prospects, infielder Rex Hudler and left-handed pitcher Chris Welsh, and Griffith immediately accepted. But Carew, despite his New York roots, didn't want to go to the Yankees either, asking instead that Griffith go back to the Angels and try to work out a deal with them.

Infuriated by this rejection, Steinbrenner called his public relations director, Larry Wahl, and dictated a statement to be read to the reporters covering the meetings: "We have great respect for Carew as a player, but if a man doesn't want to play for the New York Yankees, in the greatest baseball city in the world, and has stated that New York would not be his first choice, and that he'd be more comfortable playing someplace else, then I don't think it would be fair to our fans in New York or to the other ballplayers on our team, who have won two world championships in a row, to pursue the Carew matter any further."

ON THE SAME day that Steinbrenner and Rosen were consummating the Sparky Lyle trade back in November, Billy Martin had been involved in a barroom fight in Reno, Nevada, with a local newspaper reporter named Ray Hagar. Martin had gone to Reno as a favor to his friend Howard Wong, a Minneapolis restaurateur, to do some promotions for the Reno Bighorns of the minor league Western Basketball Association. The coach of the Bighorns, Bill Musselman, had previously coached at the University of Minnesota, where Wang had befriended him. During the course of signing autographs and doing interviews, Martin apparently took offense to some of the questions Hagar was asking about his relationship with Reggie and Steinbrenner, and a quarrel ensued in which Billy threw a punch at the sportswriter. News of Martin's latest dustup traveled fast; the next day, Martin's agent Doug Newton, who hadn't heard from Steinbrenner or anyone else from the Yankees in months as he'd tried to finalize Billy's deal, got a call from Al Rosen.

It had become apparent to Newton that Steinbrenner intended to renege on their agreement. Between the team's dramatic comeback under Lemon and all the subsequent unreturned phone calls, Newton concluded that Steinbrenner no longer wanted any part of Martin. Rosen's phone call only confirmed that.

"We've just heard about this latest incident regarding Billy," Rosen said, "and I have to tell you, Doug, we're a little bit concerned. Mr. Steinbrenner's position is that unless Billy is completely exonerated, he's not going to be coming back as manager."

"You want to run that by me again?" Newton said.

"You heard me. And even if some sort of settlement with the reporter is worked out, that won't be satisfactory to us. He's got to be completely exonerated."

Rosen was not-so-secretly delighted by this latest public scrap involving Martin, seeing it as a further validation of his decision back in August to replace Martin with his man, Lemon. However, Rosen did not realize the impact another incident—the death of Lemon's youngest son, Jerry, in an automobile accident—would have on his friend. Lemon began to drink heavily over the winter break and withdrew from the day-to-day operations of the team. It was during spring training that Rosen fully understood the degree of Lemon's suffering.

Still, before the season began, Rosen had every reason to feel optimistic about the Yankees repeating as champions in 1979. He had bolstered the pitching rotation with the free agent signings of proven veterans Luis Tiant and Tommy John, who had won a combined 30 games in 1978. Even though Lemon spent many a late night that spring drinking with friends in his favorite Fort Lauderdale haunts and seemed disinterested in the team, the spring was mostly devoid of the usual Yankees turmoil. But just 12 games into the season, after a 6–3 loss to the Baltimore Orioles at Yankee Stadium, Goose Gossage scuffled with the lumbering 6-4, 225-pound catcher–first baseman Cliff Johnson in the clubhouse shower. A seemingly harmless exchange of verbal barbs had escalated into a full-blown fight and, at one point, bracing his fall on the slippery floor, Gossage landed on his pitching hand with Johnson on top of him, spraining a ligament in the thumb of Steinbrenner's $2.75 million reliever and necessitating surgery that would sideline him for three months. Steinbrenner initially threatened to dock Gossage's salary for every day he spent on the disabled list but relented when the reliever asked what *he* would have done if someone had punched him in the face.

Johnson, on the other hand, was not spared Steinbrenner's wrath. On June 15, he was traded to the last-place Cleveland Indians, prompting Reggie Jackson to observe cryptically to the reporters, "Around here, you mess with the 'G-men' [Gossage and Guidry] and soon enough the big man with the boats is gonna get you."

By now, Al Rosen had grown weary of trading ballplayers on Steinbrenner's angry impulses. On May 22, Rosen was at home watching the Yankees game in Detroit on TV. The Yankees were leading 12–0 when, in the eighth inning, the Tigers erupted for seven runs. The primary victim of the rally was Dick Tidrow, who came on in relief of Tiant and gave up a two-run single, a sacrifice fly and a two-run double, and threw two wild pitches. It didn't matter that the Yankees held on to win the game 12–8, or that Tidrow's versatility as the setup reliever and doing spot starting assignments had made him an invaluable cog on the '76-'77-'78 teams. Steinbrenner wanted him gone.

When the call inevitably came minutes after the game had ended, Steinbrenner screamed at Rosen, "Get rid of Tidrow *now*! I don't care how you do it, or who you trade him to, but I want him off this team by tomorrow."

Given the urgency of this latest ultimatum, Rosen resignedly dialed up his old friend Bob Kennedy, the general manager of the Chicago Cubs, who had still not forgiven him for getting him to agree to take the chronic malcontent Ken Holtzman the previous year.

"What kind of cancer are you looking to unload on me this time, Al?" Kennedy said.

"I promise you, Bob, Tidrow's a good guy and I think he can still pitch," Rosen begged, "but Steinbrenner has ordered me to get rid of him. I have no choice. I've gotta move him. I'll take anyone you want to give me." (Kennedy agreed to take Tidrow in exchange for Ray Burris, a 29-year-old right-hander, who went 1-3 with a 6.18 ERA for the Yankees before Rosen sold him to the Mets at the end of the season.)

With Gossage out, the Yankees fell further and further behind in the American League East pennant race as the season moved into June. Like Gabe Paul before him, Rosen had become weary of Steinbrenner's constant harangues. Even worse, Steinbrenner was beginning to blame Lemon for the team's shortcomings. "He's just not into it, Al," Steinbrenner said after a five-game Yankee losing streak in June. "They've stopped playing for him."

Rosen tried to explain that it was nearly impossible to win consistently without a closer, but he knew it was in vain—especially since, at the end of May, Billy Martin's new lawyer, Eddie Sapir, had succeeded in getting all the charges against the ex–Yankee manager dropped in exchange for Billy issuing a public apology. A month earlier, Sapir had met with Steinbrenner in Tampa and assured him the Hagar case would be resolved to his satisfaction.

"All I'm gonna say is, he better win," said Steinbrenner.

"We will," said Sapir, "Billy will be completely exonerated, and when he is, Billy *is* your manager."

While the original agreement Steinbrenner and Newton hastily worked out for the '78 Old-Timers' Day announcement called for Martin to return as manager in 1980, the Yankees' lackluster performance in the first half of 1979 prompted Steinbrenner to make the move even earlier. At the June 15 trading deadline, he called Rosen to tell him he'd decided to make the change. By this time, given the effect that losing his son had obviously had on Lemon, Rosen reluctantly conceded that his friend probably needed to be relieved—as much from managing as from Steinbrenner. On June 18, the Yankees announced that Martin was returning as Yankees manager and that Lemon would be reassigned to scouting from his home in Long Beach, California. "I think the season can still be turned around," Steinbrenner told the beat reporters, "and Billy is the guy to do it. Last year I needed someone 180 degrees from what Billy was. This year I need someone 180 degrees different than what Lemon was."

If there was any question that Martin was once again Steinbrenner's man, it was confirmed a few days later when the owner was asked about the differences that presumably still existed between Billy and Reggie Jackson.

"No man is indispensable," Steinbrenner said. "You can't ask a manager to crawl on his knees. Certainly Billy has said all the right things [about Jackson] and done all the right things." The next day, the Yankees' press office issued a statement that said the club "felt strongly Martin had done everything expected of him in his effort to reconcile differences with Jackson and that it is clearly up to Jackson now."

Then, on June 28, another sign that Martin was in charge: Steinbrenner ordered Rosen to once again call Bob Kennedy and the Cubs about getting back Bobby Murcer. Martin had been told the Cubs were looking to dump Murcer, whom they'd obtained from the Giants a couple of years earlier. Though Murcer had failed to realize the promise he'd shown early on with the Yankees, and the Yankees would have to take on his $320,000 salary, Martin viewed him as a left-handed power-hitting alternative to Jackson.

"Much as I was opposed to getting Murcer on principle—I didn't like Billy's motives and I didn't see how he was going to help us—George didn't care about the money and saw it as a popular move with the fans," Rosen told me in 2007. "Plus, Bob really wanted to get rid of Murcer's contract and I'm sure he viewed it as payback to me for that Holtzman–Ron Davis deal."

Martin's reemergence into power with Steinbrenner troubled Rosen greatly. He knew that over the years there had been too much animosity between them to work hand in hand now, and Martin felt the same way. Things came to a head between Martin and Rosen on July 12. Martin was with the team in Seattle when, early that day, he was informed that the Yankees' game the next night with the California Angels in Anaheim had been switched from 8:30 P.M. to 5:30 because ABC had decided to make it their Friday-night game of the week. Ordinarily, it might not have seemed like any big deal, except that Nolan Ryan was scheduled to pitch for the Angels, and the twilight would make the hard-throwing right-hander's 100-mile-per-hour fastballs even harder to hit.

Martin blamed Rosen for allowing the time change. "How am I supposed to get this team back in the race when the team president was making decisions like this?" he said in a phone call to Steinbrenner in Tampa.

Steinbrenner hung up the phone and immediately called Rosen, who explained that he'd sent a memo to him about the time change along with a copy of the TV schedule two months earlier. Steinbrenner, however, wasn't placated. He quickly arranged a conference call between himself, Rosen, Baseball Commissioner Bowie Kuhn and American League president Lee MacPhail in which he insisted the game start at 8:30 and threatened to have the Yankees refuse to take the field at 5:30.

Kuhn and MacPhail reiterated that the time change had been made months ago and that ABC had a contractual right to pick up the game—which was what Rosen had been telling him all along. Steinbrenner relented somewhat.

"I don't know, I guess we have no choice but to play at 5:30, but I've got to find out about this," he grumbled. "My people lied to me."

Martin's fears turned out to be justified: Ryan took a no-hitter into the ninth inning before settling for a one-hit, 6–1 victory.

Rosen, meanwhile, took exception to being called a liar and asked Steinbrenner to stay on the line when Kuhn and MacPhail hung up.

When they were alone on the line, Steinbrenner said, "What do you want, Al?"

"I quit, George."

"What are you talking about?"

"You heard me, George. Nobody ever calls me a liar and I don't do something about it. I'm finished."

"What are you talking about, Al? Are you crazy? I didn't say that."

"You did say it, George, and it hurts deeply, and I'm just not going to tolerate it."

"Oh, c'mon, Al," Steinbrenner said. "Look, I'm coming into New York next week after the All-Star Game. Wait till I get there and we'll talk about it Wednesday."

But Rosen was tired of Steinbrenner; tired of the tirades, tired of being forced to make trades he didn't want to make, tired of dealing with Martin and tired of the New York Yankees, a team he'd hated his whole life. That Sunday, before the All-Star Game in Seattle, *Daily News* columnist Dick Young was waiting to check in at the hotel where the baseball officials and media were all staying when he overheard the conversation between Yankees general manager Cedric Tallis and the desk clerk.

"Is Mr. Rosen checking in with you?" the clerk asked.

"No," said Tallis. "You can cancel his reservation. He won't be coming."

"What's the story with Rosen?" Young asked Tallis.

"Oh, he's just taking a couple of days off," Tallis said.

Young instinctively sensed something was fishy. Rosen, after all, was a baseball man, and baseball men didn't miss the camaraderie of the All-Star Game, especially when his close friend Bob Lemon would be managing the American League by virtue of having won the pennant the year before. Young went up to his room and immediately put in a call to Rosen, whereupon he got the real story. In the next day's paper, Young wrote: *"Turns out Al Rosen is taking more than a few days off from his job as president of the Yankees. He's taking forever off. Unless, that is, George Steinbrenner can talk him out of quitting."*

Steinbrenner certainly tried.

He was sitting behind his desk when Rosen walked into his office that Wednesday morning and greeted his old friend warmly.

"Okay, Al," he said, "so what's the matter?"

"I told you, George. I quit."

Steinbrenner reached into the right-hand drawer of his desk and pulled out a standard major league contract.

"You've gotta be out of your mind," he said. "Here, take this and fill in whatever numbers and for how many years you want."

"No."

"Wait a minute," Steinbrenner said. "You mean to say you're turning down a million dollars a year for life?"

"George," Rosen said, "we're two very competitive guys, but one of us is the boss, who's always right. I'd rather be your friend than to work for you, because our friendship won't survive."

"I don't believe I'm hearing this," Steinbrenner said. "I'm calling your wife so that she can hear it."

A minute later, Steinbrenner had Rita Rosen on speakerphone.

"Hello Rita," he said. "I want you to know that your husband is crazy! I've offered him a lifetime contract for millions of dollars and he's turned me down!"

Before Rita could respond, Rosen cut in. "I may have made a lot of money, but I'd never live to enjoy it."

Hearing her husband's reasoning, Rita Rosen voiced her agreement. Steinbrenner shook his head incredulously. How could one of his best friends not want to work for him—for as much money and as long as he wanted? It was simply unfathomable.

If Rosen had any second thoughts about his decision, they were dispelled a couple of weeks later when some friends arranged a farewell lunch for him at Le Cirque. When he arrived at the restaurant, Rosen was told by the receptionist that he had a phone call. It was Doris Walden, the switchboard operator at Yankee Stadium, informing him that Steinbrenner had just called from Tampa ordering him back to his office.

"Tell him," Rosen said, "I don't work for him anymore."

ON THE AFTERNOON of August 2, 1979—an off-day for the Yankees—Steinbrenner was meeting with a couple of his financial advisors in his Yankee Stadium office when he was interrupted by his executive assistant, Jerry Murphy, informing him he had a phone call.

"God dammit, I told you I don't want to be disturbed," Steinbrenner said.

"I know, sir, but this call seems urgent. It's somebody from the sheriff's office in Canton, Ohio."

A sudden chill went through Steinbrenner.

"I'll take it."

Steinbrenner picked up the phone and as he listened to the voice on the other end, the angry expression on his face began to fade.

"Oh, no," he said. "Oh, my God. No."

After a few moments, Steinbrenner hung up the phone and turned to the two accountants.

"I'm sorry," he said, his eyes tearing up, "we have to end this meeting. There's been a terrible tragedy. We've lost Thurman . . . gone . . . plane crash. I have to get more details."

Shortly thereafter, Steinbrenner received another call from his friend Jack Doyle, the manager of the Canton airport, who provided him with details about the plane crash that had killed Thurman Munson, the 32-year-old Yankee catcher and captain. Munson, along with two instructors, had been practicing landings and takeoffs in the $1.4 million blue pinstriped Cessna Citation he'd bought just three weeks earlier. He'd wanted the plane so he could commute between New York and Ohio to spend more time with his family. As Doyle explained, the jet was much more powerful, much more plane than the props Munson had flown for the previous 18 months, and when he realized he was coming in too slow for his landing, he hit the throttle, but it was too late. The plane ripped through a row of tree-tops, tearing off a wing, before hitting the ground 870 feet from the runway, where it burst into flames. The two instructors were able to make their way out of the wreckage, but they couldn't free Munson, who was trapped in his seat, helplessly engulfed in the fire.

Steinbrenner spent a few minutes lost in thought about Munson; how the gritty captain had played through the pain in his knees and led the Yankees to the championship, hoisting the World Series trophy on the podium just nine months earlier. Then Steinbrenner's thoughts turned to Diane, Munson's widow, and the three kids. And the Yankee players. Someone would have to tell them. Arrangements. So many arrangements. The press. The game tomorrow. The funeral.

"Get everybody in here, Jerry," Steinbrenner shouted to Murphy.

The grieving would have to wait—now there were details to be worked out. Surrounded by the Yankees' front office men, Steinbrenner began doling out assignments.

Murphy, who'd become close friends with Munson, and Larry Wahl, from the public relations department, were to fly to Canton to help Diane in any way she needed. "Killer, start working on the travel arrangements. We're gonna need a charter to get the team back and forth from Canton for the funeral." Morabito, Steinbrenner said, was to start contacting the media. "Wait a minute, where's Billy?" Someone said the manager was fishing somewhere off the Jersey Shore. "Find him," Streinbrenner instructed Morabito. "You're in charge of that. Get back to me as soon as you do. I need him back here right away."

Next Steinbrenner turned to Tallis. "You and I need to start calling the players, Cedric. I'll take care of the veteran guys: Catfish, Lou, Guidry, Goose, Randolph. You start with the others." After everyone had departed on their various missions, Steinbrenner began phoning the players. Each call Steinbrenner made was more heart-wrenching than the next. "I've got some terrible news. We've lost Thurman in a plane crash." By the time he was done, dusk had begun to settle over Yankee Stadium. But there was now tomorrow to think about. The Yankees were to begin a seven-game home stand the next day with a game against the Baltimore Orioles. Thurman must be properly honored.

"This is what I want," Steinbrenner told Morabito and security chief Pat Kelly, whom he had summoned back to his office. "Tell [clubhouse man] Pete Sheehy we need the black armbands on all the uniforms, and tell him I want Thurman's locker left intact. No one is ever to use it again. It's his forever. Replace the nameplate over it with just the number 15. That's his forever, too. And when the players stand at their positions for the national anthem, I want no one in the catcher's box."

Alone again, Steinbrenner now pulled from his desk a blank piece of paper and, reaching back to his days as an English lit major at Williams, began to pen the epitaph for Munson that would appear on the scoreboard the next night and, later, on the catcher's plaque in Yankee Stadium's Monument Park: "*Our captain and leader has not left us—today, tomorrow, this year, next, our endeavors will reflect our love and admiration for him."*

"When I first walked back in there after the phone call from Canton, George's face was dissolving," remembered Murphy. "He'd had his moments with Thurman and he was very much affected. And then, as if he suddenly snapped back into reality, he went into his full George Patton mode, giving us all our marching orders. I think it was therapeutic for him. No one had much time to think about this horrible event, and he was strong for all of us."

For sure, the Yankees employees had toiled fearfully and been intimidated by their boss ever since Steinbrenner had bought the team in 1973. Even the triumphs were muted by the owner's inherent unhappiness. But in those numbing, awful days during the first week of August 1979, he was their forceful and trusted shepherd through an unimaginable tragedy. In terms of being a leader, boss and commander in chief, even 30 years later, those who were there in that time of crisis would still agree that it had been George Steinbrenner's finest hour.

9

. . .

Howser and Horses

. . .

A WEEK AFTER MUNSON'S FUNERAL, as the team was trying to get on with the season, Steinbrenner was confronted by an issue so bizarre as not to be believed. It was reported in the *Chicago Sun-Times* by the renowned columnist Mike Royko that on the afternoon of August 1, as the Yankee team bus filled up with players in the parking lot of Comiskey Park, an attractive young woman had managed to slip past security guards and board the bus, where she pulled down her jeans and, waving a blue Sharpie, asked the players to autograph her bare behind. Of course, they eagerly obliged. Royko reported that the same girl had mooned the Yankee bus the previous two nights as it pulled away from the ballpark. For her finale, she apparently wanted to do something more personal. Royko's column was based on an account from the mother of a nine-year-old Yankee fan who was seeking autographs from the players at the same time. He quoted the outraged mother as saying, "This blonde, about 20 years old and pretty, walked up, and they just let her on the bus. I couldn't believe it! They wouldn't give autographs to any of the kids, but they were signing their names on that girl's bare butt!"

The column caused quite a furor. Baseball Commissioner Bowie Kuhn demanded that the Yankees investigate the incident, and Steinbrenner, echoing Captain Renault's mock outrage about gambling in the movie *Casablanca*, responded by declaring in a statement, "If the allegations are accurate, this kind of conduct will not be tolerated. I say again, if true, I would be appalled."

Mickey Morabito, who had told one of Royko's fact-checkers that "when you travel with the Yankees you get to see everything"—a quote that Royko included in his piece—was the first to be summoned to Steinbrenner's office. Steinbrenner was also upset with Billy Martin, even though the manager had been having a drink with Morabito and White Sox owner Bill Veeck in the Comiskey Park Bards Room at the time of the incident. "He screamed at me in his office and threatened to fire me for about five minutes as I attempted to explain that Billy and I weren't there," Morabito remembered.

Steinbrenner then went down to the Yankee clubhouse and summoned all the suspected "signers" into Martin's office.

"This is just unbelievable," Steinbrenner moaned. "What's wrong with you guys? You've embarrassed this organization and you've embarrassed me by getting the goddamned commissioner on my case again."

"Oh, c'mon, George," said Lou Piniella. "What are you getting so worked up for? If you'd have been on the bus, you'd have been the first one to sign her ass and you would've signed 'George M. Steinbrenner the Third!'"

For a brief moment, everyone froze in silence. Then the room suddenly filled with laughter and even Steinbrenner forced a smile. Everyone later agreed the incident had provided a moment of welcome levity in the heavy days immediately after the Munson tragedy.

By this time, with the team in fourth place, Steinbrenner had given up on the 1979 season and begun shifting his attention to his shipbuilding business and, periodically, the Yankees' minor league operations. Shortly after the Munson funeral in Canton, he paid a visit to the Yankees' flagship farm team in Columbus. He had moved the Yankees' Triple-A ball club there from Syracuse after the 1978 season because of his strong personal ties to his in-laws, Harold and Jessie Zieg—who were prominent citizens there—and changed the team's name from the Jets to the Clippers.

For his first manager in Columbus, he'd chosen Gene Michael, despite the fact that he had no managerial experience. Michael had risen considerably in Steinbrenner's estimation since their first encounter in the spring of '73, when that hot dog had flown from the shortstop's glove and landed at the foot of the new owner. The lanky, 6-2 Michael, nicknamed "Stick" by his teammates, had played seven years for the Yankees, mostly during the dreary late '60s period when they were owned by CBS. When Ralph Houk resigned as Yankees manager after the 1973 season, he told Steinbrenner that Michael was an intelligent, winning player who had promise as a manager, coach or scout down the road. Steinbrenner remembered and, when Michael was released by the Boston Red Sox in 1976, he hired him as an extra coach for Martin. Because of that, the insecure Martin never fully trusted Michael, viewing him as Steinbrenner's man.

Michael spent most of that first season as the Yankees' "eye in the sky," an innovation Steinbrenner brought from his football-coaching days at Northwestern and Purdue by which Michael watched games from the press box and relayed information about the opposing team's defensive alignment by walkie-talkie to the dugout. Not surprisingly, the "eye in the sky" elicited frequent protests by the opposing teams and was a source of considerable embarrassment for Michael. When the Yankees visited Chicago during Michael's first season as a coach, Veeck, the ever-mischievous White Sox owner, barred Michael from the press box. The next day, when Michael bought a ticket and sat in the upper deck with his walkie-talkie, Veeck hired a circus clown to sit next to him. That fall, in the World Series against the Cincinnati Reds, Steinbrenner decided three "eyes" were better than one and assigned two scouts to sit with Michael in the press box for game one. When Reds manager Sparky Anderson found out, he complained to the umpires, who stopped play to confer with Kuhn. After an uneasy few minutes, Kuhn ordered two of the Yankee "eyes" out of the press box. After the Yankees lost the game, 5–1, a livid Steinbrenner castigated the front office staff for embarrassing him by getting caught with too many walkie-talkies.

In 1977, Steinbrenner gave Michael the title of "special assistant" and moved him into the front office, where he advised on trades and player signings. Among the recommendations Michael made was a slick-fielding first baseman, Jim Spencer, with the Texas Rangers. Michael was especially impressed with Spencer's plate discipline (a hitting attribute nobody paid much attention to in those days), and the Yankees acquired him that winter in a trade for a couple of minor league pitchers. Spencer proved to be a very useful player for the Yankees for three seasons, but Martin never liked him—and Michael, because he had pushed for Spencer, suspected this was because Martin saw him as a potential rival.

The 1979 Columbus Clippers were not supposed to fare well in the International League. Nevertheless, by late July they were comfortably in first place, prompting Steinbrenner's visit. In the taxicab on the way to his hotel from the Columbus airport, Steinbrenner was listening to the radio and was surprised to hear Michael being interviewed on a local sports station. It seemed the Cleveland Indians had just fired their manager, Jeff Torborg, and the Columbus radio man was speculating that Michael could be a candidate for the job.

"Would you be interested?" the radio reporter asked.

"Well, I'd at least like to hear what they say," Michael replied.

Hearing this, Steinbrenner instructed the cabbie to take him directly to the Clippers' ballpark, Cooper Stadium. As Michael walked into his office after pregame batting practice, he was surprised to see the Yankees owner waiting for him.

"I hear you're gonna be the next manager of the Cleveland Indians," Steinbrenner said.

"What do you mean?"

"I just heard it on the radio."

"All I said, George, was that I'd like to hear what they had to say."

"Well, you don't say that!" Steinbrenner growled. "You work for *me!*"

"I know that, George. All I said was if they called, I'd like to hear what they had to say."

"Well, you can go ahead and try," Steinbrenner said, "but I don't know why you would want to. Managers all become alcoholics. Look at Billy. Look at Lem. Look at [Baltimore's Earl] Weaver."

"To be honest, I hadn't even thought about managing anywhere beyond this year," Michael said.

"Good," said Steinbrenner, "because this is what I have in mind. At the end of the season, I want you to come back to New York and be my general manager. I'm going to put Cedric on to other things. Or, if you still want, you can go out and try to be a manager."

Michael thought about this for a moment. Even though he had no idea what the general manager's job encompassed, especially *Steinbrenner's* general manager, he liked the idea of running the baseball operations for the Yankees. He was only 41, and it was flattering to be considered by Steinbrenner for such a lofty post in the organization.

"The GM job sounds good to me," he said.

Michael's Clippers won the International League pennant by 8½ games and beat Richmond and Syracuse in the playoffs for the Governor's Cup. When he returned to New York in October, Steinbrenner gave him a $5,000 bonus for winning the International League (on top of his $25,000 salary) and told him that, as general manager, he'd make a salary of $80,000, starting immediately. But even after setting up in an office at Yankee Stadium, and though he was meeting regularly with Steinbrenner about potential trades and free-agent signings, there was no formal announcement of Michael taking over from Cedric Tallis as Yankees GM. Meanwhile, on October 25, Billy Martin got involved in another public scrap.

Martin's latest trouble occurred in the lobby of a hotel in Bloomington, Minnesota, where he was accused of punching one Joseph Cooper, described in news accounts as a 52-year-old marshmallow salesman. As in Reno, when he'd popped the sportswriter Ray Hagar, Martin was once again in the company of his friend, the restaurateur Howard Wong. Though initially telling reporters he would conduct another investigation, Steinbrenner had made up his mind that Martin was just too much of a liability; fortunately, after the last incident, the owner had made sure that Martin's latest contract allowed him to fire the manager if he got into more off-field trouble. The day after the Bloomington affair, Steinbrenner called Michael into his office at Yankee Stadium and told him he wanted him to manage the Yankees.

"But you said I was going to be the general manager," said Michael, who had seen firsthand how Steinbrenner devoured managers.

"That was before I needed a manager."

"What if I get you a manager?" Michael countered.

"Who?"

"Dick Howser."

"Howser?" said Steinbrenner. "You mean our old third-base coach? Where is he?"

"He's at Florida State," Michael replied. "He's the head baseball coach down there. Remember? You almost hired him to replace Billy once before. He's a good baseball man, and I think he'd do a good job."

"Get him on the phone."

Michael went through his book of phone numbers and dialed the Florida State athletic department as Steinbrenner put the phone on speaker. When the receptionist informed them that Howser was out on the baseball field, Steinbrenner asked to be patched through to the dugout, whereupon he introduced himself to the voice on the other end and asked to speak to Howser.

Steinbrenner and Michael listened as the voice called out, "Hey, Dick, there's some asshole on the line here who says he's George Steinbrenner."

"I can't believe it," Steinbrenner exclaimed to Michael. "That guy just called me an asshole, and he doesn't even know me!"

Michael could barely keep himself from doubling over with laughter. Once Howser came to the phone and realized it *was* Steinbrenner, he listened carefully as the Yankees owner made his pitch. Yes, Howser said, he'd be interested in managing the Yankees, as long as it was assured Martin wouldn't be back.

"I wouldn't feel right about taking Billy's job if you weren't certain of this, George," Howser said.

"Don't worry," said Steinbrenner. "I'm certain. Billy's got a lot of problems and I need someone stable."

Howser agreed to fly to New York the next day to discuss the details in person.

At their meeting at Yankee Stadium, Steinbrenner said he was prepared to give Howser a three-year contract for $80,000 per year, adding: "That's what Stick is making, and I told him you would get the same salary."

Howser said nothing.

"What's the matter?" Steinbrenner said. "Is there a problem, Dick?"

"Yeah, a little bit," replied Howser. "Eighty thousand doesn't seem like a lot of money. I kind of thought it would be more, especially being it's New York."

"Okay, then how about $100,000?"

"That sounds good."

"There you are, Stick," Steinbrenner said brightly. "I hope you're satisfied. Dick just made you an extra twenty thousand."

Howser's pluck in negotiating his first major league managing contract should have been a warning to Steinbrenner that this was a man who wouldn't be easily intimidated. Though diminutive in size—5-8, 155 pounds—Howser had a lot of bantam rooster in him. He was also very comfortable at Florida State. When they moved to Tallahassee he had assured his wife, Nancy, that Steinbrenner probably couldn't offer him enough money to go back to New York. Once they agreed to their union, Howser and Steinbrenner didn't have a lot of direct contact, primarily because Michael took pains to serve as a buffer between them. Michael saw how Steinbrenner could wear down even experienced managers such as Martin, Lemon and Ralph Houk, and he wanted to do all he could to shield Howser in his first season as a big-league manager.

When spring training arrived, it became clear that Michael had done a very thorough job rebuilding a championship-caliber team from the ruins of the 1979 season, beginning with the November 1 trade that sent first baseman Chris Chambliss, one of the cornerstone players of the 1976-77-78 World Series teams, to the Toronto Blue Jays for left-handed pitcher Tom Underwood and a promising young catcher, Rick Cerone, who would replace Munson. Later that winter, Michael signed Bob Watson, a slugging first baseman, to a four-year, $1.8 million contract, and Rudy May, another left-handed pitcher, to a three-year, $1 million deal on the free-agent market.

The 1980 Yankees under Dick Howser's leadership won 103 games, the most by any Yankee team since 1963, beating out a 100-win Baltimore Orioles team for the American League East title. They also set an all-time American League home attendance record of 2,627,417 and became the first team in AL history to play before a million fans both at home and on the road. But even with Michael's presence, the 1980 season was anything but easy for the rookie manager. Howser endured constant sniping from veterans Lou Piniella and Bobby Murcer, who were disgruntled over being platooned in the overcrowded outfield, and the loss of third baseman Graig Nettles for 89 games with hepatitis. From the get-go, Steinbrenner seemed to be even angrier than usual, lashing out at his players, Howser's management of the team and his many perceived enemies—primarily the Mets, whose spring training advertising campaign disparaged the feuding, turbulent Yankees as the "Bronx Zoo." Jerry Della Femina, the head of the ad agency that created the campaign, was quoted in the newspapers as saying, "This is a town where we had to settle for Reggie Jackson. We're looking to Mets with star quality, like Lee Mazzilli, who we believe is the big glamour player in this town—a handsome Bucky Dent who can hit and doesn't do fur commercials."

"If this guy thinks he will win fans in New York for the Mets by knocking Reggie Jackson and Bucky Dent, he's just plain stupid," Steinbrenner fumed to reporters at spring training in Fort Lauderdale. "My advice to the Mets folks and their Madison Avenue ad agency approach to the fans of New York is to forget sniping at the Yankees and the American League—the one league that never left New Yorkers high and dry—and start concentrating on players who can hit the ball, catch the ball and throw the ball better than other guys. We'll see where they are on Labor Day."

In a rare occurrence, Bowie Kuhn agreed with Steinbrenner and fined the Mets $5,000 for their ad campaign. But once the season pushed into summer and the Mets, as Steinbrenner had predicted, faded to a 95-loss, fourth-place finish, the Yankees owner turned his fire on his own team. The Yankees, in first place, lost six of their first nine games in August, including a three-game sweep at home by the fast-closing, second-place Orioles, prompting Steinbrenner to call Michael on the phone to say that Howser was blowing it. "They're not responding to him," he complained. "He's too laid-back. The umpires are killing us, and he never comes out to argue with them. "

Then, in mid-August, after the Yankees lost three of five in Baltimore at the start of a 13-game cross-country road trip to have their lead over the Orioles cut to a scant half game, Steinbrenner could no longer contain himself. For the first time, he issued a public rebuke of Howser, criticizing the manager for not sacrificing with slumping third baseman Eric Soderholm with a man on base and no outs in the ninth inning of the final game against the Orioles.

"Dick Howser is my manager, and he's done a helluva job to keep us in first place the way he has. But as a fan, I have the right to question his strategy. He knows his job rests on the bottom line, and the bottom line is winning. You've got to give Earl Weaver all the credit. He's a wizard, and our guy's a rookie manager. I wouldn't invite Weaver to Christmas dinner, but you've got to give the devil his due."

Steinbrenner was at his horse farm in Ocala, Florida, but his roar was heard all the way in Seattle, where the Yankees had begun the second leg of the road trip against the Mariners. After winning the first two games there, Howser was standing with his batting coach, Charlie Lau, and a couple of reporters in the visiting manager's office at the Kingdome.

"Did you hear from George?" one of the reporters asked.

"I don't know, should I say it?" Howser said to Lau.

"Say it!" Lau encouraged him. "Get your notebooks out, men."

Howser looked at the reporters with a twinkle in his eye and said, "You know, now that I'm competing against a rookie manager [Seattle's Maury Wills], I know it's very important for me to win. I'd hate like hell to be intimidated here after being intimidated by the other guy in Baltimore this week. If I can't be manager of the year, maybe I can at least be rookie manager of the year. Hell, that would really be something to win—especially in my first year!"

It was as if Howser had freed himself from the pressure of managing under Steinbrenner simply by speaking his mind. From that point on in the 1980 season, he seemed to openly enjoy the verbal parrying with Steinbrenner that played out in the newspapers. The next day, a package addressed to Bobby Murcer, whom Howser had been using intermittently in the outfield, was delivered to the Yankee clubhouse—prompting Dick Young to write in the *Daily News*, "the last thing Dick Howser needs is George Steinbrenner sending Bobby Murcer a first baseman's glove for his birthday, nine months before his birthday." Howser reacted with bemusement. In response to the beat writers' inquisition as to whether Steinbrenner was, in fact, ordering him to give Murcer more playing time, he said, "George has all the statistics. He obviously feels Murcer can help us at first base."

"But what do you think, Dick?" a reporter pressed.

Howser merely smiled.

The first baseman's glove disappeared, never to be seen again, and Murcer stayed in the outfield.

On September 23, Soderholm pinch-hit in the ninth inning and delivered a two-run single to key an important come-from-behind 5–4 victory over the Cleveland Indians. Afterward, Howser pointedly told reporters in his office, "I understand there were some people around here who gave up on Eric Soderholm, but I wasn't one of them."

Howser's Yankees managed to hold off the Orioles, winning seven of their last eight games to set up an American League Championship Series against their perennial AL West rivals, the Kansas City Royals. "You would have thought winning 103 games would've made George jump for joy," said Reggie Jackson, "but for some reason it didn't. He just didn't like Dick Howser's attitude, and he was never satisfied that year."

The day after the regular season ended, Steinbrenner assembled the Yankees high command at his office to strategize for the upcoming ALCS. The Yankees had beaten the Royals in the 1976, '77 and '78 American League Championship Series, but they'd lost eight of 12 to them during the 1980 season.

"We didn't bear down against these guys this season," Steinbrenner complained. "We have to be prepared."

Steinbrenner continued his critique of the team for a few minutes before he was interrupted by a tap at the door.

"Who is it?" he said.

"Monahan, Boss," came the reply.

"Oh, yeah," said Steinbrenner, motioning the team trainer, Gene Monahan, into the room. "You got it?"

"Right here, sir," Monahan said, brandishing a hypodermic needle.

"Okay, let's do it," said Steinbrenner, lowering his pants. As the others in the room watched in silent astonishment, Monahan proceeded to inject Steinbrenner in the behind with what they later learned was vitamin B-12. Over the years, this became a ritual. Usually Steinbrenner would get his injections in the trainer's room, but sometimes he'd simply have Monahan come up to his office to perform the deed. Once, Monahan had run out of his supply of B-12 and was in a bit of a panic when Steinbrenner called downstairs asking him to come up to the office with his needle.

"I don't know what to tell him," Monahan said to a couple of players. "He's gonna go crazy if I tell him I'm out of B-12."

"Don't tell him anything," Lou Piniella said, laughing. "Just fill that needle up with water and inject him with that. You could put a harpoon in that big, fat ass of his and he'd never tell the difference!"

IN THE FIRST game of the ALCS in Kansas City, Royals left-hander Larry Gura, a notorious Yankees nemesis, scattered 10 hits in a 7–2 complete-game victory in which Reggie Jackson left five runners on base. After the game, Steinbrenner stalked into the Yankee clubhouse, fuming. The players were sitting disconsolately in front of their lockers, ignoring the food laid out on the table in the middle of the room. Howser was sitting in the adjoining room with the coaches, but could easily hear Steinbrenner's stinging words breaking the solemnity.

"You guys make me sick," he bellowed. "You guys are supposed to be so damned good, and I pay you all this money, and then you go out and perform like that! You're better than Kansas City, and you better show me something—or else!"

Instead of firing up his team, however, Steinbrenner's words had the opposite effect on the players. The veterans, in particular, seethed at the idea that he would question their commitment against a team they'd beaten three times before in the ALCS. "Screw him," said one after Steinbrenner left the room.

But it was the events of the next game that set Steinbrenner off in a classic rage.

With two out in the eighth inning and the Royals leading 3–2, Willie Randolph was on first base when Bob Watson hit a liner into the left-field corner that looked certain to go for an extra base hit to tie the game. Except instead of rolling around on the artificial turf of Royals Stadium, the ball ricocheted off the wall and straight into the glove of Kansas City left fielder Willie Wilson. Randolph was chugging into third when Wilson fielded the ball, but the outfielder overthrew the cutoff man, shortstop U. L. Washington, prompting Yankees third-base coach Mike Ferraro to wave Randolph home. Since they were trailing by a run with only four outs left to them, it was the right call—except that, at the last second, Royals third baseman George Brett had alertly gone behind Washington, essentially acting as a second cutoff man, and caught the ball on the fly. Brett's throw home beat Randolph by nearly 20 feet. At that moment, the television cameras caught an apoplectic Steinbrenner in the stands, cursing and waving his arms in disgust. As soon as the game ended, he stormed the section where the Yankees' wives were sitting and screamed at Ferraro's wife, Mary, "Your fucking husband cost us this game!"

The Royals completed a three-game sweep of the series when the teams returned to New York the next night, and in the days immediately following, Steinbrenner was uncharacteristically silent in the press, leading to speculation that he was contemplating firing Howser. Or somebody. Soon after the end of the series, news leaked that the Yankees were about to hire Don Zimmer to be their new third-base coach. Zimmer was the former manager of the Red Sox, who'd lost the '78 playoff game to the Yankees, and a St. Petersburg resident who hobnobbed with Steinbrenner at the Tampa racetracks. Reached for comment by reporters at his home in Tallahassee, Howser said, "I would think I should be given the courtesy of approving or disapproving the coaches that are added to the ball club. I have to work with these guys every day, and I should be able to say who's going to coach and who's not going to coach."

After reading these remarks, Steinbrenner called Michael and informed him he was going to fire Howser.

"I'm making you the manager," he said firmly to Michael. "I want you and Howser in Tampa tomorrow. We'll settle everything up then."

"Are you sure you want to do this, George?" Michael pleaded. "I told you I don't want to manage."

"Either you manage or I'm gonna pick the next one myself. I'm not gonna have another mess like this with this little wiseass."

Michael reluctantly agreed to take the job himself. At a meeting the next day at the Bay Harbor Hotel, in Tampa, Steinbrenner told Howser of the change. Both he and Michael were somewhat surprised at Howser's reaction.

"There was none," Michael remembered. "Dick had no problem with it. He didn't argue, nothing. I had the feeling Dick just felt whatever George wanted was OK with him. He was worn out."

Howser did ask for one thing in return for leaving without a fuss, and that was a small loan from Steinbrenner for a new house he was planning to buy. Steinbrenner agreed; in fact, at the press conference in New York the next day, he would tell reporters that Howser was leaving to pursue a lucrative real estate deal in Florida. After their meeting at the Bay Harbor concluded, Steinbrenner went home and Michael and Howser retired to the hotel bar. About 45 minutes later, the bartender informed Michael that Steinbrenner was on the phone. While driving home, Steinbrenner had once again had second thoughts about firing his manager and stopped at a pay phone.

"Stick, this just isn't right," Steinbrenner said. "It's just not coming off right. Go back and see if Dick can just have a little more discipline on the team and get on the umpires' asses a little more. If he'll just do those two things, he can come back."

"Really?" Michael said, elatedly. "We can keep him?"

Michael hung up the phone and went back to Howser, telling him about Steinbrenner's change of heart. "If you'll just go out of the dugout once in a while . . . c'mon, Dick, you can do that! I want you as my manager!"

Howser listened and then replied softly, "No, Stick. I think I like it the way it is. I'll be honest: my stomach was churning all year long."

Steinbrenner knew the firing of Howser would not be popular with the fans or the media, which is why he concocted the story about the "lucrative real estate deal" to help sell it. In addition, he told his public relations director, Larry Wahl, that the press conference to announce Howser's departure would be held in his office at Yankee Stadium, and that only the beat writers from local newspapers and selected columnists should be invited. Wahl told him that such an exclusive press conference would generate even more bad publicity, but Steinbrenner was adamant, and even went so far as to turn away reporters who showed up but were not on the list.

The press conference, in which there were bite-size roast beef, turkey and ham sandwiches—along with a healthy serving of baloney—was a complete farce. Howser sat stiffly in a chair half-facing the window that looked out on the field, while Steinbrenner sat behind his big round desk at the other end of the room. He wanted Howser to stay, he told the 14 reporters present, "but Dick felt he just couldn't pass up this real estate deal."

Silence.

"Nobody wants a sandwich? A drink?"

No one responded. Steinbrenner continued. "The door was open for Dick to return, but he chose to accept this business opportunity."

A reporter asked, "But could Dick still be the manager if he wanted to be?"

"Yes," said Steinbrenner.

"Well, why don't you want to be, Dick?" the reporter persisted.

"I have to be careful here," Howser said. "That's hard to say."

"Were you fired, Dick?"

"I'm not going to comment on that."

Steinbrenner broke in: "I didn't fire the man!"

Finally, a reporter asked Howser: "Dick, do you have any advice for Stick as the new manager?"

"Yeah," Howser said, "have a strong stomach and get a good contract."

The unconvinced reporters then filed out of Steinbrenner's office, leaving the Yankees owner looking forlornly at the bartender.

"Nobody ate any sandwiches," Steinbrenner said glumly.

Steinbrenner would not see or talk to Howser again until the following February, at the New York baseball writers' 59th annual dinner, where Steinbrenner, Howser and Martin were all in attendance. Howser had won their "Good Guy" award, and the writers had arranged for Martin to fly in and present it to his successor and loyal former lieutenant. When Steinbrenner heard about this part of the program, he asked if he could give out his own award.

After presenting Howser with his award, Martin said he would also like to give Steinbrenner a "Nice Man" award. "George is such a nice man," he said, "and I never appreciated him while I was working for him. I only realized that after he fired me." He then handed Steinbrenner, who was sitting next to him on the dais, an oversized gavel. In accepting his award, Steinbrenner noted that neither he nor Martin had ever won the "Good Guy" award from the writers. "I therefore feel it's only right to present Billy with not one, but two awards," he said, pulling out from beneath the dais a pair of oversized boxing gloves and a gigantic marshmallow on which he'd inscribed: "Roses are red, violets are blue, when I eat these I think of you."

Surprisingly, Dick Howser did not stay long in the real estate business.

On August 31 of the following year, he was hired as manager of the Kansas City Royals, with whom he would win three division titles over the next five seasons and the World Series in 1985. But in July 1986, after managing the American League team in the All-Star Game, Howser was diagnosed with a malignant brain tumor. He died 11 months later, on June 17, 1987, at age 51. After a memorial service in Kansas City, Howser's body was flown to Tallahassee for burial. As his widow, Nancy, got off the plane in Tallahassee, the first person to greet her was George Steinbrenner.

IN DECEMBER 1980, Steinbrenner invited a group of sportswriters to a soiree at Tampa Bay Downs racetrack, in Oldsmar, Florida. He had purchased a 50 percent share of the run-down, 54-year-old track the previous March and immediately spent $3 million renovating it. Steinbrenner's passion for Thoroughbred horse racing predated his purchase of the Yankees. Since 1969, he had bred horses at his 860-acre farm in Ocala, Florida. Over the years, Steinbrenner's Kinsman Stable would produce more than 35 stakes champions, including 2005 Wood Memorial winner Bellamy Road, and Steve's Friend, winner of the 1977 Hollywood Derby and the fifth-place finisher in the Kentucky Derby that year. With the purchase of Tampa Bay Downs, Steinbrenner now had his own track at which to showcase his horses.

Sitting around the patio of the VIP lounge at Tampa Bay Downs that December afternoon, Steinbrenner was in a buoyant mood. "Horses are great," he told the assembled sportswriters. "They never complain, and they can't talk to sportswriters and tell them what a bum the owner is." Maybe the horses couldn't, but the employees at the track were more than capable. On opening day at the track, where the entertainment included a marching band, a fashion show, and skydivers dropping out of planes, Steinbrenner fired the general manager, Ed McKinsey, whom he had just hired away from Hialeah Park Race Track the previous May. A problem with the printing presses had caused a delay in getting the programs to the track, where they didn't arrive until the second race. McKinsey told *Sports Illustrated* that he took full blame for the printing press snafu, and that, in a meeting afterward, he and Steinbrenner had almost come to blows. "He said, 'If you were a little bigger I'd punch you out,'" McKinsey related. "I said, 'You don't have the heart to punch me out,' and he gave me a check for $19,000 and said, 'This is the least I can do.' I had given my blood to the man and he tried to dehumanize me. If it wasn't the printing press problem, it would have always been something else."

In 1983, the co-owner of the track, Chester Howell Ferguson, passed away and left his interest to his daughter, Stella Thayer, who turned out to be as headstrong in business matters as was Steinbrenner, with whom she clashed from the start. When Thayer refused to sign off on a multi-stakes deal Steinbrenner put together in 1986 with the financial backing of his friend Lee Iacocca, the CEO of Chrysler, they tried to buy each other out, finally agreeing to hold an auction between them to decide who would continue to own the track. Because Steinbrenner had invested his family's money in the track, they all had a stake in how much more it was going to cost to own it all. Thayer, on the other hand, was determined to buy Steinbrenner out no matter the price. The auction was held at the track, and according to those who were present, when the bidding reached $16 million, Steinbrenner turned to his wife and kids and said, "What do you want to do?" The answer was unanimous: "Sell."

Steinbrenner continued to frequent Tampa Bay Downs over the next two decades, occasionally watching his own horses race, but only as a patron.

Bowie Kuhn, the commissioner of baseball, was not sorry to see Steinbrenner lose ownership of the racetrack. Since becoming commissioner in 1969, Kuhn had been especially vigilant about gambling in baseball, going so far as to ban Willie Mays and Mickey Mantle from the game for taking jobs as greeters in Atlantic City casinos. Because the Galbreath family, who owned the Pittsburgh Pirates, had long held an interest in Churchill Downs, Kuhn had reluctantly given his okay when Steinbrenner first mentioned purchasing Tampa Bay Downs in 1969. But at the end of 1980, Kuhn vowed to shut the door on any future owner involvements with racetracks—a decision that was tested when Edward DeBartolo, the Youngstown, Ohio, real estate developer who had helped spark Steinbrenner's pursuit of the Cleveland Indians nine years earlier, attempted to buy the Chicago White Sox from Bill Veeck.

Kuhn had two objections to DeBartolo: he wasn't from Chicago, and he owned not one but three racetracks—Thistledown, in Cleveland; Balmoral, near Chicago; and Louisiana Downs, outside Shreveport. When Kuhn publicly expressed his opposition to the sale to DeBartolo, the multimillionaire developer accused him of being anti-Italian. An ugly spat played out in the press, and DeBartolo brought a team of lawyers with him to the winter meetings in Dallas, where the American League was to vote on the sale.

As the meeting got under way, Edward Bennett Williams, the Baltimore Orioles owner and renowned attorney who had represented Steinbrenner in the Watergate scandal, set the tone.

"Gentlemen, I've spent my life's work defending scoundrels and reprobates," he said, pausing for effect, and casting an impish wink at Steinbrenner across the table. "But this guy DeBartolo threatening us if he's not approved is outrageous. I'm prepared to bring it on."

After a few more owners, similarly angered at DeBartolo's veiled threat to sue them if he wasn't approved, delivered speeches denouncing him, Steinbrenner got up to speak on behalf of his old Ohio business associate.

"I'm here to say I've known Eddie DeBartolo for a long time and he's an outstanding citizen and a great American," Steinbrenner said. "His is a rags-to-riches story that is to be admired by us all. I know of no more honorable man."

Steinbrenner then sat down and, when it came time to cast his ballot, voted "nay" with Kuhn's 11–3 majority.

10

· · ·

Passages

· · ·

B Y THE FALL OF 1980, Steinbrenner was starting to become disenchanted with the 34-year-old Reggie Jackson, whose contract had one year remaining. He had tired of Jackson's outspokenness, especially his periodic complaints of racism and his conflicts with his teammates and Billy Martin. Reggie's heroics in the '77 World Series were now three years past—a lifetime for a what-have-you-done-for-me-lately owner like Steinbrenner—and his failure to drive in a run in the three games against the Kansas City Royals in the 1980 American League Championship Series had taken a little more luster off his Mr. October image.

Above all, with Thurman Munson gone, Steinbrenner didn't want Jackson to be the face of the Yankees. He wanted that player to be more refined, more respectful and, on the field, a complete player. He wanted a new superstar to lead the Yankees in the '80s, and with that in mind, he'd been keeping an eye on Dave Winfield since 1979.

Two weeks after the Kansas City Royals completed their sweep of the Yankees in the 1980 ALCS, Steinbrenner convened a meeting of his baseball operations staff in his office at Yankee Stadium to discuss potential trades and free agent signings for the 1981 season. In particular, Steinbrenner was eager to hear from his chief scout, Birdie Tebbetts, who had spent much of the summer of 1980 on assignment in San Diego watching Winfield, the Padres' 6-foot-6 right fielder. A four-time All-Star and National League RBI leader in 1979, the 29-year-old Winfield would be the premier player on the free-agent market and, as such, the object of Steinbrenner's utmost attention.

Winfield had always been good, signing for a $100,000 bonus with the Padres as the fourth player taken overall in the 1973 amateur draft and going directly to the major leagues without playing a game in the minors. He batted .284 with 154 homers over eight seasons for San Diego; in 1979 he batted .308 with 34 homers and 118 RBI, and became acclaimed as one of the best all-around players in the game. However, the small-market Padres knew they wouldn't be able to afford him when his contract expired the following year, so they tried to deal him away, but each time negotiations broke down, causing more and more friction between them and Winfield's hard-nosed, abrasive agent, Al Frohman. The son of a rabbi, Frohman was a retired caterer running a leisure apparel business when he first met Winfield in Los Angeles in the early '70s. Frohman helped arrange some endorsement deals for Winfield, and in return, the player introduced him to wealthy professional athletes who bought apparel from him. In 1977 they created the David M. Winfield Foundation, a tax-exempt charitable organization that provided food, recreation and education programs for disadvantaged and handicapped children in San Diego County.

"So what do you have, Birdie?" Steinbrenner asked.

Sitting around the table in his office were Gene "Stick" Michael, Cedric Tallis, Bill Bergesch and scouting director Bobby Hofman.

"Well, here's my report, George," Tebbetts said, pushing a manila envelope across the desk. "You wanted to know what kind of a player Winfield can be for us, and I would have to say he's got great physical skills unlike any player we've had here. He has flaws, like all big-swingers. He can be had, but if he's to be great, he will adjust. And even if he doesn't, he's still going to be an All-Star. He does too many things well. He's got an above-average arm. He's an excellent base runner once he gets going. He hustles and he hits with authority. Even though he's right-handed, I think he'll hit his share of homers in Yankee Stadium.

"You asked me to find out everything I could about his personal life, and I couldn't find anything other than an excessive room service bill he ran up on a Padres road trip in St. Louis. You probably know he's got a foundation for kids and that he's big in the community out there."

That night, after reading over Tebbetts's 12-page report, Steinbrenner began to form his strategy. With each year, free agents were demanding more and more money—a trend that Steinbrenner's own signings of Hunter and Jackson had helped foster—and he knew that it was going to take a whole lot more than the $2.96 million over five years Reggie had cost him. (In 1975, the year before free agency, the average baseball salary was $44,676; by 1980 it had more than tripled, to $143,756.) As he had done with Munson before signing Jackson, Steinbrenner decided that he now needed to sound out Jackson about the possibility of bringing Winfield to the team for a lot more money than any other player in baseball was making. Over dinner at Elaine's, Steinbrenner told Jackson of his intentions and listened with interest as Reggie endorsed the idea.

"I know you're looking for a big gun to hit in front or in back of me," Jackson said, "and Winfield can be that gun. As a right-handed hitter, I'm not so sure how he'll perform power-wise, because he'll be hitting so many shots to Death Valley [the deep expanse of left center field in Yankee Stadium], but basically I think he'll help us a lot. Plus, I'm not gonna be around forever, and it's probably the right time for you to start looking to groom someone who can be your horse when I'm gone."

Incidentally, Jackson leaving the team was precisely what Steinbrenner was thinking, too, but it would take another six months before Reggie began to realize the owner was intent on replacing him sooner rather than later. A couple of days after that dinner with Jackson, Steinbrenner flew to Minneapolis to meet for the first time with Winfield, who was back at his alma mater, hosting a fund-raiser with comedian Bob Hope. Over steaks with Winfield and Frohman, Steinbrenner delivered his pitch.

"We've been watching you a long time, Dave," he said, "and we feel that with a good team like the Yankees, your batting average will go up 30 points. You've been playing on losing teams your entire career in San Diego. It's time you got with a winner. We have a need for an outfielder and a middle-of-the-order hitter to complement Reggie, and you're precisely the kind of guy we want. You're an athlete who plays the whole game. I like that. And I believe you'll thrive in New York. There's a lot of business opportunities there for you that you won't be able to get anywhere else."

Steinbrenner then questioned him about that room service bill in

St. Louis. ("Right then," Winfield wrote years later in his autobiography, "I knew he'd really done his homework.") Finally their discussion turned to Winfield's foundation, with Steinbrenner pledging financial support from the Yankees. This made him the front-runner with Winfield and Frohman, as the agent had made clear that financial support for the Winfield Foundation was paramount in any negotiation with his client.

By mid-December, the list of Winfield's suitors had narrowed to the Yankees, the Atlanta Braves and their free-spending owner, Ted Turner, and, much to Steinbrenner's alarm, the Mets. At the gathering Steinbrenner had held with reporters at Tampa Bay Downs on December 5, he'd said he had no regrets at having lost out to the Houston Astros for 35-year-old free agent pitcher Don Sutton. "We didn't need Sutton," he said, "but Dave Winfield is a different matter. He's the piece to fit into the puzzle. Don't count us out on Winfield."

"The Mets are a definite threat," Steinbrenner insisted, even though the Mets had finished fifth in the NL East in 1980, losing 95 games. "That figure they're reported to have offered—a million and a half a year for eight years—I know for a fact that's legitimate. But when I really want a man, I confront him face to face. I camp at his door. I really go after him, the way I did with Reggie."

When Winfield came to New York in early December for more meetings with the Mets and Yankees, Steinbrenner was there to overwhelm him with the same full-court press he'd put on Reggie four years earlier: flowers in his hotel room, chauffeured limos, a Broadway show, dinner at "21."

"I like you a lot, Dave," Steinbrenner said as they sat in the back of the limo that was taking them to Elaine's after a show. "You've got class. I can take you places I could never take Reggie."

ON THE NIGHT of Sunday, December 14, Steinbrenner met with Frohman, Winfield and Bob Erra, the foundation's chief financial officer, at the Loews Summit Hotel in Manhattan, where the trio was staying. The Mets had bid $1.5 million per year for five years (not eight, as Steinbrenner had said two weeks before), and Steinbrenner was determined to blow Winfield over with his offer. He told Winfield he would give him $1.4 million per year, but for *ten* years—the biggest and longest contract ever for a professional athlete. In addition, he would pay Winfield a $1 million signing bonus and he would pledge $3 million to the David M. Winfield Foundation over 30 years and provide Frohman an office at the Stadium.

Winfield smiled in satisfaction at the offer, but before he could say anything, Frohman interjected that, because of the length of the contract, there needed to be a cost-of-living escalator.

"Okay," said Steinbrenner. "I'll match the rate of inflation up to 10 percent annually over the 10 years. In exchange for that, I want the option of buying out the last two years of the contract at 50 percent, or $700,000."

Winfield and his negotiators looked at each other and asked for a private caucus. Adjourning to the room next door, Erra expressed his astonishment at Steinbrenner's offer. "I don't think he realizes how a cost-of-living escalator works—that it *compounds*! By the eighth year of the contract your base salary could be over two million dollars!"

Returning to the negotiating room, Frohman told Steinbrenner he had a deal. Steinbrenner beamed. They agreed to have Dick Moss, a prominent agent who was formerly assistant executive director of the Players Association, draw up the contract and bring it to Yankee Stadium the next morning for them all to sign. At 10 A.M., Steinbrenner met with his in-house counsel, Ed Broderick, and his comptroller, Dave Weidler, and asked them to read over the contract while he went into security chief Pat Kelly's office to personally type out the addendum about the $3 million contribution to the Winfield Foundation.

At the press conference later that day, at Jimmy Weston's restaurant in Manhattan, Jackson showed up to welcome Winfield to the team. In his remarks, Steinbrenner attempted to downplay the magnitude of the deal, focusing instead on the charity aspect. "We didn't get started in youth work 15 minutes before Winfield became a free agent, you know," he said. "I really think David felt that what he does for youth could be done better from Yankee Stadium. He's totally committed to helping youngsters. I know people may not believe that, but I don't think I've ever met a finer young man. I don't question his sincerity."

The next day, Murray Chass's column in the *New York Times* reported the details of the Winfield contract, in particular the compounding cost-of-living escalator, which, based on the maximum 10 percent annually, he wrote, could make the deal worth nearly $25 million. Had Steinbrenner allowed himself to be duped? Chass's column sure made it look that way. After reading the story, an apoplectic Steinbrenner summoned Broderick to his office.

"I can't have this, Eddie!" he screamed. "I can't be made to look like that fucking little kosher caterer got the best of me! You're gonna have to take the blame for this!" Broderick knew there was no point trying to reason with Steinbrenner; no point trying to explain that they had all understood the compounding part of the cost-of-living clause, and that it wasn't likely to exceed more than 3 percent in any year, meaning the contract probably wouldn't wind up being worth much more than the $15 million face value they had figured. He understood what his job was, and that was to take the fall so his boss could save face. Accordingly, Broderick made a series of phone calls to the Yankees beat writers, informing them that he was the one who'd negotiated the contract with the cost-of-living clause, with full understanding of its potential value. In the meantime, at Winfield's urging, Broderick and Frohman quietly renegotiated the cost-of-living clause to be triggered every two years.

On Opening Day in 1981, a cold, damp, miserable April afternoon, Al Frohman showed up at Yankee Stadium expecting to watch the game from the comfort of that office suite Steinbrenner had promised him. Instead, when he arrived at the reception desk in the Stadium lobby, he was surprised to learn he'd been assigned a seat in an outdoor loge box way down the right-field line, next to the foul pole. Broderick remembered seeing him come into the foyer of the Yankees offices during the middle of the game, seeking refuge from the cold. "The guy's hands and face were white, and he was ice cold," Broderick said. "He looked awful. I told him I was taking a risk if Mr. Steinbrenner saw him in there, but the poor guy looked like he had pneumonia."

STEINBRENNER HAD SIGNED Winfield and sent Gene Michael to the dugout, but the Yankees still didn't have a president until March, when he tapped his old friend and football mentor Lou Saban. The much-traveled Saban was between football jobs, having been athletic director at both the University of Miami (Ohio) and the University of Cincinnati within a span of a year and half, when Steinbrenner called and asked him to run the Yankees.

Perhaps because he had held 18 different jobs in 33 years, Saban didn't feel it was necessary to consult with Rosen about the difference between being Steinbrenner's friend and working for the man. He would last two years before resigning from what, in title anyway, was one of the most prestigious jobs in sports, to take over as head football coach at the University of Central Florida, a fledgling Division III school. In a 2002 interview with Wayne Coffey of the *New York Daily News*, Saban told a familiar tale about why he'd had to leave Steinbrenner's employ. The breaking point, it turned out, was the same as it had been for Howard Berk a decade earlier—the postponing of a game because of rain. In Saban's case, there were already 50,000 fans in Yankee Stadium, many of them there as part of a benefit the Yankees were hosting for the family of a police officer who had been killed in the line of duty. The Yankees were leading 5–0 in the third inning when the skies opened and it began to rain about as hard as Saban could ever remember. After nearly an hour with no abatement, the phone rang in Saban's office. It was Steinbrenner, calling from Tampa.

"What the hell is going on up there?" Steinbrenner yelled. "Why isn't the game on TV?"

"It's pouring rain here, George," Saban said. "The field is inundated."

Steinbrenner hung up. Ten minutes later, he called again.

"What's going on now?"

"I told you, George, it's pouring. Water is cascading into the dugouts!"

"Well, get down there and talk to the umpires. Tell them they have to do everything they can to get the game in!"

Again, Steinbrenner hung up, only to call back in another 15 minutes in even more of a frenzy.

"Is it still raining?" he shouted.

"Yes, it's still raining, George," Saban said.

"Well, why didn't you know it was going to rain?"

"George," pleaded Saban, "I'm not the guy upstairs! I don't turn on the valves!"

"Oh, yeah, well, you're fired!"

Dumbfounded, Saban called Yankees security chief Pat Kelly, who had also been on the receiving end of Steinbrenner's rain rant all night, and the two of them polished off a bottle of Scotch in the owner's office. That night, Saban went back to his apartment and began packing his bags to go home. At 9 o'clock the next morning, Steinbrenner showed up unannounced at the Yankee Stadium offices and immediately confronted Mary Pellino, Saban's secretary.

"Where the hell is Saban?" he demanded.

"He's not here, sir," she replied. "You fired him last night."

"What the hell are you talking about? You tell him to get his ass into this office in an hour."

When Saban arrived back at the Stadium at 1:30 that afternoon, Steinbrenner was still in a foul mood over the ruined night for the slain cop and having to now honor all those rain checks, but he said nothing about the firing. Nevertheless, Saban knew it was time to go. They parted amicably a few months later and remained friends until Saban's death in 2009. "George has great feelings for people and, down deep, he's a really tender guy," Saban told Coffey. "But the one question in my life, knowing George, is that I never could quite understand how he could do a complete three-sixty in a period of 24 hours."

Still, Saban should have known what he was getting into—in his very first month as Yankees president, he witnessed several classic Steinbrenner blowups, sufficient warning as to what he could expect in his new job.

After a breakthrough season as Thurman Munson's replacement at catcher, in which he hit .277 with 14 homers and 85 RBI, Rick Cerone filed for salary arbitration, seeking a raise from $110,000 to $440,000. (Salary arbitration was a concession the owners made in a collective bargaining agreement that allowed players with at least three years of major league service to have an arbitrator determine what they'd be paid the following year.) Steinbrenner, who regarded being taken to arbitration by a player as a personal affront, was outraged. There was no way he was even going to attempt to compromise on such an exorbitant demand. Fearing he might be fired by Steinbrenner if he lost the decision, general manager Cedric Tallis elected to delegate the duties of making the Yankees' case to Broderick, the team's in-house counsel. Broderick told Steinbrenner that the Yankees should not attack Cerone but rather offer him $350,000 and try to sell the arbitrator on the fact that they recognized the catcher's considerable contributions to the team and were rewarding him by more than tripling his salary. Steinbrenner agreed, the offer was made, and Cerone rejected, preferring to present his case to the arbitrator. As soon as Broderick arrived at the hearing and saw a bunch of employees from the American Arbitration Service asking for autographs from Cerone, he knew his case was in trouble.

Indeed, the next day, he got a call from Barry Rona, one of baseball's labor relations attorneys, informing him that the arbitrator had ruled in favor of Cerone.

"What do you *mean* we lost?" Steinbrenner yelled when Broderick reached him in Tampa. "You're a fucking idiot!" Steinbrenner yelled before abruptly hanging up. A few minutes later he called back.

"OK, Broderick, you lost and it's your fault, so this is what we're going to do. Monday is the Presidents Day holiday, and everybody up there was planning to have the day off, right? Well, you tell each and every one person in the office that, because you lost the Cerone case, they all have to work a full day Monday. You got that?"

Everyone came to work that Monday, and at 1 o'clock Steinbrenner called from Tampa to say that they could all go home—except Broderick.

"So what's the lesson you've learned?" Steinbrenner said.

Broderick sighed. "Never lose an arbitration."

The easygoing Broderick was single, in his early '30s. He enjoyed the perks and prestige that came with working for the Yankees, the rubbing of elbows with celebrities and power brokers in Steinbrenner's private box, but he didn't need the job to support a family. And over time he learned how to handle his boss, so that he seemed to enjoy a unique relationship with Steinbrenner. He had met Steinbrenner through his uncle, Bishop Edwin Broderick, who was head of the world Catholic Relief Services and who, in the mid-1980s, was among a half-dozen of Steinbrenner's prominent friends to write letters in his behalf asking President Ronald Reagan to pardon him for his Watergate conviction.

"You never challenged him in front of other people," Ed Broderick said of Steinbrenner, "because leaders don't want to be made to look like they're not right. But if you got him one-on-one, you could talk to him. You could also have fun with him."

A prime example of that was the day Steinbrenner came into Broderick's office and spotted a magazine with Barbara Walters's picture on the cover. In the article, the writer described Walters's physical attributes, prompting an impish smile from Steinbrenner, who had obviously read the story.

"Watch this!" he said, picking up the phone.

"Hi, Barbara, George here. Hey, I'm reading this magazine over here in which they're describing your considerable physical attributes. How come I've never gotten to see them?"

After a few minutes of playful, lighthearted conversation, Steinbrenner hung up with Walters and looked at Broderick, chuckling.

"Well, what did you think of that?"

"I think," said Broderick, "that a guy like you, Mr. Steinbrenner, with all your wealth, power and fame, could do a whole lot better than Barbara Walters."

"What? How dare you!" Steinbrenner shrieked in mock outrage, before jumping up and chasing Broderick around his desk.

JUST BEFORE THE start of spring training, Steinbrenner managed to run afoul of the commissioner's office again when a trade he'd worked out with the financially strapped Pittsburgh Pirates for slugging first baseman Jason Thompson was rejected by Bowie Kuhn because of an excess of money thrown into it on the Yankees' part. Kuhn had set a limit of $400,000 that could be included in trades, and Steinbrenner had agreed to give the Pirates first baseman Jim Spencer, two minor leaguers and $850,000 for Thompson. When he received the letter informing him that the deal had been voided, Steinbrenner phoned Kuhn's administrator, Bill Murray, who had previously worked in the Mets' front office, and lit into him.

"I know where this is coming from, you little sonofabitch," Steinbrenner screamed. "You're just making sure to help out your Mets friends, and I'm telling you right here, you've made an enemy for life. I'll get you back for this, no matter how long it takes!"

A shaken Murray wrote a letter to Steinbrenner the next day, copying Kuhn, in which he said: *I was shocked and disturbed by your phone call yesterday immediately prior to the termination of the Thompson-Spencer deal. Your comments and threats that I had made an enemy for life were those you might expect from a gangster hit man rather than the principal owner of a major league baseball team. Your comments are completely out of character with Yankee tradition and, I'm sure you would agree, not exactly what you would like to see framed and hung on the walls of the Great Moments Room at Yankee Stadium."*

As the 1981 baseball season got under way, negotiations for a new collective bargaining agreement between the players and owners seemed headed toward an impasse over the issue of the mechanism to be implemented for free agency. Gene Michael had his own problem—putting up with Steinbrenner's daily complaints—despite the fact that the Yankees hovered within a game or so of first place through the first two months of the season. Besides Winfield, the Yankees had bolstered their lineup with the acquisition of another player from the San Diego Padres, center fielder Jerry Mumphrey, who had hit .298 with 52 stolen bases in 1980. But these additions were offset by the loss of Cerone for the first month with a hand injury and a horrendous first-half slump by Reggie Jackson.

On May 24, before a Jacket Day crowd of 53,874, the Yankees committed three errors while being humiliated 12–5 by the Cleveland Indians. After the game, Steinbrenner blistered Michael and the team, telling reporters, "I'm embarrassed and disgusted. When 53,000 people pay their hard-earned dough to come out here and witness this fiasco, I'm embarrassed. We're being killed by a number of people. I've got the facts to back me up, stats about guys not producing in critical situations." He went on to say he'd suggested to Michael moving the slumping Jackson out of the cleanup spot in the lineup, perhaps to seventh, but that the manager had resisted, claiming it would do more harm than good. "There's going to be some things happening very shortly," Steinbrenner told the *Daily News'* Phil Pepe, hinting that Michael could soon be replaced as manager.

A nine-game winning streak at the start of June vaulted the Yankees into first place in the American League East and temporarily assuaged the owner. Then, on June 12, the increasingly rancorous labor negotiations between the players and the owners broke down, and the players went on strike. The work stoppage would last 50 days, and the season did not resume until August 10. Commissioner Kuhn decided that there would be a split season, with those teams in first place at the time of the work stoppage guaranteed a berth in the postseason. Kuhn announced a revised postseason format with an extra tier of "division playoffs," from which the winners would advance to the league championship series.

But if Michael thought the assurance of the Yankees being in the postseason had given him renewed job security, he was mistaken. When his veteran-laden Yankees played sluggishly upon their return, the owner's verbal attacks resumed. After a stretch of six losses in seven games in mid-August, Steinbrenner phoned Michael from Tampa and again threatened to fire him if the team's play didn't improve quickly.

"You can't expect a veteran team like this, sitting around for six weeks, to do any work when they've won the first half," Michael protested.

"I don't know, Stick, this is just unacceptable," Steinbrenner said. "I think I'm gonna have to make a change. You're just too young. You can't get it out of 'em."

"They're going to be okay, George," Michael insisted. "This is like spring training all over again for them."

"We'll see," Steinbrenner said. "This is on you."

After that, the calls from Steinbrenner became increasingly heated, on an almost daily basis. Complicating the situation for Michael was Jackson's continued batting woes. Three weeks into the second half, Jackson's batting average was at .212 and he had hit just six homers. On August 27, Michael (perhaps under pressure from Steinbrenner?) pinch-hit for him against the Chicago White Sox with utility infielder Aurelio Rodriguez, an indignity that rivaled anything Jackson had suffered under Billy Martin. The ultimate embarrassment for Jackson, however, came the next day, when Steinbrenner ordered him to Tampa to undergo a complete physical.

"I don't know if we can make it without him," Steinbrenner told the *Times*' Murray Chass, adding that they had to find out what was wrong with Jackson, to which Reggie responded angrily, "This is just more obvious harassment."

Jackson, who was in the final year of his contract, believed that Steinbrenner's real motive was to plant seeds of doubt about his physical well-being. For months, Steinbrenner had repeatedly rebuffed Jackson's efforts to negotiate a contract extension; perhaps this was simply a ploy to lower his value. Nevertheless, Jackson was contractually obligated to take the physical, because it was stipulated in his contract—but he would do it on his terms. He told Cedric Tallis to tell Steinbrenner that he would take the physical, but rather than going to Tampa, he flew to New York to have it at NYU Medical Center, where everything, most notably his eyesight, checked out okay. Michael was not surprised. He was sure that Jackson's problems were all mental, derived from the stress of being in his free agent walk year without a contract—and he agreed with Reggie that Steinbrenner wasn't helping matters.

Still, Michael wasn't certain that Jackson could be a productive player in New York anymore, under Steinbrenner's demanding presence. Steinbrenner wasn't sure either, which is why, after being informed by Tallis that Jackson had taken the physical in New York, he said he still wanted Reggie to come to Tampa. Jackson was getting ready to rejoin the team in Chicago when Tallis reached him at the office of his agent, Matt Merola.

"Uhhh, just checking in with you, Reggie, to make sure we've got everything straight," Tallis said nervously, privately hoping Jackson had decided to comply with Steinbrenner's order. "It's all arranged for George's son to meet you at the Tampa airport. We just need your flight information."

"What the hell are you talking about, Cedric?" Jackson said. "I'm not going to Tampa. I'm going to Chicago!"

Realizing Tallis had never told Steinbrenner he wasn't going to Tampa, Jackson hung up the phone and took a taxi up to Yankee Stadium. Marching into Tallis's office, he started yelling at the beleaguered GM, "What's happened to you, Cedric? You didn't have the guts to deliver my message to him, did you?"

"I'm sorry, Reggie," Tallis pleaded. "But you've got to go. Otherwise it's going to cost me my job."

Jackson knew Tallis wasn't overstating the situation, and he didn't want to be responsible for getting him fired. He picked up the phone on Tallis's desk and called Steinbrenner himself.

"George, I'm here in Cedric's office. I just wanted you to know that I took the physical at NYU, and all the results have come back fine," Jackson said. "There's no need for me to come to Tampa. I'm going back to Chicago to rejoin the team."

"No, no, no, Reggie," Steinbrenner said. "I want you to come down here."

Jackson viewed this as more harassment from Steinbrenner. There was absolutely no reason for him to fly to Tampa and take more time out of his season. In his mind, this whole ordeal, orchestrated by Steinbrenner, had been further means to take him down. Enough was enough, he decided: their relationship was over.

"Look, George," he said, "maybe the way I've been playing is my own fault, and maybe you don't think I can play anymore. But I'm gonna play my ass off for the rest of the season, and I'm gonna show you and everybody else there isn't a player anywhere further from being finished than me. I'm off to Chicago to do my job, and then it's goodbye."

Listening as Jackson lit into Steinbrenner, Tallis shuddered. He knew he would bear the brunt of Steinbrenner's wrath after Jackson flew back to Chicago. Sadly, he had grown accustomed to this since taking over as GM when Michael moved down to the field. After a stint as GM of the Kansas City Royals, for whom he had supervised the design and construction of their much-acclaimed new stadium, he had been hired by Gabe Paul in 1974 to oversee the refurbishing of Yankee Stadium. But even after elevating him to GM, Steinbrenner never regarded Tallis as a true baseball man. Instead, in 1981, Steinbrenner took this opportunity to begin serving, essentially, as his own GM while preying on Tallis's vulnerability as a family man who needed the job. Tallis kept a set of golf clubs in his office, and his fellow Yankees executives grew concerned about his mental state when they began to see him down on the field in the middle of the day, working out his frustration by driving golf balls into the bleachers. Other times he'd be in his office, talking to himself, while putting balls into his overturned trash basket. Tallis finally resigned from the Yankees in 1982 to become the executive director of the Tampa Bay Baseball Group (which sought to bring major league baseball to the Tampa–St. Petersburg area). Away from the daily mental pounding from Steinbrenner, his quality of life improved considerably.

SENSING HE'D EXERTED his quota of creative tension on Jackson for the time being, Steinbrenner turned his attention back to Michael. Shortly after Jackson rejoined the team in Chicago, Michael got a call from Steinbrenner, renewing his threats to make a manager change. But by now Michael had had his fill.

"I'm sick and tired of your threats, George," Michael said, his voice rising. "I can't take this anymore. If you want to fire me, then get your fat ass out here to Chicago and just do it!"

"You just wait," Steinbrenner shot back. "I'll be there."

An hour later, Michael received a call from team president Lou Saban.

"Whatever it was you two guys talked about, it's off," Saban said. "He's not coming to Chicago. He wouldn't tell me what it was."

"I'll tell you what it was," Michael said. "I challenged him."

That afternoon, in the visiting manager's office of Comiskey Park, Michael challenged Steinbrenner again—only this time publicly, in the presence of the Yankees beat reporters. Unprompted, Michael abruptly shifted the topic of conversation from Jackson's physical to his own situation, saying, "I heard from George again today, and I'm tired of getting these phone calls after games and being told it's my fault if we lost. So when he said it again to me today, I said: 'Fine. Do it now. Don't wait. I don't want to manage under these circumstances.'"

At first, the writers thought Michael was just joking around with them. But as soon as he looked at them, unsmiling, and said, "I'm serious," they scurried from his office and up to the press box to feverishly type their stories. Later that night, at the hotel bar, Michael confided to Moss Klein of the Newark *Star-Ledger*, "I know I'm going to be fired for this, but I wanted to get it out there . . . what it's like to work for this guy. Howser would have gone through the same thing, but he had me as a buffer. I don't have any buffer."

Steinbrenner didn't fire Michael right away. Rather, he maintained an ominous silence, explaining during an interview on the NBC Saturday *Game of the Week* that he was still trying to make up his mind. This prompted Michael to call him in Tampa, but not for the reason Steinbrenner had hoped. In Steinbrenner's version of the phone call, which he later relayed to reporters, he told Michael he hadn't meant to threaten him but also reminded him that he was the owner of the team and that "when you take your boss on publicly, you can't just get away with it."

Steinbrenner said he was hoping that Michael would then apologize. "I begged him to say 'I'm sorry,'" he said, "but he wouldn't say it. I wasn't going to put him in front of a microphone, I just wanted him to say he made a mistake." When Michael didn't, Steinbrenner made good on his threats. "Under these conditions, I had no choice. There was no question he would do the same thing again. This was the toughest decision I ever had to make, because I nurtured him."

"I've got no reason to apologize, because I didn't do anything wrong," Michael told reporters.

Hoping to achieve the same dramatic improvement of play by his team as in 1978, when he'd fired Billy Martin, Steinbrenner once again called on Bob Lemon to bring the team home. This time, however, the results were mixed. After finishing out the "second season" 10-14 under Lemon, the Yankees won the first two games of that year's special best-of-five Division Series against the Brewers in Milwaukee, only to lose the next two games at Yankee Stadium. After the game four loss at home, Steinbrenner stormed into the Yankee clubhouse and began blistering his players. As he ranted about all the mental mistakes and shoddy base running in the 2–1 loss, Steinbrenner was shocked to be interrupted by a voice in the back of the room. "Fuck you, George!" Rick Cerone said. "You don't know what you're talking about. You don't know a fucking thing about baseball!"

Momentarily stunned, Steinbrenner glared at Cerone, and then shot back: "It's over. You're gone next year!"

(A couple of weeks earlier, still miffed that Cerone had beaten him in arbitration, Steinbrenner had singled out the catcher for the bad year he was having. "He's gotten a big head," Steinbrenner told reporters. "Suddenly, he's 'Mr. New York,' 'The Italian Stallion.' He's going to disco joints. I have a way of bringing guys down to size, and I'll bring him down or he may not be here.")

But after the Yankees responded to Steinbrenner's latest clubhouse dressing-down by dispatching the Brewers 7–3 in game five—ironically, with the help of a two-run homer by Cerone—the owner was ebullient. "They did it!" he crowed to reporters afterward. "They rose to the occasion. I can't say enough about them."

But that was the last time in that 1981 season there would be such an aura of good feelings. Even after sweeping the Oakland A's, now managed by Billy Martin, in the American League Championship Series, the team was frayed. At the victory party at Vince's restaurant, down the street from the Oakland Coliseum, a scuffle erupted between Jackson and Graig Nettles. Jackson had shown up at the party with an entourage of family and friends, who inadvertently took over the table where Nettles and his wife, Ginger, had been sitting. When Ginger Nettles came back from the buffet and didn't see her purse, her husband verbally confronted Jackson. After a heated exchange, Nettles punched Jackson, knocking him to the floor. Steinbrenner was in the hallway outside during the commotion, but when he came back in, he wasted no time in deciding who the culprit was.

"God dammit, Reggie, you're embarrassing me again," he exclaimed before ordering everyone out to the buses. The *Daily News'* Dick Young was at the party and phoned in a front-page story for the next day's editions in which he quoted Steinbrenner as saying, "I've had it up to here with Reggie. He's got to be the boss of everything. He has to be the big shot and run everything. Well, he's not going to get away with it anymore. This is it." According to Young, Steinbrenner was infuriated because it was supposed to have been a "family only" party and Reggie, in the owner's opinion, had deliberately flaunted that by bringing friends. Not surprisingly, Steinbrenner's reaction further embittered Jackson, who told Young, "I haven't liked the dude for 10 years. I'm tired of this nigger-nigger shit. I don't care if I play in the World Series or not. I don't have a contract anyway."

What is it about being careful for what you wish for?

Because of a calf injury he suffered in the Oakland series, Jackson and Lemon had already agreed that he would sit out the first two games of the 1981 World Series against the Los Angeles Dodgers, giving him a full five days of rest and therapy. After the Yankees won the first two games of the Series in New York, he was eager to become part of October again. He was especially anxious to face Fernando Valenzuela, the Dodgers' game three starter, who had been the sensation of baseball in 1981. Signed as a free agent out of the Mexican League, Valenzuela, with his herky-jerky delivery and mystifying screwball, had begun the season with 36 consecutive scoreless innings before going on to lead the National League in strike-outs and complete games. "We'll see about all this Fernandomania shit," Jackson said confidently to his teammates after game two. But when he approached Lemon before game three to confirm his availability, he found the manager's response strangely distant.

"Just to be on the safe side, I think I'm gonna hold you out one more game, Reg," Lemon said.

Jackson couldn't believe what he was hearing. He began to argue, only to be cut off tersely by Lemon: "One more day." That's when he realized it was not Lemon's decision. It had been dictated from above. "The sonofa-bitch," Jackson said to a couple of reporters. "He's so determined to take me down, now he's even taking October from Mr. October."

With Jackson on the bench and Graig Nettles also sidelined with a sprained thumb, the Yankees lost game three, 5–4, as Valenzuela pitched a complete game, giving up nine hits. Restored to the lineup for game four, Jackson went 3 for 3 with a home run and two RBI, but he also lost a fly ball in the sun in the sixth inning that led to a Dodger run, and the Yankees lost again, 8–7. The Series now tied, Steinbrenner came into the clubhouse after the game threatening all sorts of repercussions if the team didn't right itself. "For one thing," he said, "we're instituting a curfew. I want all of you in your rooms by 10 o'clock." In response to this, Lemon told reporters, "Even George's horses lose sometimes, but he doesn't go out and shoot 'em."

Despite the curfew, the Yankees lost game five in Los Angeles, 2–1. That night, David Szen, the new Yankees publicity director, was just doz-ing off in his room at the Hyatt Wilshire Hotel when the phone rang. It was Steinbrenner, asking him to come up to his suite. When Szen got there, Steinbrenner was there with team trainer Gene Monahan. Steinbrenner told him how he had been in the elevator, on his way downstairs to meet his friend and former Yankees limited partner Sheldon Guren for dinner. When the elevator stopped at the seventh floor, two drunk Dodgers fans got on. "Steinbrenner, huh?" one of them said. "Go back to those animals in New York and take those choking ballplayers with you!"

"Well, I wasn't going to take that," Steinbrenner told Szen. "I said some-thing back, and one of them slugged me with a beer bottle. I hit him back

AIMING HIGH: Steinbrenner was a high hurdler at Culver Military Academy and Williams College (pictured here). George won his share of races, but wasn't the world-class hurdler his father was, and Henry Steinbrenner never let his son forget it. *(Williams College)*

"YOU'RE FIRED": In 1955, Steinbrenner *(second from right)* got a taste of the medicine he'd be famous for. As an assistant football coach at Northwestern, Steinbrenner would be canned along with head coach Lou Saban *(far left)* and the rest of the staff after the team went 0-8-1. Years later, Saban would work for George as president of the Yankees. *(Northwestern University)*

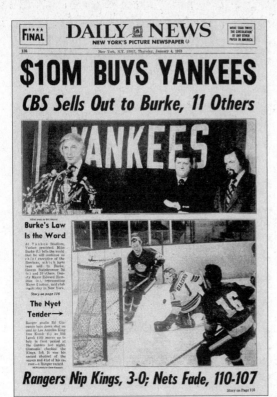

WHAT A BARGAIN: On January 4, 1973, the New York papers reported the sale of the Yankees for $10 million from CBS. Not only was Steinbrenner left out of the headline, he had to share the back page with hockey. Nearly 40 years later, the Yankees were valued at over $1 billion. *(Daily News)*

MEET THE NEW BOSS: At the January 1973 press conference to announce Gabe Paul *(center)* as the new Yankees president, George Steinbrenner *(left)* and Mike Burke *(right)* are all smiles. But it wouldn't be long before Burke discovered that Paul had been brought in by Steinbrenner to replace him in running the baseball operations. On April 25, 1973, Burke resigned as Yankees general partner. *(Daily News)*

A NOSE FOR WINNERS: George Steinbrenner's second passion after baseball was horses. Even before owning the Yankees, he had bought an 860-acre farm in Ocala, Florida, where he raised Thoroughbred horses. Over the years, he produced more than 35 stakes winners, including the 2005 Wood Memorial winner, Bellamy Road. *(Daily News)*

DO YOU KNOW "TAKE ME OUT TO THE BALLGAME"? An accomplished pianist and organist, Steinbrenner performed frequently at Williams College, and in May 1987 was a guest conductor of the New York Pops. *(Daily News)*

MR. AND MRS. BOSS: Cheering on the Yankees at a 2006 spring training game. For the first 30 years that he owned the Yankees, George Steinbrenner and his wife, Joan *(left)*, were rarely seen, much less photographed, together at games, and it was no secret that their relationship was strained. Standing in the center is Norma King, wife of longtime advisor Clyde King. *(Daily News)*

THE CLEVELAND CONNECTION: Growing up an Indians fan in Cleveland, George Steinbrenner idolized Al Rosen *(right)*, the Indians third baseman and 1953 American League MVP. Rosen would later work for Steinbrenner as Yankees president, but after just a year and half (1978–79) he quit, turning down a lifetime contract. *(Daily News)*

BUYING A LEMON: Though he enjoyed the occasional laugh with Bob Lemon, Steinbrenner mostly harangued the Yankees manager and his coaches until he fired Lemon 14 games into the '82 season. It was the second time Steinbrenner had fired Lemon as Yankees manager, but unlike Al Rosen, Lemon accepted a lifetime contract as a scout. *(Daily News)*

ON TOP OF THE WORLD AGAIN: In 1977, Steinbrenner celebrated the first Yankees championship since 1962, with Yogi Berra *(left)* and manager Billy Martin *(right)*. *(Daily News)*

TASTES GREAT, LESS FILLING: In the summer of 1978, George Steinbrenner and Billy Martin shot a beer commercial in which they spoofed their rocky relationship. After they argued over the merits of Miller Lite, the commercial ended with George telling Billy, "You're fired!" and Billy saying, "Oh, no, not again!" Three weeks later, George fired Billy for real. *(Daily News)*

HERE WE GO AGAIN: Steinbrenner fired Martin for a second time in 1979. There would be three more firings, but their tumultuous relationship would end on Christmas Day 1989, when Billy Martin died in a car crash.

IN THE LINE OF FIRING:
Steinbrenner fired Dick Howser
(right) even after the Yankees
had won 103 games in 1980, and
then tried to convince reporters
that Howser had quit to pursue a
real estate deal in Florida. Gene
Michael *(left)* replaced Howser
in the dugout in 1981, but was
himself fired halfway through the
season. *(Daily News)*

THE MELEE IN L.A.:
Following the Yankees' loss to
the Dodgers in the 1981 World
Series, Steinbrenner got into a fight
with two Dodgers fans in a hotel
elevator in Los Angeles, injuring
his left hand. *Daily News* columnist
Dick Young dictated the story (as
recounted to him by Steinbrenner)
over the phone in time to make the
front page of the final edition *(left)*.
(Daily News)

BACK TO THE FUTURE: In January 1985, *The Sporting News* arranged a photo shoot to display the uniform collection of Yankees limited partner Barry Halper *(far left)*. Rickey Henderson is wearing (appropriately) Ty Cobb's Detroit Tigers uniform *(front row, left)*, while Steinbrenner *(front, center)* is dressed as legendary Yankees owner Jacob Ruppert, with Yogi Berra to his left and John Montefusco, Mike Armstrong and Jeff Torborg standing behind them. *(Rich Pilling)*

MUSICAL BENCHES. In 1987, Steinbrenner fired Lou Piniella *(right)* as manager, moved him upstairs as general manager, and then replaced him with Billy Martin *(left)*. Halfway through 1988, he fired Martin for the fifth time and replaced him with Piniella, whom he fired when the season was over. *(Daily News)*

WITH FRIENDS LIKE THESE . . . : George Steinbrenner and Dave Winfield smiling broadly after announcing in September 1989 the end of their long-standing feud over the Winfield Foundation. An arbitrator had agreed with most of Steinbrenner's charges about the foundation's wasteful spending, and the dispute was resolved with Winfield cutting a check for $30,000 in reimbursement and another $229,000 in delinquent payments to the foundation. *(Daily News)*

HE RUINED MY LIFE! Howie Spira, who was paid $40,000 by George Steinbrenner for providing dirt on outfielder Dave Winfield, was later accused of extortion by the Yankees owner. He was found guilty and sentenced to 30 months in a federal penitentiary. *(Daily News)*

YER OUT! Baseball commissioner Fay Vincent *(above, right)* declared a lifetime sentence on Steinbrenner for associating with Howie Spira, an admitted gambler. The papers saw this as the end of the Steinbrenner era *(right)*, but ultimately the Boss got himself reinstated to baseball, and Vincent was fired by the owners. *(Alan Solomon)*

MANHATTAN ★ ★ ★ SPORTS FINAL

DAILY ◉ NEWS

NEW YORK'S PICTURE NEWSPAPER®   Tuesday, July 31, 199

GONE!

The Boss gets the thumb: Loses control of the Yankees

FULL COVERAGE BEGINS ON PAGES 4 & 5

THE EGOS HAVE LANDED: Reggie Jackson claimed that a candy bar would be named after him if he played in New York. He was right. Despite their contentious relationship, in the late 1990s Steinbrenner eventually brought Mr. October into his inner circle of Yankees advisors. (*Daily News*)

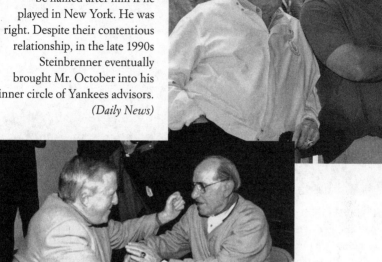

WELCOME HOME, YOGI: When Steinbrenner fired Yogi Berra (*above, right*) as Yankees manager after only 16 games of the 1985 season, Berra vowed he would never come back to Yankee Stadium unless Steinbrenner sold the team. For 14 years he kept that vow, until January 5, 1999, when a peace accord was brokered at Yogi's museum in Montclair, New Jersey. (*Daily News*)

BACK IN THE SADDLE: Despite advice from Yankees president Jack Lawn to "come back humble," Steinbrenner posed for the cover of *Sports Illustrated* as Napoleon returning from exile. (*Getty Images*)

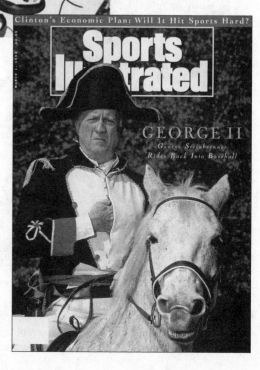

Clinton's Economic Plan: Will It Hit Sports Hard?

Sports Illustrated

GEORGE II
George Steinbrenner Rides Back Into Baseball

SHORTSTOP ON A SHORT LEASH: In December 2005, Steinbrenner complained about Yankees captain Derek Jeter *(left)* staying out "until 3 A.M. in New York City, going to a birthday party. . . . That doesn't sit well with me." Steinbrenner and Jeter would later tape a Visa commercial, which ended with the Boss and the star shortstop dancing together in a conga line. *(Daily News)*

LIVE FROM NEW YORK, IT'S THE BOSS: Steinbrenner hosted *Saturday Night Live* in October 1990. In one scene, he appeared with his pants down in front of a female sportswriter. The same night Steinbrenner appeared on the show, Lou Piniella won the World Series as manager of the Cincinnati Reds. *(Daily News)*

TRUE DIVAS: George Steinbrenner's love of music extended to the opera; two of his close friends, Beverly Sills and Robert Merrill, were icons of the Metropolitan Opera. Merrill regularly performed the national anthem at Yankee Stadium on Opening Day and Old-Timers' Day and during the postseason wearing a Yankees jersey with the number ½ on the back. *(Daily News)*

THREE AMIGOS: Throughout the 1970s and 1980s, two of George Steinbrenner's closest friends were Robert Merrill *(center)* and the legendary broadcaster Howard Cosell *(right)*. *(Daily News)*

THE GODFATHER OF TAMPA: In his adopted south Florida hometown, George was a regular at Malio's, where the Boss held court with his friends and Yankees officials. Malio Iavarone *(left)* even named a room for Steinbrenner and reserved it for him, as well as a separate phone line. It was in this room in February 1999 that Steinbrenner and the Yankees consummated the David Wells–for–Roger Clemens trade. *(Malio Iavarone)*

GEORGE'S GIRLS: Iconic TV journalist Barbara Walters *(above)* first met George Steinbrenner in Cuba during the 1970s. She was there to interview Premier Fidel Castro, and Steinbrenner was there on a secret mission to scout Cuban baseball players. *(Daily News)* New York restaurateur Elaine Kauffman *(below)* befriended Steinbrenner in 1973, when he first came to New York. He spent many a night in her restaurant wooing free agents such as Reggie Jackson and Dave Winfield, and celebrating championships.

THE HOUSE THAT GEORGE BUILT: Steinbrenner often complained about Yankee Stadium, built in 1923. Finally, in 2006, New York City issued $1.2 billion in bonds to construct a new Yankee Stadium across 161st Street from the old stadium. In August 2006, a frail Steinbrenner took part in the groundbreaking with Mayor Michael Bloomberg *(right)* and other city officials. *(Daily News)*

LEAVING HOME: In its final season the old Yankee Stadium hosted the 2008 All-Star Game. It was also an occasion for Yankees fans to pay tribute to George Steinbrenner, who had presided there as the team's owner over six world championships. Prior to the game, Steinbrenner toured the stadium in a golf cart with his family, including his older daughter, Jennifer *(right)*. *(Daily News)*

WHO'S THE BOSS?
For the first six years, George Steinbrenner had a better relationship with Joe Torre *(right)* than with any of his 13 previous managers, helped considerably by the fact that Torre had won four world championships from 1996 to 2000. But when Torre stopped winning championships, the relationship soured, and in 2008 it ended badly, like all the others. *(Daily News)*

KINGS OF NEW YORK: After winning back-to-back world championships in 1977 and 1978, George Steinbrenner had to wait 18 years for another. But once Joe Torre *(right)* won in 1996, the parade down New York City's Canyon of Heroes became a yearly event, as the Yankees repeated their victory in 1998, 1999 and 2000. Here Steinbrenner and Torre celebrate with the team's self-proclaimed number one fan, Mayor Rudy Giuliani *(center). (Daily News)*

YES MAN: Forming his Yankees Entertainment and Sports Network and building a new Yankee Stadium helped George Steinbrenner turn his initial 1973 investment of $168,000 into a business worth more than $1 billion, and enabled him to amass the highest payroll in baseball.

STEINBRENNER: THE NEXT GENERATION: As Steinbrenner's health continued to fail after 2006, it became necessary for him to relinquish control of the Yankees and "let the young elephants into the tent," as he was fond of saying. In 2008, Steinbrenner's youngest son, Hal *(right)*, took over as managing general partner of the Yankees, joining team president Randy Levine *(center)* and CEO Lonn Trost *(left)* as the brain trust of operations. *(Daily News)*

THE PROUDEST YANKEE: Steinbrenner strolls the grounds of the Yankees' spring training complex in Fort Lauderdale, Florida. *(Linda Catafo/Daily News)*

and knocked out a couple of his teeth. Then I got into it with the other guy. I left 'em both on the seventh floor. I'm okay, but we're gonna have to round up the press. They'll need to know the story."

As soon as he had sat down in the hotel dining room, Steinbrenner's hand started to throb. He went back to his suite and called Monahan and the team physician, Dr. Jack Bonamo. Upon cursory examination, Bonamo determined that Steinbrenner had broken a bone in his right hand and would have to go to the hospital to have it put in a cast.

"No way," Steinbrenner had protested. "You can do it here, Doc. I'm not going to the hospital."

"But I don't have any of the materials here," Bonamo said.

"Well, just tell Gene here what you need and he'll go to the hospital and bring everything back here."

Armed with a list of medical supplies, Monahan and his assistant Barry Weinberg took a cab to a nearby hospital, where they were met with unexpected resistance from an emergency room receptionist.

"This woman flat out refused to let us have anything we needed," Monahan recalled in a 2008 interview. "So I finally told Barry: 'Do whatever you can to distract her, even if you have to get into a big argument with her'—which he did. While they were arguing, I ran behind the desk and grabbed all the materials off the shelf and we dashed out of the hospital with them."

It took Bonamo about 30 minutes to patch Steinbrenner up and wrap his wrist, after which the owner called Szen to summon all the reporters to his suite. By the time they arrived, it was nearly 2 A.M. New York time, past most of their newspapers' final deadlines.

As Steinbrenner, his hand heavily bandaged in a makeshift cast, began recounting his tale to the stunned reporters, Dick Young suddenly got up from his chair, walked across the room, picked up the phone from the desk and began dialing. It was apparent that Young, wearing a bathrobe, was still groggy from being woken up after having indulged in a few red wines at the hotel bar. He hollered into the phone, "This is Young; get me rewrite right now! I'm out here at the World Series and Steinbrenner's been in a fight. I gotta dictate something."

"Wait a minute, Dick!" Steinbrenner exclaimed. "What are you doing? I told you this is just a briefing for you guys. It's not to be written!"

"This is news," Young shot back. "A thing like this you don't keep out of the newspaper."

As Steinbrenner and the rest of the reporters looked on helplessly, Young began dictating:

"Yankee president George Steinbrenner was attacked—"

"Wait a minute, Dick," Steinbrenner said, "I'm not the president of the Yankees. I'm the *owner* of the Yankees!"

"Oh, yeah," Young muttered. "Change that to say 'Yankee *owner* George Steinbrenner . . . was attacked in the elevator of the Los Angeles hotel where the Dodgers are staying, by two men—"

"The *Dodgers?*" Steinbrenner said. "The Dodgers aren't staying here. *We're* staying here!"

All of a sudden Steinbrenner, who had insisted the story not be written, was now serving as Young's editor as the 63-year-old veteran baseball scribe continued to dictate details of the elevator incident to the *Daily News*. When Young described Steinbrenner as using "a left-right combo, sending the guy sailing out of the elevator onto the corridor floor," everyone in the room began giggling at the absurdity of the situation.

"Then Steinbrenner said he picked up the first man, who was slumped against the elevator wall, and threw him on top of his companion."

Young's story appeared on the front page of the next day's *Daily News* under the headline STEINBRENNER KOS 2 IN BRAWL.

The team was sitting on the bus outside the hotel the next morning, waiting to go to the Los Angeles airport for the trip home, when the owner himself got on, sporting his heavily wrapped hand and the Band-Aid on his forehead where he'd been wounded by the beer bottle. They'd heard about the scuffle and tried to conceal their smiles. Nettles slunk down in his seat, hoping the owner wouldn't see him. Too late. Steinbrenner strode down the aisle, stopping at the third baseman's seat, and demanded, "Where the hell were you when I needed you last night?"

Given that opening, the quick-witted Nettles replied: "I was in bed, George. Don't you remember you told us we all had to be in by ten o'clock!"

In the years that followed, Steinbrenner's elevator fight became legend.

Ever-skeptical reporters, convinced Steinbrenner had made up the whole tale—neither of the two fans ever threatened to sue—would speculate endlessly as to what really happened: Steinbrenner punched a wall after the game five loss; he got in a fight with his wife; he made up the story to inspire his team. Whether he cleaned the floor with his two assailants, as Young so colorfully described, is subject to conjecture. But Dave Szen remembered hearing one of the two fans, identified only as "John M.," being interviewed on the sports talk radio station KABC in Los Angeles the next day. His story was similar to the one Steinbrenner told, except the fan said Steinbrenner must have hurt his hand when his punch landed on the elevator door as his friend ducked.

In a 2008 interview, Jack Bonamo told me, "George's right hand was swollen around the knuckles with abrasions on the fourth and fifth metacarpals, consistent with having been in a fight."

Unfortunately for Steinbrenner, the fight did not inspire the Yankees to a World Series comeback over the Dodgers. Nor did it alleviate any of the tension and unrest plaguing the team that year, much of it the result of Steinbrenner's incessant criticism and manic behavior. All it did was set the stage for the final indignity of the 1981 season: the apology.

Upon returning home to Yankee Stadium and sitting out a day of rain, the Yankees were thrashed 9–2 in game six. In only the fourth inning, Lemon pinch-hit Bobby Murcer for his starting pitcher, Tommy John, with the score tied 1–1. John was astounded by the decision and could be seen waving his arms in disgust in the Yankee dugout when Murcer flied out, leaving runners at first and second. The next inning the Dodgers scored three runs off reliever George Frazier and tacked on four more in the sixth.

Right after that four-run Dodger sixth, I was sitting in the press box when I felt a tap on my shoulder. It was Irv Kaze, the Yankees' VP of media relations.

"Have you got a minute?" Kaze asked. "George wants to see you in his office."

I couldn't imagine what this could be about—had I written something that angered Steinbrenner?—but I certainly wasn't going to pass up what figured to be an exclusive in-game rant from the Yankees owner. I followed Kaze down the corridor behind the press box to Steinbrenner's office. The curtains had been drawn across the windows looking onto the field and the room was dark. Steinbrenner was sitting at his desk, and across the room were Ed Broderick and his friend Bill Fugazy.

"It's pretty awful, isn't it?" Steinbrenner said.

"It's not real good," I said.

"Well, I just want to tell you, Billy, I'm embarrassed. These players have embarrassed me and embarrassed New York, and I want the fans to know that. Here, take a look at this."

He shoved a piece of a paper across the desk. It was an official Yankees press release, with the Yankees logo across the top, on which he had typewritten, "*I want to sincerely apologize to the people of New York and to the fans of the New York Yankees everywhere for the performance of the Yankee team in the World Series. I also want to assure you that we will be at work immediately to prepare for 1982. I want also to extend my congratulations to Peter O'Malley and the Dodger organization—and to my friend, Tom Lasorda, who managed a superb season, playoffs and a brilliant World Series. Sincerely, George M. Steinbrenner.*"

I finished reading and looked up.

"Well, what do you think?" Steinbrenner asked.

"I don't know, George," I said. "You're the owner. If this is the way you feel . . . I just don't know how the players are going to react."

"I don't give a shit what the players think," he snapped. "They let me down. They let New York down."

Not surprisingly, the players were outraged by the apology, which Steinbrenner had distributed in the press box as soon as the game was over. A few months after his 2008 induction into the Hall of Fame, Goose Gossage said to me, "George was the greatest owner I ever played for, but he was crazed that whole postseason in '81, and after all the shit he pulled in the World Series, with the Reggie benching, the elevator fight and the apology, I said to myself: 'In two years I'm out of here.'"

Of all the players, perhaps only one shared Steinbrenner's embarrassment. Dave Winfield went 1 for 22 with one RBI in his first World Series. A couple of days after the final game, he stopped by Yankee Stadium on his way out of town and went up to Steinbrenner's office, where he found the owner sitting at his desk with his chin in his hand, still seemingly brooding over the loss.

"I just wanted to tell you, Boss, I owe you one," Winfield said. "We'll get 'em next year, that's a promise."

Steinbrenner managed a weak smile.

"Yeah," the owner agreed. "That's a promise."

He never dreamed it was a promise that would take another 15 years to keep.

11

. . .

Chaos: Reggie's Revenge, Umpire Wars and Pine Tar Follies

. . .

ALMOST FROM THE MOMENT he finished penning his apology to the fans, George Steinbrenner became consumed with overhauling his baseball team for the 1982 season. "I'm tired of sitting around waiting for the three-run homer," he declared to his baseball people after the last game of the Series. "We're gonna change that."

The core of the '77 and '78 championship teams needed to be replaced, he decided—most of all Reggie Jackson, who finished the abbreviated '81 split season with a .237 average and 15 homers in 94 games. The success of the Philadelphia Phillies and Kansas City Royals, who both played on artificial turf and relied on quick players rather than sluggers, had further convinced Steinbrenner that speed, not power, was the way to go in baseball in the new decade. On November 4, the Yankees pulled off a shocker of a deal by acquiring All-Star Cincinnati Reds outfielder Ken Griffey, a career .307 hitter, for two unproven minor league pitchers, Brian Ryder and Freddie Toliver. Even more shocking was the whopping three-year, $2.475 million free-agent contract they gave another Reds outfielder, Dave Collins, two days before Christmas. Though the 29-year-old Collins had hit a respectable .272 in 1981, he was considered an ordinary slap-hitting corner outfielder who had tailed off precipitously from 79 steals in 1980 to 26 in '81. It turned out that Steinbrenner had been motivated to sign him after hearing that the Royals, now managed by Dick Howser, were hot to sign him. (This amused Howser, who would later tell reporters that the Royals weren't prepared to go beyond one year for Collins.)

After taking six weeks to think about it, Steinbrenner announced during the baseball winter meetings in Florida that Bob Lemon would return as manager. Steinbrenner, who'd considered making Lemon the fall guy for the '81 World Series loss, was impressed by the manager's healthy, trimmed-down appearance. (Lemon had reported to the winter meetings 24 pounds lighter, down to a svelte 210, after swearing off hard liquor.) "When I met Lem here, I couldn't believe my eyes," Steinbrenner said to reporters. "He looked great and so well rested, and he lost all that weight! I was uncertain as to what I was going to do, but when he asked me for one more year, that was it. He's always been there for me when I needed him, so I owed him. This time, he'll get a full season, no matter what."

Steinbrenner also announced that "Stick" Michael, who had become a scout after being replaced by Lemon in September, would return as manager for the 1983, '84 and '85 seasons.

Before the start of spring training, Steinbrenner, without consulting with anyone, gave aging outfielders Lou Piniella and Bobby Murcer new three-year contracts. By rewarding Piniella and Murcer for past performance, it appeared Steinbrenner was hedging his bet on the "speed game" he had seemed so eager to implement. Birdie Tebbetts, Steinbrenner's chief scout, was dumbfounded by the decision. "All this time, he told me he was phasing those two guys out," Tebbetts complained to me one day that spring. "If I'd known he was gonna bring them both back, I'd have never recommended Griffey and Collins. Where are we supposed to play all these guys?"

Lemon wondered the same thing. With Piniella, Murcer, Winfield, Jerry Mumphrey, Oscar Gamble and now Griffey, there was certainly no room in the outfield for the $800,000-per-year Collins, who was instead handed a first-base glove, a position he'd never played before, when he reported to camp. "They gave me this guy and told me to play him, but what the hell am I supposed to do with him?" Lemon said with exasperation to reporters. "We got better guys than him at every position!" Collins was equally bewildered. All spring he would ask reporters, "Why did they want me here? Are they trying to trade me?"

Actually, Collins's place on the team was hardly Lemon's biggest concern that preseason. Steinbrenner ordered everyone into camp a week early, whereupon they were handed navy blue jumpsuits instead of uniforms and introduced to Harrison Dillard, the '48 and '52 Olympic high hurdles gold medalist, who put the team through running drills. They would not don pinstripes until the actual games began. "Those sweatpants were so damn heavy, they wore you down," remembered Piniella, "and we weren't allowed to touch a bat for the first two weeks. If you wanted to take a little hitting, you had to go down the street and pay $10 to use the public cages!"

With Dillard conducting running drills, culminating each day with 45-yard sprint races in which he'd pair off two players at a time and put a stopwatch on them, the Yankees' "track camp" got the attention of the national media that spring—though not exactly the kind of attention Steinbrenner had anticipated. After the first few days, Mike Lupica wrote a column in the *Daily News* mocking what he dubbed "the Bronx Roadrunners"—which sent Steinbrenner into a rage. (It was Lupica who a couple of years earlier had first referred to Steinbrenner as "the Boss," a nickname that soon became the owner's permanent title. "It came to me after reading Mike Royko's book *Boss*, about Chicago's Mayor Daley," Lupica explained. "Here was this blustery old machine politician laying waste to anyone who got in his way, and I said to myself: 'That's our guy! He runs Yankee Stadium the way Daley ran Chicago!'")

Lupica's column was written in the form of a letter from New York to "George (Boss) Steinbrenner, Commander-in-Chief, New York Yankees." *"Sorry I haven't been able to join you down there in Florida as you were hoping,"* it read, *"but I expect to arrive shortly because I, like you, am really into track and field."* Lupica concluded the column by poking Steinbrenner: *"You know how I swoon at those photographs of the designer jogging outfits."*

"The little sonofabitch isn't even here!" Steinbrenner growled to his PR director, Irv Kaze. "This isn't funny! I want his credentials pulled when he gets here. And tell all the other writers they better not write any more smart-ass shit about what we're doing here if they ever want to get a return phone call from me!"

(Kaze was let off the hook when Lupica didn't show up at camp until a couple of weeks later, by which time Steinbrenner had forgotten about the column.)

For the rest of the spring, Steinbrenner was in a constant state of agitation, fueled no doubt by the Yankees' desultory (9-16) play in the Grapefruit League. They failed to steal bases the way he'd envisioned, and they weren't hitting as many home runs as they had in the past. After each loss, Steinbrenner would order Lemon and all the coaches to a meeting in his executive trailer alongside Fort Lauderdale Stadium, where, for two hours, he would harangue them about the team's failure. This forced the writers to hang around until midnight after night games, our only source of entertainment being to watch Joan Steinbrenner power-walking around the trailer as she waited for her husband to finish berating his coaching staff.

By midspring, Lemon was once again hitting the hard stuff. One night he was with a couple of reporters at the restaurant across the street from the Yankees' hotel, where he ordered a Canadian Club and water.

"Oh, I'm sorry," the waitress said, "but we only serve wine or beer here."

Frowning, Lemon rolled his eyes and said, "For Chrissakes, don't tell me the asshole owns *this* place too!"

Realizing that his attempt to implement a "speed game" had been a colossal waste of time and energy, Steinbrenner had begun frantically reshuffling the roster. He acquired Butch Hobson, a washed-up third baseman, from the California Angels, with the idea of having him platoon with the switch-hitting Collins at first base and hopefully provide a little power at the position. And on March 30, Steinbrenner acquired right-handed pitcher Doyle Alexander from the San Francisco Giants. Although Alexander had won 25 games for the Giants over the previous two seasons, his dour disposition did not endear him to his teammates or to reporters. Indeed, the Yankees were able to get him only because he'd become embroiled in an acrimonious salary dispute with the Giants, which was resolved when Steinbrenner gave him a four-year, $2.2 million contract extension to approve the trade to New York. The Alabama-born Alexander hated New York, but for that kind of money he was willing to go anywhere. Lemon was in his room at the Galt, watching his favorite TV show, *Barnaby Jones*, when I called him for comment on the trade.

"I hear you got yourself a new pitcher, Lem," I said.

"Oh?" Lemon replied. "I'm just the manager here, and the last person to know anything. Who am I getting?"

"Doyle Alexander."

After a few seconds of silence, I heard a sigh on the other end of the phone. "Just what I need, another hemorrhoid."

By the time the '82 season began, Lemon was already a beaten man. The meetings, the nightly phone calls from Steinbrenner, and the constant threats had worn him down. Riding together in a taxi on our way to dinner at Miller's Pub in Chicago on the opening road trip of the season, Lemon said to me, "I've had it, Meat. I can't take this guy any longer. No matter what I do, I can't please him. I'm gonna quit."

"Quit? What are you talking about, Lem?" I said. "You can't be serious."

"Serious as I've ever been, Meat. I'm only telling you this 'cause you've been a good friend. I don't need this aggravation. Life is too short."

"You can't quit, Lem," I said. "If you do, you're liable not to get your money, and I'd hate for that to happen to you. You've got to play it out. If nothing else, wait till he fires you. At least then you'll get paid for all the aggravation he's given you."

"I'll think about it," Lemon said.

It turned out Lemon only had to think about it another few days. After winning two games in Chicago, the Yankees came home and lost three out of four to the Detroit Tigers. With their record at 6-8, Steinbrenner announced he was replacing Lemon with Michael—so much for that "full season, no matter what." But at least Lemon got paid, and not only that, got paid for life: Steinbrenner gave him a lifetime scouting contract for $50,000 per year.

As Lemon's case illustrated, Steinbrenner could be heartless and magnanimous in almost the same gesture. And when it came to people in need—often people with no connection to baseball or the Yankees, whom he met either in person or through friends or the media—his benevolence knew few bounds.

A couple of months before the '82 season began, Steinbrenner was having lunch in Manhattan with his friend Jim Fuchs, the former world shot-put record holder and '48 and '52 Olympian. On the news that morning,

Steinbrenner had seen the funeral of a slain New York City policeman, and had been particularly struck by the visage of the officer's widow, flanked by her four small children, accepting a folded American flag.

"Who's gonna pay for those kids' education?" Steinbrenner said to Fuchs.

"I don't know," Fuchs said.

"We have to do something."

"What do you have in mind?"

"We'll start a foundation, and you'll run it."

"How do you start a foundation?" Fuchs asked.

"You go out and raise a lot of money and then you give it away!"

"Well," said Fuchs, "I do have a lot of wealthy friends. I'll get 100 of them to give $1,000 apiece."

"That's good," said Steinbrenner, "and for my part, I'll donate the entire gate receipts from one of our games. I've got the perfect game to do it with. On April 27 the Angels come to the Stadium. It'll be Reggie's first time back. We should have a real big house. It'll be a great night!"

From that casual lunch, Steinbrenner formed the Silver Shield Foundation, which, from 1982 until 2000, paid for the college educations of over 200 sons and daughters of New York City police and firemen, New York Port Authority officers and New York, New Jersey and Connecticut state troopers killed in the line of duty. In the aftermath of 9/11, it paid for 700 more, and after that it expanded its bounds to accept corporate donations. By 2010, the foundation had an endowment of nearly $4 million.

Michael's first game in his second term as Yankees manager, April 27, happened to be that same night Jackson made his return to Yankee Stadium wearing the uniform of the California Angels, with whom he'd signed as a free agent on January 22. To that point in the season, Jackson was hitting .173 with no homers—numbers that, ordinarily, would have earned him a seat on the bench against a lefty as formidable as Ron Guidry. But Angels manager Gene Mauch had been in baseball since 1943 and understood that this was a unique circumstance. Calling Jackson aside before the game, Mauch said: "Don't worry, Reggie. I know you have to be in there tonight."

Mauch's instincts told him that Jackson's desire to prove Steinbrenner wrong would somehow bring out Reggie's flair for the dramatic. It happened in the seventh inning, just before the rains came to end the game early. Having singled and scored the go-ahead run on a suicide squeeze in the fifth inning, Jackson came to bat in the seventh inning with the Angels leading 2–1 and Guidry still dealing. Reggie could hear the 35,458 fans—who had stayed in the rain—cheering for him, as if it were 1977 all over again. On his first pitch, Guidry hung a slider over the plate. Jackson's eyes widened as he swung mightily and launched a towering drive to right field that just kept on rising until it struck the facing of the upper deck and fell back onto the field. As Yankee right fielder Ken Griffey calmly retrieved the ball and tossed it back into the infield and Jackson began his tour of the bases, the crowd erupted, the roar crystallizing into a chant of "Reg-gie! Reg-gie! Reg-gie!" When Jackson finally crossed the plate and disappeared into the dugout, the crowd, still standing, began pointing toward the owner's box on the mezzanine level, and a new chant took hold: "Steinbrenner sucks! Steinbrenner sucks! Steinbrenner sucks!"

Watching this scene from his box, Steinbrenner was devastated. After that inning, the rain started to come down harder and the umpires called the game, declaring the Angels 3–1 winners. Minutes later, Steinbrenner sent word to the clubhouse that he wanted to see Michael and his coaches in his office. This was not the ending Michael had envisioned for his first game back as manager. As Michael walked through the door, Steinbrenner was sitting behind the big round desk, scowling.

"You're killing me, Stick!"

Michael couldn't believe his ears. "My first friggin' game and I'm killing him?" he thought.

Once Michael and his staff had taken their seats around the desk, Steinbrenner started in.

"I can't believe what went on out there tonight!" he moaned. "How could they do this to me? How could these fans, who I've done so much for, turn on me like this?"

As he continued, the coaches desperately tried to contain their laughter until, at one point, Steinbrenner spotted bullpen coach Jeff Torborg covering a smirk on his face with his hand.

"What are you laughing about?" he roared. "You think this is *funny*?

How would you like it if 40,000 people were yelling 'Torborg sucks! Torborg sucks!'?"

After dismissing Michael and the coaches, Steinbrenner called stadium security chief Pat Kelly into his office and ordered him to go down to the visiting clubhouse and inspect Jackson's bats. Even though it was against baseball laws for home team officials to be tampering with property in the visiting team's clubhouse, Kelly dutifully obliged. With a couple of other team officials in tow, he went into the empty clubhouse and began rummaging through the bats in Jackson's locker until he found a particularly light one. Kelly sawed off the top of the bat and discovered it to be filled with cork. When Kelly reported his find to Steinbrenner, the owner became even more infuriated.

"We're gonna report this and get this game back!" Steinbrenner declared.

"You can't do that, George," Kelly protested.

"Why not?"

Kelly and the others then explained that, for one thing, what they had done was contrary to baseball protocol regarding the sanctity of the visitors' clubhouse. For another, they couldn't be sure that Reggie had ever used the bat in a game and to attempt to discredit Reggie for this one home run might cast doubt on all the home runs he'd hit for them. Steinbrenner reluctantly agreed, and Kelly locked the bat up for safekeeping before having it destroyed. Jackson apparently never complained that the bat was missing from his locker. In the months afterward, Steinbrenner was periodically quoted cryptically in the newspapers that he had firsthand knowledge of players using corked bats.

After Reggie's revenge homer, the 1982 season got worse. The Yankees continued to founder, and Steinbrenner continued to panic and make bad trades.

But if there was one player who epitomized the disaster of the 1982 season, it was Doyle Alexander, who produced exactly one win in exchange for Steinbrenner's $2.2 million. In his third start of the season, against the Mariners in Seattle, Alexander was the victim of a five-run third inning in which four of the runs were unearned, prompting Michael to pull him from the game. Enraged at being yanked so early, Alexander proceeded to punch the dugout wall with his pitching hand, breaking a knuckle. The self-inflicted injury sidelined him for six weeks and cost him $12,500 in a fine levied by the team. He returned in midsummer and, on August 10, gave up three homers and six runs in the first three innings of a 10–1 drubbing by the Tigers in Detroit.

In the middle of that game, Bill Bergesch, the longtime front office executive assistant who had become Steinbrenner's de facto general manager after the resignation of Cedric Tallis, came into the Tiger Stadium press box and sheepishly began reading a statement that the owner had dictated from Tampa: *"After what happened tonight, I'm having Doyle Alexander flown back to New York to undergo a physical. I'm afraid some of our players might get hurt playing behind him. He's given up eight homers in 38 innings and, in his last two starts, 11 runs in five innings. Obviously, something is wrong and we intend to find out."*

Though they weren't very happy with Alexander, the Yankee players were outraged at Steinbrenner's belittling statement. "Doyle's getting a physical," Goose Gossage told reporters after the game, "but George needs a mental."

As if the season couldn't get any more embarrassing for Steinbrenner, after the game on the night of July 28, a Brookfield, Connecticut, family was kidnapped at knifepoint in one of the Yankee Stadium parking lots, which were owned and operated by the Kinney Company, and dumped in the middle of Harlem. Steinbrenner did not learn of the incident until two days later, when it was splashed across the front pages of the New York tabloids, whereupon he ordered his in-house counsel, Ed Broderick, to summon all the front office execs—in particular security chief Pat Kelly—to his office. Steinbrenner instructed them to take a seat around his big round desk— with the exception of Kelly, whom he ordered to stand facing the wall.

"All my years here, I've never had anything as terrible as this!" Steinbrenner bellowed at Kelly's back. "This can't be allowed to happen! What are our rights here with Kinney?"

As the fifty-something Kelly, who'd previously been a New York cop assigned to the maritime division, turned to offer his thoughts, Steinbrenner snapped, "Broderick, will you tell him to turn around? I don't want to see the tugboat captain."

The session lasted about 15 minutes, with Kelly facing the wall the whole time, before Steinbrenner dismissed them with orders to call the family and offer the Yankees' regrets for what had happened.

As stadium manager and chief of security, Kelly was a frequent recipient of Steinbrenner's abuse and was often made to perform humiliating tasks. Once, when Steinbrenner got a piece of gum stuck on the bottom of his shoe while walking from the team parking lot to the Stadium, he forced Kelly and team president Gene McHale to spend three days patrolling the Stadium, scraping up gum from the sidewalks and corridors. Jim Naples, the VP of guest services, whom Steinbrenner put in charge of the office in their absence, remembered Kelly's reaction to this punishment. "I got a phone call from Kelly, who was obviously feeling pretty good, and he said, 'This is fantastic, Jimmy! You're up there taking all of George's shit and we're over here at a saloon. Have a nice day!'"

In early August, the Yankees played a doubleheader against the Chicago White Sox at Yankee Stadium. After losing the opener, 1–0, they were clobbered, 14–2, in the second game, in which they committed numerous errors and mental mistakes. During the middle of the game, Steinbrenner ordered public address announcer Bob Sheppard to read a statement saying that all fans in attendance would be awarded free tickets to future Yankee games.

"As soon as I heard that," said Gene Michael, "I knew I was fired."

Sure enough, nearly two hours after the second game—at 1:05 A.M.— with the Yankees now in fifth place with a 50-50 record, reporters received a one-paragraph press release announcing that Michael was being replaced. The new manager would be the organization's special pitching instructor, 57-year-old Clyde King, Steinbrenner's trusted aide and troubleshooter, whom many in the Yankees organization, particularly Billy Martin, had over the years come to consider a trouble*maker*.

Unlike the year before, when Michael challenged Steinbrenner to fire him, this time he felt betrayed by the owner for not being allowed to finish the season, never mind the next three, as Steinbrenner had promised.

For two days, Michael holed up at his house in Upper Saddle River, New Jersey, refusing all calls. When Steinbrenner was finally able to get through to him, it was a very different conversation from the first firing. This time, Steinbrenner was the one doing the apologizing.

"This one hurt, George," Michael said. "I didn't deserve this, and you know it. I think I'm a good manager, but you wouldn't let me prove it."

"Oh, c'mon, Stick," Steinbrenner said. "I'm not blaming you. I'm sorry I had to do this, but the team is going nowhere and I just felt I had to do something."

"Well, I still want to manage, George."

"I understand you're upset," said Steinbrenner, "but why would you still want to manage and be constantly second-guessed by me when you can come back up to the front office and become one of the second-guessers?"

THE YANKEES FINISHED the 1982 season in fifth place in the American League East, with a 29-33 record under King. In all, the team went through three managers, five pitching coaches, three hitting instructors and 47 players as the mad shipbuilder tried everything to right his sinking vessel. Despite the dismal finish, King expected Steinbrenner to bring him back for 1983, and, over lunch in Boston with me and Moss Klein, from the Newark *Star-Ledger*, at the end of September, the GM outlined his plans for trades, free-agent signings and coaching changes. Unbeknownst to him, events in Oakland were about to scuttle his plans. When we got back to our hotel rooms, there were messages from the Oakland A's beat writers informing us that Billy Martin had just trashed his office in a drunken rage directed at A's general manager Sandy Alderson. Just as he'd done in his previous tours with the Minnesota Twins, Detroit Tigers and Yankees, Martin had clashed with Oakland's ownership just a year after guiding the A's to an unexpected American League West title.

Steinbrenner had missed the passion Martin brought to the team and his ability to connect with the fans; Billy, who was in arrears with his taxes and owed money to two ex-wives, was once again in dire need of the kind of financial relief Steinbrenner and managing in New York could provide him. Martin's agent, Eddie Sapir, negotiated a unique five-year, $2.5 million contract with Steinbrenner that gave Billy a say in all personnel decisions and, in the likely event that he was fired, a limited list of jobs—broadcaster, scout, assistant to the owner—he could work for Steinbrenner in lieu of managing. "There will be times Billy and I disagree," said Steinbrenner, standing next to Martin at the press conference on January 11, 1983, to announce his third hiring as manager of the Yankees, "but this time it will be different, because we will communicate better with each other. Besides, I feel Billy will stir up enough turmoil and excitement without me."

The two men then played out a skit, which, given their headstrong personas, was a more accurate portent of the future than either of them probably wanted to admit.

"I'll be handling all the trades," Martin said.

"What do you mean?" Steinbrenner interrupted. "That's not right. I'm handling the trades!"

"That's not the way we said, George."

"Damn right it is!" Steinbrenner shot back, "and if you don't like it, you're fired!"

"You haven't even hired me yet!" Martin said, laughing at the punch line.

The fact that Steinbrenner had a cartoonist's depiction of Martin arguing jaw-to-jaw with an umpire as the cover for the 1983 Yankees press guide was indicative enough of the kind of confrontational season he expected—and would get.

Meanwhile, at the winter meetings in Honolulu that December, Steinbrenner went about restocking the Yankees roster for '83 with more expensive free agents. He made by far the biggest deal for any player on the market that winter when he signed outfielder Steve Kemp, who had been with the Chicago White Sox, to a five-year, $5.5 million contract. It would prove to be an ill-advised signing, as the left-handed-hitting Kemp's power was predominantly to right center, the deepest part of Yankee Stadium. Also costly for Steinbrenner was the spat Kemp's signing touched off with White Sox owners Jerry Reinsdorf and Eddie Einhorn, who were upset at having one of their best players taken from them for a lot more money than they thought he was worth.

"I think we should consider putting another franchise in New York, like in the New Jersey Meadowlands," Reinsdorf told reporters at the winter meetings in Hawaii, where the Kemp signing took place. "[Steinbrenner] is totally irresponsible. He's got to start unloading now, but nobody would take those salaries from him unless they're imbeciles." Reinsdorf, who was later fined $2,500 by Commissioner Bowie Kuhn for his remarks, managed to extract a measure of revenge against Steinbrenner a few days later by out-bidding the Yankees owner for the services of the most coveted pitcher on the free agent market, left-hander Floyd Bannister. After watching Reinsdorf and Einhorn chortling on TV about bagging Bannister for five years, at $4.5 million, Steinbrenner could not resist firing back.

"I watched those two pumpkins on TV, and they can say all they want, but the fact is that's going to prove to be the most lucrative contract ever given a pitcher," he said, later referring to Reinsdorf and Einhorn as "the Katzenjammer twins." This prompted Kuhn (whose term as commissioner was not being renewed by the owners) to levy an even bigger fine—$5,000—which evoked a predictable response from Steinbrenner: "How the commissioner in his infinite wisdom decided that I should be fined twice as much as the other guys, I don't know. I'm sorry one of his last official acts was fining us. I'd have liked to see him go out a different way."

The feud between Steinbrenner and Reinsdorf would compel both of them to deliberately screw each other in a couple of future Yankees–White Sox trades before they finally called a truce and actually became allies. Later that season, at the '83 All-Star Game gala, hosted by the White Sox in Chicago, Reinsdorf got onstage with a microphone and asked Einhorn: "How do you know when George Steinbrenner is lying? Whenever he moves his lips."

"I was looped," Reinsdorf told me in 2008, "and as I said it I looked out into the audience and saw Bowie, and asked: 'How much is that one gonna cost me?' He held up five fingers."

Reinsdorf taking a verbal shot at Steinbrenner while under the influence was nothing compared to the drunken rage the Yankees owner brought out in Bill "Killer" Kane at the Yankees' spring training hotel in March '83. Kane had somehow managed to endure as the traveling secretary despite constant nitpicking from Steinbrenner over mostly trivial issues regarding the team trips. On this particular morning, however, Steinbrenner was upset about a spate of stomach flu among the players following a two-day trip to New Orleans and had concluded it was a result of the food they'd eaten on the United Airlines charter. He'd been trying for months to get out of his contract with United and saw this as his opportunity. When Kane walked into the executive trailer at the Fort Lauderdale ballpark, Steinbrenner was waiting for him.

"I've had enough with United!" he screamed at Kane in front of all the secretaries. "You get rid of them! You hear me?"

"George," said Kane, "I've told you we can't get out of this contract. I've booked our trips for the whole first half of the season already!"

"I don't care. *Un*-book them. Or else I'll get rid of you, too."

"You know what, George? You do that! I'm sick of your shit, yelling at me in front of all these people."

With that, Kane stormed out the door, got in his car and went to the nearby racetrack, Pompano Downs, where he proceeded to spend the rest of the day playing the horses and getting a load on. That night, thoroughly inebriated, he came back to the team hotel, took the elevator directly up to the top floor, staggered down the corridor to Steinbrenner's suite and began pounding on the door.

"Come out of there, you fat, fucking Fauntleroy!" he shouted. "I'm gonna kick the shit out of you right here!"

A startled Steinbrenner came to the door in his pajamas and attempted to calm Kane down.

"What's the matter with you, Killer? Don't you know you're disturbing my wife?"

"Why should I give a shit about your wife, when you don't give a shit about my wife?" Kane slurred.

"All right," Steinbrenner said. "You're disturbing everybody on this floor. Go back downstairs to the lobby and I'll get dressed and meet you down there in a few minutes."

When Steinbrenner got down to the lobby, he found Kane sitting in a chair, sound asleep. Steinbrenner shook Kane, who woke up and took a swing at the owner, missed, and lurched onto the floor. The hotel clerk rushed from behind the desk.

"Are you all right, sir?" the clerk said.

"I dunno," Kane moaned, looking at Steinbrenner. "I think I hurt my back."

"Do you want to file a report?"

"Yeah, yeah, but first I gotta go to the hospital."

"Ah, geez, Killer," Steinbrenner said. "C'mon. We've had fights before. You're okay. Let's forget about this."

In a 2008 interview, Kane laughingly recounted how, at the hospital, he was able to get a doctor he knew to give him an X-ray of another patient's bad back—which he brought to work the next day. "George never bothered me again after that," Kane said. "It got me another seven years as road secretary. But George knew he was wrong. He knew he was a spoiled brat, and he knew I had a right to be pissed about being screamed at in front of all the secretaries like that."

STEINBRENNER RAN AFOUL of Bowie Kuhn several more times—and for substantially larger penalties—before the commissioner officially left office at the end of 1984. During an '83 spring training game in Fort Lauderdale between the Yankees and the Montreal Expos, Steinbrenner was standing along the fence next to the Yankees dugout when National League umpire Lee Weyer called a Yankee out at first base. "National League homer!" Steinbrenner screamed, within earshot of *New York Post* reporter Mike McAlary, who dutifully scribbled down the remark in his notepad. "That's the way [National League president] Chub Feeney tells them to do it. If it's close, give it to the National League!"

Upon reading McAlary's account the next day, Kuhn reacted swiftly, fining the Yankees owner $50,000. Steinbrenner's war on umpires, which he'd inflamed with that silly caricature of Billy Martin arguing with one on the cover of the press guide, was further ramped up on May 27, when Dave Winfield was brushed back by a pitch, setting off a fight between the Yankees and the visiting Oakland A's. As Winfield charged Oakland pitcher Mike Norris, he was intercepted by catcher Mike Heath, whom he put in a choke hold. Both benches cleared and a wild melee broke out; when order was restored, only Winfield was ejected by home-plate umpire Derryl Cousins.

Watching the game on TV from Tampa, an enraged Steinbrenner

phoned Yankees PR director Kenny Nigro in the press box and told him to get a pen and paper. For the next five minutes Nigro feverishly scrawled up and down and into the margins of a piece of yellow legal paper as Steinbrenner dictated a blistering attack on Cousins and his partner, John Shulock, both of whom, he noted, had been awarded their jobs after serving as replacements during the recent umpire strike. "I was scribbling furiously until my wrist started aching," Nigro recalled, "but he just kept dictating. Finally, when he was done, he asked me to read it back to him. I started stammering, which set him off even more."

After somehow organizing Steinbrenner's rant into a cohesive statement, Nigro distributed it in the press box, where, it so happened, one of the occupants that night was Bob Fishel, the former Yankees PR director who was now assistant to American League president Lee MacPhail. Upon reading Steinbrenner's release, Fishel immediately called his boss, who in turn dictated his own release, which said in part, *"Mr. Steinbrenner's intemperate blast at the integrity of the American League umpires is completely unacceptable and will result in disciplinary action."* When told by Nigro of MacPhail's threatening response, Steinbrenner showed no contrition. Instead, he decided he would have the last blast and dictated yet another release, this one slamming the American League president: *"We are all free to express our opinion,"* Steinbrenner said, *"unless Lee MacPhail has authored a new Constitution or Bill of Rights of the United States."*

Though, as Nigro said proudly, "we outdueled them 2–1," Steinbrenner's two press releases earned him a one-week suspension from MacPhail. (Nigro's term as Yankees press chief lasted only for the 1983 season, after which he resigned, issuing his own press release in which he jokingly said he was checking into a rehab center. The one thing he told me he'd always remember about his experience with the Yankees was the red phones Steinbrenner had installed in everyone's office at Yankee Stadium shortly after buying the team in 1973. "Whenever those phones rang," Nigro said, "it was unbelievable. People would literally leap over desks and chairs in order to grab them on the first ring!")

Steinbrenner was hardly chastened by this suspension, something that became clear a couple of months later when he and MacPhail locked horns again over a "sticky" situation that became part of baseball lore. On

July 24, a sunny Sunday afternoon at Yankee Stadium, the Yankees were leading the Kansas City Royals, 4–3. With a runner on first base and George Brett at the plate, the Royals were down to their last out against the Yankees' dominating closer, Goose Gossage. But just as he'd done so many times against the Yankees in those ALCS wars from 1976 to '80, Brett was able to get around on one of Gossage's patented heaters and launched it into the right-field bleachers for a go-ahead two-run homer. But wait. As Brett circled the bases and trotted into the dugout, Yankees manager Billy Martin and catcher Rick Cerone approached home-plate umpire Tim McClelland.

"You need to check Brett's bat," Martin told McClelland. "Look at how far up the pine tar goes on it. That's an illegal bat!"

Two weeks earlier in Kansas City, Yankees captain Graig Nettles had noticed that Brett's bat had pine tar extending about 20 inches above the tip of the handle. Nettles was aware of the little-known Rule 1.10(b), which stated that pine tar on a bat could not extend beyond 18 inches from the tip of the bat handle. When he alerted Martin to this, the manager had said, "Let's just keep this to ourselves for now, but we may have to use it if he does something against us down the road."

After measuring the pine tar on the bat, McClelland concurred with Martin. No question, it exceeded the legal length. Home run nullified. As soon as the umpire made the "out" signal, an enraged Brett came charging out of the dugout and had to be physically restrained by crew chief Joe Brinkman. The Yankees had won—and with the help of the umpires! What the team had not counted on was that MacPhail, upon receiving the Royals' formal protest, deliberated for four days before deciding that, while the pine tar on Brett's bat probably was a violation, the umpires, in nullifying the home run, had not acted in "the spirit of the rule." MacPhail upheld the Royals' protest (and thus the Brett homer), declared the game suspended with the Royals leading 5–4 and ordered that it be picked up with two outs in the top of the ninth inning at Yankee Stadium, on August 18, an off-day for both teams.

Steinbrenner was predictably outraged by MacPhail's decision. "I like Lee," he said to reporters in response to the decision, "but I feel sorry for him. He made a very dumb decision. It was a putrid decision. He's opened up a Pandora's box and left his umpires out to dry."

First, Steinbrenner threatened to forfeit the game, claiming MacPhail had made such a mess of things that he didn't want to take the off-day away from his players. Threatened with further sanctions if he did, Steinbrenner then reversed course and said the Yankees would play the game out beginning at 2 P.M., adding that he planned to charge $2.50 admission and invite busloads of kids from the summer camps to "enjoy a festive occasion at the ballpark." This, too, met with resistance from MacPhail, who noted that the Royals were playing a night game on August 17 and, by rules, were not required to play a game the next day before 6 P.M.

"It sure tests our faith in our leadership," Steinbrenner said of MacPhail. "If the Yankees lose the American League pennant by one game, I wouldn't want to be Lee MacPhail living in New York. Maybe he should go house-hunting in Kansas City."

In the meantime, a number of fans had filed lawsuits against the Yankees for charging a separate admission for the game's resumption—lawsuits that MacPhail and Commissioner Bowie Kuhn suspected Steinbrenner actually welcomed in an effort to further delay completing the game. The pine tar follies would rage on in the courts in Manhattan and the Bronx with various lawsuits until the morning of August 18, when Bronx Supreme Court judge Orest V. Maresca granted a preliminary injunction barring the game's resumption. This prompted baseball's attorneys to rush downtown to a Manhattan courtroom, where, at 3:34 P.M., Justice Joseph Sullivan over-ruled Maresca, allowing the game to go on. After all this, the conclusion of the game turned out to be a complete mockery. When the Yankees took the field, Martin had left-handed Don Mattingly playing second base and Ron Guidry in center field. The Yankees got an out and then went down quietly, 1-2-3.

"It was a wild day," MacPhail recalled to me years later, "made wilder by George finding a friendly judge in the Bronx." Still, the final chapter wouldn't occur until two days before Christmas, when, after a hearing at his office, Kuhn's last act as commissioner was to impose financial penalties totaling $300,000 on Steinbrenner for his comments about MacPhail and other detrimental acts to baseball throughout the pine tar affair. At the time, it was the largest fine in sports history.

Amid Steinbrenner's continuing battles with the baseball hierarchy, the 1983 season was not going well on the field for the Yankees, once again fraying his relationship with Billy Martin. His vows "this time it's going to be different" and "this time we understand each other" and "this time we'll communicate better"? By June 15, he'd forgotten all of them. After losing four of the first five games of a road trip to Milwaukee and Cleveland, the Yankees' record stood at 29-30 on June 14, and rumors were swirling that Martin was once again on the firing line. Word was Steinbrenner had found out that Martin had defied his order to hold a workout for the team in Milwaukee on the off-day before the first game of the trip. Two days later, Martin was caught on a local telecast carrying on with his girlfriend (who would later become his fourth wife) during the Yankees' 6–2 loss to the Brewers. Instead of his customary perch on the top step of the dugout, Martin was sitting on a stool alongside the dugout, right in front of the visiting club box, where his girlfriend, Jill Guiver, conspicuous in a bright yellow sundress, had a front-row seat. The cameras periodically caught her passing notes through the fence with her toes to the smiling Martin. At one point, a frantic WPIX-TV producer, Don Carney, rushed into the press box and asked the writers if they were going to report Martin's actions, saying, "I'm very reluctant to show any of this."

Usually, when Steinbrenner was feuding with a manager, he would make himself unavailable while allowing his adversary to either dig himself deeper or weather the storm on his own. When I called him on this occasion, however, he surprised me by getting right on the phone. I asked him how much validity there was to the rumors that he was upset over Martin's behavior.

"I'm not happy about a lot of things I'm hearing about Billy," Steinbrenner said. "He promised me he was going to have them work out in Milwaukee and he didn't, and look what's happened. We're playing like shit. I can't have this. I think I'm gonna have to make a change."

"You're going to fire Billy?" I asked.

"He's giving me no choice. But I've got an idea that I'd like your thoughts on. What would you think about Yogi as the manager?"

Yogi Berra? Yogi, then the bench coach, was a nice guy, as different in demeanor from Martin as you could get. Aside from Art Fowler, Martin's pitching coach and drinking companion, he was also Billy's most trusted aide.

"That's an interesting one," I said. "If you fire Billy, you're going to have to replace him with someone equally or more popular with the fans, and Yogi certainly qualifies in that regard. I know the players respect him, but you're aware that he was already fired once before as Yankee manager?"

"Yeah, but that was 20 years ago, and I wasn't the owner," Steinbrenner snapped. "So what do you think? You like the idea?"

"Hey, if this is what you think you have to do, what's not to like about Yogi?" I said.

I knew Steinbrenner well enough to know I wasn't the only person he might be sounding out about this. This was not something I felt I could sit on, so I wrote in the next day's *Daily News* that Billy was in trouble again with George, that he was on the verge of being fired for his transgressions in Milwaukee and that his likely replacement would be Yogi.

Even though he had not fully made up his mind to fire Martin, Steinbrenner got the result he wanted. The Yankees were floundering in fifth place, but they were all over the newscasts—and Martin's agent, Eddie Sapir, was on the phone begging for a meeting. That night, Steinbrenner met with Sapir and Martin at the Pewter Mug restaurant in Cleveland. He didn't want Martin at the meeting, but Sapir insisted, saying that Billy had a few things he wanted to discuss with Steinbrenner as well.

In response to Steinbrenner asking about his behavior in Milwaukee, Martin said, "These allegations that I'm not keeping my mind on the game are unjust. There's no way, George. You're listening to too many other people. I've got this team playing hard, and my head is in the game."

"Now, now, Billy, just calm down," Sapir said. "We asked for this meeting to clear the air about everything, and there's no need to get worked up at George."

"It's okay," Steinbrenner said. "If Billy feels he wants to get some things off his chest, let him say them. This meeting wasn't because you were going to be fired, Billy. You have my commitment to manage the team for the rest of the season. I'm still not happy about the results so far, especially the pitching, and while I'm confident you can get this turned around, we may need to go a different direction with the pitching coach."

The next morning, the lobby of the Stouffer's Hotel, where the Yankees were staying, swarmed with TV crews colliding with each other in pursuit of Sapir, who, standing in the middle of room, could be heard shouting triumphantly: "Billy has been vindicated! Reports of the girl were unfounded!"

Nevertheless, the firing of Art Fowler as pitching coach, and his replacement by the duo of minor league pitching coach Sammy Ellis and bullpen coach Jeff Torborg, was Steinbrenner's sadistic way of punishing Martin and beating him down without again getting rid of him altogether. Steinbrenner loved Martin's fire and defiance, but felt he had to remind him that he was just the manager.

Martin was wounded now, as evidenced by his drink-fueled bad behavior after the team got home to Yankee Stadium. On the afternoon of the first game of a home stand against the Brewers, Martin was late arriving at the ballpark, his haggard appearance and red eyes suggesting that he was coming directly from a bar, brooding over the firing of his best buddy, Fowler. Brushing past reporters, he went into his office and slammed the door. A few minutes later, he stepped back out of his office and stood glaring at a woman at the far end of the clubhouse, sitting on a table taking notes. Marching across the clubhouse, he confronted the woman and demanded to know what she was doing.

The woman identified herself as Deborah Henschel, a reporter for the *New York Times*, who was working on a research project, surveying the Yankee players on the All-Star Game voting.

"Researcher? Kiss my fucking dago ass!" Martin shouted at her. "What are you researching, dressed like a slut like that? You're just a hussy. Now get your ass out of here!"

The next day, Steinbrenner received a call from the *Times'* corporate relations department informing him that Henschel had filed a formal complaint against Martin and the Yankees. Implicit in the call was the veiled suggestion of a lawsuit.

"This is the first I'm hearing of this," Steinbrenner said, "but I assure you there will be a full and thorough investigation. In the meantime, you have my apologies."

Upon hanging up, Steinbrenner called downstairs to the clubhouse and asked the attendant to tell third-base coach Don Zimmer to come up to his office. Zimmer and Steinbrenner were longtime friends from Tampa, where they spent a lot of time together at the racetrack, and he was the only coach on Martin's staff whom the owner had hired himself. Because of that, Martin distrusted Zimmer—which meant that Steinbrenner summoning him to his office put the coach in a very awkward position.

"I need to ask you about what happened in the clubhouse yesterday, Zim," Steinbrenner began. "I know you were one of the ones closest to the scene, because other people have told me that. I just want to know, did Billy tell that woman to kiss his dago ass?"

Zimmer, who had begun to sweat, was privately thankful Steinbrenner put the question to him the way he did, leaving out the more salacious words Martin had used to insult the woman.

"Well, uh, yes, I guess you could say he did," Zimmer replied.

"All right, I can handle that," Steinbrenner said. "I appreciate your being honest with me, Zim."

Zimmer, presuming the interrogation to be over, began to get up. Steinbrenner put up his hand.

"There's one other thing I need to know, Zim," he said. "Do you think we can win this with Billy?"

For a moment, Zimmer didn't respond. "George, you're asking the wrong guy!" he said before turning and walking out the door.

Zimmer would tell me years later that this was the most uncomfortable five minutes he'd ever experienced in baseball. As much as Martin made him feel like an outsider on his staff, Zimmer wasn't about to be a party to getting him fired. Steinbrenner also met with Henschel and apologized to her for the manner in which Martin had yelled at her, before confiding: "This whole thing is very embarrassing to me and the Yankees, and I don't know what else to tell you except that Billy is just mad in the head. I frankly don't know what to do with him."

Much as his instincts told him Billy was too unstable to get through the season, another part of Steinbrenner wanted to believe that Martin still had the capacity to lead the team to victory, as he'd done amid all the stress and turmoil with Reggie Jackson in 1977. However, it hadn't helped Martin's fragile psyche when Steinbrenner, on July 1, announced the hiring of Murray Cook, the Pittsburgh Pirates' 42-year-old scouting director, as the new Yankees general manager. Martin interpreted the Cook hiring as another layer of authority between him and Steinbrenner and a reneging on the owner's promise to him that he would have a say on all the trades and signings.

For Martin, the 1983 season was just as rife with conflict with the league as it was for Steinbrenner. True to his depiction on the cover of the press guide, Martin got himself in trouble twice during the first week of the season. First, he was fined $5,000 by MacPhail for criticizing umpire Dan Morrison in the season opener. Then he was ejected for arguing with another umpire, Vic Voltaggio, on April 2. MacPhail also warned Martin that he would be suspended if his comportment didn't improve. It didn't. Eight days after his ejection by Voltaggio, Martin got into three separate arguments with home-plate umpire Drew Coble in a game in Texas and, after finally being ejected, kicked dirt all over him. That drew a three-game suspension and another $5,000 fine. On August 5, Martin was suspended for another two games after calling umpire Dale Ford a "stone liar."

It was as if Steinbrenner had created a monster. For all his fire at the umpires, however, Martin was unable to ignite his team. The Yankees were in fourth place in mid-August. They went 9-4 on a road trip in late August and early September, putting them in second place in the American League East and setting up a four-game showdown with the first-place Baltimore Orioles at Yankee Stadium. On September 9, behind Guidry's seven-hit pitching, the Yankees beat Baltimore, 5–3, in the first game of the series, before a capacity crowd of 55,605, to pull within four games of the Orioles. That was the closest they got. The next day, the Orioles swept them in a doubleheader before taking the series finale, 5–3. After the game, a disappointed Martin cited injuries, particularly those to outfielder Steve Kemp, outfielder/first baseman Ken Griffey, second baseman Willie Randolph, catcher Butch Wynegar and shortstop Andre Robertson, none of whom played in more than 118 games, as the primary reason for the Yankees' inability to catch the Orioles.

"Right now, I'm not going to be critical of anybody," Steinbrenner told the *Daily News'* Phil Pepe at the conclusion of the disappointing series. "I promised I would not interfere this year, and I haven't."

True to his word, this would prove to be Steinbrenner's last public statement on a season in which the Yankees wound up third in the AL East at 91-71, seven games behind the Orioles, who went on to win the World Series. Though Martin managed to last the entire season and the Yankees' attendance increased by more than 215,000 from 1982, it had taken an exacting toll on the manager and the owner alike. Between them, Steinbrenner and Martin had accrued $370,000 in fines and three suspensions from the baseball hierarchy for their transgressions against umpires and league officials.

IN THE WEEKS after, Steinbrenner was silent about Martin and Yankees baseball operations. On November 7, 1983, Steinbrenner's father, Henry, died at age 79 in Westlake, Ohio, after a lengthy battle with Alzheimer's disease. Steinbrenner made no public comment on the passing of his father, and the service was private. It was also around that time that Steinbrenner announced he was closing AmShip's shipyard in Lorain, Ohio, and moving it to Tampa. Though the company had recently won a $300 million contract to build five tankers for the Navy, Steinbrenner said the Lorain shipyard had lost $30 million over the previous five years, and he blamed the unions for ignoring his warnings that their work rules were so archaic and their wage rates so high that the company could save 30 percent of its labor costs by moving to Tampa. The shutdown of the 87-year-old shipyard resulted in the loss of 1,500 jobs in Lorain and incurred the wrath of U.S. senator Howard Metzenbaum (the Cleveland parking lot magnate who'd been part of Steinbrenner's investor group in his bid to buy the Cleveland Indians back in the early '70s). Said Metzenbaum to the Cleveland *Plain Dealer* after the announcement of the Lorain shipyard closing: "[Steinbrenner] had called me with syrupy, sweet promises that he would do everything he could to keep jobs in Lorain. As usual with George Steinbrenner's promises, they soon turned into castor oil."

Steinbrenner defended his decision to move his operations out of Lorain, telling the Associated Press: "We feel sorry for those people, believe
me. Nobody feels worse about the closure on the lake than I do, because it's
part of me. I battled for three years to keep that yard open, but nobody can
run a business that's losing that much money. I kept warning the unions. If
they had come right up and agreed to changes . . . it might well have been
different."

Henry Steinbrenner had invested a lot in the Great Lakes, but he had
also taught his son to be a hard-nosed businessman, so it would be pure
conjecture to say how the old man would have felt about his son's decision to abandon the region, where the Steinbrenners had been a fixture
since 1885, when George's great-great-grandfather Peter Minch founded
the Cleveland Ship Building Co.

AFTER THANKSGIVING 1983, Steinbrenner told reporters that he would
decide who would manage the Yankees in 1984 by the winter meetings.
But those winter meetings, held in Nashville December 5–8, came and
went with no word on the Yankees manager. New GM Murray Cook did
make one minor deal there, sending first baseman Steve Balboni, a onetime
minor league slugging prodigy, to the Kansas City Royals for relief pitcher
Mike Armstrong.

A week after the winter meetings, Steinbrenner called Eddie Sapir to
Tampa to discuss Martin's future with the Yankees. "I've thought this over,
Eddie," Steinbrenner said, "and I've just decided that in the best interests of
the team I'm going to invoke the option on Billy's contract and reassign him
to the front office, where he'll serve as a special advisor to me."

Sapir never asked why Steinbrenner was making the change. Nor did
he make any effort to plead for Martin's retention. He knew this was merely
going to mean extra money and extra years of security for his client. He also
knew that, in good time, Martin would be back managing again.

The next day, at a Yankee Stadium press conference, Steinbrenner introduced Yogi Berra as the newest manager of the Yankees.

12

. . .

An Icon Scorned

. . .

Y OGI BERRA HAD EVERY reason to feel apprehensive about becoming George Steinbrenner's latest manager. His ascension to
the job, on December 16, 1983, marked the tenth managerial
change by the impulsive and demanding Yankees owner in just eight years.
At 58, Berra's legacy as a Yankee icon was secure. He had won three Most
Valuable Player awards, played on 14 World Series teams and been a 14-
time All-Star, and he was arguably the most beloved and respected Yankee
of all time. Yet he elected to risk all of the goodwill he had earned from the
fans and media by agreeing to work for the man who'd just fired his friend
and former teammate, Billy Martin, for the third time.

In a column in the *New York Post* (where he'd moved from the *Daily
News*), Dick Young seized on how Berra had gone from venerable to vulnerable: "The reason George Steinbrenner is naming Yogi Berra manager
is that George wants to be the manager," Young wrote. "George realizes he
made a bad deal with Billy, agreeing to stay away from the clubhouse, away
from the phone, away from the players. With Yogi in the manager's office,
George can be manager again. He can enjoy life. He can tell Yogi who
should lead off and who should catch. George can re-connect the phone to
the dugout too. That was the fun George missed last season."

Steinbrenner reacted to Young's column (which was headlined GEORGE
WILL USE YOGI AS PUPPET IN DUGOUT) by writing a humorously indignant letter to the editor of the *Post* defending Berra's honor: "I really think Dick

Young owes Yogi Berra an apology because in picking on Yogi Berra, you're picking on one of the finest men in baseball. As far as I'm concerned personally, I still like Dick Young even after the article. I'm not sure I'm going to invite him to Christmas dinner this year, but then again I may have to have him over for dinner if he keeps picking Marvis Frazier to knock out Larry Holmes."

It was a mostly tongue-in-cheek poke at Young, not nearly as stinging as the verbal barbs Steinbrenner so frequently leveled at baseball officials, other owners or umpires, probably because the owner knew deep down that Young was right. Even Berra's wife, Carmen, voiced reservations over his giving up the easy life of a bench coach and thrusting himself squarely into Steinbrenner's line of fire. At the December 17 press conference at Yankee Stadium, Berra explained: "My age had something to do with it. I've achieved just about everything a man can achieve in this game. I've won the Most Valuable Player award, I've made the Hall of Fame and I've won two pennants as a manager [with the Yankees in 1964 and the Mets in 1973]. But I've never won a world championship as a manager, and I felt that this club is capable of winning one."

Otherwise, Berra echoed much of the same familiar rhetoric of the three previous press conferences at which Steinbrenner had named Billy Martin manager. "I'm sure I'll argue with George about things, probably," Berra said, "and then I'll find out, I guess, whether I can win one. But I can accept losing an argument, too."

It had to be a bit disconcerting for Berra to see Martin's agent, Eddie Sapir, at the press conference. Sapir was there, he said, to assure everyone that relations between Martin and Steinbrenner were just fine, despite their latest parting. "Billy is available," Sapir told the writers. "Billy is disappointed he won't be managing the Yankees next season, but George has helped Billy tremendously and has been a real friend to Billy."

Steinbrenner, standing next to Sapir, insisted that Martin had not been fired but rather "shifted" to an unnamed position in the front office. When pressed as to whether Martin might resurface as manager, Steinbrenner answered with the old cliché "Nothing is sure but death and taxes."

So, with Billy Martin's shadow hovering ominously over him, Berra's second voyage as Yankees manager was launched with no guarantees from the owner that it wouldn't end as abruptly and rudely as the first. (In 1964, Berra was fired after just one season as manager by then-owners Dan Topping and Del Webb.)

Then, just two days into the job, Berra learned he'd lost his closer, Goose Gossage.

Throughout the tumultuous 1983 season, Gossage, in the final year of his contract, had expressed disenchantment with the Yankees' constant state of upheaval under Steinbrenner. In particular, Gossage had no use for Billy Martin, going all the way back to his first Yankees spring training camp, in 1978, when Martin had ordered him to deliberately throw a pitch at the head of Texas Rangers outfielder Billy Sample. He also took offense at the owner's periodic blasting of players, both privately in the clubhouse and very publicly in the newspapers. In a memorable clubhouse tirade in 1982, preserved for the ages by a radio reporter's tape recorder, a frustrated Gossage lashed out at the New York media for their eagerness to quote Steinbrenner ripping the players. "You motherfuckers with the fucking pens and fucking tape recorders," he said, "you can turn it on and take it upstairs to the fat man! Okay?"

By the end of the 1983 season, Gossage had made up his mind to leave the Yankees. But after declaring for free agency right after the World Series, he was surprised when no other team called him with an offer. At first he thought it was a confirmation of the rumors of owner collusion that had been circulating around baseball, but then he realized it was a matter of the rest of the clubs believing that Steinbrenner would spare no cost to retain him. That's what Steinbrenner had counted on as well, but he also believed that replacing Martin with Berra would entice Gossage to re-up with the Yankees.

The day after the Berra press conference, Steinbrenner called in Gene Michael and pitching coach Jeff Torborg and instructed them to go on a recruiting mission to La Jolla, California, where Gossage was staying with his agent, Jerry Kapstein.

"Goose likes and respects you two guys," Steinbrenner said. "So I want you to go out there and convince him he needs to stay with us."

"Much as I loved Yogi, I wasn't going back," Gossage said in a 2009 interview. "Still, when Gene and Jeff called me and asked if they could come out and see me, I agreed. I felt they deserved to hear it from me directly."

Indeed, when Michael and Torborg arrived at Kapstein's office, they had no idea the meeting was going to be so brief.

"I'm really sorry you guys had to come all the way out here for this," Gossage said. "But there's nothing you can say to me that's going to change my mind. I'll be honest: I've just had enough of all the bullshit that goes on there. I've grown stagnant there. I know George will probably offer me a generous deal to stay, but I want you to know I have no interest in a contract offer from the Yankees. I need a change of scenery."

Michael and Torborg looked at each other in astonishment. "It felt like I'd been punched in the stomach," Torborg later said.

That night, Gossage issued a statement confirming he'd informed the Yankees of his intentions not to return. Two weeks later, on January 6, it was announced that Gossage had signed a five-year, $25 million contract with the San Diego Padres, for whom he would play a pivotal role in their first trip to the World Series in 1984, with a 10-6 record and 25 saves.

THOUGH STUNG BY the loss of Gossage, Steinbrenner refrained from bad-mouthing the closer, vowing instead to find an equally capable replacement. A month later, however, the loss of another pitcher, who never even threw a pitch for the Yankees, would send him into a volcanic rage that would ultimately lead to the end of Murray Cook's tenure as general manager. The pitcher was Tim Belcher, a highly touted right-hander from tiny Mount Vernon Nazarene College, in Ohio, whom the Yankees had selected and signed as their first pick in the secondary phase of the January amateur draft. What they didn't realize was that once Belcher signed his contract, he had become part of their organization and was subject to the newly created free agent compensation pool in which teams who lost free agents could be indirectly compensated by selecting unprotected players from any of the other major league clubs.

On February 8, the Oakland A's announced they were selecting Belcher from the Yankees' unprotected list as compensation for having lost free-agent pitcher Tom Underwood to the Baltimore Orioles earlier that winter. Cook was stunned. "How can they do that?" he asked the American League administrator. "How could we protect Belcher when he wasn't even in our organization when the protected lists were submitted?"

It did seem as though the Yankees had a valid argument, and the Players Association joined forces with them in filing an official protest with the league. Since all the affected clubs—Oakland, Baltimore and the Yankees—were in the American League, the decision was left to AL president Lee MacPhail, whose decidedly acrimonious relationship with Steinbrenner was now well documented, to arbitrate the case. After hearing all the arguments, MacPhail determined that the A's had acted within the rules and, while he sympathized with the Yankees' plight, he said it was a mistake to sign Belcher before February 8 and allow the A's to take him through a loophole.

Cook was in his Yankee Stadium office when he received the news of MacPhail's decision in a phone call from the league president. Upon hanging up, he called his assistant, Dave Hersh, and Yankees in-house counsel Mel Southard into the office, where they proceeded to bolster themselves with a bottle of Scotch while waiting for the phone call that would inevitably come from Tampa.

"I can't believe how fucking stupid you are," Steinbrenner railed when he called Cook not long after. "How could you make a mistake like this? I should have known you were too inexperienced to be a general manager. They love fucking us over there at the American League office, and you played right into their hands!"

Before Cook could begin to offer a defense, Steinbrenner hung up. The next time Cook heard from him was two days later, when the owner called to inform him that he was to stay in New York for the first couple of weeks of spring training and that, when he did report to Fort Lauderdale, he would be consigned to the executive trailer to handle paperwork. "I don't want to see you on the field watching the games or evaluating players," Steinbrenner said.

On April 9, ten months after he'd been named general manager, Cook was demoted to scouting director and replaced by Clyde King. All that spring, Cook was the palest person in camp, and for years afterward, whenever someone would arrive for spring training from the cold north, the writers would joke that he had a "Murray Cook tan."

WHEN THE PITCHERS and catchers reported for spring training on February 17, Yogi Berra announced a decision that he and Steinbrenner had reached a month before: 25-year-old Dave Righetti would replace Gossage as the Yankees' closer. The left-handed Righetti, whom Al Rosen had acquired as the "extra player" in the Sparky Lyle trade with the Texas Rangers back in 1978, had enjoyed meteoric success in just 2½ seasons as a starter, winning Rookie of the Year honors in 1981, pitching a no-hitter against the Red Sox on July 4, 1983, and amassing 33 victories all told. But as Berra explained to the writers in making the announcement that first day, "He throws hard and can get strikeouts for two to three innings; he's never given up a home run in the first two innings of games he's pitched, and he has the ability to warm up faster than any of the other starters." Later that day, pitching coach Sammy Ellis, Righetti's mentor, confided to me, "I'm afraid for his longevity as a starter. With his delivery, every time I watch him throw, I brace myself for his arm exploding. I really believe this is the best thing for his arm."

While Righetti's conversion from starter to closer proved to be an overwhelming success—he would go on to record 248 saves over the next eight seasons—the 1984 season, under Berra's direction, was, at best, mixed. When Berra said he thought the team he'd been handed could win it all, he did not know that left fielder Steve Kemp and shortstop Andre Robertson would never fully recover from the injuries they'd incurred the season before, or that Steinbrenner would order the trading of team captain Graig Nettles, and that 35-year-old Toby Harrah would prove to be a woefully inadequate third base replacement for him. (At the start of spring training, Steinbrenner observed that the 38-year-old Nettles, who'd slumped to a .232 season with just 18 homers in 1983, "is in the twilight of his career" and not worth the $500,000 salary he was earning. The two exchanged snipes all spring until March 30, when Nettles approved the deal that sent him to his hometown San Diego Padres for pitcher Dennis Rasmussen. "Maybe San Diego will help me, because twilight comes later there," he quipped. "With the time difference, I could add three years to my career.")

In addition, Berra didn't know his 33-year-old pitching ace, Ron Guidry, would struggle through his worst season with an earned run average of over 4.00 for the first time. The Yankees were suddenly an old, decaying team, and it showed as they staggered into the All-Star break with a 36-46 record, 20 games out of first place.

Not surprisingly, Steinbrenner was frantic and began chipping away at Berra's coaches. On June 17, he demoted bullpen coach Jerry McNertney to the minors as punishment for Righetti accidentally cutting his finger on the jagged edge of a water cooler in the bullpen. Convinced Righetti had actually been in a fight, Steinbrenner personally interrogated everyone who'd been in the bullpen at the time, threatening to subject each of them to a lie-detector test. When the stories checked out, the frustrated Steinbrenner cited McNertney for his failure to impose discipline in the bullpen.

Then, at a meeting in his Yankee Stadium office with Berra and his coaches and Clyde King just prior to the All-Star break, Steinbrenner sought to cast further blame on his coaching staff for the state of the Yankees' season.

"This is just unacceptable," he moaned to the group. "I've given you guys everything you asked for and this is what I get? This is the team you wanted, and look how they're playing! All of these guys, they're all stinking up—it's embarrassing . . . and who's to blame for that? This is your team, and it's on you guys for the way they're playing!"

As Steinbrenner continued, the coaches kept glancing at Berra, who was sitting silently across the big table, his head down, clenching the arms of his chair to the point where his knuckles were turning white. Finally, at about the fifth mention of "your team" by the owner, Berra rose from his chair and glared menacingly at Steinbrenner.

"I've heard enough of this shit!" Berra shouted. "You keep saying this is my team? That's a fucking lie and you know it! This is *your* fucking team. You put this fucking team together. You make all the fucking moves around here. You get all the fucking players nobody else wants. You put this fucking team together and then you sit around and wait for us to lose so you can blame everybody else because you're a chickenshit fucking liar!"

Now it was the coaches' faces that were turning white. No one had ever seen Berra so enraged. As he started heading for the door, Berra abruptly reversed course and leaned over the desk. Flipping a pack of cigarettes off the desk right onto Steinbrenner's chest, he yelled, "You want me to quit? I'm not quitting. You'll have to fire me!"

As Berra stormed out of the room, leaving his cigarettes, Steinbrenner sat stone-faced. Finally, as the others in the room squirmed nervously in their seats, Steinbrenner shook his head and managed a weak smile.

"I guess the pressure's starting to get to him," he said softly before adjourning the meeting.

Instead of firing Berra, Steinbrenner listened to him, allowing him and GM Clyde King to bring up a contingent of youngsters from Triple-A Columbus: shortstop Bobby Meacham, third baseman Mike Pagliarulo, outfielder Brian Dayett and pitchers Dennis Rasmussen and Joe Cowley. The infusion of youth proved to be just the tonic for Berra's desultory team. From the All-Star break to the end of the season, the Yankees went 51-29, the best second-half record in baseball. And though it was not nearly enough to catch the runaway American League East champion Detroit Tigers—who got off to a record-setting 35-5 start to the season and never looked back—the Yankee resurgence, led by another of Yogi's youth brigade, 23-year-old first baseman Don Mattingly, who edged out Dave Winfield, .343–.340, in a down-to-the-last-day race for the batting title, convinced Steinbrenner to give Berra another chance with this group in '85.

The Yankees' second-half surge in '84 also earned Clyde King the confidence of Steinbrenner. For the first time since Gabe Paul had been head of baseball operations, Steinbrenner gave his general manager a free hand, beginning with the December '84 winter meetings in Houston, where King pulled off a series of deals that would prove beneficial to the Yankees, if not to Berra. In addition to shedding some expensive, faded veterans like Rick Cerone and Steve Kemp, King netted, among others, Rickey Henderson, the game's premier base stealer and five-time All-Star outfielder from the Oakland A's; a young relief pitcher from the Atlanta Braves named Brian Fisher, who turned out to be an excellent setup man for Righetti; and Ron Hassey, a lefty power-hitting backup catcher from the Chicago Cubs.

Indeed, the team that assembled in Fort Lauderdale the following spring appeared to be championship caliber. In his annual state-of-the-team spring training address on February 20, Steinbrenner said, "Yogi will be the manager this year, period! A bad start will not affect Yogi's status. I have put pressure on my managers in the past to win at certain times, but that will not be the case this spring."

Just before the Yankees left New York for spring training, Steinbrenner had agreed to do a photo shoot at Yankee Stadium with Berra and others for the cover of *The Sporting News*, which was doing a feature story on the uniform collection of the renowned baseball memorabilia collector and limited Yankees partner Barry Halper. For the occasion, the group donned period handlebar mustaches while wearing authentic uniforms of legendary, long-ago Hall of Famers Ty Cobb, Cy Young, John McGraw and Pud Galvin. For his part, Steinbrenner posed as Jacob Ruppert, the owner of the Yankees in the '20s and '30s, decked out in a tuxedo, bowler hat and bushy gray handlebar mustache. The picture made for a classic *Sporting News* cover, with Henderson appropriately wearing the uniform of Cobb, whose all-time base-stealing record he would one day eclipse. But after the shoot concluded, Steinbrenner was in a foul mood. It seemed three prominent Yankees who'd committed to take part, Lou Piniella, Willie Randolph and Don Baylor, were no-shows and had to be replaced at the last minute by Torborg and pitchers John Montefusco and Mike Armstrong.

"I come all the way up here to do this, and those three guys don't show up?" Steinbrenner fumed to Halper. "Well, that's okay. I'll take care of them. The next time Randolph wants any favors for his family, he can forget it. The same thing for Baylor, who's always asking me for extra tickets. Fuck 'em!"

After an uneasy minute of silence, Halper sought to break the tension by asking: "What about Lou, George?"

"Piniella?" Steinbrenner replied. "Oh, don't worry, I'm gonna *really* fuck him. I'm gonna make him the manager!"

(After retiring in June '84, Piniella had come on as Berra's batting coach, and while he did aspire to one day become a manager, he and Steinbrenner had not yet had any substantive conversations about it.)

As events quickly played out that spring, the *Sporting News* photo shoot proved to be the last time Berra would have much interaction with either Steinbrenner or Henderson. Midway through spring training, Henderson sustained an ankle injury that prevented him from playing most of the exhibition games and had him on the disabled list to start the season. Without Henderson as their leadoff catalyst, the Yankees' season began with a three-game sweep at the hands of the Red Sox in Boston. They won the next four, but then a string of five losses in their next seven games, including another two of three to the Red Sox at Yankee Stadium, had Steinbrenner poised to renounce his spring training vow about his manager. Though Henderson returned after missing the first ten games, it was too late for him to help Berra.

The end came on Sunday afternoon, April 28, in Chicago, after just 16 games. During the course of the Yankees' 4–3 loss to the White Sox, which completed a three-game sweep, Steinbrenner, who was watching on TV in Tampa, phoned GM Clyde King in Chicago and ordered him to perform the execution. Much as he admired and respected Berra, King did not attempt to talk Steinbrenner out of it. Rather, after the game, which dropped the Yankees' record to 6-10, King made his way down to the visiting clubhouse, entered the cramped manager's office and asked the reporters to leave.

"This is about as a hard a thing as I've ever been asked to do," King said to Berra, "but George feels we need to make a change."

"Some full season," said Berra, shrugging. "Whatever he wants; it's his team. He coulda told me himself, though. Who's gonna be the manager?"

"Billy," King said glumly.

Outside in the clubhouse, the Yankee players reacted to the news with disgust. Don Baylor kicked over a trash can. Don Mattingly could be heard throwing other canisters against the wall in the shower room. Only Henderson, who'd played for and been spoiled by Martin in Oakland, showed pleasure over the change, blissfully singing and whistling in the shower room, oblivious to the glares from his teammates.

Later that afternoon, the team flew to Texas, where Martin and Sapir were waiting at the team hotel to hold a press conference with the writers. The next day, Martin addressed the disgruntled players in the clubhouse prior to the game against the Rangers.

"I know you guys are mad about what's happened," Martin said, "but don't be mad at me. Y'all got Yogi fired, I didn't. Y'all haven't been playing the kind of baseball y'all are capable of, making a lot of mistakes, not doing the little things you need to do to win ballgames. That's all gonna change now, and we're gonna get back into this race and win this thing, 'cause I'm not gonna let you get me fired."

Meanwhile, as Martin took the Yankee reins for the fourth time, Berra went back to his home in Montclair, New Jersey, where, for the next few days, he brooded about the disrespectful way he'd been fired by Steinbrenner. It was bad enough, he thought, to have been given only 16 games, most of them without Henderson, but the sonofabitch didn't even have the guts to tell him personally. The two previous times he'd been fired as manager, in '64 with the Yankees and '75 with the Mets, the owners or team chief executives had been the ones to personally convey to him their regrets at having to do what they felt they had to do. With Steinbrenner, there hadn't even been the courtesy of a phone call. So be it, he thought. He would never have anything to do with the guy again. And as long as Steinbrenner owned the Yankees, he would never set foot in Yankee Stadium again, either.

Unlike Steinbrenner's vow that Yogi would manage for a full season, this was a vow that would be kept. For 14 years.

UNDER BILLY MARTIN, the '85 Yankees—with a healthy Henderson hitting .314 and stealing a club-record 80 bases and Don Mattingly continuing his rise as one of the elite players in the game by leading the American League with 145 RBI—gradually played their way back into contention, making it into second place on July 12. From there it became a two-team race as they tried to catch the Toronto Blue Jays, whose manager, Bobby Cox, had grown up in the Yankee system as a player and minor league manager and then a coach for Martin in 1977. The whole season came down to nine days in September, beginning with a disastrous four-game showdown with the Blue Jays at Yankee Stadium. Before the first game of the series, on September 12, Steinbrenner decided it was time for one of his "Knute Rockne fire up the troops" clubhouse addresses.

As the players sat at their lockers, Steinbrenner stood in the middle of the room and said, "This is the most important series of the year. We've got to sweep! This is a test of Yankee heart and Yankee pride! We can't let Toronto shame us in our own ballpark. This is the whole season right here!"

"That sure relaxed everyone," Dave Winfield said later.

That game got off to a bad start when a singer named Mary O'Dowd butchered the Canadian national anthem, forgetting both the words and the tune, before rushing off the field in tears while the fans booed. Upstairs in his box, Steinbrenner went ballistic, demanding to know who had hired her. He was calmed by the close Yankee victory, 7–5, but the next day he gathered his front office staff in his office, where he picked up his rant about "this insult to our Canadian friends." The Yankees would issue an apology for O'Dowd's horrendous performance, he told them, and he ordered his secretary to call down to the pressroom and have public address announcer Bob Sheppard come up to the office.

The 74-year-old Sheppard, the "Voice of God," who had served as the PA announcer for the Yankees since 1951, was not accustomed to being interrupted during his pregame routine of a meal and a Manhattan, and when he came to the phone he said politely to the secretary: "Tell him I'll be up as soon as I finish dinner."

When informed by the secretary of Sheppard's response, Steinbrenner squinted.

"He said *what*? Who does he think he's working for here? I oughta fire him right now!"

Nevertheless, a good 15 minutes went by before Sheppard appeared in Steinbrenner's office, by which time the owner was more consumed with what he wanted in the apology.

"Now, this is what I want you to say," Steinbrenner began, reading from a release he'd written up.

"I've already taken the opportunity to write something," Sheppard interrupted him, pulling a piece a paper out of his jacket pocket.

Startled, Steinbrenner grabbed the paper and began reading it over.

"This is fine," he snapped, "but I want to add a few things."

"I don't think that would be a good idea," Sheppard said softly. "It needs to be succinct."

For the first time in the memory of anyone in the room, Steinbrenner was left both disarmed and speechless. They had never seen anyone stand up to him with such confidence.

Following their first-game win, the series became nothing but despair for the Yankees—and triggered outright lunacy in Steinbrenner. The Blue Jays won the next two games, then staged a six-run third-inning rally to win the series finale, 8–5, building their AL East lead back up to 4½ games. During the late innings of the previous night's 7–4 loss, in which his third and fourth hitters, Winfield and Baylor, were a combined 0 for 8 with one double-play grounder, Steinbrenner startled the press corps by charging into the press box and plopping himself down in the empty seat between Moss Klein of the Newark *Star-Ledger* and Murray Chass of the *Times*. He then began to recite a litany of his own players' negative hitting stats, disparaging almost everyone on the team, including himself.

"We've been out-owned, out-front-officed, out-managed and out-played," he fumed. "We need the big performances from Winfield, Griffey and Baylor—the guys who are making the big money. My big-money players aren't playing like money players. Where is Reggie Jackson? We need a Mr. October or a Mr. September. Dave Winfield is Mr. May!"

A couple of weeks later, the mounting hostility between Steinbrenner and his highest-paid player came to a head when Winfield, the Yankee player rep, clashed with the owner in the clubhouse over a letter from Commissioner Peter Ueberroth, urging the players to participate in a drug-testing program. At the time, the Players Association and Ueberroth had been in negotiations over the program, and the commissioner's personal appeal to the players was viewed by the union's executive director, Donald Fehr, as a preemptive union-busting tactic. As such, when Steinbrenner arrived to personally distribute the letter to the players in the clubhouse, Winfield stopped him.

"The Mets have already voted unanimously in favor of this," Steinbrenner said (falsely, as it turned out). "So I want everyone here to do the same. I'll even stand there and piss in the bottle with all of you. We need to have this. But don't forget, I'm the guy who signs your paychecks."

"Excuse me!" Winfield interrupted. "But what you're trying to do here is override the negotiation process. It's my responsibility as the player rep to pass out these letters."

"Not for long," Steinbrenner shot back.

"Is that some sort of threat?" Winfield countered. "Because you and I both know I'm not going anywhere next year but right here."

"We'll see about that," Steinbrenner snapped.

"Yeah," said Winfield, "we'll see about that."

Glaring at Winfield, Steinbrenner tossed the stack of letters onto the table in the middle of the room, walked into Billy Martin's office and slammed the door as the players started their meeting. When the meeting was over ten minutes later, Steinbrenner told the clubhouse attendant to have Winfield come into the manager's office.

"I'm not happy with what went on out there," he said. "We can't be having these sort of public confrontations. It's not good for team morale."

"Not good for team morale?" Winfield said. "You're a fine one to talk about team morale, after blasting us the way you did after the Toronto series. You may employ us, but I'm in that locker room every day, and I know what goes on in there and how the players feel. You don't."

Steinbrenner didn't like this. "I'll talk to you tomorrow," he said, before exiting the clubhouse.

The next day, when Winfield arrived at the clubhouse, he was told Steinbrenner wanted to see him in his office. Unlike the last time he'd been in the big man's office—when they had consoled each other in the aftermath of the crushing '81 World Series defeat—this encounter further emphasized just how badly their relationship had deteriorated.

"I've thought about what happened in the clubhouse yesterday," Steinbrenner began, "and I didn't like it. I don't think we're ever going to be able to resolve our differences. You've been insubordinate and you've challenged my authority in front of the team. I can't have that. I can't have you throwing me out of the clubhouse. I'm the leader. I'm the admiral. There may be vice admirals, but I'm the only admiral around here. I can't have anyone thinking you own this team. That's why you need to pick a team that you'll agree to be traded to and I'll get on it right away."

"I'm not interested in that," Winfield replied. "I like it fine right here."

"I can make it hard for you," Steinbrenner threatened.

"Like how, benching me?" Winfield asked.

"You have to understand, I'm always hard on the biggest guy on the team. I feel that's the way to motivate the other players. I'm a football guy, and that's how the great coaches in football do it."

"Well, as you can see, I don't seem to respond to that," Winfield said. "I'm a baseball guy. So how do you propose we resolve this issue?"

"I don't know," Steinbrenner said. "I think we need to have another clubhouse meeting."

They decided to address the team together that night, declaring a truce. Winfield spoke first, asserting that he and Steinbrenner agreed on two points: "We both want a winner, and we both feel there is no place for drugs in baseball. And I want to assure you," he added, "that what happened in this clubhouse yesterday between me and Mr. Steinbrenner was *not* a confrontation."

Winfield sat down, and the players began gathering their bats and gloves for pregame batting practice. Before they could leave the clubhouse, however, Steinbrenner called them to attention once again.

"That's right," he said, "everything Dave said is right. But as long as you understand there's only one admiral on this ship!"

DEMORALIZED AFTER LOSING three of four to the Blue Jays, and by the ripping they'd received from their owner in the papers, the Yankees went on to lose five more games in a row. Their season was over. All that was left was the latest disintegration of Billy Martin, which began in Detroit on September 18 when Martin consternated both his players and the media by ordering left-handed-hitting Mike Pagliarulo to bat right-handed against the Tigers' junk-throwing lefty Mickey Mahler. (He struck out looking.) Martin never fully explained his reasoning, but even Tigers catcher Bob Melvin was caught off guard.

"What in the hell are you doing?" he asked.

"I'm *trying* to get a base hit," Pagliarulo replied.

Three nights later, in the bar of the Cross Keys Hotel, in Baltimore, where the Yankees were staying, Martin got into a drunken fight with Yankees pitcher Ed Whitson.

The fight began when Martin approached Whitson's table after teammate Dale Berra, Yogi's son, told him the pitcher was becoming agitated about something.

"I'll see what the trouble is," Martin said.

Suddenly, Whitson and Martin began grabbing each other and throwing punches, toppling to the floor as Gene Michael and catcher Ron Hassey rushed over from another part of the bar to break it up. When they were finally separated, Martin began shouting, "That guy's crazy! I just tried to help him! Can't he hold his liquor?"

This further infuriated Whitson, who began advancing at Martin again as they were being shoved out the door and into the parking lot. It was there that Whitson shoved Martin to the sidewalk and kicked him in the groin with his cowboy boots. "Okay, now I'm gonna kill you," Martin moaned as he stood up. But before Martin could get to him, Dale Berra grabbed Whitson and slugged him in the mouth in response to the pitcher tearing his V-neck sweater. Whitson broke loose again, tackling Martin to the pavement in front of the hotel entrance. When order was finally restored, Martin was left with a broken arm and a bloodied nose.

Although witnesses testified that Whitson had in fact started the fight, and Martin was ultimately exonerated by Steinbrenner, the change of managers had not produced his desired results. And while the season ended on a celebratory note with Phil Niekro, the 46-year-old knuckleballer whom King had re-signed as a free agent the previous winter, pitching a four-hit, 8–0 shutout over the Blue Jays for his 300th career win, Steinbrenner had again become convinced that Martin was simply too unstable to continue managing. But who, this time, to succeed him?

By now Lou Piniella's presence on the coaching staff was seen by everyone as a confirmation that Steinbrenner was grooming his "favorite son" (as reporters and players often referred to him) to become manager. Nevertheless, Steinbrenner knew the risks involved with replacing the still-popular and experienced Martin with someone who'd never managed before at any level, so he sought to keep his fingerprints off it. "I'm leaving the decision on the manager up to Clyde King," he insisted the day after the season ended. "There will be absolutely no stipulations or input from me."

He couldn't possibly have believed the New York media was going to buy that.

In his column in the *Post* a couple of weeks later, when still no decision had been announced, Dick Young wrote sarcastically: *"I do hope somebody has called George Steinbrenner by now to let him know that Clyde*

King named Lou Piniella to manage the Yankees next season, or the first part thereof."

In his *Daily News* column, Mike Lupica imagined a dinner conversation between Steinbrenner and his best friend, Bill Fugazy, in which Steinbrenner asked innocently: *"Fu-gie, I wonder who Clyde will choose?"*

On October 27, the morning before the seventh game of the World Series between the Kansas City Royals and the St. Louis Cardinals, the Yankees confirmed their worst-kept secret: Lou Piniella was being promoted from batting coach to manager. But rather than in a formal press conference at Yankee Stadium, the announcement was made via a conference call to reporters in Kansas City, with King and Piniella in New York. Conspicuous by his absence at either venue was Steinbrenner. It seemed almost as if King was embarrassed to be making the announcement. He dutifully reiterated that the choice of Piniella had been his and his alone, yet curiously could not confirm whether Martin had been informed of his latest dismissal.

When asked what role Martin would now have with the team, King said, "I have no idea."

13

. . .

A "Favorite Son" Exiled

. . .

W HEN CLYDE KING OFFERED Lou Piniella the job as manager, he was expecting it to be a fairly simple process. How
foolish of him to think that anything orchestrated from afar
by Steinbrenner wouldn't come with unexpected complications. Sitting in
his office at Yankee Stadium on October 26, King said, "We're prepared to
offer you $150,000 per year, Lou."

"Oh, I can't do that, Clyde" Piniella said. "That's what I'm making as a
coach!"

"Uh, no, you aren't," King said. "I checked it out. You're being paid
$75,000 as a coach."

"I think maybe you need to talk to George. Ask him about the account
from American Ship that he pays me another $75,000 out of."

After nearly 15 years with the Yankees, the 61-year-old King had a
pretty good idea about the often stealthy manner with which Steinbrenner
conducted business—especially when it came to taking care of the people
with whom he had close relationships. But this arrangement caught him
by surprise. Piniella's $150,000 salary was $50,000 more than those of the

next-highest-paid coaches in baseball at the time, the result of an extension of the three-year, $1.1 million "golden parachutes" Steinbrenner had bestowed on him and Bobby Murcer after the 1981 season. On the books, Piniella was making the same as any other coach in baseball. Nobody had to know that AmShip was supplementing his salary with an equal amount.

Steinbrenner always felt a special affinity for Piniella, who was born in Tampa and had become a local icon. They shared a mutual friend in Malio Iavarone, the owner of the town's hot-spot restaurant, populated by the local sports and political cognoscenti. Piniella had grown up playing baseball with Iavarone, while Steinbrenner had become his biggest customer soon after arriving in town from Cleveland in 1973. "Lou is like a son to me," Steinbrenner would say, to which Malio would reply, "Well, he's like a brother to me."

Lou, however, sometimes resisted the owner's attempts to impose discipline on him—as he did on the day they first met in 1974.

Upon reporting to his first Yankees spring training camp in Fort Lauderdale after having been acquired in a trade from the Kansas City Royals the previous December, Piniella was greeted by the clubhouse man, Nick Priore, who informed him that, before he could be issued a uniform, he needed to go across the way to the executive trailer and see Steinbrenner.

"Is there something wrong?" Piniella asked.

"You just gotta talk to the big man," Priore said.

Steinbrenner was sitting at his desk when Piniella entered his office.

"I was told I needed to see you," he said.

"Yeah," Steinbrenner said, "you need to get a haircut. I can't see your neck with that long hair, and I need to be able to see it."

"But, sir," Piniella said. "I always wear my hair long like this."

"Not here you don't. We have a policy about that. Same thing with facial hair—beards and long mustaches."

"Well, I don't understand it," Piniella said. "What's the big deal? I mean, as far as I've always been taught to believe, didn't even Our Lord Jesus Christ have long hair and a beard?"

At that, Steinbrenner cracked a smile. Leaping up from the desk, he grabbed Piniella by the scruff of his collar. "Come here with me," he said, guiding him out the door and around to the back of the trailer, where there was a small lake.

"You see that lake?" Steinbrenner said. "If you can show me you can walk across that lake, you can wear your hair as long as you want it!"

Recounting the story years later, Piniella said, "All George needed to do was to have the clubhouse guys explain the hair policy to me, but this was his way of letting me know right up front who the boss was."

Nevertheless, Piniella proved to be the one Yankee who could get away with chiding and poking fun at Steinbrenner in public. During one of Steinbrenner's patented clubhouse addresses about hard work and sacrifice, in which he talked about his youth spent working on the docks in Cleveland, Piniella interrupted, "Oh, c'mon, George. Everybody knows the only times you ever were down on the docks were when you were gassing up your daddy's yacht!"

Usually, Piniella's impudence would serve to disarm Steinbrenner, if only for the moment. Steinbrenner treated Piniella like a son, and aside from the occasional wiseass effrontery, he expected obedience and respect. It gave him a great deal of private satisfaction to believe that Piniella was, down deep, always in need of his approval—a father-son relationship not unlike the one he had known with his own father—and this didn't change after Steinbrenner named him manager.

As part of that three-year, $1.1 million contract he had signed after the 1981 season, Piniella was required to report to spring training at 200 pounds, and if he didn't, he'd be fined $1,000 a day until he got down to it. Piniella didn't think anything of the clause, barely even noticed it when he signed the contract. Then, one day in early January '82, he was awakened at his house in Tampa by the ringing of the doorbell at 8 A.M. It was Hopalong Cassady, whom Steinbrenner now had working as a minor league coach and fitness instructor for the Yankees. On this day, the grinning Hoppy was garbed in a sweat suit and sneakers and holding a huge gym bag.

"Hoppy?" the startled Piniella said as he opened the door. "What are you doing here?"

"I'm here to work you out," Cassady said. "The Boss wants you coming into camp in shape. We're going over to the University of South Florida where they've got an obstacle course and Nautilus machines. So take this gear, get dressed and let's go."

Shrugging, Piniella donned a sweat suit and sneakers and climbed into Cassady's car. When they arrived at South Florida, Cassady took him out to the track, where he had placed a bunch of tires and ropes around the oval.

"It's an obstacle course," Cassady explained. "You run through the tires, drop down for five push-ups, get up, continue running all around the track, through the tires and ropes that are spaced out. See how they're zigzagged? You're gonna need to be able to get through it in under three minutes. Then we'll know you're in shape!"

"Wait a minute," Piniella said. "That's a quarter-mile track, Hoppy! The best runners in the world need at least a couple of minutes to cover this, and that's without running through tires and ropes and doing push-ups in between."

"Don't worry," said Cassady. "By the time we're done these next couple of weeks, I'll have you breaking three minutes! I'm considerably older than you, and I can do it."

Piniella thought about that for a few seconds while gazing out at the imposing obstacle course.

"You know what, Hoppy?" he said. "I don't believe you can do this thing in three minutes."

"You bet I *can*!"

"Okay," said Piniella. "What's that expensive brandy you like? Carlos One? I'll buy you a bottle of Carlos One if you can do this obstacle course in three minutes."

"You're on," said Cassady, handing Piniella the stopwatch.

With that, Piniella grabbed his newspaper, climbed up into the stands and gave the signal to Cassady to start running the course. Watching the 47-year-old former Heisman Trophy winner huffing and puffing around the track, periodically dropping to the ground to pump off five quick push-ups, Piniella smiled in amusement. Finally, when Cassady crossed the finish line, Piniella held up the stopwatch and grinned.

"Sorry, Hoppy," he said. "You missed by nearly a minute. You're just gonna have to do it again tomorrow, if you want that Don Carlos."

And so, every morning for a week, they would get to the track and Piniella would take the stopwatch and stroll up into the stands, where he'd sip his coffee and read the paper as Cassady ran the obstacle course. As Piniella recalled to me years later: "I never had to do the obstacle course, but Hoppy got me back in the afternoons, working the hell out of me on the Nautilus machines."

Still, Cassady failed in his mission: Piniella weighed in at 207 pounds on the first day of spring training. When this was reported to Steinbrenner, he told assistant general manager Bill Bergesch, "You let Piniella know I'm gonna start docking him $1,000 a day until he gets that weight down. That was our deal!" As the spring wore on and Piniella still hadn't gotten down to 200 pounds, Steinbrenner ordered manager Bob Lemon to start playing him every day, for the full nine innings, in both the "A" games and "B" games in the Grapefruit League. Finally, on March 16, Piniella blew a gasket.

Calling the beat reporters together before the Yankees' "A" game against the Montreal Expos in West Palm Beach, Piniella paced up and down the first base line and began to vent.

"I am utterly disgusted with George Steinbrenner and his policies," he fumed. "I have been playing baseball for 20 years, and I have never conducted myself in any other way but professionally for the New York Yankees. Now I'm being treated like a 19-year-old, and I find that insulting. I'm not happy with the damn fines. I'm like Smith-Barney. I've worked hard for my money. To be treated suddenly like Little Orphan Annie is ridiculous!"

When told of Piniella's tirade, Steinbrenner laughed.

"Sometimes Lou Piniella needs to be treated like a 19-year-old," he told reporters. "Everyone in Tampa will tell you that. I've got the weight requirement right here, in black and white. He knew what he was signing. If I'm a man and my employer is paying me $350,000 a year, which is more than the president of the United States is making, and there are ten million unemployed people earning nothing in this country, I'd sure as hell take seven pounds off and honor that contract!

"Someday soon Lou Piniella will be out of baseball and in business. Boy! He'd last ten days in business!"

Of course, that day would never come—Steinbrenner made sure that it didn't. Steinbrenner recognized in Piniella the same fire and special connection with the fans that Billy Martin had. This was part of his calculus when he decided to give Piniella, at age 38, that three-year contract. The owner knew Piniella was smart, especially when it came to baseball. On numerous occasions through the years, he had sought Piniella's opinion on players or the state of the team. More important, in Steinbrenner's eyes, Lou was *family*. He wanted him to stay with him, to mold him into a great leader through the same tough love his father had given him.

That began in the spring of 1986, when Piniella embarked on his first season as Yankees manager. Over the winter, Steinbrenner had concentrated his efforts on the off-season roster improvements for his new manager. Specifically, he had his eye on Britt Burns, a 6-5, 220-pound left-handed pitcher with the Chicago White Sox. Only 26, Burns had already won 70 games in the big leagues, including 18 in 1985. Despite that, Steinbrenner had heard that the White Sox might be interested in trading him before his contract ran out. What he didn't know was that the White Sox had leaked that rumor themselves, and that they had done so because, unbeknownst to anyone else in baseball, Burns was suffering from a congenital hip condition. "I think you better trade me," he told White Sox board chairman Jerry Reinsdorf, "because I'm not sure if I'm going to be able to pitch much longer."

Although he and Steinbrenner had made amends for their costly series of run-ins back in 1983, Reinsdorf thought the Yankees owner had gotten the better of him in a trade the previous August, in which the Yankees dealt the White Sox fading infielder Roy Smalley in exchange for two minor league pitchers, one of whom, Doug Drabek, was a top prospect. Reinsdorf had been widely criticized by the Chicago media for giving up Drabek, and now he saw a chance to get even with Steinbrenner.

"George called me to ask me about Burns, and I kept telling him I didn't want to trade him," Reinsdorf recalled in a 2008 interview. "I kept offering another pitcher, Rich Dotson, and he kept saying he had to have

Burns. I wasn't about to tell him that, in between starts at the end of the season, Burns was walking around on crutches."

Reinsdorf finally agreed to trade Burns in exchange for catcher Ron Hassey and right-hander Joe Cowley (who had been 12-6 for the Yankees in 1985), subject to Burns passing a routine physical administered by the Yankees. When the Yankees' team physician, Dr. Bonamo, examined the X-rays of Burns's hip, he was aghast. He had never seen a hip so deteriorated on an athlete, and at a meeting in Steinbrenner's office with GM Clyde King and the baseball operations group, he expressed his concerns.

"I would have to tell you, as your team physician, George, do not under any circumstances trade for this player," Bonamo said. "I can't be any more emphatic about this. I'm looking at these X-rays and they're awful. If nothing else, at least let me bring him in and check him out personally."

"No, no, no," said Steinbrenner. "We can't do that. People will recognize him, and we've got to keep this deal under cover."

"Who would recognize Britt Burns?" Bonamo asked incredulously. "It's a very bad hip, and it's not gonna last, in my opinion."

"Okay," said Steinbrenner. "Everybody understand this?"

As the rest of the group nodded in agreement, Steinbrenner thanked Bonamo for his appraisal and dismissed him from the meeting. Then, turning to the others in the room, he said, "What does he know? He's just a doctor. We're baseball men! This kid Burns is an ace pitcher, and they don't come along every day."

Thus, Steinbrenner went ahead with the deal.

During the second inning of his second spring training start in 1986, Burns limped off the mound, wincing in pain. The next day, after Burns had consulted three hip specialists, Steinbrenner announced to the reporters that the pitcher was going on the 60-day disabled list and would likely have to undergo a hip replacement. His career was over before he ever pitched a game for the Yankees. Yet despite the disastrous turn of events, Steinbrenner insisted he would not seek any restitution from the White Sox.

"There's no way Chicago could have known," he insisted to the media. "There's no way I could blame them. My relationship with the White Sox owners is a good one. They're two of my closest friends in baseball."

"I never admitted to George I knew about Burns's condition," Reinsdorf told me. "I think he just figured that I'd gotten even with him. You have to understand, that was the morality I found back then when I came into the game. Everybody was out to screw everybody, and they all knew it."

Losing Burns was one of many ominous developments for Piniella in his first spring as manager. Another was the sudden reemergence of Billy Martin, who'd been invited to camp by Steinbrenner to serve as a special advisor. Martin became a constant presence that spring, sitting with the owner at all the exhibition games. He was particularly critical of the young left-handed pitcher Dennis Rasmussen, whom Piniella was hoping to keep on the staff as his fifth starter. Though 6-7 and 225 pounds, Rasmussen did not throw particularly hard, and Martin viewed him as "soft," an opinion he never tired of voicing to Steinbrenner.

If Piniella thought there'd be a honeymoon period before Steinbrenner started telling him how to manage, he was mistaken. Before the very first exhibition game of the spring, against Earl Weaver's Baltimore Orioles, Piniella had just posted the lineup, which did not include Don Mattingly, Rickey Henderson or Dave Winfield, and was sitting in his office when Steinbrenner burst in.

"What's with this lineup and all these guys I never heard of?" Steinbrenner demanded. "You're going up against Weaver and playing all these kids? We can't have this! You're going to get embarrassed in your very first game!"

In truth, it was Steinbrenner who was worried about being embarrassed. He'd invited his friends Bill Fugazy, Donald Trump and former Chrysler chairman Lee Iacocca to Fort Lauderdale for the inaugural spring training game, and instead of Henderson, Mattingly and Winfield, they were going to see a bunch of nobodies.

"George, I'm not changing the lineup or the pitchers," Piniella said. "They've already been posted. It's a long spring, and I need to see these kids."

"I would think you'd want to win your first game," Steinbrenner grumbled before departing to join his pals in his rooftop box.

Happily, the Yankees won the game, and afterward Steinbrenner poked his head in Piniella's office and offered his grudging congratulations: "You got lucky today!"

Without Burns, whom he had counted on to anchor the Yankees pitching staff, Piniella was now looking at a rotation projected to include 32-year-old Ron Guidry, the knuckleballing Niekro brothers, Phil and Joe, who were 46 and 41, respectively, and Ed Whitson, the fragile 30-year-old Tennessean who had flopped the previous season, his first in New York, after being lured from the San Diego Padres by Steinbrenner with a five-year, $4.5 million free agent contract. Whitson's ERA jumped from 3.24 to 4.88 in '85, and the booing from Yankee fans so intimidated him that he began to take an alternate route, under the stands, to get to the Yankee bullpen in right field before games. The "insurance policy" for this uncertain rotation was the 43-year-old Tommy John, who was in camp on a trial basis after being released by the Oakland A's in midseason the year before.

This was why Piniella desperately wanted the 26-year-old Rasmussen on his staff. Unfortunately, in one of his last starts of the spring, Rasmussen fell victim to a strong wind and the small ballpark in Pompano Beach. With Steinbrenner and Martin watching from the box seats next to the Yankee dugout, he gave up a three-run homer to pint-sized Texas Rangers infielder Curtis Wilkerson. As Rasmussen trudged off the field, Steinbrenner hollered at him: "I've seen enough! It's off to Columbus for you!"

After the game, Piniella tried in vain to dissuade Steinbrenner from banishing his young pitcher. It was only because of a back injury suffered by John a week later that Rasmussen earned a reprieve and made the team after all. But even that came with a caveat from Steinbrenner: If he wanted to keep Rasmussen, Piniella had to release the popular Phil Niekro, because Martin and the other scouts all said he had nothing left. "That was the hardest thing I ever had to do as a manager," Piniella said. "Phil had no idea it was coming. After all he'd done, in a Hall of Fame career, coming off two straight 16-win seasons, he didn't think he had to prove anything." The one consolation for Piniella was that Rasmussen went on to lead the Yankees in victories in '86, at 18-6. No other starter won more than nine, while Niekro won 11 for the Cleveland Indians.

The aging and iffy pitching bore out Piniella's concern as injuries beset Guidry and Joe Niekro (who were a combined 10-21 after May 10). In addition, problems arose for Piniella at two key positions, shortstop and catcher. After showing so much promise as a rookie in 1984, Bobby Meacham collapsed both offensively and defensively, forcing Piniella to audition several more shortstops before finally solidifying the position with Wayne Tolleson, acquired July 30 from the White Sox in a multiplayer deal. That trade, in which the Yankees also got 25-year-old catcher Joel Skinner, was viewed by many in the media as Reinsdorf's "make-up" to Steinbrenner for the Burns deal. Butch Wynegar, who'd been Piniella's regular catcher, suffered a breakdown and had to be placed on the restricted list in August with what was described as "mental fatigue." Considering the upheaval of Yankee player personnel, it was somewhat of a miracle that the rookie manager was able to bring the team home in second place, 90-72.

By far Piniella's biggest problem, however, was the festering feud between Winfield and Steinbrenner. Now five years into a contract that Steinbrenner had regretted almost from the moment he signed it, Winfield's failure to be the next Reggie was compounded by the fact that Steinbrenner believed the Winfield Foundation was being grossly mismanaged. As a result, beginning in 1982, he'd withheld those $100,000 annual contributions to the foundation that were stipulated in the contract. This prompted two separate lawsuits by Winfield, seeking to collect the back payments. And so, when Winfield's batting average dipped to .228 in early July and he went 4 for 25 with no homers or RBI during a stretch in which the Yankees closed out a home stand with five losses in seven games, Steinbrenner pounced.

Following an 8–3 loss to the Detroit Tigers at Yankee Stadium on July 2, Steinbrenner called Piniella to his office. "I want you to bench Winfield," he said. "He's killing us. He's just not the same player we thought he was."

"Oh, c'mon, George," Piniella pleaded. "Dave's a professional hitter. He's gonna come around."

"You heard me," Steinbrenner said. "We can't afford to wait for him to come around. If he's not producing, we have to get somebody else in there who will. Get him out of the lineup."

Piniella reluctantly obliged, but could not bring himself to tell Winfield. Instead, he merely posted the lineup in Chicago the next day with Dan Pasqua, a second-year left-handed hitter, in Winfield's place in the outfield.

When Winfield saw it, he was furious. "What's this?" he said to Piniella. "I understand if you want to give me a day's rest, but don't I at least deserve the courtesy of being told in advance instead of coming to the ball-park and being surprised in front of everybody?"

"I'm sorry, Dave," said Piniella. "I should've told you. You probably know this is out of my hands."

"So when am I gonna play?"

"Just give me a couple of days." Piniella sighed.

When Piniella was asked about the benching, he said, tellingly, "If it were up to *me* . . . to *me* . . . I would put Dave's name in the lineup every day and let him produce. There's nothing more I would like better than that, and I told Dave that."

After missing two games, Winfield got back into the lineup and began hitting, ultimately lifting his batting average to .262, with respectable pro-duction numbers of 24 homers and 104 RBI. Nevertheless, Steinbrenner remained on the offensive. In his column in the *Post* on August 25, Dick Young quoted the owner as suggesting that the reason Winfield wasn't liv-ing up to his $1.8 million salary was that he was devoting too much time to his foundation. "Dave is not the player he used to be," Steinbrenner said. "He's good but not that good."

Winfield's response? "That's right. I'm better!"

THEN THERE WAS Billy Martin. Still very much a presence at Yankee Stadium, Martin was honored on August 10 when the Yankees retired his number 1. But as the team foundered out of contention during the final months of the season, there was surprisingly little talk about Martin be-ing recycled again. On several occasions Steinbrenner groused to reporters that perhaps he'd made a mistake in hiring Piniella without any previous experience managing a ball club. But other than a transparent column in the *Daily News* by Steinbrenner's friend Howard Cosell, in which Cosell wrote that Piniella had mismanaged "ten or more games" during the course of the season, it still seemed likely that Steinbrenner intended to give his rookie manager another year. (Curiously, Cosell did not offer any specifics of those "ten or more games," and when Piniella confronted Steinbrenner about having leaked the column, he adamantly denied it.)

Right after the '86 season, Clyde King, citing a need to spend more time at home with his family in North Carolina, stepped down as general manager and turned his attention to scouting and working with the pitchers in the Yankees farm system. His handpicked replacement was 44-year-old Woody Woodward, a former shortstop in the major leagues whom King had hired away from the Cincinnati Reds, where he'd been an assistant GM a couple of years earlier. King had shielded the laid-back, soft-spoken Woodward from Steinbrenner's manic demands, but now, as with all the previous Yankees general managers, his life would become a daily living nightmare. In Piniella Woodward found a kindred spirit during the 1987 season, which proved to be the nadir of both of their baseball careers. Piniella often joked about the stash of aspirin bottles and other pills for stress and high blood pressure that Woodward kept in his desk drawer at Yankee Stadium. "Poor Woody," he joked to reporters. "His desk drawer was like a pharmacy up there!"

As in 1986, the 1987 Yankees were plagued by injuries. Twelve different players spent time on the disabled list before it was over, including Rickey Henderson for 55 games. By the end of the season, Piniella had fielded a team-record 48 players. Only two starting pitchers, 44-year-old Tommy John (13-6) and 34-year-old Rick Rhoden (16-10), were with the team for the entire season. The back problems that would ultimately force Don Mattingly to retire prematurely in 1995 first surfaced in 1987, sidelining him for 18 games. (Yet this somehow did not stop him from homering in eight consecutive games, tying a major league record, or from setting another by hitting six grand slams.)

It was not until after the All-Star break that the injuries finally began taking their toll. At the break, the Yankees were 53-34 and in first place, with a comfortable three-game lead over the Toronto Blue Jays. After beating the Chicago White Sox, 6–2, in the final game of the first half, Piniella was sitting in his office at Yankee Stadium when the phone on his desk rang. It was Steinbrenner, calling from Tampa.

"I just won you the pennant, Lou," he declared. "I got you Steve Trout!"

Trout, an injury-prone 30-year-old left-hander, had been having a decent season (6-3, 3.00 ERA) for the last-place Chicago Cubs. He came from good baseball bloodlines—his father, "Dizzy" Trout, was a two-time 20-game winner with the Detroit Tigers in the '40s—but it soon became apparent to Piniella that the old man's nickname more than applied to the son. When he got to New York, Trout, who'd spent his entire career in Chicago with mostly losing teams, was completely overwhelmed. His inability to throw strikes (37 walks, nine wild pitches and 27 strikeouts in 46⅓ innings overall) drove Piniella to the point of exasperation. Finally, after being kayoed after just 2⅓ innings by the Milwaukee Brewers on September 22, Trout surrendered. As he handed the ball off to Piniella, he said disconsolately, "I'm just not worth a shit, Lou. You better get me out of here."

Not only did Trout not win Piniella the pennant, he never even won a game for the Yankees.

In spite of the injuries and misguided acquisitions, like Trout and defensively challenged catcher Mark Salas (who committed 10 passed balls after being acquired from the Minnesota Twins in June for pitcher Joe Niekro), the Yankees managed to hang on to second place until August 6, when a stretch of seven losses in eight games dropped them to third, where they would stay for the rest of the season. After watching in disbelief one game in which Trout surrendered five walks and three wild pitches and Salas was charged with a passed ball, Piniella invoked a bit of gallows humor by telling reporters, "Watching Trout and Salas out there today, I thought maybe they were betting on the game! I wanted to get in on the action! I told Salas: 'I bet you're having a lot of fun here. You've gotten to know everyone in the front-row seats behind the plate on a first-name basis!'"

Following an 8–5 win over the Detroit Tigers on August 2, the last day of a home stand, Steinbrenner called Piniella up to his office, where they started talking about the state of the team. Piniella complained about Salas's catching and Henderson's lingering stay on the disabled list, while Steinbrenner countered by saying he wanted Piniella's primary situational left-handed reliever, Pat Clements, replaced on the roster by another reliever, Al Holland, whom he'd signed in April '87 as a favor to agent Tom Reich, one his longtime friends and periodic "advisors." It didn't matter that Holland had pitched so poorly that spring that he had to be demoted to Columbus, where the manager, Bucky Dent, recommended he be released. Steinbrenner wanted him up. "I was looking through my binoculars at Clements warming up in the bullpen out there today, and I've never seen an athlete look so scared," Steinbrenner said. "And I know athletes, having coached football at Northwestern and Purdue."

"Clements is the least of our problems, George," Piniella protested. "My catcher can't catch, Trout can't pitch, I can't get Henderson on the field and you're only interested in taking care of your agent friends!"

"Never you mind that," Steinbrenner shot back. "You stick to managing. I've gotten you everything you asked for!"

"That's bullshit and you know it," Piniella said before heading down to the team bus to the airport and then on to Cleveland.

The next night, the Yankees were shut out, 2–0, by the Indians. After the game, Steinbrenner called the Yankees' PR man, Harvey Greene, in the press box and instructed him to tell Piniella to be in his hotel room the next day at 2 o'clock for a phone call.

Even though he knew Steinbrenner was famous for ordering his underlings to wait in their hotel rooms for phone calls that never came, Piniella fully intended to be there for this one. But after a few drinks with lunch at the Pewter Mug that afternoon, Ed Rosenthal and Mickey Friedman, two of Steinbrenner's limited Yankees partners from Cleveland, talked Piniella into going shopping instead, and he later went directly to the ballpark. There he endured a horrendous 15–3 loss in which Salas committed three more passed balls and Holland, in his debut, surrendered five walks and six runs in 1⅔ innings of relief.

The next day, Piniella phoned Woodward to discuss getting another catcher.

"I can't talk to you, Lou," Woodward said.

"What do you mean?" Piniella asked incredulously.

"I'm not allowed to. He's ordered all of us in the organization not to talk to you."

"You gotta be kiddin'!"

"I don't know what to tell you, Lou. You're just going to have to call him and take it up with him. I just know I can't talk to you. If I do, I'll be fired."

Instead of calling Steinbrenner, Piniella took his case to the media. That night, he summoned the writers together in the visitors' clubhouse in Detroit (where the Yankees had moved on from Cleveland). "For three weeks now, I've been trying to get a catcher, Joel Skinner, called up from Columbus," he said. "Lately I've intensified my efforts, but he still hasn't made it on the Columbus shuttle. When I asked my general manager about it, he informed me he can't talk to me."

Upon hearing Piniella's complaints, Steinbrenner immediately went on the offensive. After first placing a letter of insubordination in Piniella's file, he dictated a statement over the phone to Harvey Greene, who, like his predecessor, Ken Nigro, on the night of the dueling press releases in 1983, frantically scribbled Steinbrenner's words on the front and back of a piece of paper and up into the margins. His arm began to ache as the owner continued to ramble. The result was a bizarre, almost comical "statement": *"Reacting calmly to what he termed 'inaccurate newspaper reports aimed at creating sensationalism rather than in reporting the facts', New York Yankee owner George Steinbrenner confirmed that he had not planned to talk to Yankee manager Lou Piniella in the near future."*

Having established that point, Steinbrenner used the rest of the statement as a public flogging of Piniella over the missed phone call: *"The simple fact is that Piniella didn't even bother to come back from lunch—if that's where he really was—to get a call from his boss at 2:00 P.M. I don't know of too many guys—even sportswriters—who, if their boss told them to be available for a call at a certain time, wouldn't be there!"* Then Steinbrenner proceeded to completely undermine Piniella's relationship with one of his key players: *"As far as the Rickey Henderson matter is concerned, Woody called me and told me that Piniella wanted to disable Henderson right away because he was 'jaking' it, his teammates were mad at him and he [Piniella] wanted guys who wanted to play and he would win it all without Henderson. I told Woody to get me a doctor's report—that I wouldn't disable a man as punishment. . . . I said we should talk to Lou. We did, and Piniella told us he wanted Henderson traded as soon as possible. Both Woody and I agreed—'no way,' and we told him so. . . . Dr. John Bonamo told us on Thursday that Rickey might be ready for the weekend in Detroit. Then on Saturday he reversed that completely and said Rickey's leg was sore with some swelling and told us the prognosis was not good. I went into the training room personally—told Rickey of our plans— patted him on the back and then told some writers that Rickey was indeed hurt, that he was not jaking it, and that we would disable him."*

Bonamo recalled that episode as being the most trying of his nine-year term as Yankees team physician, and the turning point that led to his resignation.

"George told me I was to check Rickey out and tell them whether he was capable of playing," Bonamo said. "They had a letter all prepared to suspend him if I said he could play. I said to myself: 'This is really getting out of control.' George never crossed the line with me about making up medical reports. If he had, I'd have been out of there. But this was the closest he came, and I told him shortly thereafter I wanted my life back."

Steinbrenner concluded the statement by saying: *"As far as me not talking to Piniella, that's pure horseshit—ask Woody. . . . A couple of the players think I should not get involved as much as I have been all year to this point—fine. That's okay with me. I've got other things to do. They think they can do better that way, that's just fine. I'll keep the whole month of October open, anxiously awaiting the World Series at Yankee Stadium."*

But Steinbrenner's attempt to put Piniella in his place and drive a wedge between him and his star players backfired. After the players read the statement in the clubhouse in Detroit that afternoon, Don Mattingly and Don Baylor set fire to it in the shower room. The next day, all the New York newspapers lambasted Steinbrenner for essentially destroying his manager and blowing up the season. Mattingly was quoted as saying, "We're behind Lou 100 percent. The only positive thing about the statement is [Steinbrenner] said he's gonna butt out. That's the way we like it." And in a column in the *Daily News* under the bold banner headline BUTT OUT! Mike Lupica wrote: *"The manager asks for pitching help and the owner gives him the likes of Steve Trout and Al Holland."*

For his part, Piniella was devastated. The next night, the Yankees were clobbered 10–1 by the Royals in Kansas City. After the game, Piniella asked me to accompany him to the Longbranch Saloon, a bar and restaurant downtown in which he had a part-ownership. "Why is he doing this to me?" he said. "Doesn't he want to win? This is a mess now. He's killed whatever chances we had of winning. But do you know what really gets me? I really loved this guy. He did a lot for me and my family, and I can't forget that. But I can't forget this either."

In all probability, the season was lost anyway. Henderson did not rejoin the team until September, by which time the Yankees were in third place, five games off the pace after an 11-17 August. At the same time, shortstop Wayne Tolleson went down with a shoulder injury while the catchers, Salas, Skinner and Rick Cerone, had a combined .208 batting average. On August 28, Piniella and Steinbrenner broke their freeze with a summit meeting at Yankee Stadium, after which Steinbrenner said, "I think Lou now understands that when the boss says he's going to call at a certain time, you should be there to take the call." In the meeting, which Steinbrenner had requested, Piniella asked the owner to issue a retraction of his "bum" reference to Salas. "I guess Lou didn't use that word," Steinbrenner said. "That's not a word he uses. It's one I do use, so I probably misquoted him."

Steinbrenner gamely proclaimed that he and Piniella were "in this thing together" and that "I want to win as badly as Lou does." But each knew too much damage had been done, both to the team and their relationship. In mid-September, Piniella confided to friends that he could no longer work for Steinbrenner. At the end of the year, the Yankees announced that Piniella was moving up to become general manager with a new three-year contract, and that Billy Martin would be taking over as manager, his fifth stint in charge of the team. Nobody was surprised about Billy's return, but Piniella's friends were astounded that he would continue to work for Steinbrenner and felt he had sold out his principles.

"What happened," Piniella told me years later, "was that Woody wanted to go to Philadelphia to become the Phillies' general manager, and George told him the only way he'd let him go was if I'd be the GM. Plus, my family all wanted to stay in New Jersey, where my kids could finish high school."

But it wasn't long after he had bailed out Woodward that Piniella began asking himself, "Why did I do this?" As general manager he now found himself occupied with the task of trading Dave Winfield at Steinbrenner's insistence. The closest he came to a deal of even near equal value was the Houston Astros' offer of Kevin Bass, a power-hitting right fielder seven years younger than Winfield. When Steinbrenner was told of the Houston offer, he ordered Piniella to go to Houston with Gene Michael and scout Bass for a few days.

"But I don't want you sitting with all the other scouts," Steinbrenner said. "They'll all know what's going on. You guys go down there and dress in raincoats and bring umbrellas so nobody will recognize you, and then get a couple of seats in the upper deck, far away from everybody else."

Piniella remembered barely being able to contain his laughter over the phone. How much more conspicuous could he and Michael be, sitting all alone in the upper deck, with umbrellas and raincoats—in the Astrodome!

Having witnessed firsthand the toll that the job had taken on Woodward, Murray Cook, Cedric Tallis, Al Rosen and Gabe Paul before him, Piniella had no illusions about being able to work any better with Steinbrenner in his new capacity. He quickly tired of being the middleman between Steinbrenner and Martin, whose relationship—predictably—began to deteriorate again as soon as the 1988 season began. "It just wore me down," Piniella told me, and on May 29 he resigned, with the GM duties turned over to his assistant, Bob Quinn. His term as GM lasted barely seven months.

But he would be back much sooner than anyone expected, thanks to Billy Martin's unerring ability to find trouble and run afoul of Steinbrenner. On May 6, Martin was beaten up outside a Texas strip club after a loss to the Rangers, exasperating Steinbrenner. "Billy and the drinking," he complained to me a couple of days later. "I don't know what I'm going to do with him, but this can't keep going on like this." I took that to mean Billy was once again on the way out the door. On June 23, following a 2-7 Yankee road trip that knocked them out of first place, Steinbrenner called Piniella into Yankee Stadium and told him he wanted him to take over the team from Martin. He said he would tear up his old contract and give him a new three-year deal at $400,000 per.

"I need you to do this, Lou," Steinbrenner said. "It was a mistake on my part, thinking Billy could handle it. He's just too unstable. I promise I won't interfere. You'll have a free hand this time."

Piniella foolishly believed him. The team was beset with the same problems as his '86 and '87 teams: an aging, inefficient pitching staff, injuries, constant changes in player personnel, the lack of a quality shortstop, and general unrest in the clubhouse. The clubhouse conflict was, as usual, a direct result of Steinbrenner's periodic sniping at players in the press, this year for their inability to make any headway on the AL East division leaders, the Toronto Blue Jays. It came to a head on August 21, when Don Mattingly unloaded on the owner following a 4–2 loss to the last-place Seattle Mariners at Yankee Stadium.

The customarily low-key Donny Baseball had had a couple of spirited verbal clashes with Steinbrenner in the past—over the Yankees' renewing of his contract in 1986 and his winning a $1.975 million salary arbitration decision in 1987—but those disputes weren't viewed as having created any lasting hostility between the two. After losing the arbitration case to Mattingly, Steinbrenner said, "The monkey is clearly on his back now. I expect he'll carry us to a World Series championship. He's like all the rest of them now. He can't play little Jack Armstrong of Evansville, Indiana, anymore. He goes into the category of the modern-player-with-agent looking for bucks."

Mattingly kind of laughed that off as George being George, but Steinbrenner kept up the zings as the first baseman's continuing back problems sapped his production in 1988. Then all of Mattingly's frustration bubbled over that August afternoon.

"You come here, you play and you get no respect," Mattingly said to a gathering of reporters in the Yankee clubhouse. "You get money and that's it. They think money is respect. Call us babies, call us whatever you want—if you don't treat me with respect, I don't want to play for you. They treat you like shit. They belittle your performance, make you look bad in the media. After they give you the money, they can do whatever they want to. They can beat you over the head and you just take it."

Throughout the uncharacteristic diatribe, Mattingly never mentioned Steinbrenner by name, but the reporters had absolutely no doubt as to who he was talking about.

What particularly irked Mattingly was the fact that the Yankees, despite all their injuries and pitching problems, were still only six games out of first place and yet Steinbrenner continued carping at them. "It's hard to come to the ballpark when you're not happy playing," he continued. "I can't imagine any other club in baseball being treated like they're not in the race. It's just not right. No other club should be treated like we're treated."

The next day, Steinbrenner dismissed Mattingly's complaints in a statement from Tampa. "I think he should have never said what he said," the statement said. "But he's young. When he signed, he guaranteed a pennant and unless things turn around, he's gonna have to eat some crow. It's a very convenient thing for the team because they have an involved owner who they can blame."

Behind the scenes, Steinbrenner had called Piniella to talk about issuing a dual statement in which Piniella would also criticize Mattingly for speaking out.

"I want you to authorize this statement and sign it," Steinbrenner said.

"I'm not doing that, George," Piniella said. "That would finish me with my players."

"Yeah, well, you better decide who you're working for—the players or me."

Steinbrenner decided not to issue the dual statement, but it was clear to Piniella that nothing was ever going to change between the two of them. It had been a terrible mistake to agree to be recycled like Billy Martin and the rest of them. Apparently Steinbrenner felt so too, as he never filed Piniella's three-year contract with the league office. It wasn't until mid-September that Piniella found out from someone in the Yankees offices the contract was never filed. Instead of calling Steinbrenner himself about it, however, he called me and asked if I would poke around and see what I could find out.

"This is typical of the kind of shit he's always pulling," Piniella said.

On September 19, I placed a call to Steinbrenner in Tampa and asked him about the contract.

"It's true I haven't filed it with the league office," he said, "but I have my reasons."

"I don't suppose you want to share with me what those reasons are?" I said.

"I'll tell you," Steinbrenner said, "but you can't write this, because it's a very sensitive matter."

"During the course of going through the financial records, I discovered that Lou had been stealing from me," Steinbrenner said.

"Stealing from you?" I said. "How could he be doing that?"

"Well, there's an entry in the books listing $10,000 worth of Scandinavian furniture sent to Lou's home. I never authorized anything like that. If

Lou's stealing from me, I've got to let him go for the good of the organization. He's like a son to me, and I'm certainly not going to prosecute him, but he's got to go."

In Steinbrenner's theater of the bizarre, this was the topper. He was terminating Lou Piniella for allegedly stealing furniture from him, and he wanted me to be the messenger by writing in the paper that Lou was in trouble with Steinbrenner over a personal matter and wasn't long for his job. I hung up the phone thinking there had to be a logical explanation for all of this, and wondering why Steinbrenner would bring this up with me and not Piniella. If he wasn't going to talk to Piniella about it, I was.

The next day Steinbrenner flew back to New York for a meeting with his limited partners at Yankee Stadium. After the meeting, I happened to see Ed Rosenthal, one of the Yankees limiteds, standing at the batting cage.

"What are you hearing about our boy Lou?" I asked him.

"He's gone," said Rosenthal. "George is really down on him. If I were you, I'd be getting ready to write Dallas Green is the next Yankee manager. I hear the deal's all but done."

Steinbrenner's selection of Green, the strapping 6-foot-5 taskmaster who'd managed the Philadelphia Phillies to the 1980 world championship before moving over to the Chicago Cubs as general manager, was not all that surprising. It had been widely rumored that Steinbrenner had reached out to Green earlier in the season as a possible replacement for Martin if Piniella wouldn't agree to take the job again. The die was obviously cast, and my conversation with Piniella about the furniture would have to wait. The next day, under the headline BRONX BOMBSHELL, the *Daily News* ran a front-page story with my byline, quoting sources as saying Dallas Green would be hired to replace Piniella as Yankee manager at the end of the season. There was no mention of furniture.

When I walked into Piniella's office at Yankee Stadium that night, he was understandably upset.

"Why couldn't you have waited to write this until the season was over?" he asked me.

"I wish I could have, Lou," I said. "But it couldn't wait. Too many other people were starting to know about it."

Much as I wanted to ask him about the furniture, given his mood, I didn't want to seem like I was accusing him of anything, so I made my exit. A week went by and, after the Yankees lost two out of three to the Red Sox to fall into fourth place, Steinbrenner and Piniella had what the manager, speaking with reporters, called a "clear-the-air" meeting at Yankee Stadium. After this session with the writers, I got Piniella privately in his office and asked him whether, during his meeting with Steinbrenner, there had been any mention of off-the-field issues of concern to the owner.

"Oh, you mean that shit about the furniture?" he said.

"Uh, yeah," I said, suddenly feeling as if an anvil had been lifted from my shoulders. "What is it with that furniture?"

"Do you believe that sonofabitch thought I was stealing furniture from him?" Piniella exclaimed. "I'm making $400,000 a year! What the fuck does $10,000 worth of furniture mean to me?"

Piniella explained to me that, when he agreed to take over for Martin, he was told that one of his extra duties was to do a five-minute pregame radio show for which there was no compensation. This was part of the record $50 million package WABC had paid for the Yankees' radio broadcast rights the previous winter. Though he had never had to do a radio show in his previous stint as manager, Piniella was aware that other managers were paid as much $50,000 extra to do radio shows.

"I'm not doing it unless I get paid," he told Arthur Adler, the Yankees' VP of business.

They worked out a compromise in which Adler arranged to compensate Piniella for the show with advertisers' merchandise. Handing him the Scandinavian furniture catalog, Adler told Piniella to have his wife, Anita, pick out what she wanted.

Of all the executives, from in and out of baseball, to pass through the Yankees in the '70s and '80s, none understood Steinbrenner better than Arthur Adler. Adler's association with Steinbrenner began in 1977, after the Manchester Broadcasting Co., which owned the Yankees' radio rights, declared bankruptcy, leaving the Yankees with zero radio broadcast revenue after their championship season. Adler, who owned a marketing business, had been selling all the advertising for Manchester, and Steinbrenner asked him if he would continue handling the Yankees' radio rights. Adler suggested that he and Steinbrenner become partners, with Steinbrenner paying all the production costs and announcer salaries and Adler selling all the advertising. Steinbrenner would get 75 percent of the advertising revenue and Adler 25 percent. The first year of the partnership, the Yankees netted $750,000 (as opposed to zero the year before), and by 1986 their net radio revenues were over $6 million.

That was when Steinbrenner told Adler he wanted to sever the partnership.

"You're making too much," he said, to which Adler replied: "Well, maybe, George, but you're making five times what I'm making!"

The truth was, Adler loved being around the Yankees' broadcasts, where Phil Rizzuto was a humorous diversion from his day-to-day business dealings with Steinbrenner. Rizzuto, the Hall of Fame Yankee shortstop of the '40s and '50s, was the lead announcer on the TV and radio broadcasts. His habit of veering off the game and riffing about his personal life and those of his friends invariably drove Steinbrenner into a frenzy. As such, Adler never allowed himself to stray far from the famed red phone installed in the Yankee Stadium production booth.

"George loved Rizzuto, and Phil, I think, really feared George," Adler said in a 2007 interview, "but he nevertheless couldn't resist getting George upset by talking about things on the air that had nothing to do with the game."

Once, Rizzuto's broadcast partner Fran Healy, who was in on the joke, said, "So, Phil, I hear you and your wife, Cora, took a little trip this afternoon?"

"Yeah, Healy," Rizzuto said, "we went to the Amish country in Pennsylvania and wound up in a place called Intercourse. Intercourse, Pennsylvania! Would you believe it? It was pretty hot there, and by the end of the day we were all sticky and sweaty."

Listening in his booth, Adler cringed as the red phone began ringing.

"This is outrageous!" Steinbrennner screamed. "We're gonna be pulled off the goddamn airwaves! Shut him up, will you?"

"What do you want me to do?" Adler said. "I can't control him."

He was right about that. Nobody could control the incorrigible Scooter. Once, on a West Coast road trip, Rizzuto ran into an old World War II buddy who had lost one of his feet. The guy was wearing a prosthetic foot that he had invented himself. Rizzuto invited him up to the booth for that night's Yankees-Angels game. Shortly after it got under way, Rizzuto decided to put his buddy on the air and invited him to launch into a dissertation about his prosthetic foot invention.

"The problem," related Adler, "was that Phil hated going on the West Coast trips, and he'd tried in vain to get out of that one, only to be told that George insisted he be there. So this was Phil's way of tweaking George and me for making him go on the trip. The other thing was, Phil didn't believe anyone was ever listening to the broadcasts back in New York at one o'clock in the morning."

As Rizzuto and his friend carried on about the prosthetic foot, completely ignoring the game, Steinbrenner called Adler at home in a fury.

"I don't care how you do it," he screamed, "but get that fucking guy with him off the air!"

Adler immediately phoned Brian Fergenson, the radio engineer in the Anaheim Stadium press box, and relayed Steinbrenner's order: "Get him out of the booth!"

"I can't," Fergenson said. "Phil's got his chair jammed up against the door so it won't open. Nobody can get in there!"

It wasn't long after that Steinbrenner began to excuse Rizzuto from going on the West Coast trips.

A few weeks after severing their radio advertising partnership in December 1986, Steinbrenner called Adler with a new proposal. He had just fired his VP of accounting and business, Dave Weidler, and now he wanted Adler to essentially take over all the Yankees' business operations.

"I reminded George that I had my own marketing business, but he insisted that I take this job," Adler related. "I didn't know anything about the Yankee business operations outside of the radio, TV and marketing end of it, so the first thing I did was get ahold of the previous year's budget and go through it item by item."

As Adler began perusing the budget, he stopped at one particular item: "Black Muslims, $20,000."

"I went in to George and asked him what this was all about," Adler said, "and he cut me off, saying: 'Never mind, just pay it.'"

Adler later learned from other longtime Yankees employees that, soon after Steinbrenner bought the team, he'd complained in the papers about all the vandalism and graffiti around Yankee Stadium. Someone from the Black Muslims, the separatist, sometimes militant organization, came to him and said that, for an annual "contribution," they'd put an end to the vandalism.

And as Gabe Paul had noted on his tapes, during the 1976 World Series, Steinbrenner had also considered extending the Black Muslims' work to address the problem that was Mickey Rivers's wife, Mary.

Another curiosity Adler didn't dare question—even though it cost the team tens of thousands of dollars—was Steinbrenner's penchant for manipulating the attendance figures for his own purposes. After the crosstown Mets won the world championship in 1986, Steinbrenner was insanely jealous. He couldn't have the Mets outdrawing him, so, beginning in 1987, Adler or ticket manager Frank Swain would have to call down to Tampa after the sixth inning of every game at Yankee Stadium to report the attendance figure before they could announce it. If Steinbrenner didn't like it, he would simply make up a new number, which was then given to the public relations director to be announced in the press box. In order to keep books straight, the Yankees ticket department devised a secret code in which all the changed figures would end in the number 7.

"It was truly bizarre," said Adler, "especially when you consider the visiting team shared in the gate receipts, which George was deliberately making higher than they really were. But that was George. He couldn't stand being one-upped by the Mets, and he didn't care what it cost him."

It did not take long for Adler to realize there was a decided difference between working *with* Steinbrenner and working *for* Steinbrenner. Once in his employ, Adler was no different from any of the other front office minions who were made to march to the owner's beat. This included the requirement that he be at the Yankee Stadium offices 52 weeks of the year, including holidays. Steinbrenner himself authorized vacations, and more often than not would at the last minute revoke permission while conjuring up some sort of emergency situation. In November 1987, Adler arranged a trip with a group of major league players to St. Maarten to conduct base-ball clinics and play a couple of exhibition games. When he arrived at his hotel on the island, the busboy noticed a message envelope under his door. Adler instructed the busboy to leave it on the floor and, only after a couple of cocktails with his wife, Shelly, on the veranda did he finally pick up the envelope. The message, marked "urgent," said he was to call Yankees president Bill Dowling at home, no matter the time.

"He wants you back here right away," Dowling said when Adler called him. "There's some problem with the WPIX and SportsChannel TV contract and you've got to be back in the office tomorrow to handle it. I can't do it."

"Well, I can't do that," Adler said. "I've got all sorts of commitments here, and I'm not leaving."

"You've *got* to!" Dowling said desperately. "What am I gonna tell him?"

"Here's what you tell him," Adler said. "I was driving a car from the airport to my hotel. It was a dark road. A goat ran out in front of me. I swerved the car and it went into a ditch. My wife hit her head on the dashboard. We went to the hospital, where they determined she's had a concussion, and I can't leave her here. Got it?"

"Okay," said Dowling. "Car . . . dark road . . . goat . . . ditch . . . hospital . . . concussion. I'll try. Why are you doing this to me?"

It's uncertain what Dowling told Steinbrenner. But knowing Steinbrenner as he did, Adler then took further steps to cover himself. Upon hanging up with Dowling, he called the St. Maarten sports commissioner.

"How many hospitals are there on this side of the island?" he asked.

When informed there were two, Adler said, "Okay. I need a favor. I need you to have my wife listed as a patient in both of those hospitals."

The next day it was reported to him that both hospitals had received deliveries of huge floral arrangements for Shelly Adler. For weeks afterward, whenever Adler saw Steinbrenner at the Yankee Stadium offices, the owner would ask, "How's your wife doing?"

"That was George's way of letting me know that he admired people who could be as clever as he was," Adler said.

Inevitably, Adler's relationship with Steinbrenner ended the way most did: badly. Adler's new deal with Steinbrenner called for him to receive 15 percent of all the revenue he brought to the Yankees, and by 1988 he was making over $1.5 million per year from the TV and radio advertising, Yankee Stadium signage and *Yankees Magazine*, which he'd founded. Steinbrenner felt that was too much. On July 4 of that year, Steinbrenner's birthday, the two had a heated exchange in Steinbrenner's office at Yankee Stadium. Steinbrenner accused Adler of stealing money from him. It wasn't true, of course, and the enraged Adler lunged at him. Lurching backward, Steinbrenner tripped on the chair shaped like a giant leather glove next to his desk and toppled to the floor, and Adler stormed out. Over the next two years, the two sued and countersued each other before finally reaching a settlement.

"What it came down to," said Adler, "is that George believed all of the Yankees revenues should be his."

DALLAS GREEN WAS named Yankees manager in an October 8 conference call to reporters. Once again, Steinbrenner did not participate in the call. Instead, he was meeting with Piniella in Tampa, where they discussed how his again ex-manager would serve the remaining two years of his contract under the terms of a personal services clause the owner had inserted in it. Like Billy Martin on his hiatus from managing, Piniella, they decided, would move to the broadcast booth to work as a color analyst.

Steinbrenner had promised not to stand in Piniella's way if another team offered him the chance to manage again. That, too, proved to be an empty promise. In mid-May, the Toronto Blue Jays fired their manager, and Pat Gillick, Toronto's general manager, sought to hire Piniella. But there was no way Steinbrenner was going to allow Piniella to manage in the same division as the Yankees, least of all for Gillick, whom he still resented for leaving the Yankees years earlier. After allowing Piniella to interview with Toronto, Steinbrenner informed Gillick that he wanted compensation, specifically one of the Blue Jays' four top pitching prospects: Todd Stottlemyre, David Wells, Duane Ward or Alex Sanchez. Gillick, who suspected that as soon as he said yes to any of them, Steinbrenner would then tell him he needed more, passed.

After the 1989 season, Piniella became the manager of the Cincinnati

Reds (whose owner, the eccentric Marge Schott, took special pride in her Nazi memorabilia collection and appeared daily on the field before games with her pet St. Bernard; Piniella's friends warned that he was going from one cuckoo's nest to another). Steinbrenner didn't demand any compensation from Schott, figuring there was no way Piniella, managing a small-market team in the other league, a team that had just finished in fifth place and had a crazy, tightfisted owner, would ever come back to haunt him.

Nobody expected Piniella to guide the Reds wire-to-wire to the National League West title in 1990, or that his team would sweep Tony La Russa's heavily favored Oakland A's in the World Series. While Piniella was managing the final game of the World Series, Steinbrenner was in New York appearing as the host on *Saturday Night Live*. Steinbrenner clearly relished playing the buffoon—in one sketch he stood up from behind a desk to confront a female sportswriter, wearing only his skivvies and socks.

Behind the scenes, however, the *Daily News*' Bob Raissman, the only reporter covering the show, witnessed a vastly different Steinbrenner than the public ever saw.

"He was all by himself, in the semi-darkness at the back of the set, playing a piano and softly singing 'The Shadow of Your Smile,' " Raissman recounted. "It was eerie. He just seemed to be in total peace with himself."

Hours after managing the Reds to a 2–1 victory over the A's, Piniella was still sitting at the desk in the visiting manager's office of the Oakland Coliseum, basking in the afterglow of his finest achievement in baseball. I had filed my column for the *Daily News* and stopped in to offer him my congratulations.

"Quite a ride," I said. "You sure paid your dues for this. I hear George was on *Saturday Night Live* tonight, pulling down his pants. Did he send you a telegram?"

"Not that I've seen," Piniella said. "He's too busy with his acting career."

"I've got to write a follow-up column tomorrow," I said. "Anything else you want to say?"

Piniella smiled weakly.

"Yeah, there is something, something I've been meaning to say for a long time: George, I can manage!"

14

. . .

Tale of the Tapes

. . .

O N A COLD FRIDAY night in mid-January 1984, the New York chapter of the Baseball Writers' Association gathered at the Shea Stadium Diamond Club for its annual roast. For this occasion, the writers decided to hold a reunion of the seven New York Yankees public relations directors who had served under George Steinbrenner, beginning with Bob Fishel.

On the dais before each man was a small cardboard tombstone inscribed with his name and the years he served, underneath the large letters R.I.P. "They should have all the managers up there too," observed Yogi Berra. Steinbrenner, who had also been invited, initially indicated that he might attend. But as the event drew closer, he put out word through his emissaries that he would be occupied with other business that night. So too, the writers discovered, were most current Yankees employees.

Moss Klein, the chairman of the New York baseball writers that year, remembered getting a telephone call a couple of days before the roast from Doug Melvin, the Yankees' assistant director of scouting. "He called me from, I think, a telephone booth outside of Yankee Stadium," Klein said, "and told me that George had forbidden everyone from attending under threat of firing and that he was checking up on everyone."

Sure enough, only a handful of Yankees employees were allowed to attend the event, including their present PR man, Joe Safety, and Gene McHale, the team president. McHale's primary duty was to make sure the only Yankees attendees were those Steinbrenner had approved. "Mr. Steinbrenner was always tentative about coming," Safety explained to the writers. "He's involved in a lot of heavy things right now in Tampa."

Safety wasn't offering an alibi for Steinbrenner. Unbeknownst to the writers, Steinbrenner had something much more serious on his mind than a silly roast by his former PR men.

BY THE LATE '80s, Steinbrenner's two principal entities, the Yankees and American Shipbuilding Co., both of which were thriving at the beginning of the decade, had begun experiencing hard times. The Reagan administration's decision to eliminate government subsidies had proved to be a death knell to the shipbuilding industry, causing more than 40 American shipyards to go out of business between 1984 and 1989. (Ironically, on January 19, 1989, Reagan pardoned Steinbrenner for his 1974 conviction for illegal campaign contributions to President Nixon. The pardon stunned even Steinbrenner's closest friends, since there was no indication of any close relationship between the Yankees owner and the president, though he did acknowledge that some of his Republican friends, including Bill Fugazy, had written letters to Reagan on his behalf.)

From 1987 to '89, AmShip reported losses of $21.7 million and its stock plummeted from a high of $17 a share to $2. In order to keep it from joining the ranks of other closed-down shipyards, Steinbrenner was forced to start pumping his own money into the company in exchange for stock. He bought AmShip's private plane for $891,000 and in 1989 gave the company $3 million. Thus, in a dramatic shift of financial resources, the company whose hefty profits had allowed Steinbrenner to purchase the Yankees in 1973 was now being kept on life support through money from the Yankees.

In particular, Steinbrenner was subsidizing AmShip with the revenue from the record $50 million ABC radio rights deal he got for the Yankees in 1987 and his TV rights bonanza in April 1986, when, through his friend Sonny Werblin, the former owner of the New York Jets and CEO of Madison Square Garden, he was introduced to Art Barron, the president of Paramount Entertainment, and Bob Gutkowski, the president of Madison Square Garden Network.

In the 1980s, the Madison Square Garden Network, which televised the

NBA's New York Knicks and the NHL's New York Rangers games, was a basic service on most local cable TV systems, with the exception of Cablevision (which dominated the Bronx, Long Island and New Jersey), where it was a pay channel. Paramount's parent company, Gulf+Western, which owned the Garden, the Knicks, the Rangers and the network, had enlisted Barron and Gutkowski to take the fight to Cablevision to liberate the MSG Network from pay status.

"The only way to do that," Gutkowski told me in a 2008 interview, "was for us to get baseball."

At the time, Steinbrenner was in the midst of a 15-year deal with Cablevision, which televised 75 Yankee games on its own SportsChannel network. But Gutkowski had heard there was a clause in the contract in which the Yankees, two years hence in November 1988, could buy back the rights for $6 million. It was with this in mind that Barron and Gutkowski, in April 1986, approached Steinbrenner, who was sitting in Suite 200 of the Garden during a Knicks playoff game.

"Through all our discussions, George never came right out and confirmed the clause," Gutkowski said. "All he said was he was free to make a deal. He was pissed at Cablevision because his revenues from his deal with them weren't coming close to their initial projections. That was because they'd been based on the Yankees being on pay TV, which a lot of people back then still couldn't afford."

What Gutkowski and Barron proposed to Steinbrenner was a deal in which the MSG Network would televise 75 Yankee games in both 1989 and '90 and then 150 Yankee games beginning in 1991, all on basic cable. For this, they said, they were prepared to pay Steinbrenner $493.5 million over 12 years. It was a staggering amount of money that sent shockwaves through baseball, since no team in any sport was getting anything remotely close to that for their TV rights. But as Gutkowski said, "We had to have baseball to make the network a viable entity. Our summer programming had been reruns of *The Untouchables*, for God's sakes! It was a landmark deal in that both parties came out big winners, and it changed the industry, all because George had the foresight to put that buyout clause in his Cablevision contract."

But while the Yankees' TV and radio deals were bringing in previously unimaginable revenues, on the field the team was failing as badly as AmShip. The Yankees hadn't been to the postseason since 1981, and Steinbrenner had made ten managerial changes and employed six different general managers. The team had finished in second place in 1986, fourth in 1987 and fifth in 1988. This is part of the reason that Steinbrenner went outside the Yankee family and hired 54-year-old Dallas Green, the straight-talking, old-school disciplinarian who was credited with literally browbeating the Philadelphia Phillies to the 1980 world championship.

"What surprised me most when I got hired was that George allowed me to bring in all my own coaches, who were all non-Yankee people," Green said in a 2008 interview. "I knew in the past he always wanted to have his guys in the clubhouse, but I guess he was seeing how his ways hadn't been working."

One of Green's first actions upon taking over the Yankee reins was to call Don Mattingly. Mattingly had experienced a difficult 1988 season. Back problems had curtailed his home-run and RBI production from 30 and 115 to 18 and 88, respectively, and this was compounded by his escalating hostilities with Steinbrenner. Green had gotten wind that Steinbrenner was quietly calling around to other clubs to determine Mattingly's trade value, and this was something he wanted to nip in the bud.

"I need to know if you want to play here, Donny, or if all this stuff with George last year has soured you on the Yankees," Green said.

"No way," said Mattingly. "I've got my issues with George, but I still want to be here. This is the organization I grew up in, and I don't want to go anyplace else."

"I'm glad to hear that," said Green, "but if you do want to stay here, you need to call George and straighten this out with him. He's getting ready to shop you around, and you're one of the guys I really need here."

Mattingly called Steinbrenner in Tampa, but the conversation did not go very well.

"I appreciate you calling me, Donny," Steinbrenner said, "but I'm telling you, I can't have you popping off like that in the papers. You have to understand I'm your boss, and I expect and deserve respect."

"Respect," said Mattingly, "is what I'm talking about here, Mr. Steinbrenner. I came into camp each year in shape and on time. I play every day banged up, and you complain about the team and belittle my performance."

"I pay you well," Steinbrenner said. "I have a right to say what I feel."

"Money is not respect!" Mattingly shot back. "That's what I said last summer. You think just because you pay us a lot, that's respect. Well, it isn't."

"Well, if you don't think it is, then good luck to you," Steinbrenner said before hanging up the phone.

Mattingly remembered turning to his wife, Kim, after the phone conversation ended so abruptly and telling her to start packing up the house. But as he reflected in a 2008 interview, that conversation, however acrimonious and final it seemed at the time, was actually the turning point in his relationship with Steinbrenner.

"From that point on," Mattingly said, "I never had another problem with him. You couldn't just let George beat you up. He respected me for speaking my mind and standing up to him."

MATTINGLY WOULD STAY, but another of Steinbrenner's employees, Harvey Greene, who had been media relations director since 1986, was plotting his escape. Greene held the dubious distinction of having lasted longer on the job than any of Steinbrenner's previous PR directors, but it had come with a price. He'd developed a nervous cough and, for reasons he never explained, could be seen devouring loaves of bread in his Yankee Stadium office. By the spring of 1989, Greene was fried. He'd endured as the messenger and middleman through all of Steinbrenner's bouts with Lou Piniella, Billy Martin and Dave Winfield; had obediently forsaken countless dinners with friends to stay in his hotel room waiting for phone calls from the owner that never came; and only once had taken a vacation. He longed for a job that would restore some normalcy to his life. Hell, he longed just to *have* a life again.

Then, in the last week of February, Greene heard that the Miami Dolphins of the NFL were looking for a new media relations director and he dashed off a letter requesting an interview. A few days later, he got a call from Tim Robbie informing him that his father, Dolphins owner Joe Robbie, would like to meet him. Greene checked the Yankees' spring training schedule and said he could come down to Miami the following Tuesday, an off-day for the Yankees. Even though he assumed there would be nobody in camp that day, Greene dutifully showed up at the executive trailer and worked alone at his desk until it was time to slip out for his noontime meeting with Joe Robbie. He was in the process of changing into a new suit in the trailer bathroom when he heard the thumping of feet outside. Peering through a crack in the door, he was stunned to see Steinbrenner. What was he doing here? How would Greene get out of there now?

Greene was starting to sweat. Looking up, he noticed the open window over the toilet. Was it big enough to squeeze through? Thank God, it was! Once on the ground behind the trailer, Greene had to make his way to his car in the parking lot on the other side of the trailer without being spotted by Steinbrenner. He crawled under the trailer, continuing on his knees behind a couple of parked cars until he got to his own.

"I often wondered," he told me in a 2007 interview, "if George ever looked out the window and saw the car easing out of the parking lot with no driver."

Greene's meeting with Joe Robbie went so well that the Dolphins' owner, an icon in Miami, offered him the job on the spot. Now he just had to resign. The next day, Greene approached Steinbrenner in the executive trailer and informed him that he'd been offered the job with the Dolphins and that he was going to accept it.

"You did this without telling me?" Steinbrenner said.

"Uh, yes," said Greene. "It just came up."

"Well, we'll see about this."

With that, Steinbrenner ordered his secretary to get Joe Robbie on the phone. As Greene sat across the desk from him, Steinbrenner launched into a diatribe at Robbie.

"I can't believe you would try to do something like this to me, Joe," Steinbrenner said. "Stealing one of my employees behind my back? So much for our friendship. That's okay. You know that baseball team you're trying to get for your stadium down there? Well, I'm on the expansion committee, and I don't think you're gonna get it."

Listening to this, Greene's head began to ache.

"I couldn't believe I'm sitting there listening to two titans of industry arguing over a PR man who was me!" Greene said.

Robbie didn't back down, and the two finally agreed to let Greene stay with the Yankees until Steinbrenner had found a replacement. Of course, even that proved to be a somewhat hollow promise on Steinbrenner's part. It wasn't until May 1, after auditioning a pair of PR interns all spring, that he finally settled on Arthur Richman, a veteran major league exec who'd spent the previous 26 years in the Mets' front office. On his last day, Greene made a point to visit Dallas Green's office in order to thank him for all his help and cooperation.

"Good luck and congratulations, Harvey," Green said, patting him on the shoulder. "I'm probably not far behind you."

LIKE ALL THE others before him, Dallas Green thought he knew what he was getting into when he agreed to manage the Yankees. In fact, he and Steinbrenner were so much alike—they both believed in discipline and confrontational motivation—that they might have gotten along well if the feud between Steinbrenner and Winfield hadn't burst into full-scale warfare in January 1989. That month, both men filed suit over the owner's refusal to make what was now $450,000 in payments to the Winfield Foundation.

In Steinbrenner's 25-page suit, filed in U.S. District Court in Manhattan, he charged that Winfield had failed to make his own $370,000 payments to the foundation and that only a portion of the foundation's money was going to programs in the New York City area, while tens of thousands of dollars were being wasted on limousines, unnecessary branch offices in California and Minnesota and foundation-paid "board meetings" at various resorts. In addition, Steinbrenner alleged that Winfield had past associations with gamblers—a serious charge in baseball—and that he had made substantial loans, "in one case charging 700% interest" to someone he knew was engaged in gambling.

Where did all this come from? The veteran Yankees beat reporters had a pretty good idea. For over a year, when the Yankees were on the road, Murray Chass of the *Times*, Moss Klein of the *Star-Ledger* and I had been getting late-night phone calls in our hotel rooms from a whiny-voiced man who described himself as a disgruntled former employee of Winfield at the foundation. "You know me," he'd say darkly. "I've been around the

ballpark, and I have credibility. . . . I have a lot of information on that bas-
tard Winfield. . . . It's going to come out. . . . He's a bad guy who destroyed
my life. . . . You need to check into the foundation. See where the money
is going. . . . It's a fraud . . . the whole thing." After several calls, he began
identifying himself as Howie Spira, whom the writers knew as a freelance
radio reporter who showed up frequently with his tape recorder at Yankees
and Mets home games, always nattily dressed in sharkskin suits. For the
most part, the writers dismissed him as a crackpot and a nuisance with an
ax to grind.

But the 29-year-old Spira hadn't been calling just them. Since 1986, he
had been calling Steinbrenner, who, at first, regarded him with skepticism.
But Spira persisted, and Steinbrenner grew more and more interested in
what he had to say, especially since much of it fed right into his own be-
liefs about Winfield and the foundation. Spira acknowledged that he was a
gambler who'd conned bookies into extending large lines of credit to him
because of his association with Winfield. He told Steinbrenner that he had
received two loans from Winfield totaling $21,000, for which he had to pay
back $26,500. But what especially piqued Steinbrenner's interest was Spira's
claim that during the 1981 World Series, in the middle of Winfield's 1-for-
22 slump, his agent, Al Frohman, had concocted a death threat scheme as
an excuse for his performance. According to Spira, Frohman told him they
"had to protect Dave" and ordered him to call Ed Ingles of CBS Radio in
New York to inform him of a death threat letter sent to Winfield. When
the FBI investigated, Spira said to Steinbrenner, he told them that Frohman
himself had drawn up a letter that read: "Nigger, if you play tonight you are
going to be shot and killed right on the field." Winfield's agent, Jeff Klein,
said he had no knowledge of the letter's origin. In April 1988, the New York
newspapers reported that the FBI, which had obtained affidavits from five
people saying the death threat letter "was fabricated by someone close to
the player," elected not to pursue an investigation. Meanwhile, the only
proof Spira was able to provide to substantiate his claims about Winfield
charging him usurious interest on the loans was a copy of a $15,000 check
made out to him from Winfield, which he showed to all the local TV stations after his association with Steinbrenner became public.

Nevertheless, Spira's allegations intrigued Steinbrenner. After consulting with his attorneys and his top security advisor, Phil McNiff, the former FBI bureau chief in Tampa, who had joined AmShip in the early '80s, Steinbrenner elected to go ahead and use Spira's information as the basis for his countersuit against Winfield. After Steinbrenner filed his lawsuit in January 1989, New York attorney general Robert Abrams announced that he was launching a probe into allegations of irregularities at the Winfield Foundation. Through all of this, Steinbrenner had assured Spira in vague terms that he would "take care of him" for all his assistance. Spira later said he interpreted this as meaning a job and a place to live in Tampa, and money—lots of it.

"I'm not going to go out and serve hamburgers," Spira later told reporters. "That man owes me."

Throughout 1989, Spira was relentless in keeping the pressure on Steinbrenner to reward him, calling McNiff, Yankees president Bill Dowling and Steinbrenner himself on an almost daily basis, only to be put off. Once, when he called Steinbrenner's house in Tampa, Joan Steinbrenner answered the phone.

Repeating his complaint about being constantly put off by Steinbrenner, Spira got no more satisfaction from his wife.

"I don't understand why you keep bothering his house," Joan Steinbrenner said. "I have nothing to do with his life except his children. . . . I don't even know what it was, but it couldn't have been anything too bad. You're still alive and walking."

"Barely, ma'am," said Spira.

"Oh, I don't think my husband would do anything to hurt you."

"No, ma'am. I was supposed to work for your husband."

"Well, there are millions of people who were supposed to work for my husband who don't work for my husband."

"But the difference is, your husband gave me his word, and we worked on something together."

Joan finally cut Spira off, saying, "Howard, I think you need to see a doctor. I really do," before hanging up on him.

In response to Spira's claim that he had been promised a job and compensation, Steinbrenner's attorney, Kenneth Warner, was evasive with the media about any agreement between the two, saying only that Spira "was one of several people" who provided allegations against Winfield. As the dispute continued to rage in the newspapers, with Winfield's character now being called into serious question for the first time, Mike Lupica proposed in his *Daily News* column that the two parties submit their dispute to binding arbitration. Surprisingly, both Steinbrenner and Winfield agreed. "I remember the ink was barely dry on the newspapers the next morning when Steinbrenner called me and said, 'I'm in!'" Lupica recalled. "It was as if he was saying: 'Bring it on!'" On January 24, it was announced that former assistant U.S. attorney Michael Armstrong, a prominent New Yorker, had volunteered his services to arbitrate the case under the condition that a gag order be imposed on both parties until he reached his decision.

Consumed with these problems over the off-season, Winfield did not have time that winter to maintain his customary conditioning program. In addition, he'd been experiencing back pain that got worse after he reported to spring training. Finally, an MRI revealed that he was suffering from a herniated disc. His season was over before he'd played a single game for Dallas Green. On March 24, Winfield's agent, Jeff Klein, issued a statement confirming that Winfield had undergone back surgery in Los Angeles. At the same time, the Yankees (no doubt at Steinbrenner's direction) announced that Winfield was "still seeking options" and was "day-to-day."

When Green signed his contract, he thought he was going to have Winfield and Claudell Washington (who hit .308 with 11 homers and 64 RBI in '88) in his outfield; Jack Clark, who'd led the team in homers in '88, as his DH; and Rick Rhoden (who was 12-12 in '88) as a proven starter. "But then," he told me in a 2007 interview, "George didn't re-sign Washington and traded away Clark and Rhoden for a bunch of prospects and players of no consequence without even consulting me. All of those moves were payroll-driven. Finally, I lost Winfield and all of a sudden it was not a very good team anymore."

In an effort to curtail media criticism that he was allowing the Yankees to become also-rans before the season even began, Steinbrenner, on March 21, announced the hiring of former Pittsburgh Pirates general manager Syd Thrift as his new VP of baseball operations (Bob Quinn was demoted to administrative status). The 60-year-old Thrift had transformed a last-place Pirates team that lost 202 games between 1985 and '86 to an 85-win pennant contender that drew a record 1.8 million fans in 1988. A clash of egos with Pirates team president Carl Barger led to his stormy departure in September 1988, and he'd been sitting at home in Fairfax, Virginia, running his real estate business, when Steinbrenner called.

"This job is too much for one man," Steinbrenner said at the introductory press conference for Thrift. "It's not the same game anymore. Syd, Bob, Dallas and Clyde King will make the moves they want to make. The fellow who will have less work than ever will be myself."

"It took me 40 years to make this team," a beaming Thrift said. "I always had a feeling I would end up here."

As it turned out, Thrift didn't even make it through a whole season with the Yankees. He resigned on August 29 for "personal reasons." The personal reasons were that Steinbrenner had driven him to the verge of a nervous breakdown. Lou Piniella, who spent the 1989 season in the Yankees' broadcasting booth before moving on to Cincinnati as manager of the Reds, became one of Thrift's closest confidants.

"Poor Syd," Piniella told me years later. "After a month on the job, he'd developed this nervous twitch with his eyes. A few weeks after that, he was sweating all the time and his eyes were still twitching. Then one day he started breaking out in hives. I said, 'Syd, what's wrong with you?' Finally, toward the end, his hair started falling out. I felt really bad for him. He said to me: 'Lou, I gotta get out of here. This guy's *killin'* me!'"

Rickey Henderson, the premier leadoff man in the game, was also disgruntled, and he showed it by demanding a contract extension that would pay him in excess of $2.7 million per year, higher than any Yankee in history, in order to forsake free agency at the end of the season. In an interview during spring training, Henderson said his teammates in '88 had regularly drunk too much on team flights. In another interview, with the *Daily News'* Michael Kay, he said, "If I was white, they'd have built a statue here for me already." Henderson later denied saying this, telling a group of reporters in the Yankee clubhouse, "I never even talked to Steven Kay," evidently confusing him with Reggie Jackson's agent.

On June 21, Steinbrenner approved the trade of Rickey Henderson to the Oakland A's for two relief pitchers, Eric Plunk and Greg Cadaret, and a singles-hitting left fielder, Luis Polonia, who, that August, would be arrested for allegedly having sexual relations with a 15-year-old girl in the Pfister Hotel in Milwaukee and was sentenced to 60 days in jail at the end of the season.

To his credit, Green was somehow able to keep this dysfunctional team close to .500 ball as they went into the All-Star break. Beneath the surface, however, he was fast losing the players—and Steinbrenner as well. Green's blunt style, which had served him so well in Philadelphia in 1980, quickly wore thin with the '89 Yankees. On the first West Coast road trip, in mid-May, after starting off losing three out of four to the California Angels, Green told reporters, "We stink, and I told them so. Some of them must have had their heads in Disneyland or somewhere. They didn't play with any life or any indication they had their minds on the game." On the charter flight to Oakland, many of the players donned Goofy hats with big ears and sang a parody of the Mickey Mouse Club theme song, substituting lyrics of "We do stink! We do stink!" for "Mick-ey Mouse! Mick-ey Mouse!"

Initially, Steinbrenner supported his tough-talking manager. "When Dallas said 'they stink,' he's right," Steinbrenner told Michael Kay of the *News*. "Dallas is the only reason we're still in the hunt. He's trying to turn babies into men. If they're going to attack Dallas, they'll have me to deal with. I'm the one who's getting gypped here. I ought to get all their agents in a room and tell them they're playing for a sucker."

But after the All-Star break, when the team lost 10 of 13 to finish July, Steinbrenner began changing his tune. Following a pair of final-at-bat 6–5 losses in Detroit on June 28 and 29, Steinbrenner told Tom Pedulla of the Gannett Westchester-Rockland papers: "I feel like the principal in *Hoosiers* when he questions the coach and the coach says: 'Don't worry, I know what I'm doing.' I just hope this has the same ending as *Hoosiers*."

Things came to a head on August 2, following a ten-inning loss to the Minnesota Twins in the second game of a doubleheader. The Yankees had failed to cash in on a bases-loaded, none-out situation in the ninth inning. In his column the next day, the *Daily News*' Phil Pepe quoted Steinbrenner fretting, "A manager has to find a way to score in those situations."

It was not Green's nature to allow such a direct slap from the owner to pass without rebuttal, and his was both pointed and classic.

"The statement that 'Manager George' made about game situations is a very logical second guess," Green told reporters. "And hindsight always being 20-20, that's why managers get gray. My boss always chooses to use the papers to discuss the coaching staff, rather than face to face, and that's not fair. If he's using this as a motivational tool, he's wasting his time."

By this time, Green wanted to get fired and, to the delight of the reporters, kept up a daily barrage of insults aimed at Steinbrenner. The end came in Detroit on August 18, although Steinbrenner had made up his mind two days earlier, following a third-straight loss to the Brewers in Milwaukee. That night, Lou Piniella was asleep at his home in Allendale, New Jersey, when the phone rang. On the other end was Steinbrenner telling him to get on a plane for Columbus, Ohio, the next morning. He was to meet Gene Michael, who was scouting there, and Bucky Dent, the manager of the Yankees' Triple-A farm team.

"You'll bring Stick and Bucky with you to Detroit, where I'll meet you," Steinbrenner said. "You're taking over the team from Dallas."

After hanging up, Piniella scratched his head and turned to his wife, Anita.

"I'm not sure I heard what I just heard," he said. "I think George just told me he wants me to manage the team again."

"You *can't*," Anita protested.

"You're right," Piniella said, "I can't."

He immediately called Steinbrenner back.

"I can't do this, George," he said. "Two times was enough. I won't be recycled again. You're just gonna have to find someone else, or else let Dallas finish out the season. I'm done managing for you. It can't work. I think you know that."

Surprisingly, Steinbrenner didn't push the issue with Piniella. Instead, he decided to promote the 37-year-old Dent, who was in his fifth season as a manager in the Yankees' minor league system. Dent remembered being surprised and apprehensive when Steinbrenner called to inform him he was to fly to Detroit the next day to take over as manager from Green, and that Michael would be accompanying him to serve as his bench coach.

"I really didn't want to take the job," Dent said in a 2008 interview. "I knew the club was in pretty bad shape, but what was I gonna do? I said to him, 'I appreciate the opportunity, Mr. Steinbrenner, but I just hope you'll be patient with me.' "

Now all Steinbrenner had to do was get rid of Green. For that, he would go at him where he knew he was most vulnerable: his coaching staff.

The night of August 17, Steinbrenner flew from Tampa to Detroit, arriving too late to watch the Yankees' 2–1 win over the Tigers. The next morning he summoned Green to his suite in the Pontchartrain Hotel, where the team was staying.

"I've been thinking about this, Dallas," he said, "and I've decided I want to make some coaching changes."

"Just a minute, George," Green said. "I said at the beginning of this thing you were very gracious to let me have my own coaches. If you're not satisfied with my coaches now, you might just as well fire me."

"Well, I'm gonna make the changes anyway," Steinbrenner said, ignoring Green's challenge.

"I can't stand by and let that happen, George," Green countered. "Fire any of my coaches, you have to fire me. That's the way to do it. You've done this before. It just never works. It's disruptive, that's all."

"Okay," said Steinbrenner, "but I want you to know, this is very hard on me. I even talked to my wife about it."

Unlike with all their previous verbal clashes in the papers that had led up to this moment, there was no acrimony in the room, just resignation on both sides. In truth, Green, who, like Syd Thrift, had begun taking high-blood-pressure pills, was ready to hit the road. This had not been at all what he bargained for, and he was tired of fighting the fight. Before he went, however, he wanted one favor from Steinbrenner, and that was for the Yankees to retain Frank "Hondo" Howard, the 6-foot-8, 300-pound batting coach who had been an All-America basketball player at Ohio State in the '50s, when Steinbrenner was taking graduate courses there.

"That's no problem," said Steinbrenner. "You know I love Hondo."

The two shook hands and Green walked out of the room, his parting words to Harvey Greene back in May having proved prophetic.

After Green departed, Steinbrenner called Frank Howard up to his suite to tell him that Green was leaving, but that Steinbrenner would like him to stay in the organization. Green had just told the owner that Howard was "going through a tough time," so he was not prepared for the big man's response.

"Mr. Steinbrenner," said Howard, "I came to the dance with the big boy, and I'm goin' home with him. No, thanks."

"I respected the hell out of Hondo for doing that," Green told me in 2007. "I don't think there's ever been a guy in baseball more loyal or with more integrity than Hondo. George could charm the hell out of you in a room, but in a baseball stadium he was a pain in the ass and an ogre. But I give him credit. He made the Yankees what they are, just not when I was there."

The news of Green's firing, Steinbrenner's 17th managerial change in 17 years of owning the team, did not please the media or Yankees fans. If Steinbrenner thought that replacing him with the popular Dent, home-run hero of the 1978 playoff game against the Red Sox, would excite supporters, he was greatly mistaken. When the team returned home on August 21, a new chant, "George must go! George must go!" could be heard in Yankee Stadium on a regular basis.

When Dent took over, the Yankees were 56-65 and in sixth place. The team got off to a 2-11 start under the new manager, then rallied with a 15-10 September to finish in fifth place, 14½ games behind. Their overall 74-87 record was the Yankees' worst since 1967, when they were owned by CBS. Winfield had missed the entire season, Henderson was gone, and the team had used 16 different starting pitchers over the season, two of them (Andy Hawkins and Dave LaPoint, with a combined record of 21-24) expensive free-agent acquisitions who didn't come close to living up to the money Steinbrenner had given them. There was little hope of the team improving anytime soon.

At the end of the '89 season, Bob Quinn, who had reassumed the duties of general manager after Syd Thrift resigned, quit in order to take a similar position with the Cincinnati Reds. Quinn had the distinction of making one of the worst trades in team history, at Steinbrenner's insistence, of course, in which the Yankees sent 23-year-old minor league right fielder Jay Buhner, the best power-hitting prospect in the organization, to the Seattle Mariners for Ken Phelps, a 34-year-old left-handed-hitting first baseman.

The deal had been pushed by Lou Piniella, then the manager, and Billy Martin, who was serving as Steinbrenner's front office assistant. Quinn was adamantly opposed to giving up on Buhner, but Martin contended that the kid had holes in his swing and would strike out too much in the majors. And Piniella insisted the Yankees needed a left-handed power bat. After putting off making the deal for a couple of days, Quinn got a phone call from Steinbrenner just before the July 31, 1988, trade deadline. "I don't want to hear any more about it, Bob. You're a fucking plodding tortoise! I've got to go with what my two guys say. Make the goddamn deal."

Buhner went on to become a cult hero in Seattle, hitting 310 homers over the next 15 seasons for the Mariners, while Phelps, whose power was more to left center, the deepest part of Yankee Stadium, hit only eight home runs in 131 games for the Yankees in 1988–'89. The trade later became immortalized in a scene in *Seinfeld* in which the character playing Steinbrenner knocks on the door of the home of his employee, George Costanza, and is greeted by Costanza's father, played by Jerry Stiller, who says, "How could you trade Jay Buhner for Ken Phelps?"

Steinbrenner replaced Quinn on October 13 with Harding "Pete" Peterson, who had previously been general manager of the Pittsburgh Pirates. Like Bucky Dent, Peterson too had reservations about the job. After moving the Yankees' minor league department from New York to Tampa after the 1988 season, Steinbrenner had set up a sort of "Vichy" front office in his adopted hometown in which the farm director, George Bradley, was given just as much power as the GM in New York.

"I was offered the job with the understanding there would be two GMs," Peterson said in a 2007 interview. "I knew Bradley was one of Steinbrenner's guys, on the job 24 hours a day and right there in Tampa. I thought to myself, 'This is never going to work out.'"

"It was Steinbrenner's familiar 'divide-and-conquer' mentality of running the Yankees," said Peter Jamieson, an assistant general manager to Peterson in 1989, "and it made things impossible for the baseball people in New York. Basically, Bradley, being right there in Tampa, had Steinbrenner's ear and they were calling all the shots for us."

That November, Jamieson found himself in Steinbrenner's crosshairs when the Boss signed a 35-year-old free agent infielder named Dámaso

García as a favor to his friend, the agent Tom Reich. García had once been an All-Star but was now washed up and, accordingly, Jamieson, who was in charge of the player payroll budget, affixed a salary of $125,000 after his name. Steinbrenner saw this as an affront to Reich.

"How come we're paying this guy so little?" Steinbrenner said at a meeting at his Bay Harbor Hotel in Tampa. "That isn't what we signed him for."

"Well, George," said Jamieson, "the rules say if we release a player prior to 30 days before the season, we're only obligated to pay him one-fourth of his salary. I figured that would give us about three weeks of spring training to determine he was through."

"Did you just call me *George*?" Steinbrenner said.

"Uh, yes, sir," Jameson said. "My mistake."

"Who died and made you general manager here?" Steinbrenner shot back. "You can call me George after you've made your first million. Now get the fuck out of here and redo that entire budget!"

For the record, García was released after three weeks of spring training.

ON CHRISTMAS DAY 1989, Steinbrenner was at home in Tampa celebrating the holiday with his family when he caught a news bulletin on TV. Billy Martin had been killed when his pickup truck crashed in upstate New York. Steinbrenner's first reaction was disbelief. There had to be a mistake. Why, just six days earlier, they'd been together in Tampa entertaining 2,000 underprivileged kids at the annual Christmas pageant Steinbrenner sponsored and produced. They had even discussed the 61-year-old Billy coming back to manage the Yankees for a sixth time, replacing Bucky Dent at the first sign of a slump in '89.

Steinbrenner made a series of phone calls that allowed him to piece together most of the details. Billy was indeed gone. He'd been drinking all day with a pal, Bill Reedy, and as the two men drove back to Martin's house in Fenton, New York, a suburb of Binghamton, the pickup truck skidded about 120 feet on the icy road before falling into a four-foot ditch and hitting a culvert. Martin's neck was broken in the crash, while Reedy, who initially claimed to have been the driver, suffered a couple of broken bones but was otherwise okay. Neither had been wearing a seat belt.

Steinbrenner then phoned Martin's house, where Jill Martin, Billy's wife, had just returned from identifying his body in the hospital and was pouring herself a glass of scotch.

"Don't you worry, Jill," Steinbrenner said. "I'm taking care of everything."

Four days later, a funeral service comparable to any of the grandiose productions Steinbrenner put on at Yankee Stadium was held for Martin at Saint Patrick's Cathedral in New York, which Bill Fugazy was able to secure through his connections with the Catholic Church, even though Billy was thrice divorced. Among the 6,500 mourners was former president Richard Nixon, who sat next to Steinbrenner in the front pew, along with Martin's three best friends on the Yankees, Mickey Mantle, Whitey Ford and Phil Rizzuto. With thousands of fans lining Fifth Avenue outside Saint Patrick's, the funeral cortege took Martin's body on the 45-minute journey to Gate of Heaven Cemetery, in Hawthorne, New York, where he was laid to rest in a casket bearing the Yankees logo, not far from the graves of Babe Ruth and Jimmy Cagney. It could be said this was Steinbrenner's ultimate act of contrition to Billy for the five firings and all the times he dangled the managing job in front of him, like a narcotic to an addict: a funeral fit for a Yankee icon.

THE DECLINING FORTUNES of American Ship and the Yankees, combined with the death of Billy Martin, had made 1989 a terrible year for Steinbrenner. The one bright spot came on September 6, when the arbitrator in Steinbrenner's dispute with Dave Winfield agreed with most of the charges the owner had made about wasteful spending and questionable allocation of monies by Frohman and the Winfield Foundation. At a joint press conference at Yankee Stadium, a settlement of the dispute was announced, with Winfield agreeing to pay $30,000 in reimbursement for "certain monies inappropriately expended by the foundation" and another $229,000 in delinquent payments to the foundation. For his part, Steinbrenner agreed to pay the foundation $600,000 that been placed in escrow.

"Certain allegations made by Steinbrenner and the Yankees were accurate," stated the eight-page agreement. "Winfield admits he was delinquent in making his required contributions and as president of the foundation accepts full responsibility for these mistakes."

"These things are never pleasant," a gracious and conciliatory Steinbrenner said to the phalanx of reporters. "It's difficult for a man to admit he's made mistakes, but David is doing that, and that makes him a bigger man in my eyes. I will be most happy to have him back with the Yankees next season. I am calling him Mr. May, June, July, August, September and October, because that's how much we've missed his bat. I say that most sincerely."

But that was not the end of it. Still lurking behind the scenes was Howie Spira, the architect of Winfield's fall from grace. Spira watched highlights of the press conference on TV in his small apartment in the Riverdale section of the Bronx, and read with interest the newspaper accounts of the settlement the next day. He'd been calling Steinbrenner incessantly throughout the summer, always taping their conversations, but he'd been unsuccessful in convincing the Yankees owner that he should be compensated for helping him bring down Winfield. In one of the conversations, Steinbrenner told Spira that his information "didn't produce for me anything we didn't already have," but instead had "helped substantiate what we found."

But Spira continued to plead for payment, citing a large gambling debt, and on January 7, 1990, against the advice of his team president and in-house attorney, Bill Dowling, and AmShip chief of security Phil McNiff, Steinbrenner agreed to pay him $40,000. "I can't give you a job, Howard, for obvious reasons," Steinbrenner said in a phone call with Spira. "So this is it. You've been harassing my family and bothering me, McNiff and Dowling to no end. I'm sorry about all your problems. Hopefully this will help you get a start on putting your life back together and get out of my life. You need to get away from New York, get away from me now and leave me alone."

In exchange for the $40,000, which was paid the next day in the form of two separate checks for $30,500 and $9,500 made out from Dowling's law firm, Gold & Wachtel, Spira had to sign an agreement of secrecy in which he agreed "not to seek or create any publicity regarding the nature of this matter." (In his testimony to baseball special prosecutor John Dowd,

Dowling later explained that the payment had been made with two checks because Spira had no bank account and needed some money right away. "The largest amount the bank would cash a check for was $9,500," Dowling said.) Yankees VP Leonard Kleinman interceded with officials at Chase Manhattan Bank, who opened an account for Spira even though he had none of the required credentials—a major credit card or even an accredited photo ID such as a driver's license or a passport.

Steinbrenner, of course, should have known Spira was never going to keep his end of the deal; was never going to be satisfied with just the $40,000; and was never going to stay quiet about it. No sooner had he received the checks than Spira was back on the phone to Phil McNiff.

"He gave me the 40; I want another 110," Spira said.

"Howard, that's extortion," McNiff replied.

"He made a deal with me," Spira said.

"You made a deal with *him*, Howard. *You* made the bargain."

"Well, why won't he give me a job in Tampa like he promised? Just because it might look bad?"

"Basically, yes," said McNiff.

Spira told McNiff that if Steinbrenner didn't come up with more money he was going to go public about the deal.

"He's not going to be happy about this, Howard," McNiff said. "He thought everything had been worked out, that he helped you. If someone gave me $40,000 to get started on a new life, I'd be very appreciative of it."

A few days later, Spira called Steinbrenner, pleading again for one more check.

"No, I'm not going to do that, Howard," Steinbrenner said. "That would be the worst thing I could do. All of these people know. You've called them all and told them, 'He's not doing this, he's not doing that.' Then suddenly if I turn around and do it again, shame on me. Well, this time it's shame on you, Howard, because you told McNiff, 'If he doesn't do this or that, I'm going to the papers with these tapes. I'll ruin him.' That's the absolute worst thing you could've done."

"I promise I won't come back again," Spira said. "Please write me one more check."

"I can't, because you've done it to me once, and if I did it, I'd be giving in to those threats that you've made. I'm telling you, Howard, no more. And don't bother my people anymore!"

"I'm forced to slit my throat, but before I do, I'm going to make everything I've been through made public to the whole world. There's nothing wrong with that, right?"

"Listen," snapped Steinbrenner, "let me tell you something, Howard. That's extortion in its purest form!"

Six days later, four FBI agents raided Spira's home in Riverdale with a search warrant for all his tapes, diaries, telephone records and correspondence with Steinbrenner. Having won his war with Winfield, Steinbrenner had now declared war on Spira.

But unbeknownst to Steinbrenner, Spira had been relating the details of his dealings with the Yankees owner to a dogged investigative reporter from the *Daily News* named Richard Pienciak. All during the 1989 season and in the months after, Pienciak had spent considerable time with Spira and his parents at their apartment in Riverdale, ultimately winning Spira's confidence and gaining access to the phone tapes. "When Howie first started calling me, I was like all the other reporters in that I thought he was a nut job with an agenda," Pienciak said. "But the more I talked to him, the more I felt there was something there to his story once you cut through all his exaggerating. At the same time, it had to be somehow corroborated. Everything was in the tapes."

On March 18, 1990, the *Daily News* dropped the bomb with an exclusive front-page story in which Pienciak revealed for the first time Steinbrenner's $40,000 payment to Spira. The story ran with photocopies of the two checks from Gold & Wachtel and transcripts from the various phone conversations between the two.

It was all out there now: Spira telling Steinbrenner he owed him. Spira begging for Steinbrenner to help bail him out from his gambling debts. And Steinbrenner finally giving in to him. When Pienciak called Steinbrenner and asked him to explain why he'd made the $40,000 payment to Spira, the owner said, "I did it because I cared about the guy, who, in my opinion, was a lost human being who cried about his parents, having used all their money, who cried about gamblers. . . . The reason I did it was absolutely out of the goodness of my heart, no other reason. I know I look stupid, for trusting a young guy, for trying to help a young guy." As for the secrecy clause in the agreement, Steinbrenner insisted he didn't care if the payment became public. "Do you think anything you do with Howard Spira can remain confidential? I have nothing to hide."

That wasn't the way Fay Vincent saw it. Vincent, a former classmate of Steinbrenner's at Williams, had been elevated from deputy commissioner of baseball to commissioner when Bart Giamatti died of a heart attack on September 1, 1989. As Giamatti's deputy, Vincent, along with John Dowd, a former trial attorney in the U.S. Department of Justice, had gathered the evidence that led to Giamatti handing down the permanent suspension of baseball icon Pete Rose on August 24, 1989, for betting on the game while managing the Cincinnati Reds. On March 24, the day after Spira was indicted by a federal grand jury in Tampa for allegedly trying to extort Steinbrenner, Vincent announced that he was looking into the payment but stopped short of calling it a full-fledged investigation.

All this was happening as the Yankees began the 1990 season under Bucky Dent. Dave Winfield was back after missing all of 1989 while recovering from back surgery. The 38-year-old slugger began the season as the Yankees' designated hitter, only to be reduced to platoon status by Dent, but a slump in late April in which he went 0 for 23 forced the manager to bench him. More than anyone, Pete Peterson was exasperated with Winfield's poor performance. Over the winter, Peterson had taken Winfield to lunch at the Plaza, in New York, to ascertain the perennial All-Star outfielder's recovery. "Don't worry, I'll be there, and I'm gonna have a typical year for me," Winfield had boasted. "You can count on it."

With Steinbrenner's full approval, Peterson began exploring trade options, even though, as a player with ten years in the majors, the last five with the same club, under baseball rules Winfield could not be dealt without his approval. Nevertheless, on May 11, Peterson reached agreement with the California Angels to trade Winfield for a serviceable 29-year-old right-hander, Mike Witt, who had been 9-15 in 1989 after five straight seasons with 13 or more wins. Peterson figured Winfield would embrace a trade from the Yankees after all he'd been through with Steinbrenner. But as Peterson and Dent were announcing the deal to beat writers who were gathered in the visiting manager's office at the Seattle Kingdome, Winfield, who had been informed of the trade by the GM while taking pregame batting practice, burst into the room and said, "Not so fast. I'm not going anywhere."

"This is our press conference, Dave. You can have your own when we're through," Peterson said curtly.

Afterward, Winfield declared he would not report to the Angels unless they gave him a contract extension. This left the trade in limbo as Winfield's agent, Jeff Klein, sought to work out a deal with Angels GM, Mike Port. In the meantime, Steinbrenner met with Winfield when the team got back to New York on May 14 and assured him that the Yankees would welcome him back if he was unable to reach a deal with the Angels. Steinbrenner further assured Winfield that he could count on being restored to the starting lineup, which was news to Bucky Dent. Then, on May 17, the Angels announced that Winfield had been signed to a three-year, $9.1 million extension. The long and stormy Steinbrenner-Winfield saga was over. A liberated Winfield told reporters, "The manager didn't think I could play, and the general manager wanted me traded. I felt strong in my position, but as long as I got the end result, I'm pleased."

It did not bode well for Dent that Steinbrenner had Winfield's side in their dispute. As the Yankees continued to lose and sink deeper into last place, Dent's position became more and more tenuous. In January, Steinbrenner had told the Yankees beat writers at a luncheon at "21": "Bucky will be the manager all year. He's one of my guys. He's won everywhere he's been in the minors, and we're gonna keep this guy around for a while. I have the greatest confidence in him. He's like a son to me."

Hadn't they heard that somewhere before?

But on June 5 at Fenway Park in Boston, the scene of Dent's greatest moment as a Yankee 12 years earlier, the Yankees lost 9–8 to the Red Sox on a squeeze play in the ninth inning. The loss was their ninth in 10 games, leaving them, at 18-31, with the worst record in baseball. When Dent got back to his hotel room after the game, he placed a call to George Bradley, the VP of player development in Tampa, requesting to have another pitcher sent up to him. The response was silence on Bradley's end of the phone.

"Is there something wrong?" Dent asked.

"George is not real happy right now," Bradley replied coldly, before hanging up.

Turning to his wife, Dent said, "I'm gonna be fired tomorrow!"

Sure enough, the next morning there was a note under Dent's door instructing him to be in his room at 12 noon for a phone call from Steinbrenner in Tampa.

At 2 P.M. on June 6, Bradley, who had flown up from Tampa, and Peterson held a press conference at the team's Boston hotel, where they announced that Dent had been fired and introduced as the new manager Carl "Stump" Merrill. A relatively unknown minor league "lifer," Merrill had been in the Yankee system as a manager since 1977, winning five league championships along the way. Stunning as the choice of Merrill was to the writers, no one at the press conference seemed more surprised than the new manager himself.

"I felt Mr. Steinbrenner would always hire a marquee name," Merrill said. "You have no idea what's going through my body right now. It has long been a goal of mine to manage in the big leagues. I just thought it was a goal that may never be reached, especially with the New York Yankees."

"I know I'll take a lot of heat for this," Steinbrenner said in a conference call later that day. "I said I wouldn't make a change, that I'd give Bucky the whole year, but I felt we had to do it. I'm a big boy. I'll handle it."

The truth was, Steinbrenner had already given up on the season. The team was a mess, and he was helpless to do anything about it, other than his customary firing of the manager, if only for cosmetic purposes. In this case, he couldn't even bring Billy Martin back for a quick fix. But for Stump Merrill, it was the opportunity of a lifetime. How could he have known that he was about to become the sacrificial lamb for an organization in chaos and an owner in big trouble with the commissioner?

15

. . .

Banished!

. . .

B Y MIDSPRING 1990, FAY Vincent was no longer just gathering
information about Steinbrenner's involvement with Spira. He was
now in the midst of a full-scale investigation, having once again
enlisted the investigative services of John Dowd. In early May, Steinbrenner,
accompanied by his attorney Bob Gold, was called in by Dowd to give his
deposition on everything that had gone down with the $40,000 payment
to Spira and the events that led up to it. For the better part of several days,
Steinbrenner answered Dowd's questions as a court stenographer named
Philip C. Rizzuti, of the Esquire Reporting Co., feverishly typed it all into
the record. A few days later, however, when Steinbrenner received a copy
of the document from Dowd's office, he was aghast. His lawyers brought
to his attention that long passages had either been altered or deleted
outright.

When Gold, who had taken his own copious notes of the proceeding
on a yellow legal pad, received his copy, he agreed. It was Gold's opinion
that the deposition was distorted to the point that in many cases it didn't
properly reflect what Steinbrenner had testified to. Dowd had also allegedly
taken pains to remove parts of the deposition that reflected badly on him,
among them his scorn for the press. *"I am not as public a person as you are,
Mr. Steinbrenner. I know how treacherous they are. [One of the prices we pay]
for being a free country is to let them out there torturing us."* Also allegedly

deleted were Dowd's pronouncements, on a couple of occasions, that Dave Winfield was *"the greatest Yankee who ever wore pinstripes."*

Gold was flabbergasted and immediately telephoned Rizzuti from his home in Connecticut.

"Did you do something that can get you in big trouble, Phil?" he asked.

Gold remembered Rizzuti responding: "Dowd made me do it. I can't discuss it."

But when Gold registered his complaints with Dowd and Vincent, they sloughed them off. Because it was an informal administrative hearing and not a judicial proceeding involving a civil or criminal case, Vincent said, the documents were not considered a deposition, and the changes made to them were "routine." Vincent was correct that it was not a civil or criminal proceeding, but baseball's rules of procedure—which serve as the articles of conduct for everyone in the game, from the commissioner on down, as part of baseball's constitution—state that commissioner's hearings "must be conducted like a judicial proceeding, with regard for all the principles of natural justice and fair play." And while they stopped short of charging unlawful behavior on Dowd's part, Steinbrenner's attorneys contended that, if nothing else, he had acted in an unprofessional and unethical manner in editing sworn testimony by Steinbrenner. Indeed, Paul Curran, one of Steinbrenner's lead attorneys, later wrote a number of letters to Vincent complaining about the investigation and Dowd's behavior while implying their intentions to sue.

Steinbrenner ultimately did file suit against Rizzuti and his employer, Esquire Reporting, but not Dowd, over the alleged tampering. But a federal judge dismissed the complaint, finding that the transcript had *not* been materially altered. Steinbrenner later dropped an appeal and issued a statement saying he did not question the "professional competence or integrity" of the firm and its personnel.

Did Dowd and Vincent have an agenda? Roland Thau, the court-appointed attorney who represented Spira in the extortion case Steinbrenner filed against him, told me of a meeting he had with Dowd in which Dowd told him that "only the commissioner could bring [Steinbrenner] down," and that "the arrogant son of a bitch has gotten away with shit for a lot of years and it was high time he was dealt with."

On June 26, Vincent, having received Dowd's report, set Steinbrenner's formal hearing for July 5. "It is not my place, nor is it the place of John Dowd, to hide anything from George," Vincent told Claire Smith of the *New York Times*. Nevertheless, Vincent did just that, refusing Steinbrenner's attorneys' request to be provided a copy of Dowd's report—another clear violation of the due process rights as outlined in baseball's rules of procedure, which further state that "judgment at a hearing must render a decision based solely upon information presented at that hearing." (It should be noted that when Vincent's predecessor, Bart Giamatti, conducted his hearing with Pete Rose, he'd allowed Rose's lawyers to preview the report Dowd had compiled on their client.)

Steinbrenner, seeking to expose the special investigator's unethical conduct, called Barbara Walters, then co-host of ABC's *20/20* news program. Soon, veteran reporter Tom Jarriel began working on a piece for the program, beginning with interviews of Steinbrenner and Bob Gold. But Vincent flat-out refused to talk to *20/20*, and Dowd, after first agreeing to go before the cameras, reneged.

According to an October 8, 1990, investigative report in *Sports Illustrated*, titled "Bad Job, Baseball," Dowd called an ABC lawyer to complain that Steinbrenner's allegations against him "were completely unfounded and untrue." Vincent, meanwhile, reportedly telephoned Daniel Burke, president of Capital Cities/ABC, to refute the story while subtly reminding him that Cap Cities/ABC owned 80 percent of ESPN, which had a $400 million contract with Major League Baseball to televise games, something he didn't exactly deny. "If there was such a call," Vincent later told *Sports Illustrated*, "I'm not going to talk about it."

The story never aired, but Steinbrenner had at least succeeded in calling to the attention of his fellow baseball owners for the first time the kind of "investigative" methods used by Dowd. A few months later, Bob Gold was boogie-boarding with his daughter on Cisco Beach, in Nantucket, when he noticed a tall, heavyset man in a dark suit, carrying a briefcase, approaching him on the beach. It was John Dowd. Gold could not believe his eyes as Dowd walked right up to the water's edge, the surf splashing over his expensive leather shoes.

"How could you do this to me, Bobby?" Dowd said. "I thought we were friends."

"John," said the incredulous Gold, "I can't believe you came all the way up here to seek me out just to tell me that. You're a fucking madman!"

In the days leading up to his hearing with Vincent, Steinbrenner tried to remain upbeat and confident he would be exonerated. Ira Berkow, a sports columnist for the *New York Times* who had been particularly critical of Steinbrenner in the past, remembered a bizarre interview he had with the owner in his Yankee Stadium office.

"I had started to ask him about his feelings about the whole investigation," said Berkow, "and he put his hand on my shoulder, ushered me into his office and began talking about Attila the Hun; what Attila the Hun did and how Attila the Hun handled things."

Berkow finally said, "George, what in the world are you talking about?"

Steinbrenner reached into his desk drawer and produced a small hardcover book titled *Leadership Secrets of Attila the Hun*.

"That's the guy who pillaged and plundered," Berkow said.

"Well, he wasn't perfect," said Steinbrenner, "but he did have some good things to say."

"Like what?" Berkow asked.

Flipping through the pages, which Berkow noticed contained several passages that had been underlined in red, Steinbrenner mused, "Here, look at this: 'Chieftains must work hard to establish discipline and morale, then to maintain them within the tribe.' Or this one: 'It is the custom of all Huns to hold to strong personal honor. This is a cardinal virtue. One's word must prevail over all other considerations.'"

"But, George," said Berkow, "you don't follow all this advice."

"What I'm saying," said Steinbrenner, "is that we can all learn from this."

After their session, Steinbrenner handed the book to Berkow, assuring him that he had another copy back in Tampa with the same underlined passages. He then inscribed it: "To my good friend, Ira. You, I know, are deep enough to understand this! George."

On the weekend before July 4, Steinbrenner celebrated his 60th birthday at his Ramada Inn hotel in Ocala, Florida. It was quite a gala affair, with over 200 guests and a pair of orchestras. The highlight of the event was a video showing the opening scene of the movie *Patton*, in which the general, played by George C. Scott, is standing in uniform in front of a giant American flag. But as the camera zoomed in on Patton's face, it turned out not to be "Old Blood and Guts" but rather Steinbrenner himself, provoking roars of applause and laughter from the audience.

ON JULY 4, Steinbrenner's actual birthday, Vincent outlined for Claire Smith of the *New York Times* how he expected the next day's hearing with the Yankees owner to go. Smith reported that Steinbrenner would be allowed to call witnesses and that Vincent had requested a list of them, purportedly following the guidelines set by Giamatti in the Rose hearing. Vincent would not reveal to Smith who Steinbrenner might call to testify, saying only that the length of the proceedings "really depends on them. It's their show." Vincent assured her that he and Dowd had nothing to hide from Steinbrenner and would be conducting the hearing with utmost fairness in conjunction with all the due process principles, as outlined in the rules of procedure.

Vincent also announced that he was fining Steinbrenner $225,000 for violating Major League Rule 3J, "with respect to tampering in the trade of outfielder Dave Winfield from the Yankees to the Angels last May." This was in regard to Steinbrenner's public comments that the Yankees would welcome Winfield back in the event he was unable to reach a satisfactory contract agreement with the Angels.

At 9:30 A.M. on July 5, Vincent convened the hearing at the 30 Rockefeller Plaza office of Judge Howard R. "Ace" Tyler, the commissioner's attorney and advisor. Besides the 68-year-old Tyler, a former assistant U.S. attorney and federal judge, Vincent's team included Dowd; baseball's general counsel, Tom Ostertag; head of security Kevin Hallinan; and deputy commissioner Steve Greenberg. Steinbrenner's legal team was headed by Curran, a former U.S. attorney for the Southern District of New York, and Steve Kaufman, a noted New York trial attorney.

Vincent began by delivering a lengthy dissertation refuting Curran's claims of bias against Steinbrenner. After that, Kaufman presented a detailed chronology of the events that had brought all of them to this hearing, all the while making the case that Steinbrenner's association with Spira had been made known to baseball (and, in particular, Hallinan) and that his $40,000 payment made to Spira, though an error in judgment and against the advice of counsel, was neither illegal nor against the best interest of baseball. Kaufman noted that an IRS investigation of the Winfield Foundation had found that 80 percent of the foundation's funds, overseen by Winfield's agent, Al Frohman, were being expended on administration. In other words, he said, "the foundation was not exactly being conducted by the United Way." Kaufman then took special pains to separate the gambling issue—which he knew Vincent was going to pursue—from Steinbrenner.

"This is not a Leo Durocher case," Kaufman said, referring to the former Brooklyn Dodgers manager who, in 1947, was kicked out of baseball for a year by then-commissioner Happy Chandler for associating with gamblers. "Mr. Steinbrenner was told by Mr. Spira that [Spira] gambled while he was at the Winfield Foundation. But [Steinbrenner] did not associate and do business with him other than to take information from him, which he sought to substantiate and corroborate the unlawful activity that had occurred [at the foundation]."

Once he concluded his opening statement, Kaufman reiterated to Vincent his team's intention to call a number of witnesses, but suggested that, for this proceeding, normal courtroom protocol be put aside. Instead of Steinbrenner being their last witness, he said, "we welcome the opportunity to have him as the first witness, because I think you should be satisfied to anything that may be of concern to you. As we go forward, we may want to call him back again, but that's why we're putting him on first."

Vincent agreed.

Steinbrenner's team strongly suspected that Vincent, taking his cue from the Dowd report, which they weren't allowed to see, would seek to tie Steinbrenner's payment to Spira to the gambling angle, as that would carry a lifetime sentence for violating baseball's cardinal rule. On the surface, that seemed to be a stretch, if for no other reason than that the only actual proof of Spira being a gambler was Spira's own word—which Vincent himself had called worthless a number of times.

Indeed, Vincent pressed hard on Spira's gambling, and Steinbrenner, much to his attorneys' dismay, was anything but a strong and steady witness under the heat of the commissioner's interrogation.

The flashpoint moment of the hearing was when Steinbrenner, asked by Vincent if there was one single factor that had prompted him to make the $40,000 payment to Spira, threw Lou Piniella and former Yankees employees Pat Kelly and Dave Weidler (who had been fired for alleged financial improprieties) under the bus.

"[Spira] scared me, and he really scared my children," Steinbrenner said, "and then there was the matter of the Kelly-Weidler situation and Piniella situation. The Piniella family is very close to me, and I think the world of Lou Piniella. But when [Spira] said that he threatened to sell information, as I recall he told me, on Lou Piniella and his sports betting habits, I didn't want to see baseball or Lou Piniella dragged through something the way it would have been sensationalized." He then added that Spira had also threatened to go public with the Kelly and Weidler scandal, in which Steinbrenner claimed they had taken various Yankee Stadium giveaway items, "selling them or giving them to this fellow who had a warehouse." (Weidler publicly and adamantly denied Steinbrenner's suspicions, saying any accusation that he stole from the Yankees was "false and untrue.")

At the time, Piniella (whose "sports betting habit" consisted of frequenting the racetrack, many times with Steinbrenner himself) had just replaced the banished Rose as manager of the Cincinnati Reds. When reports of Steinbrenner now linking *him* to gambling at the hearing leaked out a couple of weeks later, he was understandably outraged. "George calls me his friend?" Piniella said. "With friends like that, who needs enemies? The fact is, if someone told him something like this about me, you'd think he'd come to me and ask me about it. Did he? Never. What does that tell you? Hell, George fired me twice and even accused me of stealing furniture. He always talks about how much he likes me and my family. This sort of raises my doubts, I'll tell you that."

Vincent asked Steinbrenner, "Did anyone say to you, 'George, suppose this guy takes the money and pays off gambling debts. You are now an owner in baseball financing a gambler'?"

"Well, I didn't," said Steinbrenner. "I never thought of that. Nobody ever mentioned that to me, commissioner."

"And I am saying to you: Why didn't you call me, get help from other people, before you did something which your advisors told you not to do?" Vincent asked.

"I told you, nobody, for the whole time from '87 on, from the commissioner's office ever told me to stay away from this guy," Steinbrenner replied, in reference to the fact that he'd alerted former commissioner Peter Ueberroth of his association with Spira and that Hallinan, the commissioner's security chief, had interviewed Spira at length. "If it was a mistake to make the payment, I made the mistake. But the thing I'm having trouble understanding is that this Spira was in the foundation for years. Why aren't [Winfield and Spira] . . . I mean, you've got me [here]. Literally, I feel like I'm on trial. Okay. If I am, why aren't they on trial?"

Vincent's response was to remind Steinbrenner of the taped conversation with Spira in which he said, "You told me the gamblers were after you and they were going to kill you because of the money you owed them. I wanted you to get out of New York so you could get away from them."

"Take the money and get out of New York," Steinbrenner reiterated.

"Nothing else," said Vincent, further clarifying Steinbrenner. " 'I gave you the money to do that.' "

"To take the money and get out of New York," Steinbrenner repeated. "Not to pay gamblers. I got to really say to you, Fay, that's honest to God what I said."

Vincent's grilling of Steinbrenner would go on for two days. At its conclusion, Kaufman reminded Vincent of his intention to call his next set of seven witnesses, all of whom, he said, were hostile to Steinbrenner in varying degrees but who could "provide live testimony of crucial facts" that had not been available to Steinbrenner. One of them was to be Rizzuti, the court stenographer who, Steinbrenner contended, had, on Dowd's orders, altered Steinbrenner's sworn testimony to the investigator.

Vincent's response astounded Kaufman.

"I have no intention of cross-examining any of the people that you might call as witnesses," he said. "I don't want to have the record cluttered with testimony that I don't think is relevant. So, obviously, since I run this meeting, I reserve the right to decide what witnesses are relevant."

This, along with refusing to share Dowd's report with Steinbrenner's attorneys, was another abuse of due process on Vincent's part. Still, Vincent was largely applauded by the press—particularly by the *New York Times*—for finally bringing to justice the serial baseball miscreant and bully that was Steinbrenner—"who had gotten away with a lot of shit for years," as John Dowd had noted.

So instead of continuing on with the hearing, Vincent went to Cape Cod to begin his deliberations, accompanied by Dowd and deputy commissioner Steve Greenberg. Vincent had told the *Times* that he would need a couple of weeks to formulate his decision. "That was 'Fay the Faker' at his best," said one of Steinbrenner's other attorneys, Dominic Amorosa. "It's a wonder why he even bothered with the sham of a hearing."

On the morning of July 30, Steinbrenner and his attorneys went to the commissioner's office at 350 Park Avenue, where Vincent handed them his 50-page decision. He was suspending the Yankees owner for two years, followed by a three-year period of probation. Steinbrenner's attorneys concluded that Vincent had been worried that if he had suspended Steinbrenner for life, the maximum penalty in baseball, which was reserved for those found guilty of gambling on the game or directly involved with gambling in baseball, he would certainly have been sued on the grounds that he'd violated baseball's rules of procedure. As it was, Curran was prepared to sue anyway, but Steinbrenner wasn't interested.

However, Steinbrenner did have a problem with the wording of his sentence.

"I can't have the word 'suspension' attached to any of this," he said to Vincent. "I'm concerned about my position [as vice president] with the Olympic Committee. I don't want to lose that too. Isn't there some alternative here, Fay?"

Vincent could not believe his luck. Why, yes, he said, there was an alternative. Steinbrenner, he said, could voluntarily resign as Yankees managing general partner, remove himself from the day-to-day operations of the team and go on baseball's permanent ineligible list. He would also have to agree not to sue baseball.

For nearly 11 hours, as the sides worked on fine-tuning the agreement, Steinbrenner's lawyers implored him not to sign. "For some reason, he just couldn't grasp the fact that it was a lifetime deal he was agreeing to and that he was signing away his right to sue," said Amorosa.

Shortly before 8 o'clock, as hordes of reporters waited at the nearby Helmsley Palace Hotel for the decision to be announced, Vincent lost patience and sent word to Steinbrenner's camp that he was going to release his original decision. As Curran and Kaufman looked on in exasperation, Steinbrenner signed the agreement. Afterward, Vincent would tell Murray Chass of the *Times* that he "found some aspects of his decision very strange." There was no compromise, Vincent added. "I had the cards. I could've decided to go with Plan A, but I'm a reasonable man and I gave him an option."

What was it that possessed Steinbrenner to trade in a two-year suspension for a lifetime sentence? Did his commitment to the Olympics outweigh his love for the Yankees?

Steinbrenner had first joined the U.S. Olympic Committee in a volunteer leadership capacity in 1985. In 1988, while watching the dismal performance of the U.S. Olympians in the Calgary Winter Games (six medals total, the only two golds by skaters Brian Boitano and Bonnie Blair), Steinbrenner told USOC president Robert Helmick that something had to be done to restore America's Olympic honor. Helmick agreed and named Steinbrenner to chair a special Olympic Overview Committee. If there was one thing Steinbrenner knew how to do, it was raise money, and money was what he deemed necessary for American athletes to win consistently on the international stage.

In February 1989, Steinbrenner issued a 21-page report that he had prepared at his own expense. It cited the need for a significant increase in financial support to athletes through tuition assistance, a job opportunities program and direct payments through marketing and corporate sponsorships.

The committee adopted Steinbrenner's suggestions. After that, armed with new corporate and marketing sponsorships, U.S. athletes saw their stipends from the USOC rise from $2,500 each to over $100,000 apiece. Their overall performance rose too. After winning those paltry six medals in Calgary in 1988, the U.S. achieved 11 medals in the 1992 Albertville, France, Winter Games, and in 2002 won 34, including 10 golds, in Salt Lake City. And Steinbrenner's Olympic effort really paid off in 2010, when the U.S. team broke its own record for medals in the winter games.

Though Steinbrenner never admitted this publicly, people close to him believed that the Olympics were always his first love, even more so than the Yankees. The one-on-one, individual competition was, after all, in his blood. A love for hurdling had been instilled in him by his father and, from his formative years at Culver and then at Williams, he competed against other athletes and against the expectations of Henry Steinbrenner. Henry had been a world-class hurdler, and he never let George forget it.

"People have said that George was obsessed with winning, and that's obviously true," said Harvey Schiller, who worked alongside Steinbrenner as an executive director of the Olympic Committee in the '80s. "But I just think George always loved America more than anything, felt totally committed to those kids wearing the red, white and blue, and was extremely nationalistic."

WHEN HE ANNOUNCED his decision to the throng of reporters at the Helmsley Palace Hotel at 8:27 P.M., Vincent confirmed that Steinbrenner had agreed "to be treated as if he has been placed on the permanent ineligible list" and that he had also agreed not to challenge the sanctions in court. In a separate 11-page summary of the decision handed out to reporters, Vincent said that Steinbrenner's $40,000 payment to Spira and their "undisclosed working relationship" constituted conduct not in the best interests of baseball.

Vincent set August 20 as the date by which a new general partner of the Yankees would have to be appointed, subject to his approval. "This sad episode is now over," he said. "My decision in this case and this result will serve, I trust, to vindicate once again the important responsibility of the commissioner to preserve and protect our game."

News of Vincent's decision was quick to reach Yankee Stadium, where the Yankees were in the seventh inning of their game against the Detroit Tigers. There were only 24,037 fans in the ballpark, many of them listening on their transistor radios and passing along the report that Steinbrenner had been permanently removed as the owner and general partner of the team. Suddenly, a chant erupted: "No more George! No more George! No more George!" Steinbrenner, who left Vincent's office after signing the agreement and went back to his suite at the Regency with Bill Fugazy, didn't learn about this final insult until he watched the local 11 o'clock news that night.

Steinbrenner's first choice to be the new Yankees general partner was his oldest son, Hank, who in 1986 and '87 had served in the front office under the tutelage of general managers Clyde King and Woody Woodward before going back to the family horse farm in Ocala. The 33-year-old Hank loved baseball but had no desire to be his father's puppet general partner in New York. Steinbrenner next proposed Yankees VP and CEO Leonard Kleinman, a nomination that was swiftly rejected by Vincent, who cited an ongoing investigation of Kleinman's involvement in the Spira affair.

With time and candidates running out, Steinbrenner convened a meeting of Yankees partners in the Cleveland law offices of Daniel Mc-Carthy, himself a partner, on August 15, and emerged with the surprise announcement that Robert Nederlander, another of the limiteds, was his choice to assume the duties of Yankees general partner. The 57-year-old Nederlander had been one of Steinbrenner's original limited partners in the Yankees, along with his older brother Jimmy, the Broadway theater owner and producer. Robert was surprised to be tapped to run the Yankees, and sounded very much as though he did not think the gig would last very long. "Hopefully, Mr. Steinbrenner's son or son-in-law will get involved with the New York Yankees," he told reporters. "They're bright, young people. I look forward to have them come in and work with us over a period of time."

All that was left was Steinbrenner's formal letter of resignation as Yankees general partner to Vincent. He undertook that painful exercise six days later. At 9 A.M. on August 21, Vincent received a two-paragraph note from Steinbrenner informing him of his resignation, effective at 12:01 the next morning. In addition, Steinbrenner wrote, Jack Lawn, the former chief of the Drug Enforcement Agency for President George H. W. Bush, would be joining the Yankees as president and chief executive officer and would oversee the operations of the team until Nederlander was formally approved as general partner by the other baseball owners. (Thus, just as he had done with his dual general managers, Steinbrenner had now established a two-

headed front office hierarchy, with Lawn and Leonard Kleinman both serving as operations chieftains.)

That afternoon, Steinbrenner's last at Yankee Stadium, Arthur Richman, the Yankees' VP of media relations, hastily arranged a farewell luncheon for the owner. As Lawn remembered, it was not at all a melancholy
or maudlin affair. He and Gene Michael were both asked by Richman to
say a few words about Steinbrenner and, finally, George himself got up and
expressed his appreciation to all the Yankees employees, as well as his support for the new men in charge. The luncheon ended with Steinbrenner's
minions forming a line to shake his hand and say goodbye on his way out.

That night Steinbrenner watched from his private box as the Yankees
beat the Toronto Blue Jays, 6–5, in 11 innings, bringing their sorry record
to 50-70. After the game, he was led out of the Stadium through the outfield
loading dock, where his limo was waiting, to avoid the throng of reporters
congregated at the main entrance. Pausing to look back at the Stadium before stepping into the limo, Steinbrenner's eyes began to well up.

How had it come to this? AmShip, which he'd single-handedly built
into a thriving industry leader, was teetering on the verge of bankruptcy,
and now, incomprehensibly, he'd lost his baseball team too. Where once
he'd been the prince who'd rescued the Yankees from the inert ownership
of CBS and restored them to greatness, now he was vilified. His only consoling thought was that at least Henry Steinbrenner wasn't around to tell
him what a failure he was.

16

. . .

The Comeback

. . .

AFTER SUCCESSFULLY RIDDING BASEBALL of the menace that was George Steinbrenner, Fay Vincent now set his sights on prosecuting the Yankees owner's accomplice in crime, Leonard Kleinman. As chief operating officer of the Yankees, Kleinman had, according to Spira, arranged for Chase Manhattan Bank officials to circumvent their customary banking policy and set up an account for Spira's $40,000 payment from the Yankees boss. The bespectacled, bookish Kleinman had been Steinbrenner's tax attorney in Cleveland and Tampa when, in 1990, he was summoned by the Boss to New York to oversee the Yankees' business operations. Kleinman's arrogant and evasive demeanor engendered both contempt and fear from the other Yankees front office execs, who saw him as Steinbrenner's hatchet man.

The day after Steinbrenner left Yankee Stadium for the last time to begin his self-imposed lifetime banishment, Vincent announced that he was now officially examining Kleinman's role in the Spira matter, setting the Yankees COO's hearing for September 6. Kleinman reacted angrily to the announcement, telling reporters that the commissioner's allegations were "utterly false, improper and made in bad faith." But in pursuing a case against Kleinman, Vincent unwittingly created for himself a whole new, even more nettlesome adversary in Robert Costello, a New York attorney and former federal prosecutor, hired by the Yankees to represent their COO. Now that he was no longer involved with the Yankees, Steinbrenner spent much of his time conversing with his lawyers and grousing about Vincent's continued harping in the newspapers about the restrictions of his permanent ban. Finally, he began to realize what he'd done to himself. In a meeting with his attorneys, Paul Curran and Steve Kaufman, he complained about the unfairness of the whole process and how they needed to sue the commissioner on those grounds. "That's what we intended to do, George," said Curran, "but you signed those rights away when you signed that agreement."

Was there no way at all to undo this? To turn it around on the grounds that Vincent had violated baseball's rules of procedure and denied him due process? This was the topic of a phone conversation Steinbrenner had with Costello shortly after the latter had been hired to defend Kleinman in Vincent's continuing probe.

"It's like Steve and Paul told you, George," Costello said. "You gave up your right to sue when you signed the Major League agreement and again when you signed your agreement with Vincent."

"I don't care," Steinbrenner said. "I still want to sue. The guy fucked me!"

"*You* can't sue, George," said Costello, "but someone who hasn't signed the Major League Agreement can."

"Who could that be?" Steinbrenner asked.

"For one, Leonard Kleinman," Costello said. "You would have to nominate him as your choice to succeed you as Yankees general partner, and Vincent will surely reject him, thus giving Kleinman a cause of action to sue."

"But Kleinman isn't even a limited partner," Steinbrenner said.

"You can make him one by simply giving him a share of the team."

"A share of the team?" Steinbrenner protested. "This stuff is worth a lot of money! I can't just give him a share!"

"It can be one one-thousandth of a point, George," Costello said. "It doesn't matter how big the share is. As long as it's a smidgen, you can then nominate him to be managing general partner."

"And then what?" Steinbrenner asked.

"And then," Costello said, "Vincent will automatically assume Kleinman is your stooge and stop it, giving Kleinman grounds to sue, whereby, in discovery, we'll be able to bring out all of the things Vincent did to deprive you of your due process. It'll all be out there. And the rest of baseball will know the true story. Your fellow owners will see what Vincent did to you and realize he would do the same to them."

"All right," Steinbrenner said, "I'll do it. But you better be right. I don't want that little shit Kleinman running the Yankees."

"Trust me," said Costello. "I know Vincent. He'll take the bait."

"He better," said Steinbrenner, "because if you're wrong, I'll throw you out the fucking window."

This conversation took place before Steinbrenner had nominated his replacement as general partner. Sure enough, Vincent rejected Kleinman, which led to Steinbrenner's nomination of Nederlander. In the meantime, on the day before his scheduled hearing, Kleinman filed a $22 million lawsuit against the commissioner and John Dowd in a Manhattan federal court, alleging that "Vincent's course of conduct from the very beginning of his involvement in this matter demonstrates that he has harbored a prejudice against Kleinman and Steinbrenner and a desire to find a way to exclude them from being involved with the Yankees." The suit further charged that Vincent and Dowd had conducted an unfair and biased investigation of Steinbrenner and that Dowd had tampered with transcripts of witness testimony. "[Vincent's] initiation of the charges against Kleinman was done in bad faith with the intent to undermine his contract with the Yankees and to prevent him from succeeding Steinbrenner as Yankee general partner." Kleinman's suit against Vincent and Dowd, like Steinbrenner's against the stenographic agency, was ultimately dropped.

At the time, the media viewed the Kleinman suit as just another nuisance on the part of the Steinbrenner camp. Most of Steinbrenner's fellow owners were privately glad he'd been tossed out of baseball. His big spending on free agents had driven up salaries, and his constant battles with league officials, umpires and most of the other owners themselves had established him, in their eyes, as baseball's Public Enemy Number 1. If Vincent had screwed him, so be it. He deserved it, and their game would be better off without him.

• • •

IN THE MEANTIME, the team Steinbrenner left behind was well on its way to a last-place, 67-95 season, their worst record since 1912. On his way out the door, Steinbrenner had made two other announcements: Stump Merrill was getting a two-year contract extension as manager, and Gene Michael was being promoted from scout to general manager. In effect, it was "co–general manager," as George Bradley would be moving to New York to work side by side with Michael as VP of baseball operations. Although it seemed almost an afterthought on Steinbrenner's part to return Michael to the role of GM, it would later prove to be the most significant decision the deposed Yankees owner ever made for the organization.

Michael faced a daunting task. His best player, Don Mattingly, seemed helpless to regain his MVP form because of his debilitating back condition, and closer Dave Righetti, the team's most consistent pitcher since 1981, was eligible for free agency. Michael thought that, at 31, Righetti's skills had begun to erode: seven years removed from the birthday present he gave Steinbrenner in no-hitting the Boston Red Sox at Yankee Stadium on July 4, 1983, Righetti's saves as a closer had been gradually declining and his ERA had risen to a career-high 3.57 in 1990. Nevertheless, Righetti's agent, Bill Goodstein, was working the media with abandon, declaring his intention to get a five-year contract for his client. At one point, the new general partner, Robert Nederlander, obviously concerned about the public relations fallout of losing Righetti (not to mention the second-guessing he'd get from Steinbrenner), suggested to Michael that they offer a four-year deal to Goodstein.

"Are you kidding?" Michael said. "I don't even want to offer him three years! I love Dave. He's been a great Yankee, and he was unselfish in agreeing to become a closer, but I think he's got two years left, tops. I'll only go the extra year because he's meant so much to us."

As a hedge against Righetti leaving, Michael signed 34-year-old free agent right-hander Steve Farr, who had been both an effective closer and setup man for the Kansas City Royals during the previous five seasons. (Farr would save 78 games over the next three seasons and proved to be the first of many enlightened acquisitions by Michael.)

However, at the winter meetings in Chicago that December, Michael and George Bradley clashed in an embarrassing fashion, revealing a dysfunctional Yankees front office operating at cross-purposes. Late on the afternoon of the fourth, San Francisco Giants general manager Al Rosen announced he'd signed Righetti (whom he'd originally acquired for the Yankees in the Sparky Lyle trade with the Texas Rangers all those years ago as Steinbrenner's GM) to a four-year, $10 million contract. At the time of the announcement, Michael, who had yet to make his final two-year offer to his closer, was at a cocktail reception with Nederlander, privately expressing his relief at not having had to go three years for Righetti. But before Michael was able to sample his first hors d'oeuvre, I interrupted him, asking for an explanation as to why the Yankees had just signed their second baseman Steve Sax to a whopping four-year, $12.4 million contract extension at the same time they were letting Righetti go. Michael was dumbfounded.

"I don't know anything about that. I have to check on this," he said, before dashing out of the room with Nederlander, a look of panic on both their faces.

The 30-year-old Sax, coming off a bad season in which he'd hit a career-low .260, had been publicly angling for a contract extension even though he had another year to go before he was eligible for free agency. Behind Michael's back, George Bradley had given Sax what was then a record deal for a second baseman.

"We probably didn't have to sign Sax, but we did," Michael said uneasily to a throng of New York reporters later that night. "We don't know if it's the right move. Only time will tell."

Privately, however, Michael was enraged—and became even more so when he heard that Bradley and Righetti's agent, Goodstein, had called in to WFAN, a New York radio station, from their hotel rooms, and were mutually commiserating over the departure of the popular pitcher.

"I know if George here had been doing the negotiations, David would still be a Yankee," Goodstein said, to which Bradley replied, "You're probably right."

Not long after Bradley got off the air, Michael confronted him in his room. "How dare you criticize me in public like that!" he shouted. "You sign Sax behind my back and then go on 'Fans' [sic] radio with that fucking Goodstein and make me out to be the villain with Righetti? I'm telling you right now, George, it's going to be either you or me! I'm not going to put up with any more of this!"

Because Sax's agent was Tom Reich, Steinbrenner's pal, there were strong suspicions among the media and Yankees front office execs that Bradley had acted on the banished owner's instructions. Former Yankees GM Bob Quinn, then with the Cincinnati Reds, told reporters, "My analysis is that the Sax signing was done to offset Righetti leaving, in Steinbrenner's eyes. That's how George works, and I know him as well as anyone. He's a great attention diverter."

The next day, Steinbrenner took the opportunity to turn his front office chaos into another indictment of Fay Vincent.

"Don't blame Gene Michael or George Bradley," Steinbrenner said when called by reporters. "Blame Fay Vincent. If I were involved, this never would have happened."

Steinbrenner went on to insist there was a clause in his agreement with Vincent that permitted him to negotiate with free agents. "I have no intention of twisting the agreement," he said, "but there are four areas where I have the absolute right to be involved, areas where he can't say no. They involve 'extraordinary and material affairs,' and certainly Righetti qualifies. I was turned down by the commissioner. He gives no reason. He just says it's irrelevant."

(For the record, Michael's assessment of Righetti proved to be correct; the left-hander had three poor seasons in San Francisco before being released.)

Michael ended the year with a New Year's Eve signing of free agent right-hander Scott Sanderson, who would win 28 games over the next two seasons. But his most gratifying moment that off-season came on February 6, when Nederlander announced the firing of George Bradley. Pushed into taking sides between Steinbrenner's two warring GMs, Nederlander bravely chose Michael. Two weeks later, Michael made another free agent deal, one that raised eyebrows throughout baseball, when he announced he was bringing in 31-year-old left-handed closer Steve Howe, a six-time offender for drugs and alcohol, on a minor league contract. Perhaps at another time, the Yankees wouldn't have brought in a player with a reputation as damaged as Howe's, but these were desperate times for the Yankees, in which elite players were no longer inclined to cast their lot with them, no matter how much money they offered. Before succumbing to drugs and alcohol, Howe had been a Rookie of the Year and an All-Star with the Los Angeles Dodgers. As Michael explained to reporters, "I know he can still pitch and I hope he's straightened his life out. He'll have to prove himself, but in our situation I think he's worth the gamble."

As MICHAEL CONTINUED patching the Yankee roster, behind the scenes Steinbrenner was ramping up his campaign to undo his lifetime ban by Vincent. The previous fall he had added a couple of new attorneys, Arnold Burns and Randy Levine, to his legal team, both of whom had recently worked in the Reagan Justice Department. Steinbrenner had met the two at a law enforcement luncheon in Brooklyn at which he was the headline speaker. Burns was a high-profile lawyer in New York and a former deputy U.S. attorney general, while Steinbrenner's interest in Levine was piqued when he learned of Levine's long-standing relationship with Bud Selig, the influential owner of the Milwaukee Brewers.

Despite periodic outward support of Vincent's handling of Steinbrenner's case by some owners, Levine, in his discussions with Selig, detected a growing disenchantment with the commissioner by another faction of owners. Those owners, the so-called hawks in the previous spring's rancorous labor negotiations with the players' union, were miffed that Vincent had overstepped baseball's executive council and injected himself into the stalled talks, making a series of overtures to the union in an attempt to end the 1990 spring training lockout. At Steinbrenner's behest, Levine and Burns, along with Steinbrenner's Tampa attorney, Bob Banker, began researching all of Vincent's actions as commissioner as they pertained to adhering to baseball's rules of procedure in the Steinbrenner case. In addition, they began engaging in a series of meetings and phone conversations with Selig and his attorney Bob DuPuy, Chicago White Sox owner Jerry Reinsdorf and Atlanta Braves chairman Bill Bartholomay regarding the power structure of baseball and the Steinbrenner situation.

"It was a very tense time in baseball," Levine remembered. "There was beginning to be open warfare between a lot of the owners and Vincent, as well as the owners and the union. We were trying to determine what was in the commissioner's power and what was in the power of baseball's executive council. By ignoring the rules of procedure as he did in George's case, we all agreed Vincent had abused his power."

In early February 1991, baseball's executive council (which consisted of the commissioner, the two league presidents and four owners from each league) received a 135-page report compiled by Reinsdorf and Bartholomay, based on the petition submitted to them by Steinbrenner's lawyers, Levine, Burns and Banker, detailing all of Vincent's violations of the rules of procedure, specifically in regard to the Steinbrenner investigation. "Vincent could have put away Hitler, Stalin and Saddam Hussein and not gotten as much positive publicity he did in getting rid of George," Reinsdorf told me. "But there was significant concern among the owners about the procedure he used."

Vincent, who had just returned from a 2½-month health leave when details of the petition were reported in an exclusive *Daily News* story, was quick to respond. Ironically, he invoked Reinsdorf's reference to the Iraqi dictator.

"I can't think of anyone other than Saddam Hussein I'd rather have making all these complaints," Vincent told the *Daily News*. "It's very difficult to be explaining complicated matters such as this. How do you go about explaining due process and how we did it?"

Steinbrenner, Vincent maintained, had admitted two things under oath: that he did not notify the commissioner's office of his involvement with Spira and that he made a $40,000 payment to Spira, a known gambler. "I didn't have to take into account any other testimony," Vincent insisted. "If anything, I gave [Steinbrenner] the benefit of the doubt. I based my opinion on two instances of misbehavior. When I initially gave him a two-year suspension, I thought I was being fair."

Still, the executive council's decision to review Reinsdorf's report was ample reason for concern for Vincent. The executive council did not have the power to overrule the commissioner's decisions, but it could apply sufficient pressure on him to provide Steinbrenner with a new hearing.

Steinbrenner's case was aided by the extortion charges he'd filed against Spira. It was here, his lawyers maintained, that they would prove the $40,000 payment had been made by Steinbrenner in good faith, with no ulterior motive, and that he had refused Spira's demands for more. They were confident Steinbrenner would come off as an even more sympathetic figure in the trial, and ultimately they were right.

The Spira extortion trial began in April in a Manhattan federal court. For the first few days, Spira's defense attorney, David Greenfield, who had gained permission from the judge to introduce Steinbrenner's 1974 conviction for illegal campaign contributions into the proceedings, did a masterful job of painting Steinbrenner as an influential power broker, perjurer and convicted felon. Citing Steinbrenner's coercion of his employees at American Ship to lie to the grand jury about the illegal contributions, Greenfield asked, "So did you concoct and orchestrate a story to protect your business interests?"

"I pleaded guilty to what that says," Steinbrenner replied, shakily.

"For those first couple of days, Greenfield kicked the shit out of George," remembered Bobby Gold, one of Steinbrenner's attorneys. "That's when we took him across the street to the Vista Hotel and made him sit down and read all the discovery material that had been given to Greenfield by John Dowd. He had to be coached as to what was coming and how to respond to it."

Steinbrenner's attorneys all seemed to agree that the case turned in their favor when prosecutor Gregory Kehoe introduced a glassine envelope containing a list of names and phone numbers that had been seized by the FBI in a raid of Spira's house.

"Are you aware of what the FBI seized?" Kehoe asked Steinbrenner.

"No."

"Look at this envelope," Kehoe said, "and see if you recognize anyone you know."

Upon perusing the list, Steinbrenner's eyes suddenly welled up and he began to sob uncontrollably.

"Are you okay, sir?" Kehoe asked.

"Yeah," Steinbrenner mumbled, pulling out his handkerchief.

At that point, one of the U.S. attorneys turned to Gold, who was sitting in the second row, and whispered, "You little prick! How many days did it take you to teach him to do that?"

In fact, Steinbrenner hadn't known until he saw the list that one of the phone numbers on it was that of his 84-year-old mother, Rita.

"It demonstrated the full extent of how he was being extorted and the lengths Spira had gone to intrude into his life," Gold said.

The jury ultimately agreed. On May 8, 1991, Howie Spira was convicted on five of six charges involving his extortion of Steinbrenner. He would later be sentenced to 30 months in a federal penitentiary, along with three years' probation, counseling and 200 hours of community service. As he was led from the court in handcuffs, Spira said, "I hope George Steinbrenner never gets his team back and that God at least knows what he did to me."

For his part, Fay Vincent was publicly unmoved by the Spira extortion conviction.

"The federal case against Mr. Spira has no relationship at all to any baseball matter, including Mr. Steinbrenner's status as it pertains to his agreement with the commissioner," Vincent said in a statement.

STEINBRENNER'S VICTORY OVER Spira was about the only thing the Yankees won in 1991. On the field the team was only slightly less moribund than the year before, finishing 71-91, in fifth place. It was an especially trying season for Gene Michael, who found himself facing off with Steinbrenner and team captain Don Mattingly over separate issues.

According to the terms of his agreement with Vincent, Steinbrenner was permitted to participate in Yankees matters in four general areas: media agreements, stadium lease business, bank financing and partnership meetings. That last area, one limited partner observed, "was a loophole that George drove a Mack truck through." Though he was prohibited from being directly involved in any baseball matters, Steinbrenner was able to make his feelings known at the quarterly meetings between Yankees partners and thereby obliquely impose his will.

At other times, Steinbrenner used the press to make his wishes known to Michael, as he did on August 24, 1991, as the general manager was struggling to close a deal with the overall number-one pick from that June's amateur draft, 19-year-old left-hander Brien Taylor, and his high-powered agent, Scott Boras, for a bonus of about $850,000 to $900,000. That day, Steinbrenner was quoted by Steve Marcus and Jon Heyman of *Newsday* as saying, "I just don't know what my people are doing or what they're thinking. If they let him go, they ought to be shot."

This, of course, emboldened the resolve of Boras and Taylor's mother, Bettie, and the negotiations dragged on until August 26, when Michael capitulated to a record $1.55 million deal. The next day, Steinbrenner was back on Michael's case in *Newsday*, telling the same two reporters, "Never in my wildest dreams would I have paid a kid a million and a half. I said I'd love to see [the Yankees] sign their first-round draft choice. I never said 'go spend a million-and-a-half.' No goddamn way! I'm getting damned tired of people spending my money like this."

Michael was tempered in his response to Steinbrenner's criticism, taking pains to note that at least he'd been able to hold the line on giving Taylor a major league contract (as Boras had vigorously sought), which would have limited the Yankees' control of the pitcher to just six years, when he would be eligible for free agency.

"If he was here, he would have signed him," Michael said of Steinbrenner. "I guarantee you. He probably would have signed him with a little more showmanship because he's better at that than me. But he probably wouldn't have gotten him off the major league contract, as I did. I didn't want to defend myself, but I will. I don't rip him. I don't do that."

But in a later closed-door meeting of the Yankees partners, Michael lit into Steinbrenner when the owner renewed his criticism of the Taylor signing. "You don't know what the fuck you're talking about, George," he said. "If it wasn't for all that stuff you said in the papers, we could've signed the kid for a lot less."

"I think Stick really impressed the partners that day, standing up to George the way he did," said Marvin Goldklang, one of the limited partners. "We were all kind of taken aback, as we weren't used to seeing George challenged like that, and Stick asserting himself like he did made you feel like he knew what he was doing."

Earlier that month, Michael found himself squarely in the middle of a public relations fiasco with Mattingly that ultimately led to Merrill's undoing as manager. With the Yankees in a slump of 15 losses in 20 games, Michael sensed a lack of discipline on the team, represented by Mattingly's hair, which now went past his collar, in violation of the grooming rules

Steinbrenner had instituted in 1973. Michael ordered Merrill to tell Mattingly to get a haircut or else face a fine and a benching. Mattingly refused, and was subsequently benched by Merrill and fined $250, touching off a brouhaha with the fans and the media that embarrassed everybody involved.

The day after the benching, Michael rescinded the fine and all but apologized to Mattingly, saying the penalty was "too severe" and stating that he had "overreacted. I made statements to Stump before the game that if Mattingly didn't get his hair cut, he shouldn't play. I didn't mean that minute, or before the game. It was a miscommunication between Stump and myself, but Donnie was wrong in refusing."

Mattingly, who was tired of losing and dissatisfied with the direction the ownerless Yankees seemed to be taking, later revealed to reporters that he had asked Michael to trade him, and used the incident to further criticize the organization. In response, Steinbrenner told reporters, "I won't get into second-guessing Stick or Stump, but anytime in the past when Donnie's hair has been long, I'd put my arm around him and say, 'What happened to your barber? Did he die?' "

The biggest loser of the 1991 season wound up being Merrill, who was fired by Michael the day after the season ended. In Steinbrenner's absence, Merrill had been the only Yankees manager to last a whole season since Lou Piniella, in 1987. But even after suffering the ignominy of being blamed for the shortcomings of an organization in disarray, Merrill found himself under further siege. A few days after being fired, he was summoned to the commissioner's office. It seemed Vincent's bird dogs were convinced Merrill had been in steady communication with Steinbrenner during the season, a charge he adamantly denied.

"What part of the word 'no' don't you understand?" Merrill told Vincent's interrogators.

"Well, if you insist you didn't talk to Steinbrenner," said one of the inquisitors, "why don't you just tell us who did?"

"I don't know," Merrill insisted. "Even if I did, why should I tell you anything? That's your job, not mine."

In a 2009 interview, Merrill admitted he was uncharacteristically belligerent at the hearing with the commissioner's men. "It was probably the worst time of my life," he said. "It was the first time I'd ever been fired, the first time I'd ever failed, and now these guys were questioning my integrity."

For the rest of October through the World Series, Michael anguished over whom to hire to be his manager. Billy Martin was no longer waiting in the wings, and Lou Piniella was managing the Reds in Cincinnati. Michael felt that Merrill's lack of major league experience had hurt the team, and his first instincts were to find someone who had had some success as a major league manager. He interviewed Hal Lanier, who had won a division championship with the Houston Astros in 1986, and Doug Rader, who had won 91 games with the California Angels in 1989. But the limited partners didn't like either option. "They're both kind of in that category of recycled managers who got fired someplace else," said Marvin Goldklang, who then urged Michael to consider Buck Showalter, the team's third-base coach under Merrill. "Granted, he doesn't have experience as a major league manager, but at least Showalter is one of ours," Goldklang said, referring to the fact that Showalter had come up through the Yankees system, first as a minor league player and later as manager of their farm teams in Oneonta, New York, Fort Lauderdale and Albany from 1985 to '89. Michael decided to go with the 35-year-old Showalter.

On December 6, Bob Nederlander announced that he was stepping down as Yankees general partner, leaving yet another leadership vacuum at the top of the Yankees hierarchy. Steinbrenner created more havoc by naming Daniel McCarthy, his Cleveland lawyer and another Yankees limited partner, as Nederlander's successor. The problem with McCarthy was that he, along with another of the limited partners, Harold Bowman, had also filed suit against Fay Vincent in the aftermath of Steinbrenner's banishment. In their suit, the two had complained that the value of their investment in the Yankees had been severely compromised by the removal of Steinbrenner as general partner. The suit was later dismissed by a federal district court judge in Cleveland, but Vincent hadn't forgotten, and McCarthy's term as acting Yankees general partner was to be short-lived.

Unfortunately for Michael, it was not nearly short enough. In the two months McCarthy ran the Yankees before Vincent could formally reject him (as he had Leonard Kleinman the year before), Michael was prohibited from signing any free agents. At the December winter meetings in Miami

Beach, Michael sat forlornly in his small room at the Fontainebleau Hotel, unable to make a deal for free agent third baseman Steve Buechele (whom he coveted), while Mets general manager Al Harazin, who was staying in the Frank Sinatra penthouse suite, was commanding the back pages of the New York tabloids with a series of spectacular acquisitions: Cy Young Award–winning pitcher Bret Saberhagen and sluggers Eddie Murray and Bobby Bonilla.

In early January, after weeks of media criticism of the Yankees' penurious ways, Michael got a call, not from McCarthy, but from Steinbrenner's son Hal, instructing him to fly to Los Angeles to sign free-agent outfielder Danny Tartabull. Michael didn't like Tartabull as a player, but he was the last high-profile free agent still on the market. At the time, Tartabull's agent, Dennis Gilbert, had only one other team, the Philadelphia Phillies, still in the bidding, and they were said to be topped out at four years, $20 million.

Accompanying Michael on the trip to Los Angeles was Steinbrenner's son-in-law Joe Molloy, who was married to the owner's younger daughter, Jessica, and was widely speculated to be the next in line when Vincent rejected McCarthy as general partner. After a few hours of negotiations, Michael and Molloy told Gilbert that the Yankees were prepared to offer Tartabull a five-year deal for $25.5 million. Throughout the discussion, Gilbert had been sure to let it be known that he was still in serious negotiations with the Phillies, and as he pondered the proposal, Molloy suddenly interjected: "Well, if that's not enough, Dennis, you've got to come back to us—"

"No, no, no," Michael said, cutting Molloy off. "This is *it*, Dennis. This is our final offer. We're not going any higher, so you need to decide if you're going to accept it!"

Gilbert accepted, and Michael got the player he really didn't want. He also got an unsettling introduction to what it was going to be like working for a privileged Steinbrenner son-in-law who didn't have a clue about baseball or business. It turned out neither Tartabull nor Brien Taylor lived up to the money Michael signed them for, Tartabull flaming out after one good season and Taylor never making it past class Double-A in the minors after tearing up his shoulder in a fight back home in North Carolina. But little by little, Michael was making the Yankees better with under-the-radar signings like Farr, Howe, Sanderson and catcher Mike Stanley, all of whom contributed to the slightly improved 76-86 record in Showalter's maiden season as manager, in 1992. And though it would take another four years before anyone realized it, the most significant development during that '92 season was the decision of scouting and player development VP Bill Livesey to take a 19-year-old high school shortstop from Kalamazoo, Michigan, named Derek Jeter as the Yankees' number-one pick in the June amateur draft.

As EXPECTED, ON February 28, 1992, Vincent rejected Daniel McCarthy as the next Yankees general partner. Two weeks later, Steinbrenner nominated his son-in-law, Joe Molloy, whom Vincent would later approve. Four days earlier, in one of his final acts as interim general partner, McCarthy had fired Leonard Kleinman as Yankees COO after Kleinman refused McCarthy's order to drop his lawsuit against Vincent. That Vincent expressed almost no reservations about a member of Steinbrenner's immediate family being tapped to run the Yankees was telling of other events going on behind the scenes now that both McCarthy and Kleinman were no longer part of the Yankees power structure.

Vincent was starting to feel heat from the executive council and had indicated to Steinbrenner's attorneys, Burns and Levine, that he would be open to reviewing Steinbrenner's status, on one condition: that Kleinman drop his suit. In early April, Kleinman's attorney, Bob Costello, got a call from Steinbrenner's Tampa attorney Bob Banker explaining what was in the works.

"Vincent, I think, is starting to feel some pressure from our petition with the executive council," Banker said, "but we really do need now for you to get Leonard to drop this suit. Vincent's aware of how damaging it will be for him if he gets dragged into court with this suit. That's why he won't act on George until it goes away."

From the beginning, Costello had known exactly how the Kleinman suit was going to play out—which was why he had negotiated a new contract for Kleinman with the Yankees that would compensate the COO to the tune of $1 million in the event he was fired. At 11:10 A.M. on April 24, Kleinman received $1.05 million by wire from Florida. An hour and a half later, it was announced he'd dropped his suit against Vincent. That afternoon, Vincent told Murray Chass of the *Times* that he suspected Steinbrenner might now want to discuss with him a possible return to active duty with the Yankees.

Still, it was another month before Steinbrenner got his first face-to-face meeting with Vincent since he'd signed off on his life sentence from baseball. The May 19 meeting at the Ritz-Carlton Hotel was also attended by Steinbrenner's attorney, Arnold Burns, and Vincent's deputy commissioner, Steve Greenberg. While Steinbrenner made it clear he was hoping to get his sentence reduced and eventually be reinstated now that he'd made the Kleinman lawsuit go away, Vincent would make no promises. Afterward, Vincent was uncharacteristically terse and evasive about the meeting, saying only: "We met. We talked. No decision was reached." Burns, however, felt that the very fact that Vincent had agreed to further discussions boded well for Steinbrenner eventually being reinstated. But before this happened, there would be another series of events that would further erode the owners' faith in Vincent.

On December 19, 1991, the Yankees' troubled relief pitcher Steve Howe was arrested on charges of cocaine possession in Kalispell, Montana—the seventh time that Howe had been involved in drug or alcohol problems, leaving a cloud over his head when he reported to spring training the following February. He was allowed to pitch while awaiting trial and was the Yankees' most reliable reliever for the first two months of the 1992 season. Then, on June 8, on the advice of his attorneys, he filed an Alford plea of being guilty to a charge of attempting to possess cocaine, in hopes that, by essentially pleading no contest to the charge but not the crime, Vincent would allow him to continue pitching. "It's a decision by an individual not to go to trial," explained Yankees general counsel David Sussman. "It's fair to say there's a legal distinction between an Alford plea and a guilty plea."

Nevertheless, Vincent's view of Howe was that of a serial drug offender in baseball who needed to be dealt with—severely. No sooner had Howe filed his plea than Vincent announced he was suspending the pitcher indefinitely. The Players Association immediately filed a grievance on Howe's behalf, causing Vincent to make the mistake that would prove his undoing: in a letter to the 26 owners on June 18, Vincent announced that he was revoking baseball's rules of procedure. Vincent said the rules had "no practical benefit" and that recent lawsuits against the commissioner's office had "intentionally misinterpreted them." As a result, Vincent concluded, "I am revoking them and will hereby proceed informally" and announce rules "on a case-by-case basis."

"When Vincent sent that letter, it really opened everyone's eyes," said Jerry Reinsdorf in a 2007 interview.

As part of the grievance procedure on behalf of Howe, the Players Association subpoenaed Yankees president Jack Lawn as well as Michael and Showalter to testify before baseball arbitrator George Nicolau. When Vincent learned that they'd testified, he was furious, and on July 1, an hour before the Yankees were to play an afternoon "getaway" game against the Kansas City Royals at Yankee Stadium, he summoned the three to his office at 350 Park Avenue—and informed them that they could not bring legal counsel to the meeting, yet another blatant abuse of power.

"I cannot understand how you three would voluntarily appear at the Players Association hearing without the consent of the commissioner and then, at that hearing, be critical of the commissioner's decision on Steve Howe," Vincent said.

Speaking for the three of them, Lawn responded by explaining that the Players Association had subpoena power, compelling them to testify.

"Nevertheless," Vincent said, "in making your decision to testify, you have effectively tendered your resignations from Major League Baseball." Then, looking directly at Lawn, he added, "You should have laid aside your conscience and principles in order to testify in support of the position of the commissioner on the Howe matter and not contrary to it."

As Lawn listened, stupefied at Vincent's assertion, the commissioner pressed on.

"I could not believe that you would all testify because of your interest in seeing Steve Howe in a Yankee uniform."

"That's not why we testified," Lawn said firmly. "We testified to tell the truth."

"But then why would you *want* to testify?" Vincent asked.

"Because," said Lawn, "if a month from now I pick up the paper and see that Steve Howe killed himself, at least I would have known I tried to help. As I learned in the Marine Corps, you don't abandon the wounded."

The three left Vincent's office under the impression they were going to be tossed out of baseball. When Lawn got back to Yankee Stadium, he was greeted by Bob Costello, who had been enlisted by Michael to represent him in the matter, only to have Vincent reject him as the GM's counsel. "Did he really threaten to throw you out of baseball?" Costello said.

"Yeah," said Lawn.

"What are you planning to do?"

"Fuck him," said Lawn.

News of Vincent's behavior touched off a swirl of outrage within base-ball and in the media. *New York Post* columnist Mark Kriegel wrote, "More and more Steinbrenner and Vincent look like the same guy consumed with power. As Gene Michael found out yesterday, Francis T. Vincent could bully as well as the Boss."

"This is simply another example of how the Yankees are susceptible to being pushed around these days by the power factions in baseball," Yan-kees limited partner Marvin Goldklang said to me after learning of the meeting. "I've got to believe this situation might have been handled differ-ently if George were still running the team."

Reinsdorf, expressing what was now becoming a popular sentiment among the owners, told me, "I don't know why Vincent didn't just rescind the Bill of Rights while he was at it."

In a phone call to Steinbrenner right after hearing about the meeting from Michael and Lawn, Costello chortled, "Vincent has finally cooked his goose, George. This is going to get him out as commissioner and you back in."

"Let's just see how it plays out," said Steinbrenner.

As soon as the Players Association was informed of Vincent's threat to toss the three men out of baseball, it announced its intentions of filing an unfair-labor-practices suit, this time charging the commissioner with wit-ness tampering. On July 3, Nicolau sternly warned Vincent not to take any disciplinary action against Lawn, Michael and Showalter. And on July 6, Vincent managed to alienate a whole new faction of owners when he attempted to force realignment of the National League by shifting four franchises, including the Chicago Cubs, to different divisions. On July 7, the Cubs sued the commissioner, seeking a preliminary injunction barring Vincent from enforcing his decision.

With the walls now closing in, Vincent, aware that the executive council was preparing to act on Steinbrenner's petition, called Arnold Burns to a meeting on July 23 at which he was ready to issue a reprieve for the Yankees owner. The next day, deputy commissioner Greenberg called Burns to inform him that Steinbrenner would be allowed to resume active control of the Yankees on March 1, 1993. "I know George would've preferred to come back right now," Greenberg said, "but the year and a half of litigation probably had an effect on Fay's ruling. Had it not been for the litigation, he probably could've come back in August."

Burns was elated. He immediately called in Randy Levine to tell him their mission had been accomplished. Now they had to find Steinbrenner, who was in Barcelona at the Summer Olympics, to give him the good news. It was almost midnight in Spain when Levine reached Steinbrenner in his room.

"What the fuck do you want?" Steinbrenner growled.

"Boss, I got great news!" Levine said. "We got you back! Vincent's agreed to let you resume control of the Yankees next March 1."

After a strange moment of silence, Steinbrenner replied: "It should've been *February* 1st!" before hanging up, leaving Levine flabbergasted. The next day, however, an ebullient Steinbrenner called back, expressing his gratitude to Levine and Burns for their work.

"From now on," he said, "I want you guys with me."

But if Vincent's decision to reinstate Steinbrenner was an effort to stop the bleeding, it was too late. The owners had become more and more united in their resolve against him and made that known in an 18–9 vote of no confidence at a meeting at the Chicago O'Hare Hilton on September 3. At first, Vincent refused to resign, "until the highest court in the land tells me otherwise," as he wrote in a letter to the owners. But five days later, acknowledging the futility of a fight to stay in office, Vincent did just that.

Not long after, Steinbrenner received a package in the mail at his office in Tampa. In it was a framed montage of four different New York tabloid back pages chronicling his saga with Vincent:

July 21, 1990: *Baseball Commish to George: Yer Out*

June 18, 1992: *He's Outta Here!—Vincent Bans Michael's Attorney*

Sept. 1, 1992: *Owners to Fay: Get Out!*

Sept. 8, 1992: *He's Out! Baseball Commish Fay Vincent Walks*

Underneath them was inscribed: "He who laughs last, laughs best—Bob Costello."

WITH FAY VINCENT no longer around, it was no surprise that Steinbrenner's fingerprints showed up all over the Yankees' high-profile signing of free-agent third baseman Wade Boggs in December 1992. Boggs, a Tampa native, had been a five-time batting champion with the Boston Red Sox, but now, at 34, he was coming off his worst season (in which he hit just .259) and was considered an average defender at third. As a result, he had received very little interest from other clubs, and a meeting was set up between his agent, Alan Nero, and Joe Molloy at the Bay Harbor Hotel. As he negotiated with Molloy, Nero could not help but notice Steinbrenner sitting at another table across the dining room. He was sure that the table where he and Molloy were sitting was somehow bugged.

News of the Yankees' interest in Boggs began to leak, along with word that Gene Michael and Buck Showalter had privately voiced their objections to signing him. Molloy sought to quell the speculation that Steinbrenner had been behind it.

"Absolutely not!" Molloy said indignantly to reporters after the signing was announced. "My father-in-law would not jeopardize his coming back March 1. He's waited too long to do something like that."

I happened to know different, however. I'd been sitting with Steinbrenner across the dining room conducting an interview about his imminent return to baseball, still three months away. Glancing over at Boggs, Steinbrenner said to me, "I like getting guys coming off a bad year. They have something to prove. Besides, Wade Boggs is a guy people might come out to see. We haven't had any guys like that lately."

Sure enough, no sooner had Nero tossed his briefcase on the bed of his hotel room after the meeting with Molloy than the phone rang.

"Alan?" said the voice on the other end. "This is George."

"George who?" Nero replied mischievously.

"*Steinbrenner*, you idiot!"

"Oh, I'm sorry, George. What can I do for you?"

"I just want to tell you: Be patient," Steinbrenner said. "You'll get what you want."

"How opportune is this?" Nero thought. Here was Steinbrenner under-cutting his own son-in-law. Sure enough, when Nero went back downstairs to resume negotiations, Molloy informed him the Yankees were prepared to give Boggs a three-year deal for $11 million.

Michael and Showalter had been concerned that Boggs, as a member of the hated Red Sox and Mattingly's principal rival for the batting title from 1985 to '88, would create chemistry problems within the Yankee clubhouse. As it turned out, however, he would play an integral role in the team's improvement over the next four years, earning All-Star status in each of them.

Even more important in that regard, however, was the trade Michael had made a month earlier with the Cincinnati Reds, in which he acquired Paul O'Neill, a 29-year-old left-handed-hitting right fielder, for Roberto Kelly, a 25-year-old Panamanian center fielder who had been an All-Star in 1990. At the time, the trade was roundly criticized. Kelly, a product of the Yankees farm system, was regarded as their best all-around player, while O'Neill was coming off a season in which he hit a career-low .246. But Michael believed that the right-handed-hitting Kelly was never going to develop into the kind of 25-homer-per-year power hitter the Yankees had envisioned, while O'Neill, he felt, would thrive in Yankee Stadium, with its inviting right-field fence. Michael would be proved right on both counts, and the deal would go down as one of the best in Yankees history. Michael's other major acquisition that off-season was the signing of 31-year-old free agent left-hander Jimmy Key (who'd won 116 games for the Toronto Blue Jays from 1984 to '92) at the December winter meetings in Louisville. Michael only signed Key after his first-choice pitcher on the free agent market, Greg Maddux, spurned him—or, more precisely, New York—to sign with the Atlanta Braves for $8 million less than the Yankees' offer. Just the same, Key proved to be as important an addition to the vastly improved Yankees roster as O'Neill.

As my interview with Steinbrenner that day in Tampa shifted from the impending Boggs signing to the state of baseball in his absence, he groused about the Toronto Blue Jays, who had just won the first of back-to-back world championships. The architect of those Blue Jays teams was Pat Gillick, Gabe Paul's former assistant Yankees GM. In another touch of bitter irony, one of Gillick's key acquisitions that year had been none other than Dave Winfield, who, after being signed as a free agent, batted .290 with 26 homers and 108 RBI at the age of 41. Winfield's final act for the Blue Jays in 1992 was to double home the winning runs of the World Series in the 11th inning of game six against the Atlanta Braves.

"You know, I keep hearing so much about how the Blue Jays did it the 'right' way," Steinbrenner said to me. "Now, Pat Gillick is a sound baseball man. We trained him. But when I keep hearing and reading how he did it the 'right' way, I have to laugh. What was Winfield? A free agent! What was Jack Morris [the Blue Jays' pitching ace who led the American League with 21 wins in '92]? A free agent! And *old* free agents at that! And they had the highest payroll in baseball! So how come when I was doing it with free agents and had the highest payroll in baseball, they said I wasn't doing it the 'right' way?"

"Just the same, George," I countered, "in your absence, Stick and your baseball people have started to put together a pretty decent farm system with some legitimate prospects you might want to think twice about trading away in your urgency to win right away."

In particular, I cited center fielder Bernie Williams, who had hit .308 and led the International League in triples in '92.

"I know, I know," Steinbrenner said. "I'm looking forward to seeing all those kids next spring."

"You must really be looking forward to March 1," I said.

"It's going to be a happening," Steinbrenner said. "You know, there are times when I would rather be owner of the New York Yankees than president of the United States."

I left Tampa that day thinking he had hardly mellowed in his 27 months of exile. If anything, he seemed more determined than ever to resume being the owner with the loudest roar and the biggest clout in the game. Jack

Lawn remembered how, a month or so later, Steinbrenner called him from Tampa to ask his advice about a request he'd gotten from *Sports Illustrated*.

"They're doing a big story on my return," Steinbrenner said, "and they want to put me on the cover, sitting on a horse, dressed like Napoleon. What do you think, Jack? Should I do it?"

"I think, George," Lawn replied, "you need to come back humble. Otherwise you're gonna piss off a lot of people again."

"You're the only one who said that!" Steinbrenner sniffed.

Steinbrenner did the shoot, and in the story, written by Jill Lieber, Jerry Reinsdorf is quoted as saying, "This is the most ballyhooed return since the Resurrection. Originally, I thought it was going to be a coronation in New York, but this is too massive. It's a resurrection. Vincent nailed him to the cross. This is the biggest thing to happen in 2,000 years!"

March 1 dawned sunny and seasonally warm at the Yankees' spring training complex in Fort Lauderdale. Yankees public relations director Jeff Idelson, who'd been preparing for weeks for the big event, distributed buttons inscribed with THE BOSS IS BACK to some 240 newspaper, TV and radio reporters. Originally, Idelson had planned a more circus-like atmosphere with skydivers, trained dogs jumping through hoops and a helicopter carrying a Marilyn Monroe look-alike, but had toned down the program after terrorists bombed the World Trade Center three days earlier, killing 6 people and wounding 1,042 others.

At 10:30 A.M., the 62-year-old Steinbrenner walked through the front gate of Fort Lauderdale Stadium, unannounced, and it took a few minutes before anyone even recognized him. Once they did, however, the mad stampede of TV cameras and reporters was on, following Steinbrenner as he made the rounds of the stadium during the Yankees' workout, periodically stopping briefly to kibitz with the writers and ham for the TV cameras.

Pointing at Showalter, who was standing by the batting cage observing the players taking their swings, Steinbrenner said, "This guy is a young star on the rise!" When asked if he'd changed during his 2½ years of exile, Steinbrenner said, "I'm not backing down on my commitment to winning, but I don't think you'll see me back in the swing of things like I used to be. I don't think my stamp on the ball club will be as heavy as it used to be."

A week after his triumphant return, Steinbrenner flew from Fort Lauderdale to Phoenix for his first quarterly owners' meeting in nearly two years, accompanied by Yankees in-house counsel David Sussman. As they walked into the ballroom of the Ritz-Carlton on the first day for the American League session, Sussman couldn't help but notice Texas Rangers owner George W. Bush (who a few years later would leave baseball for a higher calling) standing by the entrance, his finger over his mouth. As the 14 owners and their attorneys sat down at the long conference table in the middle of the room, Steinbrenner, oblivious to the smirks on the faces of his colleagues, began speaking with Detroit Tigers owner Mike Ilitch. After a few minutes, Steinbrenner noticed that Ilitch kept pointing to his tie. Then, as he glanced around the room, it dawned on him: With the exception of Jackie Autry of the California Angels (the only female owner), everyone was wearing Steinbrenner's trademark outfit: navy blue blazers, gray slacks, white oxford shirts and identical red-white-and-blue-striped ties.

Spotting Bush across the room, now convulsing with laughter, Steinbrenner shouted, "You son of a bitch! I know it was you who put them all up to this!"

"We just wanted to make you feel at home and part of the club again, George," said Bush. "Welcome back."

17

. . .

The Buck Stops Here

. . .

A T THE DAWN OF the 1993 baseball season, the spotlight was once again beaming down on the South Bronx. On the field, Gene Michael's team was significantly better than the one George Steinbrenner had left behind in July 1990. Off the field, Steinbrenner had returned as anything but a humbled and kinder, gentler owner.

The day before the Yankees returned home from their opening six-game road trip to Cleveland and Chicago, I called Steinbrenner at the Regency Hotel and asked him if I could accompany him on his triumphant return to Yankee Stadium for the Yankees' home opener against the Kansas City Royals on April 12. I figured it was a long shot, and was pleasantly surprised when he agreed.

"Meet me at the Regency at 8:30 sharp, and don't be late," he said. "You can ride up with me in my car and we'll talk."

I arrived at the Regency, at 61st and Park, at 8:15 A.M., and I immediately recognized Steinbrenner's Lincoln Town Car with New York plates NYY parked in front, and his driver, John Gleeson, standing next to it. "He just finished breakfast," Gleeson said. "He'll be coming right out."

A few minutes later, Steinbrenner appeared, garbed in his familiar navy blue blazer and gray slacks, with a blue-and-white polka-dot tie. (It was a year or so later that Steinbrenner began wearing white turtlenecks to hide the wrinkles in his neck.) I followed Steinbrenner into the backseat, where he began fiddling with some slips of paper he'd pulled out of his pocket, finally plucking one that bore the phone number of his friend Howard Cosell, the legendary ABC sportscaster who was terminally ill with cancer. The night before, Cosell's daughter, Hillary, had told Steinbrenner her father was simply too weak to attend Opening Day. But Steinbrenner wanted to give it one last try. He dialed the car phone.

"You cannot possibly look out your window, Howard, and not want to go to the ballpark today," Steinbrenner said. "Okay, okay. I understand, but we'll be over to see you after the game."

Before going to the Stadium, Steinbrenner was scheduled to make a guest appearance on the *Live with Regis and Kathie Lee* show with Regis Philbin, another close pal and Opening Day A-lister. During the course of his interview with Philbin, Steinbrenner was asked about baseball's burgeoning labor dispute and the game's related financial problems.

"There'll always be a $5 seat at Yankee Stadium," Steinbrenner said.

"For me?" said Philbin.

"Especially for you, Regis," Steinbrenner said. "That's what I had in mind when I invited you to the game today. I wanted to put you in the bleachers, where you could catch the first homer!"

Back in the limo to the Stadium, Gleeson pulled up at a red light, where a scalper was standing with a sign that said "I need tickets!"

Steinbrenner rolled down the window. "Yeah," he yelled, "you and about eight million other guys!"

As we neared the Stadium, Steinbrenner glanced out the car window at the huge, decrepit brick warehouse that had stood, seemingly vacant, alongside the exit ramp from the Major Deegan Expressway for all the years he'd owned the team.

"Look at that," he grumbled. "A fucking blight. I can't get this city to tear that damn thing down. All that wasted space. That could be the answer to our parking lot problems. They still owe us $7 million. They could use it to buy that and fix it up. I've got to get on them again about this."

At the front gate of Yankee Stadium, we were greeted by Jack Lawn, the VP and chief of operations, who, with his close-cropped sandy-gray hair, broad shoulders and dark blue suit with an American flag pin on his lapel, still looked like a high-ranking official in the Bush administration. Now, after nearly three years supervising the Yankees' business operations in Steinbrenner's absence, Lawn knew the drill for Opening Day.

"Welcome home, George," he said cheerfully.

"Ready?" Steinbrenner said.

"I'm following you," Lawn said.

We then commenced a tour of the entire ballpark, beginning with the Pinstripe Pub, on the field level, where Steinbrenner ordered the bartender to pour him a glass of beer from the tap. He took a sip and, nodding approvingly, offered it to me.

"No, thanks, George," I said. "A little too early in the morning for me."

"Oh, c'mon," he insisted. "It tastes pretty good. Nice and cold. Just the way it's supposed to be."

After checking out the gift shops and food court, we took the elevator up to the suite level, where we were greeted by David Bernstein, the assistant director of concessions, whose Opening Day duties included taking Steinbrenner on an inspection of all the suites. A couple of years earlier, Bernstein had experienced a most humiliating Opening Day when Steinbrenner spotted a bag of garbage on the floor outside one of the suites.

"What's that doing there?" he'd demanded.

"I dunno," said Bernstein. "One of the cleaning women must have left it there by accident."

"Oh yeah?" said Steinbrenner. "Well, just to make sure it's gone from here, you carry that bag of garbage around with you everywhere you go for the rest of the day. You got that?"

Another time, Bernstein and his boss, Joel White, were touring the suites with Steinbrenner when the owner noticed some trash on the floor of a pantry adjacent to the kitchen. Steinbrenner looked at Bernstein and said, "I don't want to hear any of your excuses for this. Get this cleaned up immediately, and if this ever happens again, you're fired." Then, turning to White, he said, "As for you, you're suspended for 30 days."

Without missing a beat, White pointed to Bernstein and said, "How did *he* get so lucky?"

"Even George laughed," Bernstein recalled years later. "Joel was one of the few guys who could get away with talking to him like that."

Fortunately, on this Opening Day, Steinbrenner found all the suites to be trash-free and sufficiently stocked with beverages and condiments, so we proceeded upstairs to the loge level and out to the bleachers. It was strange seeing Steinbrenner wandering through the bleachers, rubbing his hand along the benches to make sure they were clean, and even stranger seeing him strolling through the restrooms, turning on all the faucets and testing the soap dispensers while Lawn went into each stall and flushed the toilets. As he emerged from the first restroom, Lawn winked at me, looked skyward and mumbled out of earshot of Steinbrenner, "Forgive me, Mr. President, for what I do. I've come a long way, haven't I?"

TONY KUBEK HAD been the Yankees' shortstop in the '50s and '60s. After retiring from baseball he had worked as a highly respected color analyst on NBC's Saturday *Game of the Week* before he was hired in 1990 by Bob Gutkowski to broadcast Yankees games on the MSG Network. Gutkowski had hired Kubek in spite of the fact that Kubek and Steinbrenner had a long-standing feud, dating all the way back to 1978, when the Yankees owner took exception to an article by Kubek in the *Fort Lauderdale News*, in which he wrote that Steinbrenner "manipulates people and makes players fear for their jobs." The article had so infuriated Steinbrenner that he sent copies to all the other major league owners with a note saying, "How's this for the mouth that bites the hand that feeds it!" Later, Steinbrenner took further measures by prohibiting Yankee players from doing interviews with Kubek before any *Game of the Week* telecasts that season. Through the years, Kubek and Steinbrenner waged a kind of cold war, with Kubek occasionally making mildly critical statements about the Yankees owner, and Steinbrenner voicing his dismay at being criticized by what he felt was a disloyal former Yankee.

Still, when Gutkowski approached Steinbrenner about hiring Kubek in 1990, Steinbrenner had no objections, saying only, "I respect him as a broadcaster. All I ask is that he's fair."

But while Steinbrenner was away from the Yankees, Joe Molloy, seeking to curry favor with the owner, rekindled the feud with Kubek by collecting tapes of every remotely critical comment about the Yankees or Steinbrenner made by the announcer on the MSG Network. After the 1992 season, Molloy called Gutkowski and told him that he wanted Kubek out. Gutkowski refused.

It was after that conversation that Gutkowski learned Molloy had been collecting the tapes. As a preemptive measure, he instructed his crew at MSG to compile their own set of tapes of Kubek's positive commentaries about Steinbrenner. A week after returning to Yankee Stadium in 1993, Steinbrenner called Gutkowski and said, "Gutkowski, I'm coming up to your office. I've got a big problem and dammit, I've got tapes to prove it!"

When Steinbrenner arrived at Gutkowski's office, a stack of tapes under his arms, he found Gutkowski waiting in front of a TV with a VCR and another stack of tapes spread across an adjoining table.

"Okay, George," Gutkowski said, pointing to the VCR, "be my guest."

For the next hour, the two of them took turns playing clips of Kubek's commentary, all the while screaming louder and louder at each other.

"George's eyes were bugging and he was hollering, and I was hollering right back at him, and after a while our shouting in the closed room got so loud my assistant, who was at her desk outside, panicked and called security," Gutkowski remembered.

By the time the head of security at MSG arrived, the commotion had subsided and Gutkowski and Steinbrenner were emerging from the room, smiling and laughing, their arms around each other.

"Sometimes you just had to go at it with George," said Gutkowski. "In his own way, that was what Tony was doing all those years. I always felt, down deep, George respected Tony's toughness." (In August 2009, Gutkowski filed a $23 million damage suit against Steinbrenner, alleging that he had given Steinbrenner the concept for forming his own YES TV network and that Steinbrenner had reneged on repeated promises to Gutkowski that he would then run it. In January 2010, the suit was dismissed.)

To Steinbrenner's amazement, the 1993 Yankees had been almost completely transformed from the hopeless, last-place team he'd left behind 2½ years earlier. Of the field players, only Don Mattingly remained at first base, while Gene Michael had completely overhauled the pitching staff. Besides Jimmy Key, who would lead the staff in 1993 with an 18-6 record, another left-hander, Jim Abbott, acquired from the California Angels in December '92, won 11 games, and Bob Wickman, acquired from the Chicago White Sox in Michael's salary-dump trade of second baseman Steve Sax, was 14-4.

From the farm system, center fielder Bernie Williams, second baseman Pat Kelly (.273 with 51 RBI), catcher/first baseman Jim Leyritz (.309 with 14 homers), and right-hander Scott Kamieniecki (10-7) emerged in 1993. And with new right fielder Paul O'Neill hitting .311 with 20 homers and 75 RBI, catcher Mike Stanley contributing a strong .305 average and 26 homers, Wade Boggs hitting .302 in the leadoff spot and Danny Tartabull leading the team with 31 homers and 102 RBI as the full-time designated hitter, Showalter guided the Yankees to their first winning season (88-74) since 1988, good for second place in the AL East, seven games behind the eventual world champion Toronto Blue Jays.

ON NOVEMBER 5, 1993, AmShip filed for bankruptcy, sending its stock plummeting to 50 cents a share. At the crux of the company's demise was a contract from the U.S. Navy for the completion of two naval refueling ships, called T-AO's, that had been rusting away through months of neglect in a Philadelphia shipyard. Through the help of two of his influential friends in Congress on the House Defense Appropriations Subcommittee, John Murtha (D-Pa.), the chairman, and Bill Young (R-Fla.), Steinbrenner had been able to win the contract with a bid of $49 million, even though a competing company, Avondale Industries of New Orleans, had submitted a lower bid and had already built or was in the process of building 16 of the 18 T-AO's the Navy had under contract.

When some 12,000 tons of rusted parts began arriving at the Tampa shipyard, it soon became apparent that the construction job was going to be far more extensive than the Navy had let on. On top of that, the Tampa shipyard had no warehouse nor the planning staff to map out the work. Soon, AmShip had fallen behind in payments to its vendors and was fighting with Navy inspectors. When in early 1992 the Navy turned down Amship's request for an additional $24 million, Steinbrenner went back to his friends in Congress and was able to secure another $45 million for the two oilers from a defense appropriations bill, with the promise that they would be completed and delivered by mid-1993. It soon became apparent that AmShip wouldn't be able to make that deadline either, and Steinbrenner offered to finish the job—which he conceded had become the lifeblood of his company—with his own money. But on August 26, 1993, the Navy terminated the contract, having already paid AmShip a total of $98 million. A year later AmShip emerged from bankruptcy after selling off all its remaining assets to satisfy its debts and not long after was dissolved.

Around the same time AmShip was going belly-up, Steinbrenner began negotiating with Tampa city officials and the Tampa Sports Authority to move the Yankees' spring training operations from Fort Lauderdale to his adopted hometown. Despite opposition from some Hillsborough County commissioners to subsidizing a multimillionaire such as Steinbrenner for running a private enterprise, late in 1993 they approved a deal to commit $30 million for a state-of-the-art spring training complex directly across Dale Mabry Highway from Raymond James Stadium, where the National Football League Buccaneers play. For his part, Steinbrenner contributed another $17 million to cover cost overruns and other added amenities for the complex. Construction of what was originally called Legends Field was completed in late 1995, and provided Steinbrenner with a new base of operations now that he had vacated his AmShip offices.

Amid the backdrop of increasingly contentious labor negotiations between the baseball owners and the players union, there was an air of optimism when Showalter convened the Yankees' spring training in Fort Lauderdale in mid-February 1994. "I feel very good about what this bunch can achieve this year," the manager said. Luis Polonia, the career .291-hitting outfielder Michael had reacquired over the winter after three seasons away from the Yankees, agreed. "There's no comparison to what it was like when I was here before," Polonia said. "That wasn't even a team then. It was a bunch of guys worried about numbers and trying to get their money. Guys rooted for other guys to screw up so they'd get a chance to play."

But on February 25, the spring of good feelings was rudely interrupted by the arrival of Steinbrenner. The Boss was late to spring training, having first attended the Winter Olympics in Lillehammer, Norway, where the U.S. won its most medals ever (13), including six golds, after suffering an embarrassment two weeks before the Games when the ex-husband of one of the American skaters, Tonya Harding, orchestrated an assault on her U.S. rival, Nancy Kerrigan. Instead of enjoying the optimism permeating the camp, Steinbrenner chose to challenge his troops, singling out, of all people, Jim Abbott. Abbott, who was born without a right hand, was one of the game's all-time feel-good stories, punctuated by the September 4 no-hitter he tossed for the Yankees against the Cleveland Indians the year before. But Steinbrenner came to camp prepared to chastise him and his agent, Scott Boras, for doing too much charity work.

"It's wonderful for some of these agents and other people to start having players participate in this and that, but before you know it, they're being pulled every different way," Steinbrenner said to the assembled beat reporters. "This is particularly the case of young Jim Abbott. Jim Abbott's got to give 100 percent of his attention to baseball. During the off-season, he's an All-American boy who's going out to do a lot of extracurricular activities. Too many demands on your time are bound to show up, and so I'm going to have to ask Jim to cut down and ask all these worthy causes to understand."

Everyone was stunned. What was Steinbrenner thinking? Was this his idea of motivating the troops? By calling out Jim Abbott for doing too much charity work? This was like the Pope telling Mother Teresa, "Enough with the soup kitchens—get back in the church."

Not surprisingly, Steinbrenner was roundly panned in the next day's papers. Typical of the criticism was the *Daily News'* column by John Harper: "Way to be a sport, George. Hang around too long with Tonya in Lillehammer? You want to say Abbott was a disappointment on the mound last year, then say it. But don't insult Abbott or the legions of lives he's touched. Don't suggest he went 11-14 last year because he cared enough to regularly spend a few minutes before games with ill or handicapped children to whom Abbott represents so much hope as well as courage."

Steinbrenner was not around to respond to the outrage, as he left camp later in the day after learning of the death of his 90-year-old mother, Rita, in Cleveland. While he was gone, Abbott did his best to quell the controversy by saying he would abide by Steinbrenner's wishes after further clarifying for the Boss exactly what his extracurricular activities included. "I think there's a misconception about how much I do during the season," he said. "I do meet with kids when they write to me or come to the ballpark. It takes very little of my time, maybe five or ten minutes. Other than that, I don't do much else."

Once the '94 season got under way, Steinbrenner was hard-pressed to find fault with anyone as the team Michael and Showalter had put together wasted little time living up to their grand expectations. Beginning April 20, the Yankees won 20 of their next 24 games to take over first place in the AL East, which they never relinquished. Unfortunately for them, the season ended early, on August 11, when the players went on strike after labor negotiations with the owners broke down. When two more days of bargaining, on August 24 and 25, also failed to produce an agreement, Bud Selig, who was now the acting commissioner of baseball in the aftermath of Fay Vincent's firing, announced the owners' decision to cancel the season, including the league championship series and the World Series.

At the time of the cessation of play, the Yankees were 70-43 with a 6½-game lead over the Baltimore Orioles; Paul O'Neill, with a .359 average, was declared the American League batting champion; Wade Boggs had a .342 batting average with 11 home runs; Showalter's two catchers, Mike Stanley and Jim Leyritz, had combined for 34 homers and 115 RBI; and Jimmy Key led the majors with 17 wins. Though personally upset at this lost opportunity to return to the World Series, Steinbrenner was firmly in the majority of hawkish owners who were in favor of implementing a salary cap in baseball. Upon Selig's cancellation of the season, Steinbrenner, who, along with all the owners, was under a gag order from the commissioner, issued this statement to Yankees fans: *I can't tell you how sorry I personally am that baseball has announced the cancellation of the 1994 season. We regret that no agreement with the players could be reached and we apologize to our fans for disappointing them, especially this year in which we felt we had a good chance to be in postseason play. When baseball resumes, I can assure you that I am committed to fielding a championship caliber team at Yankee Stadium, as we did this year. I sincerely hope the labor situation will be resolved soon.*

It was no doubt of little consolation to Steinbrenner that the *New York Times*, long his harshest critic, sought to commend him for his loyalty to his fellow "hawks." Wrote *Times* columnist George Vecsey, the day after Selig's cancellation declaration: "There were few heroes among the owners, but one of the least self-centered of the owners in this long and ugly battle has been George Steinbrenner of the Yankees. Steinbrenner may be acting avariciously in his lust for a new stadium in New York, but he has consistently been willing to accept a salary tax against his high payroll because he saw it in his best interest and the best interests of baseball. Among baseball owners, he counts as an altruist."

As the labor impasse dragged on through the winter, the 28 clubs continued to go about their business in anticipation of the 1995 season, and Gene Michael made two more important acquisitions for the Yankees. On December 22, Michael pulled off a stunner of a trade when he acquired 28-year-old right-hander Jack McDowell, one of the premier starting pitchers in the American League, from the Chicago White Sox for a couple of fringe minor league prospects. The reason Michael was able to acquire McDowell, a two-time 20-game winner, for so little was that White Sox chairman Jerry Reinsdorf, the primary "hawk" among the owners, had grown weary of the rancorous yearly contract negotiations with the pitcher and was unwilling to pay him more than the $5 million that he figured to get in salary arbitration for 1995. There was also some question about McDowell's status, as he was one of 11 players who fell short of the six years of major league service time required to become a free agent because of the players' strike. Reinsdorf didn't want to deal with that issue, either, which is why he let it become the Yankees' problem and asked for so little in return.

It was not until March 31, 1995, that the players ended their strike, after U.S. District Court of New York judge Sonia Sotomayor issued a preliminary injunction against the owners, ordering them to restore the baseball work rules regarding free agency and salary arbitration, which they had revoked in February when the mediator, W. J. Ussery, declared an impasse in the negotiations. The labor dispute would go on, but both sides agreed to resume play, with a 144-game schedule in 1995, while they continued to hammer out a settlement.

On April 5, Michael swung one more deal that he hoped would provide the final element of the "championship caliber team" Steinbrenner had promised New York fans, when the cash-strapped Montreal Expos traded him their stellar 28-year-old closer, John Wetteland, for another lightly regarded minor league prospect, outfielder Fernando Seguignol. Despite their having done a superb job of scouting and player development, enabling them to fashion the best record in baseball (70-40) at the time of the work stoppage in 1994, the Expos were the club hit hardest by the strike. Between their unattractive and antiquated Olympic Stadium and an underfinanced and infighting ownership group, the Expos, who lost a reported $16 million because of the cancellation of the season, were hemorrhaging money and gradually becoming an endangered franchise. As a result, team president Claude Brochu was left no choice but to start peddling his best players who were nearing salary arbitration eligibility and free agency in order to make ends meet.

But in spite of these acquisitions, the '95 Yankees struggled to regain their mojo of the year before, falling as far back as 10½ games behind the first-place Red Sox in mid-June. They lost Jimmy Key (who'd been 17-4 in '94) to shoulder surgery on July 5, sidelining him for two months, and Danny Tartabull, their $25 million middle-of-the-order big-time power hitter, disintegrated. These failures also led to more friction between Steinbrenner and Michael.

Steinbrenner had been on Tartabull's case since spring training, noting that the slugger had missed 40 games the year before with minor injuries, and in mid-June he lowered the boom on him for managing only two home runs to that point. "Tartabull's been a major disappointment," Steinbrenner told reporters. "He's supposed to be a cleanup hitter—that's what we're paying him that kind of money for—and his batting average with runners in scoring position is under .200."

What bothered Steinbrenner was that Michael and Showalter were just as disgusted with Tartabull but chose not to blast him in the newspapers. Michael's reasoning was that Tartabull's market value was low enough; it would serve no useful purpose to further tear the guy apart. Showalter, on the other hand, was concerned about upsetting the clubhouse chemistry he'd built by publicly ripping one of his players, even though he knew Tartabull had few friends on the team.

"I'm a stand-up guy with Tartabull," Steinbrenner told Jack Curry of the *New York Times* in a July 21 interview. "He knows I think he's been a major disappointment, but I'm getting a little fed up with the whole situation of Stick and Buck saying things in meetings and then being Mr. Nice Guys to the press about him."

A few days earlier, Steinbrenner, accompanied by Bill Fugazy, had been in the Yankee clubhouse discussing Key with reporters when he appeared to take a swipe at Michael. "Well, Jimmy Key's been a great competitor and we need him back," he said. "I give all the credit to Joe Molloy for signing him."

Michael was having dinner in the Yankee Stadium pressroom when I joined him a few minutes later and made the mistake of offhandedly repeating what Steinbrenner had said about Molloy signing Key.

"He said *what*?" Michael screamed, getting up from his seat.

"I don't think he meant anything by it, Stick," I said.

"Bull *shit*!" Michael said before marching out the door and into the corridor, where, coincidentally, Steinbrenner and Fugazy were making their way back to the elevator. Confronting them, Michael raged, "I heard what you told the press behind my back about Joe Molloy signing Key, George. How could you say that? What kind of an owner does that? That's bullshit and you know it!"

"Hey, hey, Stick," interjected Fugazy. "Take it easy. You and George need to talk about this privately upstairs."

"Yeah, Stick," said Steinbrenner. "I see what you're doing here. I don't appreciate having these sorts of conversations in public like this. I'll see you later upstairs."

"Fine," said Michael. "Let's go upstairs and have this out." Then, looking at me, he added: "You come with us, Billy. I want you as a witness."

The four of us took the elevator upstairs to Steinbrenner's office, where Michael resumed his tirade.

"Look, George," he said, his voice still raised, "I know you don't believe this, but I've never sought any credit for putting this team back together, and I don't want any credit. But I'll be damned if I'm gonna let you go around giving credit to Joe Molloy for signing Key. Joe Molloy wouldn't even know if Key was left-handed!"

Steinbrenner, who had taken a seat at his desk as Michael stood over him, looked at him coldly.

"You know, Stick, I can't be having these kinds of things anymore with you. I think I'm just gonna have to make a change here."

"Fine," screamed Michael. "You want to fire me? Well then, just do it.

Right here in front of Billy! Don't threaten. Just do it! Be a man, George!"

"I'm gonna have to think about this, Stick," Steinbrenner muttered. "This is just not working out."

"You do that, George," Michael said, before leading me out the door into the press box.

Despite being challenged in front of a reporter, Steinbrenner did not fire Michael that day, though it was clear that the two were not going to be able to work together much longer. For the time being, there were the play-offs to think about; and, for all the problems with the pitching, the loss of Key and the demise of Tartabull, Showalter had managed to rally the Yankees back into contention for the American League wild card as the July 31 trading deadline approached. And when the Toronto Blue Jays (who, like the Expos, had been especially hard-hit by the '94 strike) announced they were putting their right-handed ace, David Cone, on the trading block because of his impending free agency, Steinbrenner and Michael put their differences aside and combined efforts to fill the Yankees' most pressing need.

Steinbrenner began the negotiations by calling his friend Paul Beeston, the Blue Jays' president and chief executive officer. What would the Blue Jays need to get in exchange for Cone? he asked. Beeston said they were looking for young, inexpensive pitching, at least three players, one of them ready to step into their rotation. He mentioned Andy Pettitte, a rookie left-hander who had stepped up to fill one of the spots of the injured starters in the Yankee rotation in '95, and Marty Janzen, a right-hander who had just been promoted to Double-A ball in the Yankees system after dominating hitters in the Class A Florida State League. Steinbrenner and Beeston then agreed to let their GMs, Michael and Pat Gillick, conduct the rest of the negotiations.

Michael would later remember July 28, 1995, as being one of the most exasperating but ultimately satisfying days of his career as Yankees general manager. It began with him successfully getting Gillick to focus on the 22-year-old Janzen as the centerpiece of the Cone deal, leaving Pettitte off the table. At the same time, however, Steinbrenner was calling him every 15 minutes imploring him to find a way to off-load the seemingly untradable Tartabull (who had another year and a half and nearly $8 million left on his contract), while relaying the minor league department's objections to including Janzen in the Cone deal.

"They're telling me here that Janzen's a keeper," Steinbrenner said by phone from Tampa. "You need to figure out a way to do this deal without him in it."

By this time, Michael had already gotten Gillick's tentative agreement on a deal for Cone in which the Jays would get Janzen and two other low-level minor league pitching prospects, and he was eager to quickly close it out.

"We're the Yankees, George," Michael said. "We need to win now. Cone gives us that opportunity, and we can afford to sign him. I don't know if we're going to make the playoffs, but we sure as hell won't if we don't have Cone. We can't worry about what Janzen might do down the road."

"All right," said Steinbrenner. "Make the deal. But I know Gillick. He's too smart. These young pitchers we're giving him, they better not turn out to be anything."

At the time of the Cone deal, the Yankees were in Minnesota for a series against the Twins, having just won eight of their last nine games to move into third place in the AL East, 5½ games behind the Red Sox, but only 1 behind three other teams for the wild card.

A few days earlier, Michael had been talking to Showalter in the manager's office at Yankee Stadium about the possibilities for trading Tartabull.

"You can't trade that contract to anyone," Showalter sighed.

"That's not true," said Michael. "I can trade anyone, as long as you don't care what I get back."

"Not Tartabull," said Showalter. "Nobody'll take him."

"Well," said Michael, smiling thinly, "what would you do for me if I did trade him?"

"I'll kiss your ass at home plate when I bring out the lineup cards the next day."

"Tell you what," Michael said, unbuckling his belt as Showalter looked at him in astonishment. "I'm gonna save you a lot of embarrassment by letting you do that right here!"

The only way Michael was able to trade Tartabull (who, by July 28, was hitting just .224 with six home runs) was to find a team that had a similarly underperforming, overpaid player. In the Oakland A's, who had grown equally disenchanted with outfielder Ruben Sierra, who was hitting .265

with 12 homers, with two years remaining at $5.5 million each, Michael found just such a willing trade partner. So, on the heels of the Cone deal, Michael succeeded in shedding the albatross that was Tartabull, albeit for another, potentially more expensive one in Sierra.

Steinbrenner was uncharacteristically quiet after the Cone and Tartabull deals were announced. The next day, he showed up in Minneapolis and met with Showalter, not to discuss the new players but rather to talk about Darryl Strawberry, the drug-troubled former star slugger for the Mets who was seeking to rehabilitate his career. Six weeks earlier, without consulting Michael or anyone else, Steinbrenner had signed Strawberry to a minor league contract right after the faded 33-year-old outfielder completed a suspension from February until June '95 for violating baseball's drug policy while playing for the San Francisco Giants. Much to Showalter's dismay, on July 4, 1995, Steinbrenner ordered Strawberry's recall from the Yankees' Triple-A farm team in Columbus, thus creating a designated hitter logjam with the just-acquired Sierra.

Sierra and Strawberry delivered a combined 10 homers and 57 RBI over the last two months, but it was Cone, going 9-2 in 13 starts, who proved to be the most significant factor in the Yankees beating out the California Angels by one game for the AL wild card. Waiting for them in the best-of-five Division Series was none other than Lou Piniella, who was now managing the AL West champion Seattle Mariners.

The Yankees won the first two games, in New York. During game two, which was won in the 15th inning on a home run by Jim Leyritz, Steinbrenner entered the press box and launched into an umpire-bashing tirade the likes of which the amused writer corps had not seen since 1983. The targets of his outrage were home-plate umpire Dale Scott, who, replays showed, had called Yankees outfielder Dion James out on a pitch that appeared to be inside, and first-base umpire Jim McKean, who appeared to have missed two base-running calls against the Yankees.

"The pitch was a good three inches inside," Steinbrenner fumed. "The guy just blew it! All I know is the home-plate umpire is from Oregon, and I learned long ago from my geography teacher that Oregon is next to Washington. This is awful. And the first-base umpire blew both of those calls. I asked for [supervisor of umpires] Marty Springstead to come up and look at the videotapes, but he said that was inappropriate. Well, I think getting the best officiating is appropriate."

These comments would lead American League president Gene Budig to impose a $50,000 fine on Steinbrenner, who once again enlisted the services of New York attorney Bob Costello. Costello successfully got the fine rescinded on the grounds that, under baseball's constitution, the league president did not have the authority to fine an owner. "It cost George more in legal fees to me than the fine," Costello said years later with a chuckle, "but with him it was all about the winning."

The Mariners took the next two games in Seattle. Then, in the decisive game five, the Yankees blew a 4–2 eighth-inning lead and lost 6–5 to the Mariners in 11. Showalter was roundly criticized by the media for leaving an exhausted Cone in for 147 pitches, the last being a bases-loaded ball four to journeyman pinch hitter Doug Strange that tied the game in the eighth. Showalter's issue was that he had inexplicably lost faith in his closer, Wetteland, who had given up a towering 12th-inning home run to Ken Griffey Jr. in game two during his 3⅓ innings of relief. Instead of using his closer in game five, Showalter brought back his starter from game three, Jack McDowell, for the first relief appearance of his career. With Wetteland waving his arms in disbelief in the bullpen, McDowell gave up the tying and winning runs in the 11th inning.

After the game, a furious Steinbrenner heaped praise on Piniella while leaving no doubt as to whom he blamed for the Yankees' defeat.

"I feel sorry for my team," Steinbrenner told reporters. "But we had our chances to win this thing and didn't take advantage. Give Piniella credit. We're up 5-0 [in game four]. We have to win that game. And Cone was magnificent tonight. But 147 pitches?"

When asked what changes he planned for the off-season, Steinbrenner snapped, "You'll see," before walking past the manager's office without bothering to go in.

The "rising star" (as Steinbrenner had referred to Showalter on his return to baseball back in March 1993) was now a fallen star. But before Steinbrenner dealt with Showalter, whose contract was to expire the day after the completion of the World Series, he first had to settle affairs with Michael, who had an option year on his contract. A couple of days after the Yankees' elimination by the Mariners, Steinbrenner summoned Michael to Tampa. Their meeting began with Steinbrenner informing Michael that he wanted to change the terms of the option by cutting the general manager's salary from $600,000 to $400,000.

"That's unacceptable, George," Michael said. "This job is hard enough, and I don't deserve to have my salary cut."

"So maybe we just need to figure something else out," Steinbrenner said. "I want you with me, but I'm tired of the constant fighting."

"I'll go back to scouting then," Michael said. "I don't like being confined so much in the office as you have to be as GM."

They agreed that Michael would become director of major league scouting—a position that paid $150,000. When Michael told me he was stepping down as GM, mindful of that ugly confrontation I'd witnessed in the owner's office a couple of months earlier, I was curious as to whether it was as much of a mutual decision as he was letting on. But when I called Steinbrenner, he assured me that Michael was still going to have heavy input in all of the Yankees' player personnel decisions.

"It got so I was paying him $600,000 just to argue with him," Steinbrenner said. "I'm still going to argue with him all the time, but at least now it won't cost me as much!"

Before the transition took place, Steinbrenner asked Michael to find his successor, a task that proved more challenging than either of them imagined. Michael was turned down by a number of former general managers now working as assistants or scouting directors elsewhere, as well as one former manager, Joe Torre, who had been fired by the St. Louis Cardinals the previous June 16. The Yankees? Steinbrenner? Not interested. At one point, Michael told his assistant, Brian Cashman, in exasperation: "George doesn't believe that nobody wants this job. Right now, the first guy to say yes has got it."

That person turned out to be 49-year-old Bob Watson, the former Yankee first baseman who was then general manager of the Houston Astros. The only African American GM in baseball, Watson had become disenchanted with the constant interference he was getting from Astros owner Drayton McLane. On October 23, the Yankees announced that he'd signed a two-year, $800,000 contract—the same money Michael had turned down.

With Watson onboard, Steinbrenner was now able to turn his attention to Showalter, who had said he didn't want to begin negotiations on his contract until he knew who the general manager was going to be. It turned out that didn't matter, as Showalter quickly realized that Steinbrenner was intent on punishing him as well for the Yankees' playoff failure. Taking a familiar page out of his "how to fire a manager" textbook, Steinbrenner began the negotiations by telling Showalter that he wanted to replace all of his coaches, the reason being that none of them, like Showalter himself, had ever played in the major leagues.

"This is one of the problems, Buck," he said. "You need to have guys around you who are experienced."

"I don't accept that, Mr. Steinbrenner," Showalter said. "If I'm going to manage, I need to have my own coaches. I think these guys do a good job for me."

A week later, on October 26, Steinbrenner offered Showalter a two-year contract worth $1.05 million, with the condition that, at the very least, hitting coach Rick Down had to go. Showalter, who was looking for a three-year contract, mulled it over before turning it down. He was under the impression that negotiations were still open, but Steinbrenner interpreted this as Showalter's resignation and immediately called his public relations director, Rob Butcher, instructing him to announce that the manager had decided to leave. Steinbrenner was once again skewered in the newspapers and on talk radio for parting with yet another manager—indeed, a manager who had brought the Yankees back to the postseason after a 14-year drought. In an attempt to deflect the criticism, Steinbrenner issued this statement: *"We tried but were unable to dissuade Buck. I have nothing but praise for Buck and the job he did for us. I am very upset by his leaving. I wish Buck and his fine little family nothing but the best."*

Unlike all the previous times he'd gotten rid of a manager, however, Steinbrenner had no candidates-in-waiting already working for him in the organization. Michael made it clear he didn't want the job, but agreed to help Steinbrenner find a suitable replacement for Showalter. It was Michael's belief that, despite the disappointing Seattle playoff series, the team he had put together was ready to win with perhaps a little more tweaking, and that it was important to hire an experienced manager who would not be intimidated by Steinbrenner. As Michael began the process of narrowing down the list of viable candidates, Yankees senior VP Arthur Richman took it upon himself to submit his own list of managerial candidates to Steinbrenner, including Tony La Russa, who had resigned as Oakland A's manager at the end of the year; Davey Johnson, who'd just been fired as manager of the Cincinnati Reds; John McNamara, who had previously managed five different teams in the majors; and Joe Torre. After a very brief evaluation and interview process, Michael concluded that the Brooklyn-born Torre, who'd previously managed the Mets and had also won a division championship as manager of the Atlanta Braves in 1982, was the best fit for the job, in spite of his underwhelming 894-1,003 career record. On November 2, the Yankees announced that the 55-year-old Torre had agreed to a two-year contract worth $500,000 for the first year and $550,000 for the second, which ranked in the lower echelon among major league managers.

The next day, the *Daily News* greeted Torre's return to his hometown with the back-page headline CLUELESS JOE. In the accompanying column, Ian O'Connor wrote, *"He thinks he knows, but he has not a clue. . . . The fact is, Steinbrenner is giving his team to a manager who has lost more than 1,000 games, who in 30 years as a player and coach hasn't secured a single playoff victory. Torre has won 47% of his games from the bench, Showalter 54%."*

Alarmed over the stunningly negative press for the hiring of Torre, Steinbrenner convened his Yankees high command in Tampa.

"The media's killing us," Steinbrenner said. "Are you sure Torre's the right man?"

"Torre can manage," asserted Michael. "I'm confident he can handle the job and handle New York. He's a New York guy."

"Was he the best man for the job?" Steinbrenner asked.

"I told you, George, I thought Buck was the best man for the job, but you didn't want him," Michael replied.

"What do you think?" Steinbrenner said, looking at Cashman.

"I agree with Stick, boss," Cashman said. "I always thought Buck was the best man for the job."

"All right," Steinbrenner said. "What if I got Buck back?"

Michael and Cashman looked at each other quizzically. Steinbrenner didn't say anything further about the manager situation, and the discussion turned to various trades they were contemplating. A few days later, Showalter was in Phoenix, preparing to meet with Jerry Colangelo, the managing general partner of the Arizona Diamondbacks, who was anxious to talk to him about managing the expansion team even though they would not begin play until 1998, when he got a phone call from his agent, Jim Krivacs.

"You're not gonna believe this," said Krivacs, "but I just got off the phone with George and he wants to talk to you again about coming back to the Yankees."

"He what?" said Showalter.

"He wants you back," Krivacs said. "He's coming up to your home in Pensacola tomorrow to personally make his pitch to you."

The next day, after meeting with Colangelo and coming to a tentative agreement on a seven-year, $7 million contract to manage the Diamondbacks, Showalter arrived home in Pensacola to find Steinbrenner sitting in his living room munching on cookies that had been baked by Showalter's wife, Angela.

"You need to be a Yankee," Steinbrenner said. "You need to stay here."

"I appreciate your support, George," Showalter said, "but I've already made a deal with Arizona."

"Have you signed anything?"

"Well, no. Not yet. But we have a handshake."

"What's it for?

"Seven years."

"*Seven years?* Well, I still think you need to stay with the Yankees. I want you with me."

"You've already got a manager in Torre," Showalter said.

"Don't worry about that," Steinbrenner said. "I'll just make him the president."

"Well, how do we get out of this then?" Showalter said. "You haven't changed your mind on the coaches."

"You're just being stubborn about that," Steinbrenner said.

"But Colangelo is letting me bring all my coaches with me to Arizona."

Steinbrenner sighed. "I don't know what to say. I tried, but I guess you've got to take the job out there, Buck. I'm at least glad we had this talk. I didn't like the way things ended back there in Tampa."

"Neither did I," said Showalter.

As with Billy Martin in 1978, Dick Howser in 1980, Lou Piniella in 1988 and Dallas Green in 1989, no sooner had Steinbrenner parted ways with his manager than he began suffering pangs of guilt and offered to bring him back. Managers: he couldn't live with them and he couldn't live without them. And now he'd chased off one he'd groomed himself through the Yankees' system and replaced him with an outsider, a career National Leaguer with a losing record whom the media was already calling "Clueless."

18

. . .

Torre Glory

. . .

T HE TURMOIL AND TRANSITION that engulfed the Yankees in
the weeks following the 1995 season did not end with the departure of Buck Showalter and the reassignment of Gene Michael.
There were trades to be made, free agents to be signed, a coaching staff
for Joe Torre to be assembled. And right in the middle of it all was Rob
Butcher, the 32-year-old second-year public relations director whose job it
was to arrange the press conferences where all these comings and goings
would be announced.

It would have helped Butcher do his job if he was kept in the loop
on events as they were playing out, but because of the stealthy manner in
which Steinbrenner conducted the sensitive Showalter and Michael negotiations, Butcher was about the last person to be clued in. He was helping
the Major League Baseball public relations team at the World Series in
Cleveland when he was informed by his immediate superior, Yankees VP
Arthur Richman, that Bob Watson had been hired to take over as general
manager. Richman did not know when Watson would be available to talk to
the media, and while he did know that Steinbrenner was presently engaged
in increasingly contentious negotiations with Showalter, he did not bother
to alert Butcher to this.

Although there had long been an MLB embargo on teams making major announcements during the World Series, Steinbrenner had never paid it
any heed. Butcher was now faced with the task of trying to round up all the

local media, most of whom were covering the World Series, to announce the Watson hiring. Frantic, he had his assistant back in New York write up a press release and fax it to the Indians' Jacobs Field office, then hustled copies across town to the Rock and Roll Hall of Fame, where the World Series gala was going on. Butcher knew that handing out press releases in the middle of a World Series gala was no way to announce the hiring of a new general manager, and he braced himself for the wave of abuse he would take from the partying New York media corps, especially since the Associated Press had already put the news on the wires.

"I would have never left for the World Series if I'd known the Stick and Buck things were going down," Butcher said in a 2009 interview. "After all, they'd just led us to the postseason for the first time in 14 years. Who would have believed he'd be making any changes with them?"

Only someone who didn't know the history of George Steinbrenner.

Back in New York, at Yankee Stadium, Butcher put together what became known as the "Clueless Joe" press conference (thanks to the headline the *Daily News* ran the next day), where Torre was formally introduced as the new Yankees manager. Unbeknownst to Butcher, however, there were even more developments in the works that would illustrate the confusion within the newly splintered Yankees high command.

For, as it turned out, Torre wasn't the one who, as Ian O'Connor wrote, "thinks he knows but hasn't got a clue." Bob Watson was. In their first strategy session, Torre told Watson that the Yankees' top priority was to get a defense-oriented catcher who could handle a veteran pitching staff. To that end, Torre's new bench coach, Don Zimmer, who had previously worked for the Colorado Rockies, highly recommended the Rockies' Joe Girardi. The Rockies had made it known that Girardi was available because he was due to earn $2.25 million in 1996, a salary they felt was excessive for a 31-year-old catcher who had caught over 100 games only twice in his career.

But as Watson negotiated the trade for Girardi (for whom he gave up a minor league pitcher named Mike DeJean), Gene Michael, at Steinbrenner's urging, was working on a much bigger deal with the Seattle Mariners. The Mariners were looking to decrease their payroll, and one of their highest-paid players, Tampa-born first baseman Tino Martinez, was going to be eligible for free agency after the 1997 season. Martinez had just hit a career-high 31 homers and 111 RBI, and he told Mariners manager Lou Piniella that his preference would be to play on the East Coast, if possible for the Yankees.

"Then I'll do everything I can to see to it that you will," promised Piniella, who soon thereafter met with Steinbrenner in Tampa to impress upon him what a perfect fit the left-handed-hitting Martinez would be as the replacement for the retiring Don Mattingly.

Michael spent the next three weeks working with Piniella and Mariners GM Woody Woodward putting together the blockbuster deal that would send Martinez (along with reliever Jeff Nelson) to the Yankees for two of their prize young players, left-hander Sterling Hitchcock and third base prospect Russ Davis. Watson was largely excluded from these discussions, which might have explained why he kept denying to the New York media that the Yankees were talking to the Mariners about Martinez—even after all the players involved in the deal were being reported on a daily basis. The first time Watson officially acknowledged the Yankees' involvement with Seattle was December 7, the day the deal was announced. On the same day, the Yankees announced that Steinbrenner had negotiated a five-year, $20 million contract extension with Martinez. "Now," said Watson at the conclusion of the press conference, "I need to turn my attention to re-signing [David] Cone."

This should have been the cue to Rob Butcher to remain on red alert for yet another major off-season announcement.

The negotiations with Cone dragged on until he agreed to sign with the Yankees on December 20, the same day that Butcher had been planning to leave for a quick trip home to Columbus, where his nine brothers and sisters were to gather for their first Christmas together since 1989. The reunion had been planned for months, and Butcher had twice notified Steinbrenner during the previous two weeks of his intention to go home to Ohio on December 20. He had also notified Richman and Yankees general counsel David Sussman. But on the morning of the 20th, as he was about to leave his office at Yankee Stadium for the airport, Sussman and Richman told him that he should probably wait around in case something happened with Cone. When neither of them could tell him just how long he should wait, Butcher elected to make his flight anyway.

Upon arriving in Columbus, Butcher called the office to check in, and Richman told him that Cone had indeed agreed to terms and that Steinbrenner was furious his PR man was not there to alert the media. Still, Richman said, Steinbrenner would probably get over it as long as Butcher was back in New York the next day to handle the press conference. Butcher assured Richman he'd be on the first plane to New York and then called Steinbrenner from his sister's home to explain, again, why he was in Columbus.

"This is the third time this off-season you've left your post when we had things going on," Steinbrenner said. "I can't have this."

"I'll be back first thing tomorrow to handle the press conference," Butcher said.

"Don't worry about that," Steinbrenner snapped. "I needed you and you weren't here. We'll pay you till January. In the meantime you need to find another job!"

Just the same, Butcher flew back to New York the following morning, but when he walked into Sussman's office, he was told that his sentence remained.

"George hasn't changed his mind," Sussman said. "He doesn't want you here. You're not in a union, so there's nothing you can do. I'd advise you to just go."

Butcher put his coat back on and headed out of the Stadium, but not before saying goodbye to Watson and Torre, who were having lunch in the pressroom.

"Where are you going?" Watson asked him.

"I'm going home. I've been fired."

"You're joking!" Watson said.

"I wish I was."

It took two days before word of Butcher's firing got out, but when it did, Steinbrenner was thoroughly skewered by the media for firing a $50,000-per-year PR man three days before Christmas. On the back page of the *Daily News*, Steinbrenner was depicted in an Ed Murawinski cartoon as Ebenezer Scrooge. A week later, Steinbrenner phoned Butcher in Columbus and told him that he could have his job back after all.

"I think you've learned your lesson," he said.

For Butcher, those words stung even more than "You're fired."

"As soon as he said that," Butcher remembered, "I said to myself, 'He's just being a bully again,' and I didn't need that. As much as I still wanted to work there, I didn't think I'd ever done anything that I would need to be taught a lesson."

Butcher thanked Steinbrenner and said he'd think it over. He never talked to Steinbrenner again and, after a year working for a small public relations firm promoting the Olympic Games, he was hired as media relations director by the Cincinnati Reds—a job he still held 14 years later.

THAT OFF-SEASON, STEINBRENNER signed one other pitcher he hoped would bolster the staff for 1996. This one, however, was greeted by more skepticism than enthusiasm. After all, 30-year-old Dwight Gooden had been out of baseball for most of the previous two years, having betrayed the great promise he'd shown as a 20-year-old 24-game winner with the Mets in 1985, ultimately being suspended three separate times for drug use.

Steinbrenner had always seemed to relish reclamation projects, whether it was that other fallen Mets idol, Darryl Strawberry, whom he'd signed the year before, or, in 1991, Steve Howe, whom he allowed Gene Michael to sign in spite of the relief pitcher's half dozen previous drug suspensions. And of course there were all the times he had brought back the damaged Billy Martin.

Gooden, a Tampa product, had been working out at Eckerd College, in St. Petersburg. A former Yankees clubhouse attendant, Ray Negron, had helped Gooden to enroll in a Narcotics Anonymous program, and, acting as his agent, arranged a meeting with Steinbrenner at Carmine's Restaurant, in north Tampa. As Gooden remembered it, there wasn't much of a negotiation—he didn't exactly have a lot of leverage.

"I'm prepared to give you a three-year contract," Steinbrenner said, explaining that only the first year would be guaranteed, at a base salary of $850,000, with incentives that could get it up over $1 million. "I hope you've gotten your life straightened out. I'm counting on you to help this team. I believe in you. Just don't ever make me look bad."

Gooden made good on Steinbrenner's commitment to him, throwing a 2–0 no-hitter against the Seattle Mariners at Yankee Stadium on May 14,

1996, even as his dad was awaiting heart surgery at St. Joseph's Hospital, in Tampa. He would go on to win 11 games for the Yankees in '96, earning most of his incentives, but the payback to Steinbrenner was short-lived. A shoulder injury limited his 1997 season and prompted his release by the Yankees, and after a brief comeback with them in 2000, he was released again and signed by Steinbrenner as a "special assistant" working out of the team's Himes Avenue minor league complex in Tampa. However, Gooden relapsed into drugs and was arrested and jailed in August 2005 for fleeing a DUI traffic stop in Tampa, then arrested again later that year on domestic violence charges filed by his girlfriend.

Steinbrenner remained silent during all of this, just as he had when Strawberry, to whom he'd offered a similar postcareer "special assistant" job at Himes, also wound up in a Tampa jail in 2000 after yet another drug bust. None of Steinbrenner's front office and coaching staff could understand his continued compassion for these serial drug offenders, which seemed to contrast so thoroughly with the hard-ass George Patton image he'd crafted for himself. When Don Zimmer, who'd been a close friend of Steinbrenner's for more than 25 years, left the Yankees' coaching staff after the 2003 season, he bitterly assailed Steinbrenner for his bafflingly inconsistent treatment of his underlings. "All year long, he's bad-mouthing the coaches, who only work their asses off for him, and he says nothin' about those other two guys he's paying $100,000 a year and have done nothing for it but embarrass him. Who can figure him out?"

In a 2009 interview, Gooden admitted to being ashamed at how he'd let Steinbrenner down.

"The day after my no-hitter, George was having an important meeting with his baseball people in Tampa when somebody told him about my father waiting on heart surgery at St. Joseph's Hospital," Gooden said. "He adjourned the meeting and rushed over to be at my dad's bedside to give him a pep talk and assure him everything was going to be all right. That meant more to me than anything anyone ever did."

IN HIS FEBRUARY 1996 inaugural address to the Yankees at their new Legends Field spring training complex in Tampa, Torre acknowledged the absence of any World Series appearances on his baseball résumé. Pointing to his coaches—Zimmer, Mel Stottlemyre, Chris Chambliss, Jose Cardenal and Tony Cloninger—Torre noted that they all had World Series rings. "That's what I want," he said. "But I don't want to win just one. I want to win three in a row and establish something here that's special."

His players found Torre's quiet confidence and relaxed candor refreshing, and as the 1996 season progressed, it became more and more apparent that he was just the opposite of the tightly wound Showalter, whose controlling style had worn thin on most of the veterans. In particular, Showalter's decision to give up on John Wetteland, the popular closer and spiritual leader of the relief pitchers, had left a bad taste with them. More important, Torre's ability to disarm Steinbrenner served as a welcome change to the players, who were accustomed to the owner's intrusions into the clubhouse and propensity for public critiques of their performances.

Early in the 1996 season, the Yankees had an off-day and Steinbrenner called Torre from Yankee Stadium, chastising him for not taking part in a meeting of his baseball operations people.

"Here we are, working on things to help make the club better for you, and you're out there in the woods somewhere," Steinbrenner complained, to which Torre replied: "I can't believe it, George. How did you know my ball was in the woods? I haven't been able to keep it in the fairway all day."

It didn't hurt that, after opening the season with two impressive wins in Cleveland against the defending American League champion Indians, Torre's Yankees stayed within a game or two of the American League East lead through the first month of the season before taking over first place April 30 and never relinquishing it. Of particular significance was the emergence of Derek Jeter at shortstop. Coming into spring training, there were some doubts about Jeter's ability to handle the shortstop duties after he'd led the International League with 29 errors in '95. Clyde King, Steinbrenner's longtime advisor, opined in one of the staff meetings that spring that, at 6-3, 195 pounds, Jeter lacked the necessary footwork for the position. By then, however, Torre and Zimmer, his infield/bench coach, had been impressed with Jeter's play and uncommon confidence for a 21-year-old, and the shortstop went on to reward their faith by winning Rookie of the Year honors, hitting .314 with 10 homers, 78 RBI and 104 runs scored.

That is not to say the accomplishments of 1996 came without considerable adversity.

On May 7, Cone, who was 4-1 with a 2.02 ERA, was diagnosed with an aneurysm in his pitching arm that caused him to go on the disabled list for four months. Then, on June 21, after a stirring come-from-behind 10-inning win against the Indians, Torre got a call from his wife, Ali, informing him that his oldest brother, Rocco, who'd been watching the game on TV, had died of a heart attack. At the same time, Torre's other older brother, Frank, was gravely ill at a Florida hospital and in need of a heart transplant.

There was more. Veteran outfielder Tim Raines, an inspirational clubhouse leader, missed 75 days with nagging hamstring injuries; Scott Kamieniecki, whom Torre was counting on to be the number four or five starter, missed almost the entire season with an arm injury; and, in midseason, designated hitter Ruben Sierra clashed openly with Torre, accusing the manager of reneging on a promise to give him more playing time. Torre, in turn, called Sierra a spoiled brat who never could grasp the concept of team play, and on July 31 the Yankees traded him to the Detroit Tigers for Cecil "Big Daddy" Fielder.

The Yankees won the AL East by four games over the Baltimore Orioles, but they ranked ninth in the AL in runs, twelfth in homers, seventh in stolen bases and fifth in ERA. They never won more than five games in a row and didn't have any players with 30 or more homers, 200 or more hits or 20 or more stolen bases. Other than Andy Pettitte, at 21-8, no Yankee starter won more than 12 games.

Once the Yankees reached the postseason, Steinbrenner seemed to be in a perpetually foul mood, especially after the team lost the first game of the best-of-five Division Series with the Texas Rangers at home and had to go 12 innings, with Torre using a total of seven pitchers, to eke out a come-from-behind 5–4 win in game two. On the bus ride from Yankee Stadium to Newark Airport after that game, the players were alarmed when Reggie Jackson (who was with the team in his capacity as a special advisor) suddenly stood up from his front-row seat next to Torre and began shouting at Steinbrenner, sitting in the row behind him.

"I'm 50 years old. Why do you treat me the way you do?" Jackson screamed before being grabbed and subdued by Torre.

"It was no big deal," Steinbrenner later said of the incident. "Just something between Reggie and me."

But according to Jackson, it *was* a big deal, something that had been simmering between the two ever since they'd supposedly reconciled their long-ago differences after Jackson announced he wanted to go into the Hall of Fame as a Yankee in 1993 and was welcomed back with open arms by Steinbrenner. Witnesses said Reggie's rage was precipitated when Steinbrenner questioned why he was on the bus. "The next time you want to go where you're not invited, check with me," he reportedly told Jackson.

The next day, Jackson sought out Steinbrenner at the Yankees hotel in Texas to apologize for speaking to him like that in public.

"Reggie, you were wrong," Steinbrenner said. "You can't talk to the owner of the team like that. If there's something wrong, we have to rectify it. Right now, you probably need to go on home and we'll talk later."

After the Yankees won the next two games to advance to the American League Championship Series against the Orioles, Jackson and Steinbrenner talked again by phone. This time, Jackson told the owner that after what had happened, he didn't want to come to the ALCS.

"Oh, no, no," said Steinbrenner, "you have to be here. Come to New York and we'll talk."

When, the next day, Jackson arrived at Yankee Stadium and went into Steinbrenner's suite, he was puzzled by the owner's reaction.

"He didn't say anything to me," Jackson recalled. "It was like nothing had ever happened. He just treated me like a long-lost son, but I was sorry we never had that talk. Our relationship did change, though, and after that he valued my opinions and went out of his way to keep me involved with the organization."

The Yankees split the first two games of the ALCS at home against the Orioles, only to win the next three, setting up a World Series matchup with the defending world champion Atlanta Braves, who had swept the Los Angeles Dodgers in the NL Division Series and outscored the St. Louis Cardinals 44-18 in winning a seven-game NLCS. When the Braves thrashed the Yankees, 12–1, in the opening game at Yankee Stadium, it appeared they were going to live up to their billing as heavy favorites to retain their crown. In his 1997 memoir, *Catching the Dream,* Torre recounted how, in the hours before game two, an agitated Steinbrenner came into his office and began venting about how the Yankees were in danger of being swept.

"This is a must-win game," Steinbrenner said. "I don't want to be embarrassed."

Torre, who'd been reading over the scouting report on Greg Maddux, the Braves' starting pitcher that night, barely looked up from his desk. "You better prepare yourself for losing again tonight," he said. "But then we're going to go down there to Atlanta. I managed there. Atlanta's my town. We're going to win all three down there and come back here and win the Series on Saturday."

Steinbrenner, speechless, glared at his manager before walking out of the room, shaking his head. Torre later said he couldn't believe what he'd just said either. Nevertheless, he turned out to be a prophet: the Yankees lost game two to Maddux, 4–0, before sweeping three games in Atlanta—overcoming a 6–0 deficit in game four and following that up with a classic game five in which Pettitte outpitched John Smoltz, 1–0. That Saturday night at Yankee Stadium, they delivered to Steinbrenner his first world championship since 1978 with a 3–2 win. At the victory podium in the Yankee clubhouse after the game, Steinbrenner welled up with tears as his old friend, baseball commissioner Bud Selig, presented him with the World Series trophy.

"Here he was, finally winning another championship after all he'd been through, and I could see how much it meant to him that I was the one presenting it to him," Selig recalled. "I had been the one constant person in his baseball life since 1973 and the one who brought him back from the suspension. After all we'd been through together, it was a very emotional moment for both of us."

POIGNANT AND WARM as that scene might have been, it was not long after that Selig was given another rude reminder of how Steinbrenner could be the proverbial bull in the china shop when it came to the commissioner's grand design of establishing a competitive balance between the haves and have-nots in baseball. In early March 1997, Greg Murphy, the newly minted president of Major League Baseball Enterprises, had just announced a huge new advertising campaign slated to net over $150 million in corporate sponsorships for baseball when the Yankees announced that they had independently entered into a $93 million advertising deal with the Adidas sporting goods company. The deal would allow Adidas to plaster its name on signs all over Yankee Stadium, advertise during Yankees telecasts, promote its connection to the team in local marketing, and supply footwear to the Yankees' minor league players.

The Yankees contended that the Adidas deal did not violate the Major League Baseball Properties agreement, under which all licensing money was shared equally by the clubs. "We felt we could license the Yankee logo with Adidas in certain areas where MLB didn't have the rights," said former Yankees in-house counsel David Sussman in a 2009 interview. "It was a deal equivalent to the MSG Network television deal George had done a few years earlier."

But this was not the way Major League Baseball, and Selig in particular, viewed it, and after a couple of weeks of studying the deal, they decided that it infringed on the league's deal with Russell Athletic and ordered the Yankees to cease and desist selling Yankee T-shirts with Adidas logos on them.

Steinbrenner's reaction was a familiar one: he promptly sued his fellow owners, accusing them of "collaborating in a merchandising cartel that favors the weak teams." As part of the suit, for which he hired prominent New York attorney David Boies to be the driving force, Steinbrenner singled out Selig for mismanaging the Brewers and helping to create a sort-of welfare system in baseball. Successful teams like the Yankees, he said, whose logos and brand were far more valuable than those of other teams, nevertheless had to share equally with teams that spent far less on marketing. Only four years after being reinstated to baseball, Steinbrenner had declared war on his fellow owners, some of whom had lobbied hard on his behalf.

On May 13, Selig announced that Steinbrenner had been kicked off the ruling executive council (to which the commissioner had appointed him as a kind of "welcome back" gesture after his ban from Fay Vincent was lifted) and the Yankees were barred from participating on any working committees within the game. Implicit in the punishment was the prospect of Steinbrenner's third suspension from baseball.

"You can understand why Bud feels he's been stabbed in the back by George," White Sox board chairman Jerry Reinsdorf confided to me as tensions increased on both sides. "I don't think Bud's ever been madder with an owner like he is now with George. The other owners feel the same way. They're fed up."

The cold war between the Yankees and MLB continued through the summer of '97. Eventually, Steinbrenner's lawsuit was dropped and MLB Properties achieved a settlement of the dispute by admitting Adidas as one of its official licensees.

But soon enough, Steinbrenner was involved in another lawsuit, one that would end up costing him $3 million and lead to a falling out between him and his best friend, Bill Fugazy. In the mid-'90s, Steinbrenner had agreed to outsource the Yankees' advertising and marketing to Sports Advertising Network Inc. (SANI), a firm that had been created by Fugazy's son, John, and former Yankees president Gene McHale. Under the terms of their deal, SANI was to receive a certain percentage for all the advertising and marketing business they brought to the Yankees. Since Steinbrenner and his execs had negotiated the Adidas deal on their own, they did not believe it fell under the realm of their agreement with SANI. John Fugazy and McHale thought otherwise and filed suit against the Yankees. An enraged Steinbrenner called Bill Fugazy, demanding to know how he could allow his son to do this. Fugazy protested that he had nothing to do with the suit, but Steinbrenner wasn't buying it, and for the next few years, the elder Fugazy became persona non grata around Yankee Stadium. John Fugazy won his suit against the Yankees and was awarded $3 million. As for his father and Steinbrenner, they reconciled in the early 2000s when Steinbrenner learned that his old friend had been diagnosed with Alzheimer's disease, but their relationship was never the same.

The fact that he would be allowed to reap almost all of the $93 million from the Adidas deal was no doubt of some solace to Steinbrenner after a disappointing 1997 season. The team won 96 games and Tino Martinez put up huge numbers (44 homers and 141 RBI), but it was only good enough for second place in the AL East and a wild-card berth in the postseason, where they lost in five games to the Cleveland Indians. The Yankees were just five outs away from advancing to the ALCS when Mariano Rivera, who had taken over as the closer in '97 after the departure of John Wetteland as a free agent, gave up the tying home run. Rivera would pitch 26⅓ innings in the postseason over the next two years before giving up another run.

Perhaps if Steinbrenner had been successful in wooing Roger Clemens, the '97 season might have turned out differently. The 35-year-old Clemens had become a free agent after the '96 season, following an acrimonious parting with the Red Sox, for whom he'd won four Cy Young Awards and an MVP between 1984 and '96. With permission from Clemens's agents, Steinbrenner had visited the pitcher's home in Houston in November 1996, spending a half day delivering his patented sales pitch of Yankee pride and tradition and the chance to win a world championship. He left Houston confident he was going to bring the game's premier right-handed pitcher— and a Red Sox icon, no less—to the Bronx.

A week later, Steinbrenner called his friend Paul Beeston, the president of the Toronto Blue Jays, who had just completed his own visit to Clemens's home, to compare notes.

"I don't know about you, Paul, but I really had a great visit with the guy," Steinbrenner said. "We talked Texas football and had barbecue for lunch, and before I left I signed a whole bunch of Yankee items for him."

"No kidding, George?" Beeston said. "Well, I have to say, I did even better. Before I left, I got his signature on a contract!"

"You fucking Canuck!" Steinbrenner screamed. "How did you do that? You can't afford him!"

Clemens later explained that it would have been very awkward for him to go from Boston right to the Yankees. Toronto turned out to be a temporary layover before he did join Steinbrenner's Yankees, but in his two years there he won two more Cy Young Awards and in 1997 had a 21-7 season in which he led the league in wins, ERA, innings and strikeouts.

By the end of the '97 season, Bob Watson was convinced there was no worse job in the universe than general manager of the New York Yankees. When it came to advice on trades and player evaluations, Steinbrenner invariably turned to Gene Michael, or his player development people in Tampa. The only time Watson ever seemed to hear from the Boss was when something went wrong. Michael, it seemed, was still Steinbrenner's GM, while Watson merely had the title. Gabe Paul, Steinbrenner's first general manager, had a favorite saying: "One man's shit is another man's ice cream." Bob Watson came to know what that meant.

And so, after just two years on the job, Watson went into full retreat. According to Yankees employees, during his last few months on the job, he would arrive at his office, shut the door, order out lunch and spend the rest of the day watching soap operas on TV.

The day after the New York baseball writers' dinner on February 2, 1998, Watson summoned his assistant, Brian Cashman, into his office.

"I just told the Boss I'm out," he announced. "I have to do this for my health and my sanity, and I recommended that he give you the job. I think he's gonna offer it to you. So good luck, buddy."

The 30-year-old Cashman immediately felt a rush of excitement come over him, which was quickly tempered by apprehension. After 11 years in the Yankees organization, where he'd started as an office intern and worked his way up through the ranks as an assistant, first to Michael and then to Watson, was he ready to report directly to the owner? It didn't matter that Cashman's father, John, who operated a horse farm in Lexington, Kentucky, was a friend of Steinbrenner's. Brian would be the second-youngest GM in league history, and he had seen firsthand how Steinbrenner devoured general managers with much more experience than he had.

When he went back to his office, Cashman received the call from Steinbrenner asking him to meet him at the Regency at noon. At the meeting, Steinbrenner began by telling Cashman he'd talked to both Michael and Mark Newman, the VP of player development in Tampa.

"I can go out and recycle someone," Steinbrenner said, "but Stick and Newman think you're ready. I want to know: do you think you can handle this?"

Cashman remembered his body trembling at the question before he said firmly, "I think I can, sir, but I want to prove to you I'm the right man for the job. That's why I'd like only a one-year contract."

"One year?" Steinbrenner said.

"Yes, sir. I want to show you I'm the right man, but I feel that right now, any more than one year wouldn't be right for either of us."

"Okay," said Steinbrenner, already satisfied that, if nothing else, Cashman appeared to have the right outlook. "One year it will be."

Cashman's first order of business was to complete a trade with the Minnesota Twins to bring the career .304-hitting second baseman Chuck Knoblauch to the Yankees. The Twins wanted three of the Yankees' top minor league prospects, left-hander Eric Milton (their 1996 number-one draft pick), shortstop Cristian Guzman and outfielder Brian Buchanan.

It was a hefty price, but the trade paid immediate dividends for the Yankees. Knoblauch—the team's first bona fide leadoff hitter since Rickey Henderson—hit 40 points below his career average in Minnesota, but he stole 31 bases and scored 117 runs. More important, he allowed everyone else to find their proper niche below him in the order. Most notable in this regard was Jeter, who hit .324 and scored 127 runs from the number-two hole and finished third in the American League Most Valuable Player voting.

The '98 Yankees would set an American League record with 114 victories, but their stadium wasn't nearly as robust. On April 14, a 500-pound concrete-and-steel beam suspended beneath the upper deck in left field came loose and crashed into the empty seats, touching off renewed speculation (fostered by Steinbrenner) that Yankee Stadium was falling apart. Now that Steinbrenner had his proof, he was content to let Mayor Rudolph Giuliani pick up the baton for him.

"I think George is right that the Yankees are entitled to a new stadium," Giuliani said. "This could have been a terrible tragedy. We were fortunate it happened before the gates had been opened to let the fans in."

The beam collapse forced the city to close the Stadium for a week while repairs were made and engineers surveyed every nook of the 75-year-old edifice. When the Yankees returned and the Stadium reopened, fans with tickets in Section 22, where the beam had fallen, were taken aback to find Steinbrenner sitting in Row A, munching popcorn.

"Do I look worried?" he quipped.

Steinbrenner couldn't have been happier. The beam accident had only increased his leverage with the city in his attempt to build a new ballpark, and he celebrated this good fortune by treating all the fans in Section 22 to free hot dogs and ice cream.

By then the Yankees, who'd begun the season 1-4 on the West Coast, were in the process of winning 16 of 18 games to take permanent hold of first place. They wound up winning the Eastern Division by 22 games and continued their domination in the postseason, sweeping the Texas Rangers, 3-0, in the Division Series and beating the defending AL champion Cleveland Indians in six games in the ALCS. They completed a record 125-win season with a four-game sweep of the San Diego Padres in the World Series. At the trophy presentation, Steinbrenner was even more emotional than he'd been with Selig in '96.

"This team—what can you say about this team?" he blubbered after being drenched with champagne by Jeter. "All I'm gonna say is, they're as great as any team that's ever been." He then reached into a huge ice tub, pulled out a bottle of champagne, and began shaking it while pointing it at Jeter. "What the hell?" he gasped. "There's nothing in this one!"

A few weeks after the Series, Steinbrenner met with Jeter at his Legends Field office in Tampa and presented him with a book, *Patton on Leadership: Strategic Lessons for Corporate Warfare*, with the inscription "To Derek. Read and study. He was a great leader, just as you are and will be a great leader. Hopefully of the men in pinstripes." It was a prelude to Steinbrenner making Jeter the 11th Yankees captain five years later.

So dominant and superior were the '98 Yankees that, as Torre noted in his 2009 memoir, *The Yankee Years*, even the irrepressibly negative Steinbrenner found little cause for complaint during the course of the season.

Cashman had put together a nearly perfect roster in his rookie year as GM. Besides Knoblauch, he had acquired third baseman Scott Brosius (.300 with 19 homers and 98 RBI, and the MVP of the World Series with a .471 average, two homers and six RBI) from the Oakland A's on Michael's recommendation. Then there was Cuban refugee Orlando (El Duque) Hernandez, signed at the end of spring training, who was 12-4 with a 3.13 ERA as the Yankees' number-four starter, yielding just one earned run in 14 innings as he won both an ALCS and World Series start.

But as Cashman knew firsthand from being around the Yankees front office for 14 years, Steinbrenner did not allow himself or any of his minions to dwell very long on success. Soon after the '98 World Series, Cashman began negotiating with free-agent center fielder Bernie Williams. At age 30, Williams had become a Yankees icon after three straight seasons in which he'd averaged .323 with 100 RBI. His agent, Scott Boras, had earned a reputation for getting his clients the biggest contracts in baseball by taking them into free agency. At the same time, at Torre's urging, Cashman was talking to two other prominent free agent outfielders, Albert Belle and Brian Jordan, as possible alternatives.

As negotiations with Williams stalled over Boras's demand for a seven-year contract, Steinbrenner conducted a meeting of the Yankees' high command in Tampa a couple of days before Thanksgiving to discuss the situation. Steinbrenner was very interested in Belle, who'd led the American League in RBI three times and was coming off a mammoth season in which he'd hit 49 homers and driven in 152 runs for the Chicago White Sox. The downside was Belle's truculent personality, which had alienated the media and even many of his own teammates. Still, after playing golf with Belle in Arizona, Torre insisted he could handle him.

"You're going to be sorry if you do this," Michael told the group. "He's going to be a problem in the clubhouse, where other players will be afraid to talk to the media around him, and we can't have that."

"I don't know, Stick," said Steinbrenner. "He's a helluva hitter, and 'Cash' says he thinks we can get him for five years and around $65 million. I wish you liked him a little better."

"Well, what's it gonna cost us to re-sign Bernie?" Michael asked.

"We're presently at five years, around $60 million, with him, but Boras wants seven or eight years at $15 million per, and so far he's not budging from that," Cashman replied.

"What?" Michael shrieked. "In that case, I *love* Albert Belle!"

Everyone in the room broke out in laughter, and Steinbrenner instructed Cashman to go ahead and make a five-year, $65 million offer to Belle's agent, Arn Tellem. The next day, Williams called Cashman at about the same time Tellem was informing the GM that Belle was prepared to accept the Yankees' offer.

"Is this really happening?" Williams said. "Am I really going to be forced to work someplace else after spending my entire career as a Yankee?"

"I don't know what to tell you, Bernie," said Cashman. "We're real close with Albert Belle."

"Really?" said Williams.

At that point, Bernie Williams was all but a goner. But later that day, Tellem called Cashman to say that Belle had changed his mind and was going to sign with the Baltimore Orioles. When Cashman went in to tell Steinbrenner of this development, the owner exploded.

"How could you blow this?" he screamed. "I knew I couldn't trust you to handle this job! You're just too inexperienced for these agents. I oughta fire you right now and get someone in here who knows what the hell they're doing!"

As Steinbrenner was yelling at Cashman, Williams called again, this time to inform him that the Red Sox had bowled him over with a seven-year offer worth over $90 million. With Steinbrenner listening on the speaker-phone, Williams implored Cashman to make a counteroffer.

"The Yankees are the only place I've ever been," he said, "and it's going to be very hard for me to go anyplace else. I'm not asking you to top that offer. I just need to feel you want to keep me by coming after me with the kind of offer you make to free agents from other teams that have never done anything for the Yankees."

This won Steinbrenner over. He told Cashman to bring the All-Star center fielder back into the fold for a seven-year deal worth $87.5 million. It was far more than either of them had wanted—or expected—to pay, but it worked out just fine, as Williams went on to enjoy three more All-Star seasons as a major contributor to two more Yankees world championships, while Belle sustained a hip injury that ended his career after just two seasons in Baltimore.

Around this time, it was reported that Steinbrenner had agreed to sell 70 percent of the Yankees to the media giant Cablevision for $525 million. Steinbrenner knew that revenue sharing was coming in baseball, and he needed to find an equity partner. Under the terms of the deal, Steinbrenner was to remain general partner of the Yankees and would also oversee the operations of the NBA Knicks and the NHL Rangers. The impetus of the deal from Cablevision's standpoint was the expiration in 2000 of its 12-year contract to broadcast Yankee games. By having a majority interest in the Yankees, Cablevision would essentially be guaranteed the rights to broadcast Yankee games forever. "All I'm doing," Steinbrenner insisted, "is taking on a new partner. I'm not going anywhere."

Neither was this deal, it turned out.

IN MID-DECEMBER 1998, Suzyn Waldman, the Yankees beat reporter for WFAN, got a phone call from her boss, Mark Chernoff, the station's program director, informing her of a special show they were planning to broadcast from the Yogi Berra Museum, in Upper Montclair, New Jersey. "You know what would be really great?" Chernoff said. "If you could get George to come up from Tampa to be on the show."

It had been 14 years since Yogi Berra and Steinbrenner had spoken to each other, and just as long since Yogi had set foot in Yankee Stadium. Waldman had never met Berra, but she had a long-standing, close relationship with Steinbrenner, and she saw the possibilities. After hanging up with Chernoff, she placed a call to Steinbrenner in Tampa, and an hour later he called her back.

"George," Waldman began, "I want to talk to you about Yogi."

"Yogi?" said Steinbrenner. "Oh, my God. What's wrong? Has something happened to him?"

"No, no, he's fine," said Waldman, who explained that she would be hosting this show with Berra from his museum and that she hoped to use it as a vehicle for a reconciliation between the two of them.

"I don't know," said Steinbrenner. "I've tried a hundred times to make things up with him. Maybe I could invite him to the Stadium?"

"That's not gonna work," said Waldman. "You're gonna have to come to him, on his turf. And then you're gonna have to apologize."

"Apologize?" Steinbrenner said. "Why do I have to apologize?"

"I don't know, George," said Waldman. "For whatever it was you did to him. It would sure be good for the Yankees."

"No, it would sure be good for Suzyn Waldman," Steinbrenner grumped. "I would make her larger than she already is."

"Well, that too, George," Waldman said, laughing.

Steinbrenner came around, and Waldman next went to Berra to propose the peace terms.

"How is this gonna work?" asked Yogi's son, Dale.

"He's gonna fly up from Tampa and have his limo driver take him from the airport to the museum, where he'll be at 5 o'clock sharp," Waldman explained. "That'll give them an hour to talk before going on the air."

"What if he doesn't apologize?" Dale Berra asked. "My dad's gonna expect that."

"I can assure you the man's not going to fly a thousand miles all the way up here to say 'Fuck you.' "

On the afternoon of January 5, 1999, a nervous Steinbrenner stepped off his private jet at New Jersey's Teterboro Airport. He was met by his limo driver, who, on his orders, had already made three dry runs of the 30-minute drive to the Berra museum earlier in the day. Nevertheless, when they arrived at the museum, it was a few minutes after five and Berra was waiting in the lobby, looking at his watch.

"You're late," he said to Steinbrenner.

Already Steinbrenner was on the defensive. They proceeded to a room off the main gallery of the museum, and when their raised voices could be heard, Berra's wife, Carmen, went in to join them. Fifteen minutes later, Steinbrenner and Berra emerged arm in arm, all smiles.

"It's over," Berra quipped, a reference to his most famous Yogi-ism, "It ain't over till it's over."

During Waldman's broadcast, Steinbrenner apologized—not for firing him as manager just 16 games into the 1985 season, but for having enlisted then–Yankees GM Clyde King to do the dirty deed instead of having the guts to do it himself. On July 18 at Yankee Stadium, the team presented Berra with a $100,000 check for the museum and, in the years after, Steinbrenner donated numerous Yankees artifacts to its collection, including replicas of all ten of Berra's world championship rings.

"I would've driven across the George Washington Bridge in a rickshaw to get Yogi back," Steinbrenner told the assembled press corps at the museum. Years later, Rick Cerrone, the Yankees publicity director from 1996 to 2007, who accompanied Steinbrenner to the event, recalled, "In all the years I worked for him, that was the happiest I ever saw him."

Left unsaid was the urgency on Steinbrenner's part to get Yogi back into the official Yankees family. Joe DiMaggio was terminally ill, and Mickey Mantle had died in 1995. After DiMaggio, the title of "greatest living

Yankee" would fall to Yogi. A week after making peace with Berra, Steinbrenner paid a visit to DiMaggio's home in Hollywood, Florida, where the Yankee Clipper was in the final stages of lung cancer. Only a couple of weeks earlier, Steinbrenner had announced that "Joe will certainly throw out the first ball at Yankee Stadium on Opening Day," but now DiMaggio was barely able to speak. His valet, DeJan Pesut, had spent hours sprucing him up for Steinbrenner's visit, dressing him in a shirt and tie that he could wear only by removing the collar to help him breathe. The visit lasted barely five minutes before DiMaggio had to be hooked back up to his breathing machine. "You just get better, Joe," Steinbrenner said before leaving. "I'm counting on you to be there Opening Day."

Steinbrenner returned to Tampa with no idea that yet another reconciliation was in the offing for him. On February 17, a couple of days before the opening of spring training, he and Cashman and the rest of the Yankees high command were in Tampa conducting a meeting in the private room bearing his name in Malio's Restaurant. The subject of the meeting was a proposed trade for Roger Clemens, which Cashman had brought to the group. Two years later, Steinbrenner had been proved right: the Toronto Blue Jays couldn't afford Clemens, who, under a secret side agreement in the four-year, $31.1 million deal he'd signed with them in December 1996, was exercising his right to demand a trade. It was Steinbrenner's second shot at acquiring the premier pitcher in the American League, but it was also going to mean giving up David Wells, the free-spirited left-hander whose penchant for mischief, curiously, had won the affection of the Boss and the enmity of Joe Torre and pitching coach Mel Stottlemyre.

"You guys all know how I feel about Wells," Steinbrenner said. "That's why I'm not going to cast a vote on this. At the same time, though, if everyone in the room is in favor of this deal, I won't stand in the way."

Everybody was.

As Steinbrenner and his group finished conducting their business, Lou Piniella happened to come into the restaurant to have lunch. Even though Piniella, as Malio Iavarone's best friend, and Steinbrenner, as Malio's best customer, frequently dined in the Tampa hot spot, their own relationship had been severely ruptured ever since Steinbrenner had smeared Lou's name in the Howie Spira trial by saying he had a "gambling problem."

Malio especially was outraged at Steinbrenner for that, telling him, "Lou's only gambling problem was betting on your damn horses!"

For years, Malio had been tiptoeing a fine line when Steinbrenner and Piniella were in his restaurant at the same time, but now he saw an opportunity to bring them together and finally patch things up. He knew Steinbrenner was sorry for what he'd done to Piniella, and he also knew that Lou was not one to hold grudges.

"You know, the Boss is here in his room with all his guys," Malio said to Piniella. "Why don't you go say hello?"

"I don't know," Piniella said. "I don't want to bother him."

"Oh, c'mon," Malio said, leading Piniella by the arm to the other side of the restaurant and into the Steinbrenner Room. "Look who I got here, Boss!" he said. Rising from his seat, Steinbrenner rushed over to Piniella and affixed a bear hug on him.

"It's great to see you, Lou," he said.

"You, too, Boss," Piniella said. "It's been too long."

19

. . .

Billionaire George

. . .

I N THE WEEKS AFTER initially agreeing to sell 70 percent of the Yankees to Cablevision, Steinbrenner was slowly coming to the conclusion that this was not a good deal for him. For one thing, Cablevision czar Charles Dolan was now insisting that Steinbrenner's term for continuing to run the Yankees would be limited to five years. For another, Steinbrenner realized that the only reason Cablevision was willing to pay him $525 million for a temporarily inactive majority share of the team was that their 12-year contract to broadcast Yankee games on their MSG Network was due to expire after the 2001 season and, without the Yankees, the network's primary programming would be just the NBA Knicks and the NHL Rangers. More important, if Cablevision owned the Yankees, they would not have to pay a rights fee, which promised to be significantly higher than the $40.5 million per year they were paying under the present deal. Cablevision needed the Yankees a lot more than the Yankees needed Cablevision.

For tax reasons, the deadline for completing the deal was January 1, but as the date approached, Steinbrenner decided he would not be saying "Happy New Year, partner" to Charles Dolan. In fact, it was not long after he'd made the landmark $486 million rights agreement with the MSG Network in 1989 that Bob Gutkowski, the president of Madison Square Garden, who had brokered the deal, gave Steinbrenner the idea of one day creating his own regional network—and now he was seeing the merits of it.

To do so, Steinbrenner would need a basketball or hockey team to provide the bulk of the network's winter programming. Obviously the Knicks and Rangers weren't options, but across the river in New Jersey, the Nets of the NBA, who had enjoyed only three winning seasons in 15 years, were struggling for an identity. The Nets were owned by Ray Chambers and Lewis Katz, two prominent New Jersey businessmen. Steinbrenner contacted the men, and, after a series of discussions in conjunction with the Allen & Co. investment firm, they announced in February 1999 that the Yankees and the Nets would be merging into a 50-50 corporate partnership called YankeeNets LLC. A $750 million value was put on the holding company, with the Yankees' worth established at $600 million and the Nets' at $150 million.

Although much was made of the fact that the company would be engaging in joint sales operations to market the two teams, Steinbrenner made clear that, from his end, the primary purpose of the merger was to create a regional sports network. He enlisted as chairman of the new company his old U.S. Olympic Committee cohort Harvey Schiller, who had since become head of TV sports programming for the Turner Broadcasting System. But as time went on, Steinbrenner became more and more impatient with the lack of progress being made in finding an equity partner for a new network, and he was also becoming annoyed at what he perceived as Chambers and Katz's attempts to put together sponsorship deals designed to enhance the Nets while diminishing the value of the Yankees.

Indeed, Steinbrenner and Katz got along fine in social situations, but their business relationship became quite acrimonious. On one occasion they were having lunch at the Post House restaurant in Manhattan when Katz "semi-mooned" Steinbrenner. According to Katz, the two were poking fun at each other's attire when Steinbrenner said, "The only thing I like about you is your belt." Katz got up from the table and tore off his belt, allowing his pants to slip down to reveal his boxer shorts beneath. "We both had a big laugh over that," Katz related, "but the business times with George were not so much fun."

In late December 1999, Steinbrenner had lunch at the Regency with Randy Levine, who, after working for him as part of the legal team that got him reinstated to baseball, had gone on to serve as baseball's chief labor negotiator and later as deputy to New York City mayor Rudy Giuliani.

Steinbrenner was 69 now and, with Bill Fugazy in exile from his inner circle and his other cronies from his days of late-night gallivanting in Manhattan either dead or "retired" from that lifestyle, he was spending more and more time with his family in Tampa.

"It's time I started cutting back and begin letting the young elephants into the tent," Steinbrenner told Levine, explaining that he wanted to get his son-in-law Steve Swindal (who was married to his older daughter, Jennifer), along with his two sons, Hank and Hal, more involved in the Yankees operations. "I'm going to need someone in New York to keep an eye on things for me," he told Levine. "I want you to come to work for me as president of the Yankees. I'm getting more and more fed up with this Yankees Nets thing, and I need your help. We're nowhere on the network. These guys can't do shit."

Steinbrenner realized baseball had changed drastically from when he bought the Yankees for $8.5 million in 1973, and that no one man—not even him—could oversee every aspect of the increasingly complex business operations of the Yankees the way he used to. In Levine he saw a shrewd legal mind who'd successfully negotiated an end to the ruinous 234-day baseball work stoppage in 1994–95 (after two predecessors had failed) and who was also well connected in New York political circles. Steinbrenner felt Levine would be a good partner to work with Lonn Trost, who had served as the Yankees' in-house counsel since 1997 and whom he'd just appointed chief operating officer of the team. The diminutive 5-foot-6 Trost had more than earned the promotion from Steinbrenner as one of the attorneys who had drawn up the contract with Cablevision containing the opt-out clause that led to the landmark MSG deal. But, as in-house Yankees counsel, he also came in for the brunt of abuse from Steinbrenner, who once told him half-kiddingly: "You're a little man in every way." Trost often repeated that to associates, taking it as a sort of badge of honor.

For his part, Levine could see that Steinbrenner was serious about wanting to turn the heavy lifting of the greatly expanded Yankees business over to younger hands, and he was excited at the prospect of becoming the point man in the effort to create a new TV network and procure a new stadium for the Yankees.

Levine took over as president on January 1, 2000, and immediately plunged into work on the network project. His first call was to his friend Joe Ravitch, an investment banker at Goldman Sachs, about the possibility of the bank becoming an equity partner with the Yankees. Ravitch connected Levine with Gerry Cardinale, managing director of Goldman Sachs's media-focused private equity group, who, along with his boss, Richard Friedman, a partner and head of the investment committee at Goldman Sachs, told Levine and Trost that he wanted Goldman to partner with Yankees Nets in the network.

Then Schiller, who'd been unsuccessful in finding an equity partner for the network, made the fatal mistake of portraying himself in *Forbes* magazine as Steinbrenner's boss at YankeeNets. When Steinbrenner saw Schiller's picture on the cover of *Forbes* with the headline THE BOSS' BOSS, he flew into a rage. "Who the fuck does he think he is!" he screamed to his Yankees execs. Not long after, Schiller was no longer chairman of YankeeNets.

As the programming and the equity partnership fell into place, the parties now needed to find the right person to head the fledgling network. On the recommendation of Goldman Sachs, Leo Hindery, who had previously been president of AT&T Broadband, was hired as the first chairman of the Yankees Entertainment and Sports (YES) Network and given a small equity share. YankeeNets owned a 66 percent share, and Goldman Sachs paid $300 million to YankeeNets for their 32 percent.

The next step was for Hindery to broker deals with the local cable companies to carry the new network. But while he quickly succeeded in reaching agreements with Comcast, Time Warner and DirecTV to carry YES on basic cable, Cablevision, which was suing YankeeNets for breach of contract, claiming their MSG Network had not been allowed to effectively match a bid for a new cable contract, remained a holdout. YankeeNets eventually settled the suit for $30 million during a mediation process in a New Jersey federal court, but it did not get the YES Network on Cablevision. Steinbrenner was only too happy to pay the $30 million in exchange for his cable "free agency." But in reluctantly agreeing to the settlement, Charles Dolan told Steinbrenner, "We're still never going to put you on the air."

"We'll see about that, Chuck," Steinbrenner said.

(The stalemate continued until April 20 of the following year, when, with the intervention of New York State attorney general Eliot Spitzer and

Mayor Michael Bloomberg, both sides agreed to submit their cases to binding arbitration, while Cablevision agreed to begin carrying Yankees games
on basic cable on a temporary basis, charging an extra $1.95 per customer.
A year later, the arbitration board ruled 3–0 in the Yankees' favor, and
Cablevision agreed to keep the YES Network on basic cable for an extra 95
cents per month to its subscribers.)

Once the YES Network was created, Steinbrenner saw no more reason
for the YankeeNets partnership. After years of wrangling, in early 2004,
Steinbrenner, Chambers and Katz agreed to dissolve YankeeNets and go
their separate ways. The first step was the sale of the Nets to real estate developer Bruce Ratner for $300 million. Under the terms of the dissolution
of YankeeNets, Chambers and Katz kept the money from the sale of the
Nets, while Steinbrenner regained much of the equity in the Yankees that
he'd given up to the Nets owners when the company was first formed in
1999. In addition, Chambers and Kats kept their approximately 33 percent
in the YES Network, which, *Forbes* magazine reported in August 2007,
"could be worth up to $3 billion." The Yankees then formed a company
called Yankee Global Enterprises, in which Chambers and Katz had a limited, nonvoting share.

In 2009, *Forbes* valued the Yankees at $1.5 billion, of which Stein-
brenner and his family owned just over 60 percent. Combined with his 33
percent of the YES Network and his 33 percent interest in the $500 million
Legends Hospitality concessions company—which Yankee Global Enterprises formed with Dallas Cowboys owner Jerry Jones in 2008—his Yankees assets as of 2009 were worth somewhere between $2 and $3 billion.
Not a bad return for that original outlay of $168,000 in 1973.

THE '99 YANKEES led the Eastern Division from June 9 on, finishing
four games ahead of the Red Sox, with the high point of the season being July 18, Yogi Berra Day, when David Cone upstaged Yogi's return by
pitching a perfect game against the Montreal Expos. The pitching staff
ranked second in the AL in ERA, shutouts and opponents' batting average.
Four Yankees—Derek Jeter, Tino Martinez, Paul O'Neill and Bernie Williams—drove in 100 or more runs, and Jeter had a career season, batting
.349 with 24 homers and 102 RBI.

For all the success, the season was marked by much tragedy. On March 8, Joe DiMaggio passed away in Hollywood, Florida, at the age of 84. Two days later, Torre revealed that he'd been diagnosed with prostate cancer and would be taking an undetermined leave of absence as manager, from which he returned on May 18.

Paul O'Neill, Luis Sojo and Scott Brosius all lost their fathers in 1999, and on September 9 the organization was devastated by the news that Catfish Hunter, only 53, had succumbed to Lou Gehrig's disease at his home in Hertford, North Carolina. The previous March, Steinbrenner had arranged for Hunter to come to spring training for what turned out to be his final visit with his former teammates. After calling Hunter's widow, Helen, to offer his condolences, Steinbrenner told reporters, "She's a very brave woman with a great family around her, but she has lost one of the greatest people I have ever known. Catfish was the foundation on which our tradition here was built."

The '99 Yankees won a second-straight world championship, and their third in four years under Torre, with their most dominant postseason of all, sweeping Texas in the Division Series, taking four out of five from the Red Sox in the ALCS, and then capping it all off with another sweep of the Atlanta Braves in the World Series. In the triumphant clubhouse afterward, Steinbrenner, once again teary-eyed, with his voice cracking, declared: "This was the team of the decade . . . it's sweet. We had three guys who lost their fathers this year, but they were really a mentally tough team."

"So how long can it go on, George?" asked a TV reporter.

"Forever," choked Steinbrenner, wiping his eyes.

The next season, after jockeying back and forth with the Red Sox for the AL East lead for much of the first half, the Yankees took over first place on July 7 and gradually built their lead to nine games by September 13. But then, in a slump that mystified Torre and cast doubts on their ability to make it three championships in a row, the Yankees lost 15 of their last 18 games to finish a scant 2½ games ahead of the Red Sox, with just 87 wins. Once in the postseason, however, it was as if they flipped the "on" switch again, dispatching the Oakland A's in a five-game Division Series and Lou Piniella's Seattle Mariners in six games in the ALCS. All the while, though, Steinbrenner was fretting about developments on the other side of town, where the Mets, having crept into the postseason as a wild card, had beaten both the NL West champion San Francisco Giants in the Division Series and the NL Central champion St. Louis Cardinals in the NLCS to advance as the Yankees' opponent in the World Series.

"We cannot afford to lose to the Mets," Steinbrenner said to Torre the day before the World Series was to begin. "There's just too much at stake here for us. I hope you realize this."

In truth, there was much at stake for Steinbrenner besides just the New York bragging rights. There was the new TV network to consider. He thought that losing to the Mets in spring training games devalued the Yankees; losing to them in the World Series, he believed, could mean a decrease of millions of dollars in the Yankees' value. After wins by the Yankees in games one and two at Yankee Stadium, the scene shifted to dilapidated Shea Stadium, in Queens, where Steinbrenner was immediately appalled at the shabby conditions in the visiting clubhouse, with its frayed carpeting and small wooden stools instead of chairs. At the last minute before game three, the presence of Steinbrenner's longtime gal pal Barbara Walters in the visiting-club box created a panic among the Yankees security force when it was learned that Joan Steinbrenner had decided to fly up from Tampa to attend the game. George's son Hal led the advance party to the box to move Walters before his mother got there. "She had the right tickets," said one of the security men, "but as soon as Hal saw her, he said: 'You have to get out and move to another box. You really need to get out now!'"

Embarrassed and annoyed at this unceremonious eviction, Walters reportedly said, "I always thought George had a nice son," to which Hal replied, "You must be talking about my brother. Now please leave."

After the Yankees lost game three, Steinbrenner blamed it on the fact that they weren't able to get comfortable in the clubhouse. Accordingly, after the game he ordered the Yankees' clubhouse staff to pack up all the high-backed leather chairs and the leather couch his team used at Yankee Stadium and have them transported in moving trucks over to Shea for game four. "I can't have my players sitting on these little wooden stools," Steinbrenner grumbled. "I want them to feel they're at home. Hell, they *are* at home. Just in the wrong ballpark. This place is a dump!" After all the furniture was in place, Steinbrenner went around the room doling out $100 bills to all the clubhouse attendants.

Steinbrenner was watching game four on television in the Yankees' clubhouse—from the comfort of that leather couch—when, during the eighth inning, a cascade of water came gushing from the ceiling. There had been a fire in a trash bin on the third deck of Shea, and when firefighters opened a standpipe to extinguish it, another pipe, located above the visiting clubhouse, burst, sending a deluge of dirty brown water out of the ceiling, which eventually collapsed from the weight. As the Yankees filed back into the clubhouse after their 3–2 win, they were stunned at the sight of the mess—and even more so at the sight of the principal owner of the Yankees in the middle of it all, furiously bailing the six inches of water and debris in his expensive loafers.

The Yankees wrapped up the World Series the next night with a 4–2 win at Shea. It was their 26th title, but it had been anything but easy. They outscored the Mets only 19–16 in the five games and, in the process, set a World Series record by stranding 52 base runners in the five games.

"As far as heart, there has never been a team with more heart than this one," Steinbrenner said during the clubhouse celebration afterward. Wiping a mixture of tears and champagne from his face, he saluted his troops for a job well done and then pondered their place in history.

"The Mets gave us everything we could want," Steinbrenner said. "It was the Battle of New York, and it was a great way to win. This team has done something that very few teams will ever do."

Steinbrenner's appreciation for what the team had accomplished was short-lived. A few days after the World Series, he informed Torre that he would not be giving bonuses to the coaches, and it was later reported that none of the Yankees scouts were given World Series rings. The latter slight would become known as the Yankees' "Curse of the Rings," as it would be another nine years before they would experience another World Series champagne celebration, and Steinbrenner would not be a part of it.

THE 2001 SEASON began well, with the Yankees taking first place in the division on July 3 and never relinquishing it, winning by 13½ games over the Red Sox. On the morning of September 11, Steinbrenner was at the Regency, scheduled to appear at a speaking engagement before the National Urban Coalition later that day, when he got word of the terror attacks on the World Trade Center. Associates described him as being "subdued but very much engaged" in the days following the attacks. With Commissioner Bud Selig having canceled all major league games for the rest of the week and many of the Yankee players having flown home, Steinbrenner called New York mayor Rudy Giuliani. "We want to do whatever we can," he told Giuliani, "but we don't want to get in anyone's way."

On Saturday, September 15, at Giuliani's suggestion, 13 Yankees, including Torre, Bernie Williams, Derek Jeter and Paul O'Neill, went to the Javits Center, in Midtown Manhattan, which the New York City cops and firemen were using as a holding area between shifts at Ground Zero, then visited the Armory, on Lexington Avenue and 25th Street, where the families of many of the missing victims were congregated.

Nearly seven weeks later, the city was still numb with grief as the Yankees and Arizona Diamondbacks played out games three, four and five of the World Series at Yankee Stadium, a few miles north of Ground Zero, where the bodies were still being dug out of the rubble that had once been the Twin Towers. In those three games, however, the Yankees provided an intense emotional lift to the city. With President George W. Bush throwing a defiant ceremonial first pitch—a strike, despite the constraints of a bulletproof vest—the Yankees, who had lost the first two games in Arizona, came away with a 2–1 victory behind the combined three-hit pitching of Clemens and Mariano Rivera. The next night, Halloween, they were one out away from losing game four when Tino Martinez, 0 for 9 in the Series to that point, hit the first pitch he saw from Diamondbacks closer Byung-Hyun Kim high into the right field bleachers to tie the score, 3–3. Derek Jeter then won the game an inning later with a home run on the stroke of midnight. In game five, the Yankees came back from a two-run deficit with one out to go on yet another homer off Kim—this one by Scott Brosius—and then went on to win, 3–2, in 12 innings.

Watching the delirium of the 56,018 fans in the Stadium from his private box, Steinbrenner turned to Levine and Trost and said, "Look at this! I can't believe this team's courage. They [the Diamondbacks] didn't think we'd be going back to Arizona!"

It was unbelievable—almost as unbelievable as what happened in game seven, after the Diamondbacks won game six. The Yankees had gone ahead

2–1 in the eighth inning on a home run by Alfonso Soriano. Steinbrenner, pacing back and forth in the visitors' clubhouse, was interrupted by a pounding at the door by the Fox TV camera crews and MLB maintenance workers seeking to come in and begin setting up the podium and the camera stands for the trophy presentation.

"Don't let them in!" Steinbrenner ordered.

When Phyllis Merhige, the MLB VP of club relations, attempted to explain to him the necessity of letting in the TV crew, Steinbrenner erupted in what witnesses said was a blistering, vile, expletive-filled verbal assault. It finally took Steinbrenner's old friend Paul Beeston, who was now president of Major League Baseball, to prevail upon him to let the crews in. Turning to Rick Cerrone, the Yankees' public relations director, who'd been standing off to the side during the commotion, Steinbrenner snapped, "If we lose, this is all your fault."

A few minutes later, the Diamondbacks began to mount a winning rally—against Rivera, who was undefeated in 51 previous postseason games—and all the Fox and MLB crews rushed to haul all their equipment over to the home-team clubhouse. The scene that followed, as the defeated Yankees trudged in from the dugout, was almost surreal. Here was Torre, standing in the middle of the room, addressing and consoling his players, many of whom were weeping openly, while Steinbrenner stood scowling, arms crossed, on the other side. When Torre was done and the media were allowed in, a grim-faced Steinbrenner walked around the clubhouse, followed by the writers and camera crews, spitting out congratulations to the Diamondbacks while vowing darkly that "there's gonna be changes. . . . I believe in what Ernest Hemingway said: 'The way to be a good loser is to practice it,' and I'm not gonna be practicing."

On his way out of the clubhouse, he stopped in front of general manager Brian Cashman, who had presided over four championships in five years and had just come within two outs of a fifth, and muttered, "You've had your chance. Now we're gonna do it my way."

THE CHANGES STEINBRENNER promised were not long in coming. The day after the World Series, Paul O'Neill and third baseman Scott Brosius announced their retirements. Rather than re-signing Tino Martinez, whose contract was up, the Yankees replaced him at first base with hulking, defense-challenged free agent Jason Giambi, who would later confess to having used steroids when he won the 2000 American League Most Valuable Player award with the Oakland A's. (Chuck Knoblauch, who also was not re-signed, would be revealed years later as having used steroids during his Yankee years.)

On December 20, 2001, two days after Steinbrenner completed the signing of Giambi to a seven-year, $120 million contract, Major League Baseball announced a monumental three-way transfer of club ownerships. Major League Baseball would buy the Montreal Expos from art dealer Jeffrey Loria, who in turn would buy the equally financially stressed Florida Marlins from commodities dealer John Henry, who then bought the Boston Red Sox from the estate of the late Jean Yawkey. Before purchasing the Marlins in 1999, Henry had been a limited partner in the Yankees for eight years, and Steinbrenner was particularly fond of him. So fond that when Henry sought to sell his points in the Yankees after purchasing the Marlins, the Boss refused, telling him: "Just hold on to them for now, John, because in a few years they're going to be worth a lot more, and I want you to get all you can for them."

Henry had been somewhat apprehensive about how his friendship with Steinbrenner would be affected now that he was taking ownership of the Yankees' bitter rivals. But the day after his purchase of the Red Sox was completed—and after it had been announced that former San Diego Padres owner Tom Werner and former Padres and Baltimore Orioles chief exec Larry Lucchino would be joining Henry as partners—Steinbrenner called his friend to congratulate him.

"I'm delighted for you, John, getting out of that mess in south Florida," Steinbrenner said, referring to Henry's frustrated attempts to secure a new stadium for the Marlins. "Welcome back to the American League East! We'll have some fun as rivals. But I gotta tell ya, I'm very concerned about you getting into bed with Werner and Lucchino. Those are two treacherous, phony backstabbers you've got there, John. You're a pal, but I'm telling you, I've got no use for those two bastards."

Henry was dumbstruck as he listened to Steinbrenner carry on about his two partners.

"George," he finally said, "I really appreciate you calling me, but I have to say this is the strangest conversation I've ever had. I don't think it's appropriate that I should hear any more of this."

After he had completed his all-out pursuit of Giambi, Steinbrenner made another three-year, $17 million over-market investment in oft-injured reliever Steve Karsay. Then on Christmas Eve 2001, Steinbrenner secretly met with his favorite overweight free spirit, David Wells, over lunch at Pete & Shorty's Tavern in Clearwater, Florida, just across the causeway from Tampa. Steinbrenner still felt remorse for trading Wells to the Blue Jays for Roger Clemens in February '99, and now the big left-hander, who was coming off back surgery, was a free agent again, albeit a tentative one. A few days earlier he'd made a handshake agreement with Arizona Diamondbacks general partner Jerry Colangelo for a one-year, $1 million deal (plus $4 million in incentives).

As the two munched on bite-size Shorty Burgers, Steinbrenner pulled out a piece of yellow legal paper and began scribbling some figures down.

"You don't want to go to Arizona," he said. "You need to be with me. This is what I think we can do."

Looking at the figures—two years, $6.5 million guaranteed, with a full no-trade clause—Wells's eyes widened.

"Wow, George, I can't believe this!" he said. "Why didn't you bring this up earlier? You could have wrapped me up at any time with this offer, but you waited until I had a handshake with Arizona. Good thing I didn't sign anything, huh?"

It didn't matter that Steinbrenner's signing of Wells gave the Yankees six starting pitchers going into 2002. That would be a problem for Joe Torre and pitching coach Mel Stottlemyre to sort out. What did he care if they detested Wells?

His reunion with Wells notwithstanding, Steinbrenner was unable to get past the '01 World Series loss and was in an unforgiving mood for most of that winter. Prior to spring training in Tampa, he'd prepared a memo to the staff in which he stated they would all be quartered in complimentary rooms at the Bay Harbor Hotel and could sign for all of their meals. For any meals outside, they were on their own. After sending it out, however, he called Cerrone from Tampa for his feedback.

"Are you okay with this?" he asked.

"Well, actually, no sir, I'm not," Cerrone replied. "I mean, this is essentially a seven-week business trip and you're telling us we have to eat all our meals in the hotel. And what about dry cleaning? There's nothing about how we're supposed to pay for that."

After mulling Cerrone's complaint for a few minutes, Steinbrenner called him back.

"You're right," Steinbrenner said. "I didn't fully think this out. We'll pick up the dry cleaning."

A couple of months earlier, Yankees VP Arthur Richman had leaked a story to *Newsday*'s Ken Davidoff and the Bergen *Record*'s Bob Klapisch: Steinbrenner was planning to eliminate the Yankees employees' dental benefits package. Although he was later quoted as saying "those things are a waste of money," the flap this created in the media prompted Steinbrenner to back off, and the dental benefits were never canceled.

Though he would reward Steinbrenner with a 19-7 season in 2002, the signing would come back to embarrass the Boss the following spring, when Wells published a tell-all book. In it, he claimed he'd been "half-drunk" when he pitched his perfect game for the Yankees in 1998; was critical of teammates Roger Clemens and Mike Mussina; maintained that over 40 percent of the players in baseball were on steroids (which, in retrospect, may have been true); and generally made Steinbrenner look like an out-negotiated fool at their Christmas Eve meeting.

Steinbrenner was understandably livid about the book and summoned Torre, Cashman, Trost, assistant GM Jean Afterman and Cerrone to his Legends Field office, with Levine checking in via speakerphone from New York, to decide what to do with Wells. But according to Torre, in his *Yankee Years* memoir, the session quickly regressed into a war of words between him and Steinbrenner. It began with Steinbrenner asking Torre what he suggested they do with Wells, to which Torre replied, "What I would do if I were you is call him up here and tell him to shut the fuck up." When Steinbrenner countered that Torre should be the one to say that to Wells, the manager shot back, "I'm not telling him anything. This has nothing to do with me."

Finally, after much deliberation and more angry words between Torre and Steinbrenner, they decided to fine Wells $100,000 and have him issue a public apology for the book.

The Yankees won their fifth-straight American League East title in 2002, leading the division from June 28 on and finishing with 103 victories, a comfortable 10½ games ahead of the Red Sox—but the season was a total failure as far as Steinbrenner was concerned. They were evicted from the postseason by the California Angels in the best-of-five first-round Division Series, during which the Yankee starting pitchers were torched for 56 hits and 31 runs in four games. It was clear to Torre that, with so many new hired hands from other teams now in the mix—including Giambi, reliever Steve Karsay, third baseman Robin Ventura and outfielders Rondell White and Raul Mondesi—none of whom had ever won a world championship before, the battle-hardened, selfless mentality he'd fostered with the O'Neill/Tino/Brosius group had begun to erode.

Steinbrenner had gone to Tampa when the series switched to Anaheim after the first two games at Yankee Stadium and watched the carnage of the final game (in which the Angels kayoed Wells on 10 hits and eight earned runs in just four innings) on TV. I called him two days later.

"If I had to get beat," he said, "let it have been the team that was once owned by Gene Autry, one of the finest men I ever met. Otherwise, I'm embarrassed for us. Adversity can be your greatest teacher, success your shortest lesson."

"Who said that?" I asked.

"I did."

"Oh," I said, "I thought that might have been another one from Hemingway."

"No, but as long you brought up Hemingway, I'll repeat his famous quote, because it's still my favorite: 'To be a good loser takes practice,' and I don't intend to practice."

"That's what you said last year. So can I assume you're going to be making more changes?"

"I've always believed in the old adage that it's better to trade a player one year too early than one year too late," he replied. "That was Branch Rickey."

"You seem to be taking this quite well," I said.

"I am wounded, but I am not slain, and now I shall lay down and bleed awhile. Then I will rise and fight again."

"Who said that?"

"Anon," said Steinbrenner, "as in 'Anonymous.'"

In a December 29 Q&A interview with the *Daily News*'s Wayne Coffey, Steinbrenner sounded more like the old, blustering Boss, taking his usual shots at his manager and coaching staff, but also singling out Larry Lucchino and even Derek Jeter for criticism.

A few days prior to the interview, Lucchino, the Red Sox CEO, responding to reports that the Sox had been outbid and outmaneuvered by the Yankees in their attempts to sign Cuban pitcher Jose Contreras (to whom Steinbrenner gave a four-year, $32 million contract), had famously labeled them "the Evil Empire." This was Steinbrenner's opportunity to retaliate by going public with the same ill feelings about Lucchino he'd expressed privately in his congratulatory phone call to John Henry.

"That's bullshit," he told Coffey. "That's how a sick person thinks. I've learned this about Lucchino: He's baseball's foremost chameleon of all time. He changes colors depending on where he's standing. . . . When he was in San Diego, he was a big man for small markets. Now he's in Boston and he's for the big markets. . . . He's running the team behind John Henry's back. I warned John it would happen, told him, 'Just be careful.' He talks out of both sides of his mouth. He has trouble talking out of the front of it."

Off the record with Coffey, Steinbrenner was even more vehement about Lucchino. "He's a two-faced, lying, duplicitous son-of-a-bitch," he said. "I wanted to punch him out at the last owners' meeting."

What really caught everyone by surprise was Steinbrenner's criticism of Derek Jeter. By now, Jeter was a virtual deity in New York, already acknowledged as right up there with Phil Rizzuto as the greatest shortstop in Yankees history, with four championship rings and a .317 average in seven seasons in the big leagues. Not only that, he'd just hit .500 (8 for 16 with two homers) in the losing Division Series to the Angels.

"As far as trying and being a warrior, I wouldn't put anyone ahead of him," Steinbrenner said. "But how much better would he be if he didn't have all his other activities? . . . He makes enough money that he doesn't need a lot of the commercials. . . . When I read in the paper that he's out until 3 A.M. in New York City, going to a birthday party, I won't lie. That doesn't sit well with me. That was in violation of Joe's curfew. That's the focus I'm talking about."

This evoked memories of Steinbrenner singling out the equally respect-ed Jim Abbott for spending too much time doing charity work a few years earlier. If there was one pattern in Steinbrenner's motivational style, it was to pick on the biggest star on the team, usually not long after they'd signed lucrative long-term contracts. He'd done it to Reggie Jackson, Dave Win-field, and Don Mattingly, and now he was doing it to Jeter. The year before, Steinbrenner had locked him up to age 36 with a 10-year, $189 million contract—the most money he'd ever given to a player.

Six weeks later, Steinbrenner's snipe at Jeter turned into a full-blown controversy—fueled in no small part by a case of classic tabloid journalism by the *Daily News*. Upon leaving his first pre–spring training workout at the Yankees' minor league complex in Tampa, Jeter was asked by the *Daily News*' Roger Rubin if he was bothered by Steinbrenner's remarks. "Not at all," was the short and sweet reply—but that was more than enough for the *News* to make a back-page story with the banner headline PARTY ON. It was all a bunch of silly, "slow news day" nonsense, but Steinbrenner had once again succeeded in getting the Yankees all over the news in the dead of winter—and, at the same time, he had gotten under the skin of his best player.

"He's the boss and he's entitled to his opinion," Jeter said on the first official day of '03 spring training, when the controversy had continued to drag on for weeks. "But what he said has turned me into being this big party animal. He even made a reference to one birthday party. That's been turned into that I'm like Dennis Rodman now."

Only in the world of Steinbrenner's Yankees could such a meaningless episode be turned into a multimillion-dollar TV commercial. Soon, repre-sentatives from the ad agency BBDO approached Jeter and Steinbrenner about doing a commercial for Visa. What resulted was a hilarious spot in which Steinbrenner, sitting at his desk in his blue blazer and white turtle-neck, admonishes Jeter by asking, "How can you possibly afford to spend two nights dancing, two nights eating out and three nights just carousing with your friends?" Jeter's reply is to calmly hold up his Visa credit card.

The commercial ends by flashing to a conga line in a nightclub, in which Jeter is the leader and Steinbrenner the caboose.

Steinbrenner's biggest news splash that winter was the celebrated signing of Japan's premier slugger, Hideki Matsui, to a three-year, $21 million contract. Matsui, nicknamed "Godzilla" for his decade of dominance with the Yomiuri Giants, had won three Central League MVP awards. He was introduced at a massive press conference, televised worldwide, held in the grand ballroom of the Marriott Marquis Hotel, in Times Square, on January 14. More than 500 reporters were present at the press conference, a harbinger that Matsui's presence on the team would add 50 to 100 Japanese journalists to the Yankees' traveling media corps.

With Matsui hitting .287 with 106 RBI, Giambi clubbing 41 homers with 107 RBI, and four starting pitchers—Clemens, Pettitte, Wells and Mussina—each winning 15 or more games, the 2003 Yankees waltzed to their sixth-straight American League East title, then beat the Minnesota Twins in the best-of-five Division Series. The ALCS against the Red Sox was a hard-fought, draining set of seven games that the Yankees finally won on Aaron Boone's 11th-inning walk-off homer at Yankee Stadium off Boston knuckleballer Tim Wakefield.

The 2003 World Series, against the unheralded Florida Marlins, was anticlimactic. After splitting the first two games in New York, the Yankees lost two out of three in Florida, came back to Yankee Stadium and went out with a whimper as Marlins right-hander Josh Beckett shut them out on five hits for the clincher. But as he strode briskly out of the Stadium after the game, attired in his customary blue blazer, gray slacks and white turtleneck, Steinbrenner seemed almost subdued and uncharacteristically restrained from offering criticism of his team or Torre. Rather than stopping to talk to reporters and offer a dissertation on the Series, he tersely answered questions on the fly as he made his way to his limo.

"Will there be many changes?"

"No comment."

"Will Torre be back?"

"I've said many times, yes."

"What about Brian Cashman?"

"I'm very satisfied with Joe."

It was unclear whether he'd heard the question about Cashman, but the reporters all agreed Steinbrenner was lacking the usual venom after a Yankee loss, especially one of this magnitude. Unbeknownst to Yankees officials, between games four and five of the World Series in Miami, Steinbrenner had been stricken with a severe case of the flu onboard the private yacht he'd rented for his family in Biscayne Bay. According to family sources, he had to be helped into bed by his son Hal and his longtime bodyguard, John Sibayan. He apparently staged a quick recovery, however, as he made it back for game five, which he watched for the most part from the visiting-club suite at Dolphins Stadium with the other Yankees officials.

Three days after Christmas, Steinbrenner made the 45-minute trip from Tampa to Sarasota to attend the funeral of his longtime friend Otto Graham, the Hall of Fame quarterback for the 1950s Cleveland Browns. Steinbrenner had idolized Graham from his days as a young business and civic leader in Cleveland, and his passing was a grim reminder that Steinbrenner himself was now 73.

As he sat by himself in the Church of the Palms Presbyterian-USA, watching a slide show of Graham's life, Steinbrenner began to feel a closeness in the air. God, it was hot, and it was getting harder and harder to breathe. When Graham's daughter-in-law began to deliver her eulogy, everything suddenly began to go dark and fuzzy, and Steinbrenner lurched forward as if trying to grab hold of something, then toppled onto the floor. For a few moments he lay there, unconscious, his face ashen white, as mourners rushed to his aid, loosening his tie and screaming for a doctor. Paramedics arrived a few minutes later, by which time Steinbrenner had regained consciousness.

"I'm all right, dammit!" he groaned before they lifted him onto a stretcher, carried him out of the church and put him in the ambulance that would take him to nearby Sarasota Memorial Hospital. His stay there was brief. After undergoing a battery of tests and being kept overnight for observation, he was released the next day, and Dr. Andrew Boyer, his personal physician, who had rushed from Tampa to Sarasota to supervise his treatment, issued a statement, assuring one and all that Steinbrenner was okay.

"It was nothing more than a fainting spell," Boyer said. "He's feeling well, and his general health is excellent."

If only that were true.

20

. . .

The Lion in Winter

. . .

I N THE WEEKS FOLLOWING Steinbrenner's collapse at Otto Graham's funeral, there were no sightings of him at any of his favorite Tampa haunts. "I'll give him the message," his longtime receptionist, Joanne Nastal, would say when I called for an interview, but those calls, uncharacteristically, were never returned. Occasionally, his New York publicist, Howard Rubenstein, would put out a statement, cheerily reporting that he was feeling fine and hard at work putting together the Yankee team for 2004. But the Boss himself had nothing to say—about the Yankees, Torre (whose contract was to expire after the 2004 season) or his health.

In the days preceding the incident in Sarasota, Steinbrenner had been plenty vocal about Yankee affairs—much to the chagrin of Randy Levine and Brian Cashman—as he pursued another free agent that no other teams were interested in signing, the perpetually disgruntled slugger Gary Sheffield. Because of his reputation as a chronic complainer, none of the Yankees high command wanted anything to do with the 35-year-old Sheffield, even though he was coming off a 39-homer, 132-RBI season with the Atlanta Braves. But Sheffield, the nephew of Dwight Gooden, had gone to Steinbrenner himself to pitch his wares—without an agent—and the Boss was immediately infatuated.

Cashman and Torre warned that Sheffield represented the antithesis of the team-first culture they had so carefully created with the Yankees, but Steinbrenner persisted, beginning what, predictably, became a rancorous contract negotiation. That fall, Cashman had been a handshake away from signing free agent outfielder Vladimir Guerrero, who was eight years younger than Sheffield, only to be told by Steinbrenner to beg off. All the while, Gooden was lobbying hard in Tampa for Steinbrenner to sign his nephew, which frustrated everyone in the New York office. How could a serial drug offender, someone who'd been given so many chances, still enjoy so much influence with the Boss?

"I'm handling this," Steinbrenner told his front office men. "We're doing it my way now. I'll decide who we're getting."

After initially agreeing to a three-year, $39 million contract, Steinbrenner and Sheffield got into a tussle over deferred money, and Sheffield threatened to walk away if the total value wasn't increased to $42 million. A week of not speaking to each other went by before Sheffield finally relented, agreeing to the original terms. The only consolation for Levine, Cashman & Co. was that Sheffield's behavior during the negotiations had proved them right.

Steinbrenner remained curiously unavailable for comment in mid-February, when the Yankees pulled off their biggest acquisition since they had brought Babe Ruth to the Bronx in 1920. Cashman had thought the team was pretty much set, with the additions of Sheffield, outfielder Kenny Lofton and oft-injured but frequently brilliant Kevin Brown (whom he'd acquired from the Los Angeles Dodgers for Jeff Weaver, the losing pitcher in the pivotal game four of the World Series against the Marlins). He had been content to watch as the Red Sox attempted to complete a blockbuster trade in which they would acquire shortstop Alex Rodriguez, generally acknowledged as the best all-around player in the game, from the Texas Rangers for Manny Ramirez, the best pure hitter in the game.

But as the Red Sox–Rangers negotiations snagged over who was going to pay the remaining $179 million on Rodriguez's contract, the Yankees were jolted by the news that third baseman Aaron Boone, the home run hero of their stirring '03 ALCS triumph against Boston, had torn his anterior cruciate ligament playing basketball and would require surgery that would sideline him for the entire 2004 season.

On January 25, Cashman and Levine had spent some time with Rodriguez at the New York baseball writers' dinner (where the shortstop was on hand to accept his 2003 American League Most Valuable Player award).

"What about A-Rod?" Cashman said to Levine a few days later.

"I like it," Levine said, "but at third base?"

"Well, obviously he'd have to agree to switch positions, but if he would, could we afford him?"

"I'll talk to George," Levine said. "In the meantime, why don't you go talk to Texas and see if they'd be interested in trading him to us."

After first getting permission from Rangers GM John Hart to talk to Rodriguez and then getting assurance from A-Rod that he would willingly move to third base just to be liberated from Texas, Cashman worked out a deal in which the Yankees would send their 28-year-old power-hitting second baseman, Alfonso Soriano, to the Rangers for Rodriguez, a seven-time All-Star who had just won his third-straight American League home run crown. Levine then worked out the hard part, getting the Rangers to agree to pay $67 million of the remaining $179 million on Rodriguez's contract. While all of this was transpiring, Steinbrenner was urging his men on behind the scenes, and even got on the phone with Texas owner Tom Hicks to formally seal the deal. But at the press conference at Yankee Stadium to introduce Rodriguez on February 17, he was nowhere to be seen. Instead, his son Hal and son-in-law Steve Swindal represented Yankees ownership.

The acquisitions of Rodriguez and Kevin Brown escalated the Yankees' payroll from $153 million to $185 million, some $57 million higher than the number-two Red Sox—which Boston owner John Henry found distressing.

"There is really no way to deal with a team that has gone so insanely far beyond the resources of all the other teams," Henry wrote in an e-mail to the Boston beat reporters.

This brought a swift response from Steinbrenner, in the form of a statement issued by Howard Rubenstein in New York.

"We understand John must be embarrassed, frustrated and disappointed by his team's failure in this transaction. Unlike the Yankees, he chose not to go the extra distance for his fans in Boston."

Henry replied by saying, "I kind of liken George to Don Rickles, but if Don Rickles insults you it's funny."

Never one to let someone else have the parting shot, Steinbrenner, upon hearing his former limited partner's rebuttal, fired off another statement, in which he appeared to make fun of Henry's skinny physique.

"Being compared to Don Rickles is a great compliment, because Rickles is a warm, funny and caring man. As for Henry, he reminds me of Ray Bolger, the scarecrow in *The Wizard of Oz.*"

It was vintage Steinbrenner, just not live Steinbrenner.

Nobody was more puzzled by Steinbrenner's reclusiveness than Rick Cerrone, the Yankees PR man, who hadn't had a single call from the owner since the Otto Graham funeral incident—a circumstance his 11 predecessors would no doubt have considered incredibly good fortune. Cerrone regarded the approach of spring training with a sense of dread. As if bringing in A-Rod wasn't going to create enough of a circus, there was the matter of Torre's unresolved expiring contract, which was sure to be an ongoing issue with the media, and the status of the Boss himself. What would he be like? Would he demand to be shielded from the media? Torre probably wondered, too, as he and Steinbrenner hadn't spoken since the previous season, and he'd been kept out of the loop on the A-Rod deal until it was almost completed.

Immediately following the A-Rod press conference, Cerrone, Cashman, Swindal, Hal Steinbrenner and Torre took the Yankees' charter plane back to Florida for the start of spring training. When they landed in Tampa, they were startled at the sight of a beaming Steinbrenner waiting on the tarmac to greet them.

"Great job, men," he said. "I'm proud of all of you."

"I don't know what it was," Cerrone said, "but George was a different person after the A-Rod trade. He seemed to be in an ebullient mood that whole spring. Don't get me wrong—he still had his moments when he'd snap at you or call you out for something—but he became almost fatherly. Hell, he and Joe weren't even speaking, and the next thing you know he was giving him a three-year extension."

Indeed, even Torre was caught off-guard when Steinbrenner popped into his office early one day that spring and casually asked, "What do you want to do next year?" When Torre replied that he'd like to stay on the job awhile longer, Steinbrenner said, "Fine. I'll let you and Steve [Swindal] work out the extension." On April 8, the Yankees announced that Torre had agreed to a three-year, $19.2 million deal that made him the highest-paid manager in history. Steinbrenner even seemed to rebound from his health scare. Reporters watched him interact with fans and even make light of his mortality.

"Everybody's coming up to me and yelling, 'Sign this baseball,'" he said. "You all think I'm gonna die. You want one of the last autographs."

Knowing Steinbrenner's impatience for reading scripts and having to do multiple takes, Cerrone was surprised when he agreed to appear on *The Late Show with David Letterman* in February, where he recited a top 10 list of good things about being a New York Yankee. Number 1: "You think this A-Rod deal is good, huh? We're about to sign Ty Cobb!"

For most of that spring, however, Steinbrenner limited his appearances to the clubhouse and Max's Café, the media dining room (operated by his old friend from Buffalo, Max Margulis, whom he'd lured to Tampa years earlier to serve as food and beverage manager, first at the Bay Harbor Hotel and then at Legends Field). He was seldom seen on the field, which puzzled the newspaper photographers and TV crews accustomed to his almost daily accessibility there.

After opening the 2004 season with a two-game series against the Tampa Bay Devil Rays in Japan—a trip Steinbrenner did not make—the Yankees returned home for their Yankee Stadium opener, on April 8, against the Chicago White Sox. Steinbrenner had agreed to a pregame interview with WCBS's veteran sports anchor, Warner Wolf. To get to the set, which was atop a platform in the left-field seats, Steinbrenner was transported on a golf cart under the stands, past the marching band and the military color guard. Wolf remembered how Steinbrenner appeared to struggle as he climbed up onto the platform, and how distracted he seemed by the West Point color guard and the fans shouting and waving at him. He looked to be tearing up a little.

"These fans really love you, George!" Wolf said, attempting to start the interview on an upbeat note.

"This is a very important thing . . . that we've had the strings on . . . this is the people's team—" Steinbrenner began to say.

Suddenly, he was overcome with emotion and began to cry.

"I can see it really affects you," Wolf said.

"You know . . . I'm getting older," Steinbrenner stammered. "After you get older, you do this more."

Changing the subject, Wolf said, "What about the business of baseball and how it's changed, George? You bought the Yankees for $10 million in 1973, and look what they're worth now."

"Actually, it was $8.5 million," Steinbrenner said, his voice still cracking but his emotions slightly more under control. He made it through the rest of the interview without further incident, but after he departed for his private box upstairs, Wolf thought to himself that something didn't seem right about him.

"I never told this to anyone," Wolf said in a 2009 interview, "but the more I thought about it, I realized there was something different about his eyes. Those blue piercing eyes that always looked right at you, penetrating you . . . the spark was missing from them. Instead, there was a distance, a kind of vulnerability to them."

A month into the '04 season, Steinbrenner sat for an interview in his office at Yankee Stadium with *New York Times* reporter Juliet Macur. For the first time, he spoke seriously about growing old and his own mortality. Macur reported that, periodically during the interview, he had begun to tear up.

When she asked if he had a retirement plan, Steinbrenner said, "You don't want to leave because you're a competitive human being and the juices are still flowing. So you just hope you'll go out one way—horizontal." Then, as if to emphasize that, he whispered: "Yep . . . hor-i-zontal."

Macur noted that Steinbrenner would be turning 74 on July 4, to which he responded, "My God, a guy I knew just died and he was only 60! I've been to a lot of funerals. So sure, when you see your friends die, you think about dying yourself. You never know when your time is going to come. It could be—it could be tomorrow."

It was then that Macur asked him about his crying.

"Well, I don't cry all the time," he said, explaining that his welling up with Warner Wolf on Opening Day had been the result of seeing a group of West Point cadets cheering for him. "Those men and women may be going into harm's way next year and they're applauding me? What have I done that's so great? They appreciate me for what I'm trying to do. I've never really felt that before."

"I've been different," he said toward the end of the interview. "As you get older, you can't remember everything and then you get impatient. You're not the same anymore. It's hard."

Throughout 2004, the media and Yankees staffers noticed that Steinbrenner was spending very little time at Yankee Stadium, flying in from Tampa only for big opponents like the Red Sox, and then staying out of the spotlight. After the Yankees won their seventh-straight American League East title, he was on hand for the first two games of the Division Series against the Minnesota Twins, but was back in Tampa when they won the last two games in Minneapolis to advance to the ALCS against the Red Sox. The Red Sox became the first team in major league history to come back from being down 0-3 to win a best-of-seven series, eradicating their 86 years of cursed history, and the deciding game seven at Yankee Stadium was excruciating for Steinbrenner. Afterward, Steinbrenner's nemesis, Red Sox CEO Larry Lucchino, chortled: "All empires fall sooner or later."

But unlike previous postseason losses, like the one in 1981, when he issued the apology to Yankee fans after losing to the Dodgers, or in 2001, when he stalked around the clubhouse in Arizona vowing to make changes, this time Steinbrenner did everything he could to avoid the media. To the small group of reporters camped outside the Yankees offices as he exited the Stadium, he uttered tersely: "I want to congratulate the Boston team. They did very well."

Three days later, Robert Merrill, one of Steinbrenner's closest friends, died at 85. Merrill, the Metropolitan Opera baritone for 31 years, had become equally renowned as the Yankees' "in-house" national anthem singer at Yankee Stadium. Howard Rubenstein, not Steinbrenner, issued a press release from the Yankees calling Merrill "a friend and close associate of the Yankees" who "sang the anthem at Yankee Stadium for many years and provided a true inspiration for us, the ballplayers and all of our fans."

Hundreds of Merrill's friends turned out to pay tribute at a memorial service on December 15, with Steinbrenner a conspicuous absentee. And for the rest of the winter, there was nothing but radio silence out of Tampa.

I was one of many reporters who'd been unsuccessful in numerous attempts to reach him at his office. And when the Yankees gathered for spring training in Tampa the following February, he continued to be this Oz-like figure, seldom heard from, and only in statements made through

Rubinstein. I concluded that he must be seriously ill, especially when he failed to respond earlier that month after the *San Francisco Chronicle* reported that Jason Giambi had testified to a grand jury in San Francisco that he had used steroids in 2003, the year before the Yankees signed him to a seven-year, $120 million contract.

"George is not sick," I was told by Reggie Jackson, who claimed to have visited him almost daily in his Legends Field office. "He's changed, but he's not seriously ill. Why don't you just call up there?"

Despite all my previous failed attempts, I took Jackson's advice, went up to the press box at Legends Field and called the office upstairs. Much to my surprise, Steinbrenner got on the phone and told me to come on up. As I was being escorted into his office on the fourth floor, I wasn't sure what to expect, but then I heard him hollering to his secretary about Randy Levine and Brian Cashman not straightening out some problem with Gary Sheffield's contract. At least it sounded like the old Boss.

"What do you want, Madden?" he barked.

"I want to know what's wrong with you," I said.

"Do I look sick?" Steinbrenner asked. "I'm just busy, that's all. I don't have time for all of you guys. These things . . . Sheffield's got a problem with his contract, Reggie's got a problem . . . they all call me. I've got to take care of everything here."

"So people can still get through to you?"

"What does it look like?"

"Then why have you become so reclusive?" I asked. "Any other year, the Red Sox are taking potshots at you, Giambi's got this steroids mess, and you're all over that, on the back pages."

"I'm just not gonna do that stuff anymore," Steinbrenner said, even though the day before he'd made big news with just one small sound bite, when a flock of reporters intercepted him getting onto the elevator. Someone asked if he was going to give Hideki Matsui a contract extension, and Steinbrenner shot back, "We'd like to have the player, but fuck the agent." The agent in question, Arn Tellem, also represented Giambi.

"The Red Sox can say all they want," Steinbrenner told me. "They won and they deserved it. I admit I took last year very hard. I'm still not over it. But we'll settle this on the field, not in the newspapers."

"So what about all those statements through Howard Rubenstein?" I asked. "They're not just because you've lost something off your fastball?"

"I'm telling you, those statements are really me," he said adamantly. "They're my words. I write every one of them! It's just easier that way, so I don't have to get into long discussions with everyone when something comes up."

The more he talked, however, the more I sensed a kind of distance about him. When we began to reminisce about old times, he seemed to have trouble remembering certain things and he was less expansive than usual. Finally, I said: "You know, Douglas MacArthur, one of your heroes, once said: 'Old soldiers never die, they just fade away.' Is that what you're doing?"

"That's a thought," Steinbrenner mused. "I think I'd much rather fade away than go out with a big splash."

As I got up to leave, I told him it was nice to see that he was still in control of his kingdom and that it had been a fun bull session.

"I really enjoyed this," he said to me. "We'll have to do this more often."

We never did. It was my last face-to-face interview with him. The next day, I was having lunch in Max's Café with Max Margulis, who told me, "The Boss really babies himself now. I don't think he likes to stray too far from his doctor. He keeps in this little triangle: his home to the office and to the IHOP [three miles south of Legends Field], now that Malio's has closed. He seldom if ever goes to the farm in Ocala anymore."

It was three months later that Steinbrenner agreed to his first (and last) interview for the YES Network. The taped *CenterStage* interview was supposed to be a sort of retrospective in which Michael Kay, the Yankees' play-by-play broadcaster for YES, asked Steinbrenner questions about his 32 years as owner of the Yankees. It was a disaster. Steinbrenner seemed nervous and frightened and incapable of answering Kay's questions. In many cases throughout the interview he merely repeated the question.

"Was it overwhelming [to realize] you own the Yankees?" Kay asked.

"It was overwhelming," Steinbrenner replied.

When Kay asked what he was thinking as he watched Reggie Jackson and Billy Martin fighting in the dugout in Boston in 1977, Steinbrenner said, "I didn't like that at all."

"Were you watching on TV?" Kay asked.

"I was watching on TV."

Desperately prodding on, Kay asked: "Did you go, 'Oh, my God?' "

"I said he [Martin] lost it," Steinbrenner answered.

"Was it hard?"

"It was a very hard moment."

At the end of the interview, Kay, hoping to draw Steinbrenner out by switching to a non-baseball subject, asked him to name his favorite song.

"Anything by Sinatra."

The day after the interview aired, *Daily News* TV sports columnist Bob Raissman wrote that Steinbrenner had been exposed as being a shell of the old Boss. "The steely stare has given way to hollow eyes. Arrogance and bluster replaced by the tinny-toned voice of a grandfather suddenly awakened from a nap. No energy. No animation. Steinbrenner was not registering."

Kay remembered feeling extremely depressed at the conclusion of the interview. Here was this dynamic and powerful man, unable to respond to the most softball of questions, nervously clutching his eyeglasses throughout. "I felt terribly sorry for him," Kay told me in 2009. "He kept repeating the questions, and he gripped those glasses as if they represented dear life. Eight questions in, I knew we were in real trouble."

At one point, according to Kay, YES president of production John Filippelli ordered the camera stopped and told him, "You're making him nervous by asking the questions too fast. Let it breathe."

It turned out to be the highest-rated YES *CenterStage* ever. And it never aired again.

Steinbrenner remained just as reclusive throughout the 2005 season, in which the Yankees ended the season tied with the Red Sox in the American League East. The Yankees took the division title by virtue of winning the season series between the teams, only to be knocked out of the postseason in the first round by the Los Angeles Angels of Anaheim. On the occasion of Steinbrenner's 75th birthday, the *Times'* Murray Chass called Howard Rubenstein to inquire about speaking with Steinbrenner and was told, "Mr. Steinbrenner is declining all interviews now." Rubenstein also sought to dispel the speculation that Steinbrenner was seriously ill, saying that "he lifts weights every day."

Nevertheless, Chass wrote, "*Where is the Steinbrenner who said of Ken Clay, 'he spit the bit'; of Jim Beattie, 'he looked scared stiff'; of Dave Winfield, 'we need a Mr. October or a Mr. September. Winfield is Mr. May'? That Steinbrenner no longer exists. Little wonder the Yankees are having difficulty winning with the highest payroll in sports history. It's just money; there's no passion behind it.*"

Steinbrenner's appearances at Yankee Stadium were limited to the Red Sox series, and then the only sightings of him were when he arrived and departed through the Yankees offices, where a small group of reporters kept vigil in hopes of gleaning any sort of a quote from him. "Get out of here, guys—leave me alone!" was all they got as two security guards escorted him from the Stadium after a 9–2 drubbing by the Red Sox on September 11.

Steinbrenner was home in Tampa when the Angels evicted the Yankees from the postseason for the second time in four years, knocking out Mike Mussina in the third inning of the deciding game five in Anaheim. It wasn't until the next day that Steinbrenner issued a statement through Rubinstein praising Angels manager Mike Scioscia while taking what was perceived as a shot at Joe Torre. "I congratulate the Angels and their manager on the great job they've done. Our team played hard, but we let our fans down."

According to those who communicated with Steinbrenner on a semi-regular basis, that Division Series loss to the Angels was the beginning of his disenchantment with Torre. "He had just given Torre that $7 million-per-year contract and taken the payroll over $200 million and felt he was getting cheated," one of his friends told me. "Plus, he saw that Torre had changed. This was no longer the guy who was on the balls of his ass in debt when George first hired him. He'd become wealthy beyond his wildest dreams, started his own foundation and had essentially become 'Joe Torre Inc.,' who was bigger than the Yankees. George resented that."

On the other hand, Brian Cashman, whose contract as general manager was due to expire at the end of 2005, had become disenchanted with Steinbrenner—or at least the way the Boss continued to allow the Tampa-based minor league execs to have more influence and authority than the GM in New York. In a meeting with team president Randy Levine and general partner Swindal right after the '05 season, Cashman broke down in tears, telling them he loved the Yankees but could not stay on the job under these circumstances. "You need a general manager you can trust," he said, "but ultimately it's got to be one guy. We run the draft out of Tampa, we make pitching decisions out of Tampa. We make trade decisions out of Tampa. I mean, what the fuck am I responsible for?"

After Levine and Swindal relayed Cashman's feelings to Steinbrenner, the next day he called the GM, imploring him to stay.

"I'm told you're leaving me," Steinbrenner said.

"I'm thinking about it, yes, sir," Cashman said.

"Why?"

"Because the job is not the job I thought it would be. I'm like a caretaker. We're on the verge of collapse here, and I don't want to be a part of that. You're a military guy. There's got to be a chain of command from the owner to the general manager to the manager with nobody in between. It's got to be that way or it won't work. The players, the press and the fans all have to know that."

"Well, I want you back," said Steinbrenner. "We'll just do it that way."

And in yet another sign that Steinbrenner was gradually relinquishing control and phasing himself out, he gave Cashman a three-year contract for $1.6, $1.8 and $2 million, making him the highest-paid GM in the game. Cashman also got full authority over all Yankees baseball operations, including the minor leagues and the draft.

WHILE STEINBRENNER'S HEALTH and mental well-being were clearly in decline, Randy Levine and the other Yankees executives continued to work with New York City and State officials to build a new stadium for the Yankees. Steinbrenner had been lobbying the city to build him a new stadium since the 1980s, preferably in Manhattan, while also implying that he could take the Yankees across the river to New Jersey if the city did not accommodate him.

In 1993, New York governor Mario Cuomo had announced that he was exploring a plan to redevelop a 30-acre railyard along the Hudson River between 30th and 33rd streets, on the West Side of Manhattan, for an entertainment center and possible site for a new Yankee Stadium.

Cuomo's proposal met with immediate resistance from environmentalists and Manhattan residents, as did Mayor Rudy Giuliani's 1996 plan to build a new Yankee Stadium on the site to serve as the centerpiece of New York's bid for the 2008 Olympics. By then, however, Steinbrenner had all but given up on the idea of moving the Yankees out of the Bronx, because of two remarkable developments: First, crime in New York had decreased immensely under Giuliani and his police commissioner, William Bratton, making the Bronx a much more attractive location for the team. This, plus the fact that the Yankees were now regular contenders for the World Series, meant the team was suddenly selling out Yankee Stadium almost every game. After Torre's first world championship year, 1996, in which the Yankees drew 2.25 million fans to Yankee Stadium, attendance grew substantially each succeeding year, eclipsing the four million mark in 2005.

Still, there was no getting around the fact that Yankee Stadium was nearly 80 years old and was going to require hundreds of millions of dollars in annual infrastructure maintenance. And, with a mere 18 luxury suites, it was outmoded compared with the 16 state-of-the-art ballparks that had sprung up across the major league landscape since 1991. Just days before leaving office in December 2001, Giuliani announced tentative agreements between the city and both the Yankees and the Mets for $1.6 billion in construction funds for new stadiums for each of the teams, with taxpayers footing half the tab. However, not long after taking office, Giuliani's successor, Michael Bloomberg, pulled the plug on the stadium deals, calling them "corporate welfare."

With these plans going nowhere, Steinbrenner's executive team turned to Major League Baseball's revenue-sharing agreement—which included a provision allowing teams to deduct stadium construction and operating and maintenance expenses against their revenues—as an avenue to building a new stadium. Instead of that sizable chunk of Yankees money going to the other clubs, it could be used as a sort of "tax shelter" that would enable Steinbrenner, over 40 years, to pay for the cost of a new stadium. Subsidizing this would be $1.2 billion in bonds issued by the city, agreed to by Bloomberg.

On January 18, 2006, Charles Gargano, chairman of the Empire State Development Corporation, announced the details of the new Yankee Stadium area revitalization plan. In addition to the new five-level stadium, with a capacity of 50,000 plus 57 luxury suites, which would be constructed across 161st Street from the old stadium, the city would erect four new garages, providing 4,735 additional parking spaces, along with a new Metro North railroad stop. A few months later, *Forbes* magazine, citing the new Yankee Stadium revenue-sharing deal as a primary factor, reported the Yankees to be the first sports franchise in history to be valued at $1 billion.

The day the *Forbes* story hit newsstands, I placed a call to Steinbrenner's office in Tampa. To my surprise, Joanne Nastal put me right through to him.

"I was just calling for your comment about *Forbes* valuing the Yankees at a billion dollars, George," I said. "Could you ever in your wildest imagination have envisioned this?"

"I'm truly humbled," he said. "I've been very lucky in life. . . . I've had a lot of good people with me the whole time."

When I asked him what he thought his father would have said about his original $168,000 investment now being worth $1 billion, his voice began to tremble.

"Oh . . . I don't know," he said. "I think . . . he'd be very happy."

Around the same time that spring, Steinbrenner had lunch with Lou Piniella and Malio Iavarone at Fleming's Steakhouse in Tampa. Piniella was sitting out the 2006 season after being released from the final year of his managing contract by the Tampa Bay Devil Rays, and Steinbrenner was making a final pitch to get him back.

"I want you with the Yankees, Lou," Steinbrenner said. "I need you to manage the team."

"You've got a good manager in Torre," Piniella said, "and, besides, I'm still under contract with the Devil Rays. I can't manage for anyone until next year."

"Well, then just come to work for me in the front office for the year," Steinbrenner persisted.

"I can't, George," Piniella said. "It's in my contract I can't work for any team. If you want to talk to me, it'll have to be after the season."

"All right," said Steinbrenner. "Then that's what we'll do."

THE 2006 YANKEES won a ninth-straight American League East title, but they were once again eliminated in the first round of the playoffs, this time by the Detroit Tigers. Throughout the year, Steinbrenner had been even more reclusive, avoiding contact with the media and making even fewer appearances at Yankee Stadium. Only because, at his request, I had been providing him with updates on the condition of our mutual friend Frank Dolson, who was dying of cancer, was I able to occasionally get through to him by phone. Dolson, the former sports editor and lead columnist for the *Philadelphia Inquirer*, was a lifelong Yankee fan who had met Steinbrenner while covering the Penn Relays, and after his retirement from sportswriting he'd been hired by the Boss as a special advisor. It was after the Yankees lost game three of the Division Series in Detroit to go down two games to one that I called Steinbrenner. Our friend was at the end. After thanking me for filling him in with this distressing news about Dolson, Steinbrenner suddenly launched into a rambling criticism of Torre.

"I don't know why you guys keep giving Torre a pass," he said. "He's managing us right out of the playoffs again, but nobody writes that. You're all waiting for me to criticize him. I've stayed out of this all year, just like he asked. . . . He's spending too much time with all his other things, his charity, his commercials, and not paying attention to detail with the Yankees. . . . He thinks he's bigger than the Yankees. . . . Why doesn't anybody write that?"

I didn't know what to say, especially since I assumed that Steinbrenner didn't want to be quoted directly. But after the Yankees' next game, an 8–3 trouncing that ended their season, Torre came under heavy media criticism for playing Gary Sheffield at first base, waiting too long to get hot-hitting rookie Melky Cabrera's youthful energy into the lineup, and embarrassing Alex Rodriguez by batting him eighth. I wrote a column that channeled what Steinbrenner had said to me.

"You can make the case that they didn't have enough pitching to get back to the World Series, but I can assure you George Steinbrenner doesn't want to hear it. He may walk a little slower, talk in shorter sentences and seem somewhat detached from the operation he used to rule with an iron hand from the Stadium's boardroom to the bathrooms, but that doesn't mean there won't be repercussions from the Boss in the face of yet another humiliating early playoff exit by the $200 million Yankees.

"Believe it. Faster than you can say 'Goodbye Joe, welcome back Lou,' there will be."

Although I had no knowledge of that lunch conversation they'd had back in April, Lou Piniella's contract with the Devil Rays had now expired, making him a free agent, and it wasn't at all a leap to assume that Steinbrenner would want to bring him back into the Yankee fold, either as the manager immediately or as a manager-in-waiting for the last season of Torre's contract. What I did know was that Steinbrenner was furious at Torre.

"If George wants Lou back, he'd better move fast," Alan Nero, Piniella's agent, told me that day.

I have no doubt that the old, audacious, self-assured George would have. But this Steinbrenner was no longer capable of making this kind of decision without seeking counsel and consensus from the new Yankees hierarchy, comprising Levine, Trost, Swindal and Cashman. The day after the Division Series ended, Steinbrenner had a conference call with the four of them to discuss Torre. Swindal was the first to speak, making a persuasive plea to Steinbrenner to allow Torre to finish out the final $7 million year of the contract he'd negotiated with the manager. Then Cashman noted that firing Torre after he'd taken the Yankees to the playoffs 11 straight years was bound to prompt a severe backlash in the media and from fans. Steinbrenner listened to their arguments but said he needed time to think it over. It was then that Cashman called Torre to tell him he wasn't sure which way it was going to go with the old man.

"If I were you," he told Torre, "and if you want to come back, I'd call him yourself."

Torre did, telling Steinbrenner, "All I ever wanted to do was to make you proud, Boss. I've got a year left on my contract and I'd like to work for it and not just sit at home collecting my money. But if you feel in your heart you want to make a change, that's what you should do."

Again, Steinbrenner said he needed to think it over. Finally, on October 11, four days after the Yankees lost the Division Series, Torre held a delayed season wrap-up session with the media at Yankee Stadium. Minutes before the press conference was set to begin, Torre was in his office in the clubhouse when the phone rang. It was Cashman, with Levine and Trost, calling from upstairs, and Steinbrenner on the line from Tampa. "We want you to manage next year," Steinbrenner said, adding that he expected Torre to get the team to play with more energy and enthusiasm than they'd shown against Detroit.

In the accompanying press release handed out to the media, Steinbrenner was quoted as saying, "I expect a great deal from you and the entire team. I have high expectations, and I want to see enthusiasm, a fighting spirit and a team that works together." It sounded as much an indictment of Torre as an endorsement from the Boss. Six days later, the Chicago Cubs introduced Lou Piniella as their new manager.

Nearly three weeks after Torre's press conference, Steinbrenner made a rare trip out of Tampa to Chapel Hill, North Carolina, where his granddaughter Haley, a drama student at the University of North Carolina, was performing in the play *Cabaret* on the afternoon of Sunday, October 29. Steinbrenner was accompanied by his wife, Joan, and his daughters, Jessica and Jennifer (Haley's mother), and midway through the performance he was suddenly stricken with chest pains and breathing problems and began to black out. The performance was cut short as paramedics were summoned to the theater.

Steinbrenner was taken to a local hospital, where he remained overnight and into Monday as doctors conducted more tests to determine what had happened. The day after he was released from the hospital, Howard Rubenstein issued another upbeat press release from New York: "George Steinbrenner is well and raising hell today." Rubenstein went on to say that he'd spoken to Steinbrenner "several times on Monday and today, and he is okay. He's dived back into planning next season and is quite feisty." Rubenstein wrote off this latest Steinbrenner health scare as merely a product of the absence of air conditioning and the close quarters in the auditorium.

In fact, Steinbrenner was anything but "well and raising hell," and his close associates later conceded that it was after the North Carolina incident that they really began to notice a marked decline in his mental acuity and overall health. According to sources close to the family, the doctors in North Carolina explained to Steinbrenner's wife and daughters that he had suffered a series of transient ischemic attacks (TIAs), in which a clot temporarily clogs an artery, preventing the brain from getting the blood it needs. The symptoms of such attacks are numbness and weakness in the face, arms and legs, sudden confusion, and trouble speaking and understanding, among others. Ensuing dementia could be slowed by drugs but not halted or reversed.

The family discussed having Steinbrenner undergo further treatment in North Carolina, but he refused, insisting on returning home to Tampa under the care of his personal physician, Andrew Boyer. The North Carolina doctors also strongly advised the family that Steinbrenner should no longer drive and that he needed to have someone with him all the time. The family arranged to have nurses on duty 24 hours at the Steinbrenner home on Frankland Road, in the Palma Ceia section of south Tampa.

In early February 2007, Lou Piniella and Malio Iavarone met Steinbrenner for lunch at the Palm Restaurant in Tampa. It was just a few days before Piniella was scheduled to go to Arizona for his first spring training with the Cubs, and this time Steinbrenner was accompanied by his older son, Hank, who in the mid-'80s had spent a couple of years working in the Yankees' front office before returning to run the family horse farm in Ocala.

Piniella and Iavarone were alarmed at how much Steinbrenner's physical and mental health had declined in the previous year. He could barely get around on his bad knee, and his conversation during the lunch was limited. Where once he was the life of the party, asking Piniella's opinions on all things baseball while offering plenty of his own, now there was a distinct disconnect. Mostly, he just sat there, offering little as the others talked and laughed. Afterward, a concerned Piniella took Hank Steinbrenner aside and said, "I can see what's happened to him. You've got to step forward now and get involved with the team. He needs you now."

Seven months later, a writer for *Condé Nast Portfolio*, Franz Lidz, got one of Steinbrenner's longtime pals, 84-year-old Tom McEwen, the former sports editor of the *Tampa Tribune*, to take him to the Steinbrenner home on Frankland Road, where they were granted entrance through the wrought-iron driveway gate as another car pulled out. They asked a gardener to announce their presence and waited about five minutes before Steinbrenner appeared at his front door, wearing silk pajamas, slippers and a terrycloth bathrobe. It was two o'clock in the afternoon.

"His body is bloated; his jawline has slackened into a triple chin; his skin looks as if a dry-cleaner bag has been stretched over it," Lidz wrote. "Steinbrenner's face, pale and swollen, has a curiously undefined look. His features seem frozen in a permanent rictus of careworn disbelief." But according to Lidz, the transformation of Steinbrenner's mind was even more surprising. Steinbrenner seemed unable to comprehend anything the two asked him, instead repeating, "Great to see you, Tommy." As they left, McEwen told Lidz, "I'm shocked. George doesn't even seem the same person. I figured he might be in a bad way, but I never expected this."

Lidz's piece drew outrage from Steinbrenner's friends and even some of his enemies. "I always thought George was a bully and a blowhard," one former major league owner told me, "but what that guy wrote about him was just cruel, an unfair invasion of his privacy." The Steinbrenner family blamed McEwen for having facilitated the visit (even though he appeared to have been duped by Lidz) and refused to take his phone calls. From then on, he was persona non grata at Legends Field.

Six weeks later, the Yankees were again knocked out of the postseason in the first round, this time by the Cleveland Indians. Steinbrenner's high command was once again faced with a dilemma over what to do with Torre, whose contract had expired at the end of the season. For the first time since 1997, the Yankees had not won the AL East, earning a postseason berth as the wild card. And unlike the previous year, Torre no longer had Steve Swindal as his principal champion. On Valentine's Day the previous spring, Swindal had been pulled over in his 2007 Mercedes for cutting off another car on Central Avenue and 31st Street in St. Petersburg shortly after two o'clock in the morning. He was charged with a DUI and jailed overnight.

Over the course of the next few days, reports surfaced of domestic trouble between Swindal and Jennifer Steinbrenner Swindal, who filed for divorce a month later, citing irreconcilable differences. Out of the family for Swindal meant out of the Yankees (like Joe Molloy, who in 1998 divorced himself out of the organization). This opened the door for Steinbrenner's two sons, Hal and Hank, to take more active roles in the running of the ball club.

It was the six-man group of Hal and Hank Steinbrenner, Randy Levine, Lonn Trost, Brian Cashman and Steinbrenner's son-in-law Felix Lopez (Jessica's second husband), who huddled with Steinbrenner at his home in Tampa on October 17, 2007, to discuss the Torre situation. Steinbrenner offered no opinion other than to say he was tired of paying Torre $4 million per year more than any other manager in baseball based on past performance. The Steinbrenners and Levine did not want to bring him back, but Cashman convinced them that for public relations reasons alone, they needed at least to offer him a contract. The group decided to offer him a one-year contract with a $5 million base—keeping him the highest-paid manager in the game by $2 million—with a series of incentives that, if the Yankees just reached the World Series, would top out at $8 million and automatically vest at that same number in 2009.

When Cashman called Torre to tell him of the offer, Torre did not commit either way. Rather, he said he wanted to come to Tampa and look Steinbrenner in the eye. Cashman, who was returning to New York that day, agreed to fly back to Tampa with Torre to meet with the Steinbrenners. The Yankees execs assumed that Torre, as he'd done in the past, merely wanted to get Steinbrenner's personal assurance that he wanted him to continue managing the team.

Shortly before 2 P.M. on October 18, Torre, accompanied by Cashman and Trost, walked into Steinbrenner's office on the fourth floor of Legends Field. The Boss was sitting at his desk, flanked by Levine, Hal and Hank Steinbrenner and Lopez. Hal Steinbrenner began the meeting by reiterating to Torre the group's wishes that he come back for another year, then asked Levine to go over the terms of the offer and to review Torre's previous contracts. At that point, Steinbrenner said, "I've always been fair to you. We want you to come back. I hope you accept."

Torre looked at the group coldly.

"I have to say I find this insulting," he said. "I don't believe I deserve a pay cut."

Then, looking straight at Steinbrenner, he said, "You know, George, the success of my teams allowed you to have the YES network and a new stadium, not to mention the record attendances and all the added advertising and marketing revenue. Is this fair? I can't in good conscience face my players and take a deal like this."

As Torre spoke, Steinbrenner looked at him blankly, as if not fully comprehending what he was hearing. The others were stunned at Torre's audacity. Was he delusional? Asserting that he was the one responsible for the Boss becoming wealthy beyond his wildest imagination, when in fact it was the other way around? Finally, after an uneasy silence, Hal Steinbrenner spoke up again.

"I'm sorry you feel this way, Joe," he said, "but we'd all still like you to stay with the Yankees and work with the network."

Torre did not respond. Instead, he reached across the desk, shook Steinbrenner's hand, thanked him, stood up and walked out the door. The next day, he held his own press conference in which he said the incentives in the contract were an insult and expressed dismay at there having been no negotiation. It was left to Hank Steinbrenner to return fire for his father in an October 20 interview with the *New York Post*.

"Where was Joe's career in '95 when my dad hired him?" Hank asked. "My dad was crucified for hiring him. Let's not forget what my dad did in giving him that opportunity—and the great team he was handed. You can't take credit for the success when you're going good and then not take at least some of the blame when things change."

That Cashman was given unfettered authority to hire Torre's successor—and selected Joe Girardi, the former Yankee catcher who'd previously managed the Florida Marlins, rather than bench coach Don Mattingly, the icon who, it had seemed, was being groomed for the job—was further evidence that Steinbrenner had fully retired from the Yankees operations. This was confirmed at the major league owners' meeting in New York in November 2008, when the Yankees announced that Hal Steinbrenner would become the new Yankees managing general partner. Why Hal and not his older brother, Hank? All agreed that Hal was the one with the business acumen and that Hank, despite his frequent public comments on the Yankees' baseball dealings, had no interest in spending the necessary time in New York working with Levine and Trost on all the complicated stadium, network, marketing and concessions operations.

Left unsaid was the fact that Hal's ascension over Hank further so-lidified Cashman's position as head of all baseball operations. Until then, it had been Hank who had acted as the team spokesman on player deci-sions, much to Cashman's dismay. According to team sources, two months earlier, in his negotiations with Hal on a new three-year contract, Cash-man had complained that Hank's frequent public comments were creating confusion as to just who was in charge, and that he needed to be muzzled. Coincidence or not, when Hal became managing general partner, Hank changed his cell phone number—which just about every New York base-ball reporter had—and was thereafter no longer available for comment on Yankee doings.

In Girardi's first season as manager, Steinbrenner's only appearances at Yankee Stadium were on Opening Day and at the All-Star Game in July, a commemoration of the final season of the venerable and storied old ballpark. (By this time, he'd finally surrendered to the intolerable pain in his arthritic knee and grudgingly allowed himself to be consigned to a wheelchair.) What was supposed to be a fans' tribute to Steinbrenner at the All-Star Game—a "victory tour" around the Stadium in a golf cart at the conclusion of the pregame ceremonies—was mostly lost on the capacity crowd, because the announcement of his entrance onto the field was made as part of the TV broadcast and not preceded by the familiar sound of Bob Sheppard saying, "Your attention, please, ladies and gentlemen." As the white-haired, frail-looking Steinbrenner—wearing his familiar blue blazer, blue-and-white dotted tie and huge sunglasses, and accompanied by Hal, Jennifer and his son-in-law Felix Lopez—was driven around the park, the fans applauded sporadically, as if uncertain as to what was going on.

The All-Star Game was the last time Steinbrenner would appear at the Stadium, as the Yankees, under Girardi, failed to make the postseason for the first time since 1993, leading to speculation that the new manager might well become a short-timer. But over the winter, Cashman, emulating Stein-brenner by going on a wild free agent spending spree, procured the three premium players on the market, pitchers C. C. Sabathia and A. J. Burnett and first baseman Mark Teixeira, for a whopping $423.5 million altogeth-er. And just as with Steinbrenner's '70s signings of Catfish Hunter, Reggie Jackson and Goose Gossage, Cashman's free agent foray paid off as the team handily won the AL East by eight games over the Red Sox, on their way to another Yankee championship. Sabathia tied for the league lead with 19 wins, Burnett chipped in with 13 (while also logging 209 innings) and Teixeira delivered an MVP-caliber season, hitting .292 with a league-leading 39 homers and 122 RBI while winning a Gold Glove at first base.

Steinbrenner saw only three games of the Yankees' 2009 season first-hand: Opening Day at the new Yankee Stadium, and twice from a private box at the Tropicana Dome, in St. Petersburg, when the team played the Tampa Bay Devil Rays in late summer. There had been considerable specu-lation as to whether he would be well enough to make the trip to New York for the opening of the new stadium, but, accompanied by the entire family, Dr. Boyer and his nurse, he flew up from Tampa on a charter plane and watched the game from his new suite, concealed from view. The only sighting of him by the media was after the game, when he was being spir-ited down the corridor in a golf cart on the clubhouse level beneath the stadium, surrounded by a phalanx of security guards. As he passed a group of reporters being restrained in a stairwell, one of them, Anthony McCar-ron of the *Daily News*, shouted at him, "George, what do you think of the new stadium?"

"It's beautiful," Steinbrenner replied weakly as his handlers sped him away.

ON JULY 2, 2009, Malio Iavarone, who had opened a new restaurant in Tampa, received a call from one of Steinbrenner's secretaries at the Yan-kees' complex there (which, in the spring, had been renamed from Legends Field to Steinbrenner Field). Phil McNiff, Steinbrenner's longtime security chief in Tampa, was organizing a 79th birthday lunch for the Boss and was hoping that Malio would bring along some of Steinbrenner's favorite Flor-ida stone crabs. "I'm there!" Malio said, excited at the prospect of seeing his old friend, who had turned down repeated requests from his longtime pals who wanted to visit him at the Frankland Road house. It had already been a particularly bad year for Steinbrenner. On March 29, Lou Saban, who had hired him as a college football coach and later served as Yankees president, passed away after suffering a fall in his house in Myrtle Beach, South Carolina. Then, on May 19, Max Margulis, who'd been with him since 1981, after closing up the restaurant in Buffalo, died of a heart attack at age 83 at his home in Palm Harbor, Florida. When Iavarone arrived at the fourth-floor offices, Steinbrenner was wheeled in to greet him.

"Here's Malio, Boss," one of his secretaries said.

"Oh, Malio," said Steinbrenner. "I love Malio."

But as he said it, he seemed to be looking right through Iavarone, who could tell Steinbrenner didn't recognize him. Malio hugged him and planted a kiss on his cheek.

"I love you, too, Boss," he said, before excusing himself from the party and leaving the building in tears.

"McNiff asked me to stay for the birthday cake, but I just had to get out of there," Iavarone told me. "I just couldn't play that game—that George knew everybody and that everything was just the same. It wasn't."

BY SWEEPING THE Minnesota Twins in three games in the American League Division Series and getting past the Los Angeles Angels in six games in the ALCS, Girardi's Yankees saw to it that Steinbrenner's new Yankee Stadium would host the World Series in its maiden season—against the defending world champion Philadelphia Phillies. Despite rumors that his health had deteriorated to the point that he now rarely left his house, word out of Tampa during the Twins series was that Steinbrenner would definitely be there if the Yankees advanced to the Series. On the afternoon of October 27, Steinbrenner and his family, along with Dr. Boyer and his nurse, flew up to New York from Tampa for games one and two of the Series, which began the next night.

Unlike all the previous World Series and Opening Days, the Steinbrenner private suite was empty of the usual celebrities and big-shot New York political figures. Instead, with Hal Steinbrenner now in charge, the suite was restricted to just the family, a few of Hal's associates, Yogi Berra and only the Boss's oldest friends, among them Dick Kraft, his Williams College roommate who'd worked for the Yankees in various capacities for over 30 years; Jim Fuchs, his partner in the Silver Shield Foundation; USA Today founder Al Neuharth; restaurateur Elaine Kaufman; and 87-year-old Jimmy Nederlander, his long-ago Broadway show compadre and original partner in the Yankees.

Throughout the two games, the wheelchair-bound Steinbrenner remained stationed at the big round table in the middle of the room, content to watch the action on the high-definition flat-screen TV on the wall. Prior to game two, he seemed oblivious to the sounds coming from the field of rapper Jay-Z, clad in a Yankee varsity jacket and a Yankee cap, performing his anthem "Empire State of Mind," which includes the lyric "I made the Yankee hat more famous than a Yankee can." It was a long way from Steinbrenner's world of Frank Sinatra and Robert Merrill, and just another sad reminder to his old friends that he was no longer master of his own realm.

At one point during game two, which the Yankees would win, 3–1, to tie the Series at one game apiece, Steinbrenner was joined at the big table by Jimmy Nederlander, who was also confined to a wheelchair.

"You two guys look great!" said Elaine Kaufman. "This is like a reunion tour!"

"How can I look great?" Nederlander chuckled. "I'm 90 years old!"

Everyone else in the room, sensing the poignancy of the moment, gave them space—Steinbrenner and his oldest friend, the guy who told him, way back in the beginning when he bought the Yankees, "Never forget, New York is a city of stars. You gotta have stars!" They sat together in silence, and after a few minutes Nederlander turned to Steinbrenner and said, "This is a beautiful stadium, George, but you shoulda put a roof on it so we could have concerts and shows and things in the winter."

"It would have cost too much," Steinbrenner said softly, before returning his gaze to the TV screen, "and it wouldn't have been Yankee Stadium."

When the World Series returned to the Stadium for game six, Steinbrenner was back in Tampa. According to the family, he watched the Yankees win their 27th world championship on TV. "He was very teary-eyed," Hank reported. "It meant everything to him. It was very strange, him not being here. But he's happy now."

Epilogue

. . .

Steinbrenner's Last Dance

. . .

ROUND 1:30 IN THE morning on July 13, 2010, the telephone rang in Hank Steinbrenner's Clearwater Beach home. As soon as he picked up, his sister Jessica told him that their father had been rushed, struggling to breathe and with a pain in his chest, to St. Joseph's Hospital.

Hank dressed quickly and drove the half hour through the empty streets of Clearwater, across the causeway to Tampa, and arrived at his father's hospital room where Steinbrenner was lying below a crowd of doctors and nurses while the rest of the family—his wife, Joan, his daughters Jessica and Jennifer, and Jessica's husband, Felix Lopez—looked on helplessly.

In addition to the medication treating his Alzheimer's, he had been taking blood-thinner drugs to counteract clots that were the result of his confinement in a wheelchair. A clot that had developed in his leg had now apparently moved into his chest, and the medical crew was working feverishly to contain it. "They were doing all sorts of things to him, trying to relieve his pain, dissolve the blood clot," Hank remembered. "As all this was going on, he just looked at me and said: 'Are you okay, Buddy?' That's when I lost it. I couldn't bear to be in that room, but as I started to walk out, I saw him following me with his eyes. He wasn't scared. It was almost as if, at this point, he was feeling like this was the end and accepting it."

Ultimately, the doctors could not prevent the clot from reaching Steinbrenner's heart, and at approximately 6:30 A.M., just nine days after he'd celebrated his 80th birthday, his heart stopped beating. George Steinbrenner was gone.

THERE WAS A touch of irony that Steinbrenner died on the morning of the 2010 All-Star Game. Through the years, he'd always disparaged the "classic" as a needless interruption and encouraged his players instead to use the time to rest and heal their injuries for what really mattered—the playoffs, October, the championship season. "Leave it to George to upstage the All-Star Game," cracked one Yankee executive.

Hank, the oldest of Steinbrenner's four kids, said his dad's last years were "happy" despite his incapacitation, advanced dementia and the growing number of his close friends who had passed away.

Employees at the Tampa complex said the "form of Alzheimer's disease" (which was how the doctors were then describing his affliction) had progressed to the point where he no longer recognized many of his old acquaintances. Whenever he was wheeled down the corridor underneath the stadium, past Max's Café—the media dining room that his old friend Max Margulis presided over until he died the previous May—Steinbrenner would ask in vain: "Where's Max?"

On March 8, 2010, Dick Kraft, Steinbrenner's oldest and best friend as well as his former roommate at Williams College, who also had worked for him in various capacities with the Yankees beginning in 1984, died following a brain hemorrhage that he suffered while shaving in the bathroom of his Tampa condo. He was 79. The previous fall, Mark Zettelmeyer, Steinbrenner's first cousin, one of his most trusted aides and the general manager of the Yankees' Fort Lauderdale farm team before he moved to Tampa to oversee spring training operations, died of cancer.

In the shadow of his grief, a mounting sense of isolation from the world as he knew it, Steinbrenner struggled to keep up appearances of his own vitality. "He fought going into the wheelchair furiously," Hank said.

ON FRIDAY, JULY 16, the night the Yankees opened the second half of the season, they held an emotional memorial ceremony for the Boss and the beloved "Voice of God," Bob Sheppard, the revered Yankee Stadium public-address announcer who had died, at age 99, only a few days before

Steinbrenner. After a video tribute to Steinbrenner, with the musical back-drop of Frank Sinatra's "My Way," Mariano Rivera laid two roses on home plate. A band played "Taps." Finally, Derek Jeter strode to the microphone, no notes in hand: "We gather to honor two men who are both shining stars in the Yankee universe," he said. "They'll be forever remembered in base-ball history and in our hearts."

The next day, after a private service at Trinity Garden Cemetery, about 25 miles north of Tampa, Steinbrenner was laid to rest in a mausoleum by his family.

According to Yankee officials and family associates, it was Joan Stein-brenner's decision not to have a public memorial service in which her hus-band's friends could all gather to eulogize him. Nevertheless, in the days immediately following his internment, many of them recounted their favor-ite memories of him in various media outlets.

"George was a giant of the game, and his devotion to baseball was sur-passed only by his devotion to his family and his beloved New York Yan-kees," said baseball commissioner Bud Selig, who'd known Steinbrenner as both a close friend and contentious adversary in their shared 37 years in baseball. "He was, and always will be, as much of a New York Yankee as Babe Ruth, Lou Gehrig, Joe DiMaggio, Mickey Mantle, Whitey Ford and all the other Yankee legends."

(Apparently those words were not lost on Steinbrenner's family as, two months later, a mammoth plaque, which dwarfed the monuments of Ruth, DiMaggio, Gehrig, Mantle and Miller Huggins, was dedicated in the Yan-kee Boss's honor in Yankee Stadium's Monument Park.)

Former commissioner Fay Vincent, who attempted to banish Stein-brenner from baseball for life, grudgingly hailed him as a visionary. In a *New York Times* op-ed piece on July 14, Vincent wrote: "Many of the criticisms of George hit the mark. He was intensely belligerent. He never waited to attack from the flank. Nor was he subtle. He took things on directly and sel-dom ducked a punch. And that style worked for him. George Steinbrenner made plenty of mistakes and even more enemies. But very few people have bought a team and dominated a sport with the level of his success. Given the astronomical prices of franchises today, it's doubtful that we will see his like again."

David Sussman, Steinbrenner's in-house counsel with the Yankees for eight years, shared with *New York Times* columnist Maureen Dowd his "inside" story of Steinbrenner's experiences with the *Seinfeld* show. Despite one of the principal storylines of the show, in which George Costanza (played by Jason Alexander) is employed by the Yankees, Steinbrenner apparently never watched the show. One day, Jerry Seinfeld came to Sussman with a request to use the Yankee uniform in an episode where Costanza decides to switch the material from polyester to cotton. As Sussman sought to assure Steinbrenner that the script was innocuous, Steinbrenner snapped: "I'll be the judge of that. Let me see it."

As he began reading it over, Steinbrenner shook his head.

"I thought you said this doesn't involve me?"

"It doesn't," Sussman insisted.

"Then what are all these references to 'George' here?"

Sussman, incredulous that Steinbrenner had so little knowledge of the show, attempted to explain that "George" was the Costanza character, who is Jerry Seinfeld's friend in the show.

"I thought you were smarter than that," Steinbrenner interrupted. "Don't you see? This is how they're trying to get at me! They've named their character after me. So here's what you do. Call your friend Jerry back and tell him he has Mr. Steinbrenner's permission to use the Yankee uniform, but under one condition: He changes the name of the Costanza character. In fact, have him name this character after you, David."

For Yankee president Randy Levine, it was Steinbrenner's anger and intimidation factor—especially after a particularly devastating Yankee loss—that was most memorable.

Levine recalled the Saturday night—October 5, 2002—after the Yankees were eliminated by the Angels in the American League Division Series in Anaheim. Levine had watched the game on TV at his Manhattan apartment and was getting ready to go to bed when the phone rang. It was Steinbrenner calling from the Regency.

"I want you to get your ass down here . . . now!" he bellowed.

"What's going on, Boss?" Levine asked.

"Never mind. Just get your ass down here. I'll be waiting for you in the lobby."

Fearing to ever dare question Steinbrenner or try to reason with him when he was upset about something, Levine hung up the phone, dressed hastily and dashed out of his apartment for the five-block trek down to the Regency. It was just after midnight. But when he walked into the lobby, it was empty, except for the desk clerk. For a few minutes he paced nervously until suddenly the elevator door opened and Steinbrenner emerged.

"Your fucking team sucks!" Steinbrenner shouted. "I just want you to know that! They're a fucking embarrassment!"

With that, he got back into the elevator and was gone, leaving Levine standing there, speechless.

ON DECEMBER 5, 2010, the 16-member Hall of Fame Veterans Committee—eight Hall of Fame players, four owners and four senior baseball writers—convened at the winter baseball meetings in Lake Buena Vista, Florida, to consider 10 candidates. Two days prior, Elaine Kaufman, the grande dame New York saloonkeeper who had been a confidant and best friend to Steinbrenner for 35 years, finally surrendered, at age 81, to the emphysema that had plagued her for years. The death—a final punctuation to Steinbrenner's era—brought the Boss and his cadre of oldest and dearest friends full circle, from Steinbrenner's undergraduate days at Williams to Cleveland and finally New York. Enshrinement in Cooperstown seemed nearly an afterthought.

Included on the Hall of Fame ballot was the trailblazing executive director of the Players Association, Marvin Miller; five-time Yankee manager Billy Martin; longtime general manager Pat Gillick, who won back-to-back world championships with the Toronto Blue Jays in 1992 and 1993 and another with the Philadelphia Phillies in 2008; and, for the first time, George Steinbrenner. But there would be no reunion of Steinbrenner and Martin in Cooperstown.

After nearly four hours, the group elected just one person–Gillick.

It was not revealed how many votes Steinbrenner received, other than the fact it was less than eight (with 12 needed for election). His resurrection of the Yankees from the irrelevance and mediocrity of the CBS years to seven world championships—to say nothing of the impact his television deals had on major league franchise values—were apparently outweighed in the minds of voters by his manic behavior and transgressions against baseball mankind over his nearly 36 years in the game. Steinbrenner would have pointed out, no doubt, that Gillick was his first Yankee scouting director from 1973–76, but it is doubtful if that would have been much consolation for him.

In interviews with members of the committee, the overriding opinion of Steinbrenner's candidacy was that there was no urgency to elect him on his first turn on the ballot, and that they felt more time was necessary to put his career as an owner of impact in better perspective. There are only three or four pure owners in the Hall of Fame, and as one voter pointed out: "It took Walter O'Malley [the former Dodgers owner who opened up the baseball gateway to the West Coast by moving the team to Los Angeles] thirty years to get elected."

IN THE CASE of O'Malley, who was elected to the Hall of Fame in 2007 along with long-ago Pittsburgh Pirates owner Barney Dreyfuss, he was regarded as the most powerful and influential owner in baseball until his death in 1979. The same could not be said of Steinbrenner who, because of the onset of his dementia, had ceased being an active force in baseball and the Yankees over the last four to five years of his life. Of the seven world championships that Steinbrenner presided over, no one will ever know the degree to which he really comprehended the Yankees' most recent one in 2009. The very fact that he was unable to return to New York for the Yankees' victorious game six was further evidence of just how frail and debilitated he really was—and even his family, who were all at Yankee Stadium, didn't know if he'd merely slept through it. The following spring, his visits to newly christened Steinbrenner Field had been restricted to just a few of the Yankees' spring training games.

Despite his increasingly deteriorating health, the family had put out the word that Steinbrenner would indeed be making another trip to New York for the Yankees' home opener and the presentation of their championship rings on April 13 against the Los Angeles Angels. Hardly anyone thought he'd be able to make the trip, but on the afternoon of April 12, the Steinbrenner clan all boarded the Yankee private jet in Tampa for the flight to Teterboro Airport in New Jersey. As usual, Steinbrenner was accompanied by Dr. Boyer and two male nurses, who, the next day, were beside him in the family suite at Yankee Stadium when, an hour before the game, Yankee manager Joe Girardi and Derek Jeter suddenly emerged, clad in sneakers and their Yankee pinstripe pants and blue undershirts. As they entered the room, Yankees CEO Lonn Trost handed Girardi a small velvet case and whispered: "You give it to him."

Steinbrenner, stationary in his wheelchair and staring straight ahead at the big-screen TV on the wall, with his son Hal at his right, did not see them at first. As they approached him from his left side, Hal said: "Dad, Joe has something here for you."

Reaching over Steinbrenner's shoulder, Girardi handed him the box. Steinbrenner anxiously grappled at it before prying it open to reveal the huge diamond-encrusted 2009 world championship ring. For an uneasy moment, as everyone else looked on in awe at the ring, Steinbrenner appeared confused. Finally, Jeter, standing behind him over his left shoulder said: "Don't you think you've got enough of these, Boss?"

With that, Steinbrenner's lips began to quiver and, beneath his glasses, his eyes welled with tears. Slowly, he removed the 2002 Ohio State national championship ring from his hand, a ring that Buckeyes football coach Jim Tressel had given him personally, and replaced it with what would be his seventh and last memento of a Yankee world championship. Turning his head to Jeter now, he said: "You're the best, Jetes."

As soon as the game was over—the Yankees won, 7–5—Steinbrenner was shunted into an SUV beneath the stadium with his medical team and taken back to the Regency. He flew home to Tampa the next day, never to return.

Notes and Acknowledgments

I WOULD LIKE TO THANK the more than 150 friends, associates, employees and former employees of George Steinbrenner who cooperated with me on this book. I understood when I took on this project that numerous authors through the years had made efforts to write biographies of Steinbrenner—or even proposed collaborating with him on an autobiography—only to be met with stiff resistance from Steinbrenner, his family and the New York Yankees. Because of that, I am grateful to all of those who trusted me to portray them accurately and to tell the story of Steinbrenner as it was. I was fortunate in many cases to have had a relationship with the people I talked to—and to have been there for most of the events and anecdotes they related to me—which I'm sure contributed to that trust.

As such, I have tried to be faithful to the actual conversations that take place throughout this book, all of which were obtained from one or both of the people engaged in them or by someone who was a firsthand witness to them. In addition, all of the anecdotes included in this book had at least two sources.

It took three years to complete this project, and it could not have been accomplished without the assistance of so many people:

Moss Klein, my dear friend, previous coauthor and proofreader/fact-checker extraordinaire, who served as my administrator of accuracy.

Gabe Paul Jr., who generously afforded me access to his father's diaries and tape-recorded accounts of his years with the Yankees—the mother lode of previously unmined background material that was such an important part of the first six chapters of the book.

Marty Appel, who provided historical insight and unyielding support and friendship, and whose Rolodex was an invaluable tool in the process of locating so many of the sources in this book.

Martin Dunn, editor-in-chief, and Leon Carter, sports editor, of the New York *Daily News*, who gave their full support to this project and afforded me the time to complete it.

Scott Browne, Ellen Locker, Jimmy Converso, Scott Widener, Kristina Bilello, Bruce Furman and Tony Rollo of the New York *Daily News* library, who tirelessly combed through the *News*' archives for the historical news accounts that were the basis of the book, and for helping in the locating of a number of important people who were interviewed for the project.

Peter Edelman, Jo Barefoot and Angie Troisi of the New York *Daily News* photo department, who aided in the selection and procurement of most of the photos used in the book.

Murray Chass and Phil Pepe, highly accomplished baseball writers who provided insight on the subject in the early years, 1973–78, before I came on the Yankees beat.

Sean Forman, whose Baseball-Reference.com Web site was an invaluable source of information throughout the book.

Jeff Idelson, Jim Gates and Bill Francis of the National Baseball Hall of Fame, who made available all of their resources and gave of their time to help research a lot of the material used in the book.

Michael Margolis of the New York Yankees media relations department, who helped in the research of Yankees historical material.

Phyllis Merhige and Pat Courtney of Major League Baseball, who helped in the research of owners' meetings and other MLB events that were pertinent to the book.

Bobby Goldwater, who served as both a source and a proofreader, and a valued friend and supporter.

Art Berke and Dave Kaplan of the Yogi Berra Museum, who supported and gladly served as "sounding boards" throughout the three years of working on this project.

Tom Villante, who provided insight on Major League Baseball television operations in the 1980s, as well as a couple of terrific anecdotes about CBS and Mike Burke.

Roseanne Miskau, Mike Burke's former secretary, who was extremely helpful in putting me in touch with her former boss's family and associates.

Bruce Haims and the Burke family, who allowed me access to Mike Burke's legal papers regarding the sale of the Yankees by CBS to George Steinbrenner.

Dick Quinn, Williams College sports information director, who provided research material from the subject's time on the Williams College track team as well as the photo of the subject practicing the hurdles.

Lori DuBois and Linda Hall of the Williams College library, who helped in the procurement of materials from the school's archives on the subject's writings for the college newspaper.

And last, the three people who were most instrumental in making this book possible: David Hirshey, executive editor at HarperCollins, who believed in the project and that I was the person to do it; George Quraishi, my editor at HarperCollins, who performed his magic like a skilled surgeon in enabling me to tell the subject's life story—which was substantial—as concisely as possible without losing any of the character; and Rob Wilson, my agent, who is a constant source of inspiration, encouragement and calm under fire.

Bibliography

Bashe, Philip. *Dog Days: The New York Yankees' Fall from Grace and Return to Glory, 1964–76.* New York: Random House, 1994.

Burke, Michael. *Outrageous Good Fortune.* Boston: Little Brown, 1984.

Cramer, Richard Ben. *DiMaggio: The Hero's Life.* New York: Simon & Schuster, 2000.

Falkner, David. *The Last Yankee: The Turbulent Life of Billy Martin.* New York: Simon & Schuster, 1992.

Gossage, Richard "Goose," with Russ Pate. *The Goose Is Loose.* New York: Ballantine, 2000.

Hunter, Jim "Catfish," with Armen Keteyian. *Catfish: My Life in Baseball.* New York: McGraw-Hill, 1988.

Jackson, Reggie, with Mike Lupica. *Reggie: The Autobiography of Reggie Jackson.* New York: Villard, 1984.

Kuhn, Bowie. *Hardball: The Education of a Baseball Commissioner.* New York: Times Books, 1987.

MacPhail, Lee. *My Nine Innings: An Autobiography of 50 Years in Baseball.* Westport, Conn.: Meckler Books, 1989.

Madden, Bill, and Moss Klein. *Damned Yankees: A No-Holds-Barred Account of Life with "Boss" Steinbrenner.* New York: Warner Books, 1990.

Martin, Billy, with Phil Pepe. *Billyball.* New York: Doubleday, 1987.

Schaap, Dick. *Steinbrenner!* New York: G. P. Putnam's Sons, 1982.

Tebbetts, Birdie, with James Morrison. *Birdie: Confessions of a Baseball Nomad.* Chicago: Triumph, 2002.

Torre, Joe, with Tom Verducci. *Chasing the Dream: My Lifelong Journey to the World Series.* New York: Bantam, 1997.

———. *The Yankees Years.* New York: Doubleday, 2009.

Torry, Jack. *Endless Summers: The Fall and Rise of the Cleveland Indians.* South Bend, Ind.: Diamond Communications Inc., 1995.

Williams, Dick, and Bill Plaschke. *No More Mr. Nice Guy: A Life of Hardball.* San Diego: Harcourt, Brace, Jovanovich, 1990.

Winfield, Dave, with Tom Parker. *Winfield: A Player's Life.* New York: W. W. Norton, 1988.

Zimmer, Don, with Bill Madden. *Zim: A Baseball Life.* Kingston, N.Y.: Total/Sports Illustrated, 2001.

Index